Lonely Planet Publications
Melbourne | Oakland | London

Neil Wilson

Edinburgh

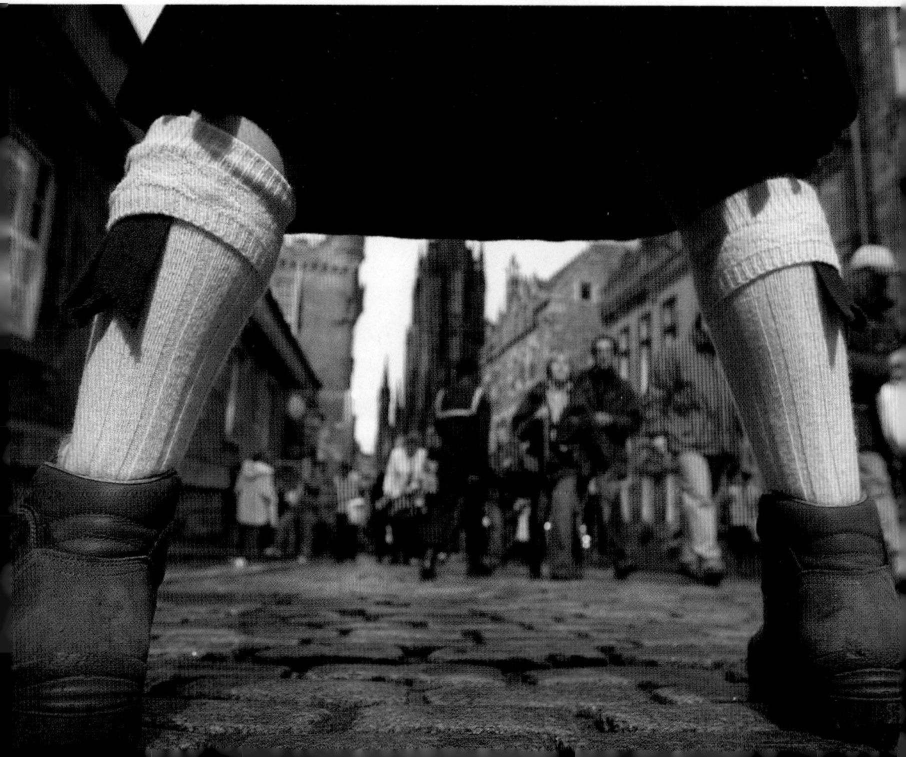

The Top Five

1 Museum of Scotland
Explore the museum's imaginative interior (p65)

2 Royal Yacht Britannia
Embark on a royal tour (p76)

3 Scottish Parliament Building
Check out the striking yet controversial building (p61)

4 Edinburgh Castle
See for miles from the city's most recognisable landmark (p52)

5 Underground Edinburgh
Visit the haunted subterranean South Bridge vaults (p49)

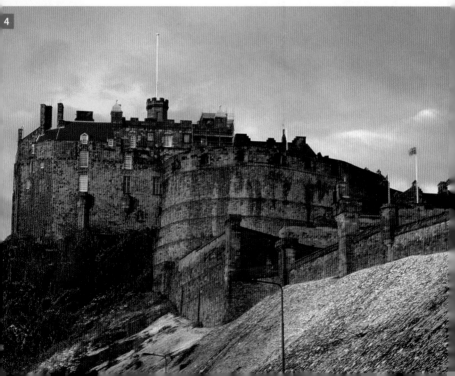

4

Published by Lonely Planet Publications Pty Ltd
ABN 36 005 607 983

Australia Head Office, Locked Bag 1, Footscray, Victoria 3011, ☎ 03 8379 8000, fax 03 8379 8111, talk2us@lonelyplanet.com.au

USA 150 Linden St, Oakland, CA 94607, ☎ 510 893 8555, toll free 800 275 8555, fax 510 893 8572, info@lonelyplanet.com

UK 72–82 Rosebery Ave, Clerkenwell, London, EC1R 4RW, ☎ 020 7841 9000, fax 020 7841 9001, go@lonelyplanet.co.uk

Printed through SNP Security Printing Pte Ltd, Singapore

Contents

The Author

Neil Wilson

Neil was born in Glasgow (boooo!) but defected to the east at the age of 18 (hurrah!) and has now lived in Edinburgh for more than 20 years. While studying geology at Edinburgh University he spent long, lazy summer afternoons exploring the closes, wynds (alleys), courtyards and back streets of his adopted city; since then, he has continued to enjoy delving into Edinburgh's many hidden corners, taking a special interest in the city's pubs and restaurants. Neil has been a full-time writer and photographer since 1988 and has written more than 40 guidebooks for various publishers, including the Lonely Planet guide to Scotland.

NEIL'S TOP EDINBURGH DAY

Even though I've lived here for most of my adult life, Edinburgh still has the power to stop me in my tracks and make me gawp, slack-jawed, at its beauty. So a good day out means walking, walking, walking, camera in hand, taking in lots of different viewpoints. I would start at the Scottish Parliament Building – I was critical of it at first, but it's growing on me – and hike up the Royal Mile to the castle, which commands great views all round, then descend through Princes St Gardens from the Esplanade (a nicer route than going down the Mound). Then it's across Princes St and north along Hanover and Dundas Sts – as I cross George St another great vista opens up, to the Firth of Forth and the Fife hills beyond. There are loads of interesting shops and galleries on the way downhill, and I might stop for coffee and a read of the newspaper at Glass & Thompson. At the bottom I'd turn left and follow Henderson Row to Stockbridge; lots of good places for lunch here, but I usually head for the Circus Café. Afterwards, there's a lovely walk along the Water of Leith to the Scottish National Gallery of Modern Art and the Dean Gallery – beautiful buildings and grounds as well as great art. Then it's up through the West End and back along Princes St for a final climb up Calton Hill to watch the sunset. I would be pretty damned hungry after all that walking, so I'd grab a taxi and treat myself to dinner; again somewhere with a view – perhaps Oloroso, or maybe the Tower.

LONELY PLANET AUTHORS

Why is our travel information the best in the world? It's simple: our authors are independent, dedicated travellers. They don't research using just the Internet or phone, and they don't take freebies in exchange for positive coverage. They travel widely, to all the popular spots and off the beaten track. They personally visit thousands of hotels, restaurants, cafés, bars, galleries, palaces, museums and more – and they take pride in getting all the details right, and telling it how it is. For more, see the authors section on **www.lonelyplanet.com**.

PHOTOGRAPHER

Jonathan Smith

Raised in the Scottish Highlands, Jon graduated from St Andrews University in 1994 with an MA in German. Unsure of what to do with his life, he took a flight to Vilnius and spent the next four years travelling around the former USSR. Having tried everything from teaching to translating Lithuanian cookery books into English, Jon resolved to seek his fortune as a freelance travel photographer. Since then Jon's byline has appeared in over 50 Lonely Planet titles, notably *Prague*, *Moscow* and *St Petersburg*. Currently based in Aberdeenshire, Jon has worked on several major book projects down the road in Auld Reekie. For him the main highlight of this particular assignment was being paid to explore Edinburgh's drinking dens (hard work if you can get it). He also attended his first ever football match, though sadly his team – Leith's 'Hibbies' – lost.

Introducing Edinburgh

Festival time. Fireworks explode in fizzing starbursts of ruby and emerald above the smoke-swept battlements of Edinburgh Castle, while cascades of sparkling fire stream down the castle walls. Swooshing rooster-tails of rockets fill the sky ever more thickly, lighting up the rapt faces of the crowds, as the thundering music swells to a climax. And you're standing there in the midst of it all, face turned towards the sky; transfixed, mesmerised, seduced, wondering what's going to happen next.

Edinburgh does that to you. Scots poet Hugh MacDiarmid described the city as 'a mad god's dream', but even the maddest of gods couldn't have dreamt up a more inspiring setting for the world's biggest, most exhilarating, most over-the-top festival.

Edinburgh is one of Europe's most beautiful cities, draped across a series of rocky hills overlooking the sea. It's a town intimately entwined with its landscape, with buildings and monuments perched atop crags and overshadowed by cliffs – in the words of Robert Louis Stevenson, 'a dream in masonry and living rock'. From the Old Town's picturesque jumble of medieval tenements piled high along the Royal Mile, its turreted skyline strung between the black, bull-nosed Castle Rock and the russet palisade of Salisbury Crags, to the New Town's neat grid of neoclassical respectability, all columns and capitals, porticoes and pediments, the city offers a constantly changing perspective. And it's all small enough to explore easily on foot.

You can always tell the character of a place by the nicknames it has earned. Appropriately enough for the city that inspired

LOWDOWN

Bus ticket 80p
Coffee £2
Don't say ... But it's not a real parliament, is it?
Essential accessory The latest Inspector Rebus novel, by Ian Rankin
Midrange double room Around £80
No-no Trying to take a photo of your pal beside the Greyfriars Bobby statue during rush hour
Population 454,000
Time Zone GMT

The Strange Case of Dr Jekyll and Mr Hyde, Edinburgh has two contradictory – but complementary – ones.

The Athens of the North, a name inspired by the great thinkers of the Scottish Enlightenment, is a city of high culture and lofty ideals, of art and literature, philosophy and science. It is here that each summer the world's biggest arts festival rises, phoenixlike, from the ashes of last year's rave reviews and broken box-office records to produce yet another string of superlatives. And it is here, beneath the Greek temples of Calton Hill – Edinburgh's acropolis – that the Scottish Parliament sits again after a 300-year absence.

But Edinburgh is also Auld Reekie, an altogether earthier place that flicks an impudent finger at the pretensions of the literati. Auld Reekie is a city of loud, crowded pubs and decadent restaurants, late-night drinking and all-night parties, beer-fuelled poets and foul-mouthed comedians. It's the city that tempted Robert Louis Stevenson from his law lectures to explore the drinking dens and lurid street life of the 19th-century Old Town. And it's the city of Beltane, the resurrected pagan May Day festival where half-naked revellers dance in the flickering firelight of bonfires beneath the stony indifference of Calton Hill's pillared monuments.

Like a favourite book, Edinburgh is a city you'll want to dip into again and again, savouring each time a different image or experience – the castle silhouetted against a blue spring sky with a yellow haze of daffodils misting the slopes below the esplanade; stumbling out of a late-night club into the pale gold of a summer dawn, with only the yawp of seagulls and the thrum of taxi tyres over cobblestones to break the unexpected silence; heading for a café on a chill December morning with the haar (fog) snagging the spires of the Old Town, and the dark mouths of the wynds (alleys) more mysterious than ever; and festival fireworks crackling in the night sky as you stand, transfixed, amid the crowds in Princes St Gardens.

UNMISSABLE EDINBURGH

- Down a pint of Deuchars IPA at the **Bow Bar** (p123)
- Enjoy dinner at **Oloroso's rooftop restaurant** (p110)
- Take a tour of the new **Scottish Parliament Building** (p61)
- Discover the **Real Mary King's Close** (p57)
- Watch the sunset from the summit of **Calton Hill** (p70)

City Life

City Life

EDINBURGH TODAY

There is a definite spring in Edinburgh's step these days. The return of the Scottish Parliament and the booming financial sector have led to low unemployment, a growing population, high property prices and new building projects everywhere.

The city has shrugged off its grey, Presbyterian image and is now fast overtaking Glasgow in the coolness stakes. A brand-development project has been put in place to promote Edinburgh around the world, and soon you will be seeing the slogan 'Edinburgh: Inspiring Capital' and the brand logo of three arching, intersecting lines everywhere from the airport arrivals hall to the sides of taxicabs. (The lines in the logo symbolically link past, present and future, but also call to mind the outline of Arthur's Seat and Salisbury Crags, or perhaps the triple cantilevers of the Forth Bridge.)

Edinburgh was designated as Unesco's first City of Literature in 2004, and there are plans to create an Edinburgh equivalent of London Fashion Week. The city ranks in the top 10 international conference and convention cities, and readers of the *Guardian* and *Observer* newspapers have voted it their favourite UK city for six years running (2000–05). There's no denying it's a great place to live – it has all the amenities of a cosmopolitan capital city, from superb art galleries and museums to top restaurants and clubs. With the addition of the Christmas and New Year celebrations to the long-standing Festival and Fringe, Edinburgh has become the party capital of Europe.

AULD REEKIE NAE MAIR

The Scottish Parliament has introduced a Scotland-wide ban on smoking in all enclosed public spaces and workplaces, effective from 26 March 2006. Unlike the ban proposed for England and Wales, the Scottish ban applies to all pubs and private clubs; hotels may provide designated smoking rooms if they wish. The penalty for defying the ban is a £50 fine.

CITY CALENDAR

Edinburgh's calendar is packed full of events and festivities; for more information check out the Festival City chapter (p20) and Holidays (p196).

CULTURE

IDENTITY

Edinburgh was once portrayed as a prim Presbyterian city full of repressed Calvinists who would no sooner speak to a stranger in the street than they would punch a church minister. Today, however, Edinburgh is the most cosmopolitan city in Scotland – it's often described as the 'least Scottish' of Scottish cities; anyone who lives here for any length of time soon finds out that many of the people they meet are not native Edinburghers, but are incomers from somewhere else.

This cosmopolitan blend means that there's no longer any such thing as a 'typical' Edinburgher…except, perhaps, in the mind of Glaswegians, who will be happy to tell you – often at great length – that their east-coast neighbours are smug, superior, stuck-up and standoffish.

As with any stereotype, there are elements of truth in the Glasgow jibes. Writing in the late 19th century, novelist Robert Louis Stevenson described the inhabitants of his home town as 'citizens of the familiar type who keep ledgers, and attend church, and have sold their immortal portion to a daily paper… To see them thronging by, in their neat clothes and conscious moral rectitude, and with a little air of possession that verges on the absurd, is not the least striking feature of the place.'

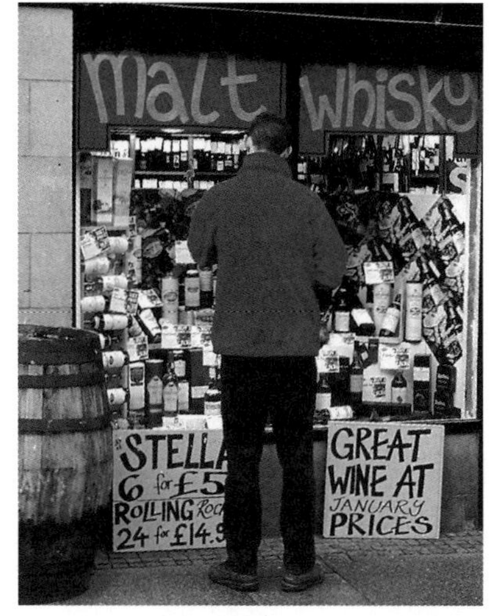

More than a hundred years later, church attendance is much reduced but 'keeping ledgers' is still one of the city's economic mainstays and the *Scotsman* newspaper is still the breakfast read of choice for the middle classes. You can still observe the neat clothes of the brokers and accountants as they tote their cardboard cups of Starbucks latte back to the office, and that 'air of possession' is reflected in an instinctive (and protective) awareness of the beauty of their city – God help any neighbour who installs plastic-framed windows in a Georgian town house. As for 'conscious moral rectitude' – just read the letters page of the *Scotsman.*

Bar-room sociologists theorise that it was Edinburgh citizens' long history of living cheek-by-jowl in close-packed tenements that led to both their polite reticence (we all have to retain some privacy, after all, and respect that of others) and their feverish obsession with the doings of their neighbours. Here's Stevenson again, with another observation that still rings true today: 'Edinburgh is not so much a small city as the largest of small towns. It is scarce possible to avoid observing your neighbours; and I never yet heard of any one who tried.'

Although they're a gregarious lot, Edinburgh folk can still display a certain reticence with strangers. In pubs you'll find that the locals are rarely the ones to break the ice, but if you make the effort to get talking you'll find them to be warm and witty company, proud of their city and happy to expound on its finer points (as well as the multifarious failings of its politicians). But whatever you do, don't refer to people from Leith as Edinburghers. Although Edinburgh's port was incorporated as part of the city in 1920, its inhabitants remain fiercely independent. They're Leithers, and don't you forget it.

Edinburgh's population of 454,000 is made up of white-collar and blue-collar workers in roughly equal proportions. In fact, with so many people employed in finance, government, education, law and medicine, the city has Scotland's largest middle-class population. This class divide is mirrored in the sporting world, where rugby is traditionally seen as the preserve of former public schoolboys, while football (soccer) is for the great unwashed. Whenever two or more Edinburgh football fans get together, the first question is, 'what team do you support?' With rugby fans, it's, 'what school did you go to?'

Immigration has added a bit of spice to the city's ethnic mixture but on a smaller scale than other European capitals. Following the 19th-century famines in Ireland, many Irish settled here, and so have a considerable proportion of English people. There are also many

HOT CONVERSATION TOPICS

- The new Parliament Building – a ground-breaking architectural achievement or the world's biggest IKEA office?
- Edinburgh: Inspiring Capital – a snappy slogan well worth spending £800,000 on or sounds like the advertising strap-line for an investment bank?
- Bringing back trams on Princes St – will the overhead power lines spoil the view?
- Edinburgh City Centre Traffic Management – a clever scheme to cut congestion or the demented ravings of megalomaniac planners?
- The new ban on smoking in enclosed public places – an infringement of human rights or a breath of fresh air?

smaller ethnic communities including Italians, Poles, Indians, Pakistanis, Bangladeshis and Chinese. There is a growing Spanish community and, since the enlargement of the EU in 2004, the Poles who adopted Scotland as their home after WWII have been joined by a sizeable new wave of younger compatriots.

LIFESTYLE

The old Edinburgh stereotype was the blue-rinsed and handbagged Morningside lady who spent her days drinking tea with her friends, shopping at Jenners for tweeds and twinsets, and twitching the lace curtains in the front room to keep an eye on the neighbours. The annual Festival Fringe was an occasion for writing letters of complaint to the *Scotsman* ('an affront to decent citizens' etc etc); and 'sex' was what the coalman delivered your coal in.

The Morningside ladies still exist – keep your eyes open in Jenners – but today the typical 30-something professional Edinburgher probably lives in a tenement flat in the Southside (paid for with a hefty mortgage), works in financial services and spends far too much time each evening circling the block in the eternal quest for a parking space. They drink wine rather than beer, latte rather than tea, and eat out at least once a week. They're obsessed with property prices, take a week or two's skiing holiday each winter and dream about owning a farmhouse in France. The average annual salary is around £24,500 (that's 107% of the Scottish national average), and the average house price in late 2005 was £178,000, so getting a foot on the property ladder is difficult.

All the same, living in Edinburgh has many benefits. The place is small enough to have a human scale, and you're forever bumping into people you know (someone once

A DOUBLE LIFE

Ever since the 18th century writers have found in Edinburgh a metaphor for the duality of human nature. The image of the orderly and elegant New Town alongside the jumble and chaos of the Old has long suggested the juxtaposition of respectable and bawdy, public and private, good and evil. And the city's vertical dimension – with its soaring monuments and sculpted façades rising above dark alleys, dripping vaults and chilly cellars – neatly symbolises an equivalent moral dimension, with lofty ideals and ambitions raised high above festering sumps of filth and depravity.

Robert Louis Stevenson became all too aware of the two sides of his own nature during his student days, when he would escape the rectitude of Presbyterian family life and the monotony of his law lectures by slinking off to the pubs and brothels of the Old Town and Leith. He explored this theme more fully in his classic story of dual identity, *The Strange Case of Dr Jekyll and Mr Hyde,* which, though set in London, is undeniably an Edinburgh novel.

Along with his own adventures, Stevenson's inspiration for Jekyll and Hyde was the story of Deacon Brodie. William Brodie (1741–88) was born to a wealthy New Town family. He grew up to be a skilled cabinet-maker and a member of the city council, mingling with high society and meeting poet Robert Burns and painter Sir Henry Raeburn. But this veneer of respectability concealed a taste for Edinburgh's darker side: by night he haunted the Old Town's drinking dens, whorehouses and cockpits, maintained two mistresses and fathered half a dozen illegitimate children. He gambled away his inherited fortune and ran up huge debts.

Brodie's status as a trusted deacon (city councillor) and cabinet-maker gave him legitimate daytime access to city shops and grand houses. Using a piece of putty, he secretly took impressions of any keys he found, and paid a criminal locksmith to make copies, allowing him to enter his victims' properties during the night and steal at will to finance his nocturnal activities.

Deacon Brodie's double life continued undetected for several years until a bungled attempt to burgle the Excise Office forced him to flee to Holland. Brodie's accomplices turned King's evidence, and he was caught in the act of boarding a ship to America. Tried and sentenced to death, he was hanged – in a wonderfully ironic twist – on an improved city gallows that he himself had designed.

Muriel Spark's classic novel *The Prime of Miss Jean Brodie* explores duality both in the contrast between Miss Brodie's two suitors – the respectable music teacher, Mr Lowther, and the libidinous art teacher, Teddy Lloyd – and in her own inner conflict between wild romance and repressed sexuality; the choice of the heroine's surname was not accidental. More recently, Edinburgh novelist Ian Rankin has admitted that the inspiration for his first John Rebus novel, *Knots and Crosses*, came from Jekyll and Hyde; his subsequent Rebus books display a continuing fascination with the darker side of human nature and the seamier side of Scotland's capital.

TENEMENT LIVING

The tenement is a distinctive feature of Edinburgh's streetscape, from the cramped, 17th-century 'lands' that line much of the Royal Mile to the regular façades and pointy turrets of the smart Victorian buildings that spread to the south of the city centre.

A tenement is a communal building, generally four to six storeys high, that is divided into flats (apartments) opening from a common stairway. Tenement flats range in size and grandeur from cramped one-bedroom places in formerly working-class areas such as Gorgie and Abbeyhill to the spacious, high-ceilinged, three- and four-bedroom apartments of genteel Marchmont and Newington.

The original tenements of the Old Town were a response to the lack of building space within the city walls: unable to expand outwards, the city built upwards. The Victorian tenements of southern Edinburgh were built in order to squeeze as many rent-paying tenants as possible onto a landowner's property. Both meant living in close proximity to your neighbours, and the 'vertical street' of the common stairway often engendered a strong feeling of community. Even now, things such as upkeep of the roof, cleaning of the stairs and payment of the electricity bill for the main-door buzzer/intercom are shared among the occupants.

Today, a spacious tenement flat in Edinburgh is a highly desirable property, especially if it retains period features such as ornate plaster cornicing and cast-iron fireplaces. At the time of writing, a three-bedroomed flat in Marchmont (just south of the Meadows) would set you back around £265,000 to £325,000.

said that Edinburgh is a city the size of a town that feels like a village, and you'll soon see what they mean). Its compact size means that getting around is easy – many people enjoy a short walk to work rather than a long commute – and the countryside is never more than half an hour away. You can go walking through the Pentland Hills or sailing on the Firth of Forth – both are only a few miles from the city centre – and the Scottish Highlands are only an hour's drive to the north.

Edinburgh's population is ageing – almost a quarter of Edinburghers are retired – but this balance is set to change as the city expands dramatically over the next 10 to 15 years; the population is expected to have increased by 50,000 in 2015.

FOOD

Eating out in Edinburgh has changed beyond all recognition in the last 20 years. Two decades ago, sophisticated dining meant a visit to the Aberdeen Angus Steak House for prawn cocktail, sirloin steak (well done) and chips, and Black Forest gateau, all washed down with Mateus Rosé. Today, the city has more restaurants per head of population than any other city in the UK, with settings ranging from cosy candlelit cellars to modern roof-top lounges.

Traditionally, Scottish cookery was all about basic comfort food – solid, nourishing fare, often high in fat, that would keep you warm on a winter's day spent in the fields or fishing, and sweet treats to come home to in the evening. Nowadays, the label Modern Scottish (see p103) has been invented to describe the lighter, more sophisticated cuisine served in many of Edinburgh's newer restaurants.

Haggis may be the national dish for which Scotland is most famous but, when it comes to what Scottish people actually cook and eat most often, the hands-down winner has to be mince and tatties. Minced beef is browned in the pan and then stewed slowly with onion, carrot and gravy, and served with mashed potatoes (with a splash of milk and a knob of butter added during the mashing) – tasty, warming, and you don't even have to chew. You'll rarely see it on an Edinburgh restaurant menu though – it's strictly a home-cooked dish.

Surprisingly few Scots eat porridge for breakfast – these days a café latte and a croissant is just as likely – and even fewer eat it in the traditional way; that is with salt to taste, but no sugar. The breakfast offered in an Edinburgh B&B or hotel usually consists of fruit juice and cereal or muesli, followed by a choice of bacon, sausage, black pudding, grilled tomato, mushrooms and a fried egg or two. Fish for breakfast may sound strange, but many hotels still offer the traditional Scots delicacy of grilled kippers (smoked herrings) or smoked haddock (poached in milk and served with a poached egg) for breakfast – delicious with lots of buttered toast.

OAT CUISINE

Oats: a grain, which in England is generally given to horses, but in Scotland appears to support the people.

A Dictionary of the English Language, *by Samuel Johnson (1709–84)*

The most distinctive feature of traditional Scottish cookery is the abundant use of oatmeal. Oats *(Avena sativa)* grow well in the cool, wet climate of Scotland and have been cultivated here for at least 2000 years. Up to the 19th century, oatmeal was the main source of calories for the rural Scottish population. The farmer in his field, the cattle drover on the road to market, the soldier on the march – all would carry with them a bag of meal that could be mixed with water and baked on a girdle (a flat metal plate) or on hot stones beside a fire.

Long despised as an inferior foodstuff (see Johnson's sneering description above), oatmeal is enjoying a return to popularity as recent research has proved it to be highly nutritious (high in iron, calcium and B vitamins) and healthy (rich in soluble fibre, which helps to reduce cholesterol).

The best-known Scottish oatmeal dish is, of course, porridge, which is simply rolled oatmeal boiled with water. A lot of nonsense has been written about porridge and whether it should be eaten with salt or with sugar. It should be eaten however you like it – as a child in the 1850s, Robert Louis Stevenson had golden syrup with his. Oatmeal is also a vital ingredient of haggis.

Oatcakes are another traditional dish that you will certainly come across during a visit to Edinburgh, usually as an accompaniment to cheese at the end of a meal. A mealie pudding is a sausage-skin stuffed with oatmeal and onion and boiled for an hour or so. Add blood to the mixture and you have a black pudding. Skirlie is simply chopped onions and oatmeal fried in beef dripping and seasoned with salt and pepper; it's usually served as a side dish. Trout and herring can be dipped in oatmeal before frying, and it can be added to soups and stews as a thickening agent. It's even used in desserts – toasted oatmeal is a vital flavouring in cranachan, a delicious mixture of whipped cream, whisky and raspberries.

Meat eaters will enjoy a thick fillet of world-famous Aberdeen Angus beef; venison, from Highland red deer, is leaner and also appears on many menus. Both may be served with a wine-based or creamy whisky sauce.

And then there's haggis, Scotland's much-maligned national dish. Haggis is often ridiculed because of its ingredients, which admittedly don't sound promising – the finely chopped lungs, heart and liver of a sheep, mixed with oatmeal and onion and stuffed into a sheep's stomach bag. However, it actually tastes surprisingly good. Haggis should be served with champit tatties and bashed neeps (mashed potatoes and turnips), with a generous dollop of butter and a good sprinkling of black pepper.

Although it's eaten year-round, haggis is central to the celebrations of 25 January, in honour of Scotland's national poet, Robert Burns. Scots worldwide unite on Burns Night to revel in their Scottishness. A piper announces the arrival of the haggis and Burns' poem *Address to a Haggis* is recited to this 'Great chieftain o' the puddin-race'. The bulging haggis is then lanced with a dirk (dagger) to reveal the steaming offal within, 'warm, reekin, rich'. Vegetarians (and quite a few carnivores, no doubt) will be relieved to know that veggie haggis is available in some restaurants.

Scottish salmon is famous worldwide, but there's a big difference between farmed salmon and the leaner, more expensive, wild fish. Smoked salmon is traditionally dressed with a squeeze of lemon juice and eaten with fresh brown bread and butter. Trout, the salmon's smaller cousin – whether wild, rod-caught brown trout or farmed rainbow trout – is delicious fried in oatmeal.

As an alternative to kippers you may be offered Arbroath smokies (lightly smoked fresh haddock), traditionally eaten cold. Herring fillets fried in oatmeal are good, if you don't mind picking out a few bones. Mackerel pâté and smoked or peppered mackerel (both served cold) are also popular.

Juicy Scottish langoustines (also called Dublin Bay prawns), crabs, lobsters, oysters, mussels and scallops are widely available in Edinburgh restaurants. Seafood soups include the delicious Cullen skink, made with smoked haddock, potato, onion and milk, and partan bree (crab soup).

Traditional Scottish puddings are irresistibly creamy, high-calorie concoctions. Cranachan is whipped cream flavoured with whisky and mixed with toasted oatmeal and raspberries. Atholl brose is a mixture of cream, whisky and honey flavoured with oatmeal, and clootie dumpling is a rich steamed pudding filled with currants and raisins.

FASHION

Edinburgh has often been dismissed as a style vacuum, especially by Glasgow fashionistas who consider their city to be Scotland's capital of chic. But things are changing, and the capital is starting to carve out a place of its own in the fashion world. Following the opening of Harvey Nichols, Louis Vuitton and Armani stores in Edinburgh, there are plans to establish the Scottish capital's own version of London Fashion Week.

In 2005 Edinburgh was listed by *Vogue* magazine as one of the top 16 fashion destinations in the world, and the Edinburgh College of Art continues to turn out a string of talented fashion graduates. Yong Hei Fong won several national awards in 2004, including the Harrods Design Initiative Award, and went on to work with Alexander McQueen and Phoebe Philo at Chloe in Paris. Browns, a leading London designer boutique, bought his entire collection.

Once a city of pinstripe suits, twinsets and tweeds, Edinburgh has become increasingly fashion-conscious in recent years, and the local Sunday newspaper supplements are filled with soft-focus spreads of the latest designer offerings. A developing taste for sharp styling and look-at-me chic is reflected in a wave of new designer boutiques, though Princes St is still a long way short of a Parisian boulevard when it comes to citizens decked out with effortless elegance.

Many of Edinburgh's clothes shops stock knitwear from the famous Pringle factory. The 200-year-old Pringle brand was a world-famous fashion name from the 1930s to the '60s (think twinsets – Pringle invented them – and diamond-pattern sweaters), but from the '70s to the '90s it fell out of the mainstream and the name came to be associated with golfers and, in the '80s, a violent faction of football fans known as 'casuals'. But Pringle was relaunched in 2000 as a designer brand and has achieved huge success: Pringle sweaters have been seen clinging to the torsos of Sharon Stone, Tom Hanks and David Beckham.

Another traditionally Scottish fashion success story is 21st Century Kilts (see p152). Designer Howie Nicholsby created the company in 1996 in order to reinvent Scotland's national costume for the 21st century. He believes that the kilt should be a garment that can be worn in all situations, not just at weddings and Burns Nights. His designs range from plain black barathea and formal pinstripe to more exotic variations like camouflage material and black leather; he himself has worn a kilt almost every day since 1999. Howie's kilts have been worn by celebrities such as Madonna, Robbie Williams, Mel Gibson and Samuel L Jackson.

SPORT

Football (soccer) in Scotland is not so much a sport as a religion, with thousands turning out to worship their local teams on Wednesdays and weekends throughout the season (August to May). Sacred rites include standing in the freezing cold of a February day, drinking hot Bovril and eating a Scotch pie as you watch your team getting gubbed.

Edinburgh's two main football teams are Heart of Midlothian (aka Hearts, nicknamed the Jam Tarts or Jambos), founded in 1874, and Hibernian (aka Hibs, Hibbies or Hi-bees), founded in 1875. On match days you'll see thousands of supporters streaming along Dalry and Gorgie Rds (Hearts) or Easter Rd (Hibs) on their way to the game (see also p145).

There's intense rivalry between the two clubs – both play in the Scottish Premier League – which reaches a peak when they play each other (the teams meet four times a year in a match known as the 'local Derby'). The big event in Edinburgh's football calendar used to be the New Year Derby, when Hibs and Hearts faced each other on New Year's Day, but the 100-year-old tradition was scrapped in 1999; match timing is now dictated by TV schedules.

Traditionally, football was the sport of Scotland's urban working classes, while rugby union was the preserve of public schoolboys, middle-class university graduates, and farmers and agricultural workers from the Borders. Although this distinction is breaking down – rugby's popularity soared after the 1999 World Cup was staged in the UK, and the middle classes have invaded the football terraces – it still persists to some extent, especially in Edinburgh.

Each year, starting in January, Scotland takes part in the Six Nations Rugby Union Championship. The most important fixture is the clash against England for the Calcutta Cup – it's always an emotive event, though Scotland has only won once in the last 10 years. The match is played at Edinburgh's Murrayfield Stadium (p146) every second year – the next one is in 2008.

MEDIA

Edinburgh has been a major publishing centre since the 18th century, and many famous names had their origins here – the *Encyclopaedia Britannica* (1768–71) and *Chambers Encyclopaedia* (1859–68) were first published in Edinburgh, and the publishing houses A&C Black and Constable were founded here. Edinburgh publishers are fewer in number these days but they include the innovative Canongate Books, led by charismatic young publisher Jamie Byng and home to bestselling authors Michel Faber *(The Crimson Petal and the White),* Yann Martel *(The Life of Pi)* and Man-Booker Prize–winner DBC Pierre *(Vernon God Little).*

Edinburgh's first newspaper – *Diurnal Occurrances touching the Dailie Proceedings in Parliament* – was printed in 1641. Today, the city is home to the Scotsman Publications, founded in 1817, which publishes the *Scotsman, Scotland on Sunday* and *Edinburgh Evening News.* Having been owned for 10 years by the wealthy and reclusive Barclay brothers (who also own the *Daily Telegraph, Sunday Telegraph* and *Spectator*), the Scotsman group was taken over in December 2005 by Johnston Press, a regional newspaper publisher that was founded in Falkirk, Scotland, in 1767.

Edinburgh pretty much invented the literary magazine in the late 18th century, and the *Edinburgh Review,* founded in 1802, is still published twice a year. Current Edinburgh-based literary magazines also include the thrice-yearly *Cencrastus* and the quarterly *Chapman.*

LANGUAGE

The language of modern Edinburgh is, of course, English. The educated Edinburgh accent at its Sunday best has a Scottish burr, but is much more clear and understandable to visitors than the broader accents of Glasgow and Aberdeen. There is, of course, a less formal Edinburgh argot, famously recorded in the expletive-strewn pages of Irvine Welsh's novel *Trainspotting,* which you'll overhear in pubs, on buses and on the football terraces. At the other end of the social spectrum, the ultimate expression of Edinburgh gentility is the Morningside accent, an over-compensated attempt to mimic the posh vowels of southern England's Received Pronunciation, in which 'girl' becomes 'gerl' and 'friend' becomes 'fraynd'. Wonderfully rendered by Maggie Smith in *The Prime of Miss Jean Brodie*, the Morningside accent is becoming rarer but can still occasionally be heard in any tearoom with more than a hint of chintz.

From the 8th to the 19th centuries the common language of the city's inhabitants was Lowland Scots. Sometimes called Lallans, Lowland Scots evolved from Old English, like modern English, and has Dutch, French, Gaelic, German and Scandinavian influences. As distinct from English as Norwegian is from Danish, it was the official language of the state in Scotland until the Act of Union in 1707, and was the language used by Robert Burns in much of his poetry. Following the Union, English rose to predominance as the language of government and of polite society. The spread of education and literacy in the 19th century eventually led to the Scots language being perceived as backward and unsophisticated; school children were often beaten for using Scots instead of English.

The Scots tongue persisted, however, and today it is undergoing a revival: Scots language dictionaries have been published, there are university degree courses in Scots language and literature, and Scots is studied as part of the school curriculum. The Scottish Parliament's website (www.scottish.parliament.uk) has a section written in Scots, and a few die-hard enthusiasts even write letters to the newspapers in broad Scots.

KEN WHIT AH MEAN?

Many old Scots words, and a few Gaelic ones, survive in common usage in Scotland, and you'll come across them in books, newspapers and even TV news reports as well as everyday speech. If you're intrigued by such Scotticisms, any Edinburgh bookshop will be able to sell you a Scots dictionary, where you can discover the delights of colourful words such as *cantrip, dreich* and *clishmaclaiver.*

Auld Reekie – Edinburgh (Old Smoky)

aye – yes/always

bairn – baby or child

ben – mountain

blether – chat

brae – hill

bridie – pie filled with meat, potatoes and onion

brig – bridge

burgh – town

cairn – pile of stones to mark a path or junction, also peak

ceilidh – pronounced 'kay-ley', dance

close – entrance

cratur – whisky

daur – dare

dene – valley

dinnae – don't

dram – glass of whisky

drap – drop

dun – fort

firth – estuary

glen – valley

gubbed – beaten soundly (as in a football match)

haar – fog off the North Sea

Hogmanay – New Year's Eve

howff – pub or shelter

ken – know

kirk – church

law – round hill

links – grass-covered, coastal sand dunes; golf course on same

neeps – turnips

provost – mayor

quaich – small drinking cup

quid – pound sterling

rood – cross

sporran – purse worn on a chain round the waist, with a kilt

tatties – potatoes

tolbooth – courthouse or jail

tron – public weighbridge

vennel – narrow street

wynd – lane or alley

ECONOMY & COSTS

Edinburgh's economy today is overwhelmingly based on the service sector, which accounts for some 90% of the city's employment, mainly in the fields of finance and tourism; in both sectors Edinburgh is second only to London. The Royal Bank of Scotland, HBOS (created in 2001 from the merger of the Bank of Scotland with the Halifax building society) and several other major financial institutions have their headquarters in the city, with many financial offices clustered in the new Exchange district on the west side of Lothian Rd. The Royal Bank has recently moved into a huge, purpose-built complex at Gogarburn, near Edinburgh Airport.

Other important service sectors include retail, education, law, local government and health. The city's growth areas are in research, information technology, computer software and biotechnology, with many businesses located in new industrial parks in the west of the city.

The traditional industries of Edinburgh's past – brewing, biscuit-making, publishing and printing – linger on in much reduced form. The international brewing company Scottish & Newcastle still has its corporate HQ in the city, but only a single brewery now survives (there were once 40), while publishing and printing also continue on a smaller scale.

The city's economy received a major boost with the creation of the Scottish Parliament in 1999. New building and redevelopment projects are taking shape all over the city and the unemployment rate (around 2%) is below the UK average.

As a visitor to the city, expect to pay around £60 to £100 a night for a double room in an attractive, central hotel, and budget around £15 a head for lunch and £25 for dinner if you plan to sample the best of Edinburgh's restaurants. Rates in both hotels and backpacker hostels can rise by up to 25% during the festival periods in August and at New Year.

Most of the city's art galleries and museums have free admission, and you can save on restaurant bills by looking for business-lunch deals and reduced-price pre- and post-theatre menus.

HOW MUCH?

1.5L bottled water 65p

1L petrol 90p

Bottle of malt whisky £25 to £30

Cappuccino £2

Dinner at the Tower £27 a head

Fashion kilt from £300

Fish supper £4

Glass of wine £2.75

Pint of beer £2.50

Souvenir T-shirt £12

GOVERNMENT & POLITICS

The Scottish Parliament is a single-chamber system with 129 members (known as MSPs), elected through proportional representation and led by a first minister, currently Jack McConnell. It sits for four-year terms and is responsible for so-called 'devolved matters': education, health, housing, transport, economic development and other domestic affairs. It also has the power (as yet unused) to increase or decrease the rate of income tax in Scotland by up to 3%. The Scottish Executive – composed of the first minister, various Scottish ministers, junior ministers and Scottish law officers – is the Scottish government, which proposes new laws and deals with the areas of responsibility outlined above, while the body of MSPs – the Scottish Parliament – constitutes the Scottish legislature, which debates, amends and votes on new legislation.

Westminster still has power over so-called 'reserved matters' such as defence, foreign affairs and social security. Scotland is represented in Westminster by 59 Scottish members of parliament (MPs) in the House of Commons, out of a total of 646. The Scotland Office, headed by the Secretary of State for Scotland, is the Westminster department charged with ensuring Scotland's interests are represented in the UK government.

In contrast to Westminster, where the main political contest is between the Labour and Conservative parties, with the Liberal Democrats coming third, Scotland has four main parties – the Labour Party, the Scottish National Party (SNP), the Scottish Conservative and Unionist Party (also known as the Tory Party or just the Tories) and the Liberal Democrats (Lib Dems); the main struggle for power is between Labour and the SNP. Smaller parties are also represented, including the Scottish Socialist Party and the Green Party.

The Conservative Party was opposed to devolution (the transfer of government powers from Westminster to Scotland), a policy proposed by the Labour Party in the hope of appeasing demands for independence. The long-term goal of Scottish Nationalists is complete independence for Scotland.

The new Scottish Parliament Building (p61) at Holyrood

In the 1997 UK general elections, Scotland returned no Conservative MPs at all; in the 2001 UK elections the Tories managed to claw back just one seat in Scotland, a figure which did not increase in the 2005 elections. In the 2003 Scottish Parliament elections, Labour won 50 seats, the SNP 27, Conservatives 18 and the Lib Dems 17; the Scottish Socialist Party took six seats and the Green Party seven.

Edinburgh's local government is in the hands of the City of Edinburgh Council, based in the City Chambers in High St. The council is popularly elected and serves four-year terms. The council's 58 seats are dominated by Labour (30 seats); the Lib Dems have 15 seats and the Conservatives 13.

ENVIRONMENT

Edinburgh earned its sobriquet of Auld Reekie (Old Smoky) in the 17th century from the characteristic pall of smoke that hung over the city, caused by the huge concentration of domestic fires. With the coming of the Industrial Revolution, pollution from factories and steam trains added to the grime. Beginning in the 1950s, a series of smokeless zones were set up that now encompass the whole city.

The last decade has seen the cleaning of soot-blackened stonework on many of Edinburgh's older buildings, in the hope of restoring them to their original colour; the Royal Scottish Academy is one of the most recent structures to shed its grime. Others have not been cleaned because of the danger of damage to delicate stonework – it may be hard to believe, but the Scott Monument on Princes St was originally pale grey in colour.

Edinburghers are proud of their city's appearance, and any development plans put forward by the city council inevitably generate a lively debate in the letters pages of the *Scotsman* and *Evening News* newspapers. The Cockburn Association (www.cockburnassociation.org.uk) was founded in 1875 with the aim of 'preserving and increasing the attractions of Edinburgh', and is still very active today, having been involved in, among other things, the creation of the City Bypass, the Water of Leith Walkway and the plans to introduce a tram system.

THE LAND

Edinburgh is draped over and around a series of hills – the deeply eroded stumps of ancient volcanoes – between the Pentland Hills in the south and the broad Firth of Forth estuary to the north. During the last Ice Age (around 12,000 years ago) a vast ice sheet flowed from west to east around Castle Rock, creating a 'crag and tail' feature on which the Old Town was built.

Holyrood Park provides a broad swath of wild countryside in the city centre, with a varied landscape of hills, lochs and moorland. Edinburgh's only river, the Water of Leith, runs from the Pentlands northwards to the Firth of Forth at Leith, along the northwestern border of New Town.

GREEN EDINBURGH

The City of Edinburgh Council is one of the UK's more daring and forward-thinking when it comes to the subject of traffic control. In the last decade it has set up a system of dedicated bus lanes with the aim of reducing traffic congestion and vehicle pollution, and developed a growing network of cycling routes. Private cars have been banned from Princes St, but the plan to introduce a congestion-charging scheme similar to that in London was abandoned by the council after city residents rejected the scheme in a referendum in 2005.

Edinburgh was the first city in the UK to introduce a car-free housing development, 2 miles from the city centre on Gorgie Rd. Space usually allocated to car parking has been given over to children's playgrounds, sports facilities and cycle paths; solar power is used to augment the electricity supply; and 'grey water' (waste water from baths and kitchen sinks) is recycled through a reed bed and reused for domestic washing.

The Water of Leith (p81) and the River Almond (at Cramond; see p77) were once industrialised and severely polluted but both have been cleaned up in the last two decades; the Almond is now so clean that otters and salmon have been sighted in recent years.

URBAN PLANNING & DEVELOPMENT

Edinburgh is growing faster than any other city in Scotland, creating problems for planners; the main issues are traffic congestion and a lack of building space, which is putting pressure on green-belt areas.

Since the rejection of the congestion-charging scheme, city planners have been tearing their hair out trying to come up with effective ways to reduce congestion, while motorists have been tearing their hair out trying to cope with the often hare-brained schemes city planners have put into effect – if you have a couple of hours to spare, just ask any taxi driver what they think about the Central Edinburgh Traffic Management scheme.

Recent transport improvements include the Fastlink – a guided busway and priority route linking the city centre with the Gyle and Edinburgh Park train stations to the west of the city – which opened in December 2004. The Edinburgh Airport Rail Link (which will tie the airport into the national rail network) should be operational by 2010.

Waverley train station is undergoing a redevelopment that will include the introduction of escalators on the Waverley Steps, linking the station with Princes St, and new high-tech bus stops throughout the city will provide real-time travel information so you know exactly when the next bus will arrive.

There are also plans to reintroduce trams to Edinburgh's streets, with lines running from the city centre to Leith in the north and Edinburgh Airport in the west; it is hoped that the first line will open by 2010.

The revamp of the Exchange financial district to the west of Lothian Rd is nearly complete, with a complex of new office buildings complementing the Edinburgh International Conference Centre and the Sheraton Grand Hotel. The next stage, still under way at the time of writing, is the building of luxury residential apartments at Port Hamilton, the easterly terminus of the Union Canal, which was reopened to navigation in 2002.

The removal of the Edinburgh Royal Infirmary in 2003 to a site on the southern edge of the city has left its old home between Lauriston Pl and the Meadows ripe for redevelopment. This prime city-centre location has been renamed Quartermile, and by 2010 it should have been transformed into a complex of offices, flats, shops, restaurants and a hotel (housed in the grand Scottish Baronial shell of the old infirmary).

Probably the biggest development in the city, however, is the plan to transform the whole of Edinburgh's waterfront, from Granton to Leith. This previously industrial area, once characterised by derelict gasometers, wasteland and the smell of chemical factories, is slated to become a dazzling Riviera of luxury apartments, hotels, shopping centres and yacht marinas by 2017.

Festival City

Festival City

Visit Edinburgh in August and you'll find yourself caught up in a phantasmagoria of festivals. The Royal Mile becomes a colourful crush of people and performers, with stilt-walkers wading through the crowds and fire-jugglers' flaming torches arcing above the sea of heads. Jazz bands and majorettes parade along a packed Princes St, Charlotte Sq is transformed into a book-lovers' village, Princes St Gardens is asprawl with sunbathers and picnickers, and the pub crowds spill out onto the pavements. The city's population almost doubles, and there is a permanent buzz of excitement in the air.

Since the first Edinburgh International Festival of Music and Drama in 1947, the city has grown into one of the biggest party venues in the world, with a crowded calendar of contrasting festivals ranging from science and storytelling to music, movies and marching military bands.

Festival high season is August, when half a dozen festivals – including the huge Edinburgh International Festival and the even bigger Festival Fringe – run concurrently, closely followed by late December, when the Christmas festival runs into the Hogmanay celebrations. All these and more are listed below in chronological order.

Edinburgh is at its prettiest in spring, when daffodils and cherry blossom brighten the parks and the weather is often at its best. May, June and September are generally the driest and sunniest months; July and August can bring heatwaves, but also a fair bit of rain, so consider carrying an umbrella or waterproof. Midwinter means short, dark days (the sun rises after 9am and sets before 4pm) and often cold weather – wrap up well for the Hogmanay festivities.

EDINBURGH INTERNATIONAL SCIENCE FESTIVAL

☎ 558 7666; www.sciencefestival.co.uk; 4 Gayfield Pl Lane, Edinburgh EH1 3NZ

First held in 1987, the Science Festival hosts a wide range of events, including talks, lectures, exhibitions, demonstrations, guided tours and interactive experiments designed to stimulate, inspire and challenge. From dinosaurs and ghosts to alien life forms, there's something to interest everyone. The Science Festival runs over 10 days in the first two weeks of April.

BELTANE

☎ 228 5353; www.beltane.org; Beltane Fire Society, 19 Leven St, Edinburgh EH3 9LH

Beltane is a pagan fire festival that marks the end of winter and the rebirth of spring. It was resurrected in modern form in 1988 and is now celebrated annually on the summit of Calton Hill. The spectacular rituals involve lots of fire, drumming, body paint and sexual innuendo (well, it's a fertility rite, after all). Bring your sparklers. Held annually on the night of 30 April into the early hours (around 1am) of 1 May.

SCOTTISH INTERNATIONAL CHILDREN'S FESTIVAL

☎ 225 8050; www.imaginate.org.uk; 45a George St, Edinburgh EH2 2HT

This is Britain's biggest festival of performing arts for children, with events suitable for kids aged from three to 12. Groups from around the world perform such classic tales as *Hansel and Gretel*, as well as new material written especially for youngsters. The Children's Festival takes place annually in the last week of May.

ROYAL HIGHLAND SHOW

☎ 335 6200; www.royalhighlandshow.org; Royal Highland Centre, Ingliston, Edinburgh EH28 8NF

Scotland's hugely popular national agricultural show is a four-day, green-wellied, Barbour-jacketed feast of all things rural, with everything from show-jumping and tractor-driving to sheep-shearing and falconry. Countless pens are filled with coiffed show cattle and pedicured prize ewes, while food and drink stalls dish out a feast, from smoked salmon to roast suckling pig sandwiches. The show is held over a long weekend (Thursday to Sunday) in late June.

PRIDE SCOTIA

☎ 556 9471; www.pride-scotia.org; 58a Broughton St, Edinburgh EH1 3SA

This annual celebration of Scotland's gay, lesbian and transgender community begins with a colourful parade along High St, down the Mound, along Princes St, then down Leith St and Broughton St, followed by lots of eating, drinking and dancing at various venues in the Pink Triangle, Edinburgh's 'gay village'. The Pride Scotia parade and festival takes place in even years in Glasgow, odd years in Edinburgh, on the last Saturday in June.

EDINBURGH INTERNATIONAL JAZZ & BLUES FESTIVAL

☎ 467 5200; www.edinburghjazzfestival.co.uk; 29 St Stephen St, Edinburgh EH3 5AN

Held annually since 1978, the Edinburgh International Jazz & Blues Festival pulls in top talent from all over the world. The first weekend sees a Mardi Gras street parade on Saturday from the City Chambers, up the Royal Mile and down into the Grassmarket, for an afternoon of free, open-air music. On the Sunday there's a series of free concerts at the Ross Bandstand in Princes St Gardens. The Jazz Festival runs for nine days, beginning on the last Friday in July (ie the week before the Fringe and Tattoo begin).

EDINBURGH MILITARY TATTOO

☎ 0870 755 5118; www.edintattoo.co.uk; Tattoo Office, 32 Market St, Edinburgh EH1 1QB

The Military Tattoo is a spectacular display of military marching bands, massed pipes and drums, acrobats, cheerleaders and motorcycle display teams, all played out in front of the magnificent backdrop of the floodlit castle. Each show traditionally finishes with a lone piper, dramatically lit, playing a lament on the battlements. The Tattoo takes place over the first three weeks of August (from a Friday to a Saturday); there's one show at 9pm Monday to Friday, and two (at 7.30pm and 10.30pm) on Saturday, but no performance on Sunday.

ONLY IN EDINBURGH

- **Beltane** (opposite) Pagan fire festival on Calton Hill.
- **Edinburgh Mela** (p23) Multicultural festival where sitars and bagpipes meet.
- **Edinburgh Military Tattoo** (above) Pomp and tradition set against an inimitable backdrop.
- **Edinburgh Festival Fringe** (p22) Nothing like it anywhere else.
- **Edinburgh's Hogmanay** (p24) World's biggest street party.

EDINBURGH FESTIVAL FRINGE

☎ 226 0026; www.edfringe.com; the Fringe Office, 180 High St, Edinburgh EH1 1QS

When the first Edinburgh Festival was held in 1947, there were eight theatre companies who didn't make it onto the main programme. Undeterred, they grouped together and held their own mini-festival, on the fringe…and an Edinburgh institution was born. Today the Edinburgh Festival Fringe is the biggest festival of the performing arts anywhere in the world, but despite its size the Fringe remains true to its origins in three fundamental respects: performers are not invited to the event (they must make their own arrangements); they make use of unusual and unconventional theatre spaces; and they take all their own financial risks – and it continues to be one of the world's most exciting and innovative drama events.

Since 1990 the Fringe has been dominated by stand-up comedy, but the sheer variety of shows on offer is just staggering – everything from performance poetry to chain-saw juggling and Tibetan yak-milk gargling. So how do you decide what to see? There are daily reviews in the *Scotsman* newspaper (one good *Scotsman* review, and a show sells out in hours) but the best recommendation is word of mouth. If you have the time, go to at least one unknown show – it may be crap but at least you'll have your obligatory 'worst show I ever saw' story to tell in the pub.

The big names play at the mega-venues such as the Assembly Rooms and the Pleasance, and charge mega-prices (from £10 per ticket and more). However, there are plenty of good shows that will only cost you a fiver and, best of all, lots of free stuff. Fringe Sunday – usually the second Sunday – is a smorgasbord of free performances staged in the Meadows park to the south of the Old Town.

The Fringe takes place over three and a half weeks in August, the last two weeks overlapping with the first two of the Edinburgh International Festival.

EDINBURGH INTERNATIONAL FESTIVAL

☎ 473 2000; www.eif.co.uk; the Hub, Castlehill, Edinburgh E1 2NE

First held in 1947 to mark a return to peace after the ordeal of WWII, the Edinburgh International Festival is festooned with superlatives: the oldest, the biggest, the most famous, the best in the world. The original was a modest affair but today hundreds of the world's top musicians and performers congregate in Edinburgh for three weeks of diverse and inspirational music, opera, theatre and dance.

The famous **Fireworks Concert**, held on the final Saturday of the Festival, is one of the most spectacular events of the year. A concert performed at the Ross Bandstand in Princes St Gardens (and broadcast live on radio) is accompanied by the carefully choreographed detonation of around 40 tons of artistically arranged gunpowder.

Tickets for the bandstand and gardens tend to sell out early but some are held back for personal callers at the Hub – these go on sale from the previous Sunday. If you don't manage to get a ticket, bring along a radio and join the crowds of locals on Princes St, the Mound, North Bridge, Calton Hill and Inverleith Park.

Tickets for popular events – especially music and opera – sell out quickly, so it's

FESTIVAL TICKETS & PROGRAMMES

The programme for the Edinburgh International Festival is usually published at the beginning of April; the Fringe programme comes out in early June. If you want to get hold of one as soon as possible, you can register online at the relevant website and a programme will be sent to you as soon as it's available (free for the International Festival, £2 for the Fringe).

You can start booking tickets as soon as you have a programme in your hands – by post, fax, phone or Internet, or over the counter at the box office (the Hub for the International Festival, the Fringe Office for the Fringe; see entries for details). Book as far in advance as possible for popular shows, or for anything you really, really want to see – there are few words more disappointing than 'sorry, it's sold out'.

You can find listings for all of Edinburgh's festivals on the umbrella website www.edinburgh-festivals.com.

best to book as far in advance as possible. You can buy tickets in person at the Hub, or by phone or Internet.

Edinburgh's annual culture-fest takes place over the three weeks ending on the first Saturday in September; the programme is usually available from April.

EDINBURGH INTERNATIONAL BOOK FESTIVAL

☎ 228 5444; www.edbookfest.co.uk; Scottish Book Centre, 137 Dundee St, Edinburgh EH11 1BG

Held in a little village of marquees in the middle of Charlotte Sq, the Book Festival is a fun fortnight of talks, readings, debates, lectures, book signings and meet-the-author events, with a café, bar and tented bookshop thrown in. The festival lasts for two weeks in August (usually during the first two weeks of the Edinburgh International Festival).

EDINBURGH INTERNATIONAL FILM FESTIVAL

☎ 229 2550; www.edfilmfest.org.uk; Filmhouse, 88 Lothian Rd, Edinburgh EH3 9BZ

The Edinburgh International Film Festival is one of the original Edinburgh Festival trinity, having first been staged in 1947 along with the International Festival and the Fringe. It is a major international event, serving as a showcase for new British and European films, and staging the European premieres of one or two Hollywood blockbusters. The Film Festival lasts for two weeks in August (usually the first two weeks of the Edinburgh International Festival).

EDINBURGH MELA

☎ 557 1400; www.edinburgh-mela.co.uk; Arts Quarter, Gateway Theatre, Elm Row, Edinburgh EH7 4AH

Swirling saris and skirling bagpipes, the swing of the kilt and the twang of sitars, curry washed down with Irn-Bru – the Edinburgh Mela is a colourful festival that celebrates Scotland's cultural diversity. Founded by the city's Bangladeshi, Indian and Pakistani communities back in 1995, the Mela is a weekend of multicultural music, dance, food and fashion, with plenty of children's activities. It's held over a weekend at the end of August or the beginning of September; the venue is Pilrig Park.

Torch-light procession, Hogmanay (p24)

SCOTTISH INTERNATIONAL STORYTELLING FESTIVAL

☎ 556 9579; www.scottishstorytellingcentre.co.uk; Scottish Storytelling Centre, the Netherbow, 43-45 High St, Edinburgh EH1 1SR

The Storytelling Centre was established in 1996 and now organises this annual celebration of the great art of spinning a yarn. Events for all ages are staged at a variety of indoor and outdoor venues, leavened with both traditional music and crafts workshops. The Storytelling Festival runs over 10 days, ending on the first Sunday in November.

EDINBURGH'S CHRISTMAS

☎ 529 3914; www.edinburghschristmas.com; City of Edinburgh Council, City Chambers, High St, Edinburgh EH1 1HQ

The newest of the Scottish capital's festivals, first held in 2000, the Edinburgh Christmas bash includes a big street parade, a fairground and a Ferris wheel, plus an open-air ice rink in Princes St Gardens. The celebrations are held over the three weeks prior to Christmas.

EDINBURGH'S HOGMANAY

☎ 529 3914; www.edinburghshogmanay.com; City of Edinburgh Council, City Chambers, High St, Edinburgh EH1 1HQ

For Scots, the New Year (Hogmanay) has always been a more important celebration than Christmas. In towns, cities and villages all over the country, people fill the streets at midnight on 31 December to wish each other a Guid New Year and, yes, to knock back a dram or six to keep the cold at bay.

In 1993 Edinburgh's city council had the excellent idea of spicing up Hogmanay by organising some events, laying on some live music in Princes St and issuing an open invitation to the rest of the world. Most of them turned up, or so it seemed, and had such a good time that they told all their pals and came back again the following year. Now Edinburgh's Hogmanay is the biggest winter festival in Europe, regularly pulling in over 250,000 partying punters.

Hogmanay events run from 29 December to 1 January. To get into the main party area in the city centre after 8pm on 31 December you'll need a ticket – book well in advance.

Arts & Architecture

Arts & Architecture

Edinburgh has long dominated the Scottish arts scene, with its many galleries, studios and theatres and an annual feast of world-class festivals (see p20). Although it plays host to a wide cross-section of the arts, it has always been above all a writer's city: as well as being a major publishing centre for more than 250 years, and having produced many of Britain's best writers, Edinburgh has its main train station named after a novel *(Waverley)*, its main shopping street is dominated by a towering Gothic monument to that novel's author (Sir Walter Scott) and there are at least four pubs named after Scott's novels. In 2004 Edinburgh was designated as Unesco's first City of Literature (see www.cityofliterature.com).

LITERATURE

Edinburgh has always been at the heart of the Scottish literary scene, from the days of the medieval makars (makers of verses; poets) William Dunbar and Gavin Douglas to the modern 'brat pack' of Iain Banks, Irvine Welsh, Ian Rankin and Christopher Brookmyre. To experience the Scottish literature scene at a reading, see p144.

POPULAR LITERATURE TODAY

Walk into any major bookshop in Edinburgh and you'll find a healthy 'Scottish Fiction' section, its shelves bulging with recently published works by bestselling Edinburgh authors such as Iain Banks, Christopher Brookmyre, Quintin Jardine, Ian Rankin, Alexander McCall Smith and Irvine Welsh.

Hailed as one of the most imaginative writers of his generation, Iain Banks burst upon the Scottish literary scene in 1990 with his dazzling debut novel *The Wasp Factory*, a macabre but utterly compelling exploration of the inner world of Frank, a strange and deeply disturbed teenager. His most enjoyable books are the thriller-cum-satire *Complicity* (1993) and the immensely likeable *The Crow Road* (1992), a witty and moving family saga that provides one of Scottish fiction's most memorable opening sentences: 'It was the day my grandmother exploded.' He also writes science fiction under 'the world's most penetrable pseudonym', Iain M Banks – his latest SF novel, *The Algebraist* (2005), got rave reviews – and he recently produced a nonfiction title, *Raw Spirit* (2004), about malt whisky.

Christopher Brookmyre's thrillers specialise in outrageous characters, preposterous plots, biting wit and lots of violence and bad language. His more recent offerings seem to have lost the plot a little, but early titles such as *Quite Ugly One Morning* (1997) and *Country of the Blind* (1998) provide laugh-out-loud entertainment. Not a suitable Christmas present for your granny, though.

Ian Rankin and Quintin Jardine have both made their names with fictional, Edinburgh-based detectives – the hard-drinking, introspective John Rebus and the glamorous, golf-playing Bob Skinner, respectively. Ian Rankin's Rebus novels are dark, engrossing mysteries that explore the darker side of Scotland's capital city, filled with sharp dialogue, telling detail and three-dimensional characters, while Quintin Jardine's books are fast-paced, tightly plotted thrillers; both outsell John Grisham in Scotland. Rankin seems to improve with every book – his latest, *Fleshmarket Close* (2005), is one of his best – and he attracts a growing international following (his books have been translated into 22 languages).

The novels of Irvine Welsh, who grew up in Edinburgh's working-class district of Muirhouse, describe a very different world from that inhabited by Muriel Spark's Miss Jean Brodie – the modern city's underworld of drugs, drink, despair and violence. Famous for his debut novel *Trainspotting* (1993), Welsh's best work is probably *Marabou Stork Nightmares* (1996), in which a soccer hooligan – paralysed and in a coma – reviews his

TOP 10 EDINBURGH NOVELS

- *44 Scotland Street* by Alexander McCall Smith (2004) began as a serialised novel in the *Scotsman* newspaper. The absorbing, humorous and elegantly interwoven stories of the inhabitants of neighbouring New Town flats have now extended to a third volume.
- *Born Free* by Laura Hird (1999) is a gritty and tragic but heart-warming tale of modern family life in one of Edinburgh's poorer neighbourhoods, which brings vividly to life an aspect of the city that tourists never see.
- *Complicity* by Iain Banks (1993) is a gruesome and often hilarious thriller-cum-satire on the greed and corruption of the Thatcher years as it follows a strung-out journalist on the trail of a serial killer through the backdrop of Edinburgh.
- *The Falls* by Ian Rankin (2001) is a gripping noir-style crime novel that stars hard-drinking detective John Rebus, Edinburgh's answer to Sam Spade, as he struggles to solve the disappearance of a student while grappling with shades of the city's dark history.
- *The Heart of Midlothian* by Sir Walter Scott (1818) is perhaps Scott's finest and most complex work. Set in Edinburgh in the first half of the 18th century, this novel deals with justice, and the lack of it, seen through the eyes of Jeanie Deans, a heroine far ahead of her time.
- *Fleshmarket* by Nicola Morgan (2003), aimed primarily at a teenage readership, is a gory tale of revenge and redemption set in early-19th-century Edinburgh that follows the adventures of a boy who gets mixed up in the murky world of the notorious bodysnatchers Burke and Hare.
- *The Prime of Miss Jean Brodie* by Muriel Spark (1962) is the story of a charismatic teacher in a 1930s Edinburgh girls' school who leads her chosen girls – her *'crème de la crème'* – in the pursuit of truth and beauty, with devastating consequences.
- *The Private Memoirs and Confessions of a Justified Sinner* by James Hogg (1824) is a postmodern novel some 150 years ahead of its time. This is both a murder story told from two points of view and an ingenious deconstruction of the religious certainties of 18th-century Scotland.
- *Skinner's Rules* by Quintin Jardine (1993) is the first in a series of well-plotted detective stories centred on Edinburgh CID chief Bob Skinner; not as dark or as satisfying as Ian Rankin's Rebus novels, but gripping nonetheless.
- *Trainspotting* by Irvine Welsh (1993) is a disturbing and darkly humorous journey through the junkie underworld of 1990s Edinburgh, pulling no punches as it charts hero Renton's descent into heroin addiction.

violent and brutal life. His much-anticipated latest novel, *Bedroom Secrets of the Master Chefs*, comes out in late 2006.

The latest Edinburgh author to hit the headlines is Alexander McCall Smith, a professor of medical ethics at Edinburgh University. He has written more than 50 books but is best known for his whimsical detective stories set in Botswana, starring the female private investigator Precious Ramotswe; the first in the series is titled *The No 1 Ladies' Detective Agency*. In recent years he has revived the art of the serialised novel in *44 Scotland Street*, the engrossing adventures of a cross-section of contemporary Edinburgh society, which first appeared in daily instalments in the Scotsman newspaper in 2004; at the time of writing a second volume *(Espresso Tales)* had appeared, and a third was in the pipleline.

FROM THE BEGINNING

There are monuments and memorials to poets and novelists all over Edinburgh. One of the more prominent is the statue of the poet Allan Ramsay on the corner of Princes St and the Mound. Though born in the Southern Uplands village of Leadhills, Allan Ramsay (1686–1758) spent most of his life in Edinburgh. His best-known work is *The Gentle Shepherd*, a pastoral comedy that was much admired by Robert Burns. The house he built for himself on Castle Hill survives today in Ramsay Garden (p92).

Another poet who earned Burns' admiration was Robert Fergusson (1750–74), who was born in Edinburgh and wrote wittily in broad Scots about everyday city life, notably in the poem 'Auld Reekie'. Tragically, he suffered a head injury after falling down some stairs and died soon afterwards in a mental institution at the age of only 24; a statue of Fergusson stands outside the kirkyard of Canongate Church (p55), where he is buried.

Robert Burns (1759–96) himself spent only a few short spells in the capital between 1786 and 1788, and again in 1791, but he was enthusiastically received by Edinburgh society, who hailed him as 'the ploughman poet'. Burns' love affair with the Edinburgh lady Mrs Agnes MacLehose inspired one of his finest love poems, 'Ae Fond Kiss'. The Burns Monument (p71) stands on Regent Rd on Calton Hill.

A contemporary of Burns, James Boswell (1740–95) was an Edinburgh advocate who is best known for his *Life of Johnson*, a biography of Dr Samuel Johnson, the English lexicographer who compiled the first dictionary of the English language. A classic of 18th-century literature, Boswell's *Journal of a Tour to the Hebrides* is a lively and engaging account of his expedition with Johnson to the western isles of Scotland.

The writer most deeply associated with Edinburgh is undoubtedly Sir Walter Scott (1771–1832), Scotland's greatest and most prolific novelist. The son of an Edinburgh lawyer, Scott was born in Guthrie St (off Chambers St; the house no longer exists) and lived at various New Town addresses before moving to his country house at Abbotsford, near Melrose. Scott's early works were rhyming ballads, such as *The Lady of the Lake*, and his first historical novels (Scott effectively invented the genre) were published anonymously; he will always be best remembered for classic tales such as *The Antiquary*, *The Heart of Midlothian*, *Ivanhoe*, *Redgauntlet* and *Castle Dangerous*. Scott almost single-handedly revived interest in Scottish history and legend in the early 19th century, and was largely responsible for organising King George IV's visit to Scotland in 1822, an event which kick-started Scotland's tourist industry.

Another Edinburgh novelist with an international reputation, Robert Louis Stevenson (1850–94) was born at 8 Howard Pl in the New Town, into a family of famous lighthouse engineers. Stevenson studied law at Edinburgh University but was always intent on pursuing the life of writer. Though dogged by ill health, he was an inveterate traveller and eventually settled in Samoa in 1889, where he was revered by the natives as 'Tusitala' – the teller of tales. Stevenson is known and loved around the world for those tales, classic stories such as *Kidnapped*, *Catriona*, *Treasure Island*, *The Master of Ballantrae* and *The Strange Case of Dr Jekyll and Mr Hyde*, many of which have been made into successful films. The most popular and enduring is *Treasure Island* (1883), which has been translated into many languages and has never been out of print.

The year after Stevenson finished dodging his law lectures at Edinburgh University, another famous writer in the making enrolled to study medicine. Sir Arthur Conan Doyle (1859–1930) based the character of Sherlock Holmes on one of his lecturers, the surgeon Dr Joseph Bell, who was famed for his powers of observation. Bell's party trick was to deduce a person's trade or occupation simply by observing them, and he applied his forensic skills and powers of deduction on several murder cases in Edinburgh. Conan Doyle (who is commemorated in a statue of Sherlock Holmes on Picardy Pl, at the top of Leith Walk) also wrote *The Lost World*, an early inspiration for *Jurassic Park*.

No list of Edinburgh novelists would be complete without mention of Dame Muriel Spark (b 1918), who was born in Edinburgh and educated at James Gillespie's High School for Girls, an experience that provided material for her best-known novel *The Prime of Miss Jean Brodie* (1961), a shrewd portrait of 1930s Edinburgh. A prolific writer, Dame Muriel's 22nd novel, *The Finishing School*, was published in 2004 when she was 86.

Norman MacCaig (1910–96), born in Edinburgh and educated at Edinburgh University, is widely regarded as the greatest Scottish poet of his generation. A primary-school teacher for almost 40 years, MacCaig wrote poetry that is witty, adventurous, moving and evocative, and filled with sharp observation; poems such as 'November Night, Edinburgh' vividly capture the atmosphere of his home city. MacCaig could often be found enjoying a pint of beer with his contemporaries Robert Garioch (1909–81) and Sydney Goodsir Smith (1915–75) in Milne's Bar on the corner of Rose and Hanover Sts, behind Princes St in central Edinburgh.

ARCHITECTURE

Edinburgh's unique beauty arises from a combination of its unusual site, perched among craggy hills, and a legacy of fine architecture dating from the 16th century to the present day.

One of the outstanding features of the Old Town is the biggest concentration of surviving 17th-century buildings in Britain, which were impressive enough to be remarked upon by Daniel Defoe (author of *Robinson Crusoe*) during a visit in 1723, when he described the

Georgian terraces in the New Town (p67)

Royal Mile as 'the largest, longest and finest street for buildings and number of inhabitants, not only in Britain, but in the world.' You can explore the interior of a 17th-century tenement at Gladstone's Land (p56) and John Knox House (p56).

ATHENS OF THE NORTH

Perhaps the most important event in Edinburgh's development was the opening of the North Bridge in 1772, connecting the Old Town to the ridge of land on which the New Town was to be built (the North Bridge you see today is a replacement built in the 1890s), allowing the city to expand outside the old city walls.

The construction of the New Town began in the east, around St Andrew Sq; you can see the oldest New Town houses at 23 to 26 St Andrew Sq. Initially, the houses were derided for their dullness and lack of imagination, and as a result of such criticism the city council commissioned Robert Adam to design a unified plan for Charlotte Sq.

Robert Adam (1728–92) was one of the leading architects of the 18th century, leaving his mark not only on Edinburgh, where he was educated, but on England, where he became architect to King George III. Having studied the antiquities of Rome during his grand tour of Europe, he transformed the appearance of country houses throughout Britain with his neoclassical designs. As well as his masterpiece on Charlotte Sq (p70), his Edinburgh works include Register House (p68), Edinburgh University's Old College (p65) and Hopetoun House (p81). You can experience the elegance of Adam's work by visiting the National Trust for Scotland's Georgian House (p70).

William Henry Playfair (1790–1857) dominated Edinburgh's 19th-century architecture as Adam had dominated that of the Georgian era. Though born in London, he moved to Edinburgh at the age of five and was educated there. His first commission in Edinburgh

TOP FIVE BEAUTIFUL BUILDINGS

- **Charlotte Square** (1796; p70) The elegantly proportioned Adam façade on the square's north side is the jewel in the New Town's architectural crown.
- **Dundas House** (1772–74; p70) A gorgeous Palladian mansion that now houses a bank; pop into the main banking hall for a look at the dome, painted cerulean blue and studded with glazed stars.
- **Museum of Scotland** (1999; p65) One of the best of the city's modern buildings, the museum's golden sandstone lines create echoes of castles, churches, gardens and cliffs.
- **Royal Scottish Academy** (1836; p69) Recently stone-cleaned, this imposing William Playfair–designed Doric temple dominates the centre of Princes St.
- **Scottish Parliament Building** (2005; p61) Ambitious, controversial and way over budget, the new Parliament Building is the most exciting example of modern architecture in Scotland.

was to complete the unfinished quad of Adam's Old College. Having inherited the mantle of Robert Adam, he went on to create many of the grand neoclassical buildings that have given Edinburgh the nickname 'Athens of the North', including the City Observatory (1818; p71), the National Monument (1829; p71), Surgeon's Hall (1832; p66), the Royal Scottish Academy (1836; p69) and the National Gallery of Scotland (1848; p68).

ARCHITECTURE OF THE OLD SCHOOL

Education has always been important to the Scots, an enthusiasm reflected in the fact that some of the grandest buildings in Edinburgh are schools. The oldest is George Heriot's School (p63), which was built between 1628 and 1650. The building was funded by George Heriot (nicknamed Jinglin' Geordie), goldsmith and jeweller to King James VI, who bequeathed most of his estate to the founding of a hospital (ie a charity school) for 'puir faitherless bairnes' (orphans). Heriot's Hospital, as it was originally known, is one of the finest Renaissance buildings in Scotland; one of the most unusual features is the sequence of numbers from 1 to 180 carved into the 17th-century flagstones in the quad – each boy had a number, and had to stand on that number each morning when lined up at roll call.

Looking north from the walls of Edinburgh Castle, you can't avoid spotting the forest of Gothic turrets and spires that is Fettes College, designed by David Bryce and built in 1870. The magnificent confection of French Gothic and Scottish Baronial styles is best seen from the top of Learmonth Ave. The school's illustrious former pupils include the Rt Hon Tony Blair, the British prime minister, and (in fiction only, of course) James Bond, agent 007. Bryce's other works include the Bank of Scotland headquarters on the Mound (p57), the old Royal Infirmary on Lauriston Pl and the Bank of Scotland building on St Andrew Sq.

Persistently in the news is the former Royal High School on Calton Hill. This beautiful neoclassical complex was built in 1829 in Greek Doric style to a design by Thomas Hamilton based on the Temple of Theseus in Athens (this was one of the buildings that gave Edinburgh its nickname, Athens of the North). In 1977 the school was converted into a debating chamber in anticipation of the creation of a Scottish Parliament in 1979, a move which was rejected until 1996. The building has lain empty ever since but a campaign has been launched to convert the school into a home for a Scottish National Photography Centre (see www.snpc.org.uk).

Other grandiose school buildings in Edinburgh include Donaldson's College (1851; by William Playfair) on West Coates and Stewart's Melville College (1848; by David Rhind) on Queensferry St.

COMPETING INTERESTS

Edinburgh's planners have often resorted to architectural competitions when deciding on designs for major new developments. The plan for the New Town (18th century) was the result of a competition won by James Craig, then an unknown, self-taught 23-year-old. Likewise, the design of the Scott Monument (19th century; p69) was the work of George Meikle Kemp, an unknown joiner and draughtsman who entered the competition under a pseudonym so as to avoid prejudice.

At the end of the 20th century an architectural competition resulted in the relatively unknown (at least in Scotland) Enric Miralles, a 45-year-old Catalan, being chosen as the architect for the new Scottish Parliament Building (p61). Though its construction was shrouded with controversy, the new building won the 2005 Stirling Prize for the best new architecture in Britain, and has revitalised a near-derelict industrial site at the foot of the Royal Mile. Nearby on Holyrood Rd is the overhanging glass façade of the Tun (p123), an energetically modern complex that includes a café-bar, offices and BBC studios, plus the award-winning Scottish Poetry Library (p144), cleverly insinuated into a cramped location.

Overlooking the Parliament Building from Regent Rd on Calton Hill is the massive, modernist pile of St Andrew's House (p71; 1936–39), one of the most impressive pieces of pre-WWII architecture in Edinburgh. Yet another result of an architectural competition, this Art Deco palace was built to house the Scottish Office – now renamed the Scottish Executive and moved to an austerely symmetrical modern building on Victoria Quay in Leith.

TOP FIVE EDINBURGH FILMS

- *Complicity* (2000) Though not as satisfying as the novel (see p27), this fast-paced thriller keeps you watching as it follows cocaine-fuelled Edinburgh journalist Cameron Colley (Jonny Lee Miller) on the trail of a serial killer.
- *Greyfriars Bobby* (1961) Walt Disney's film version of the life of Edinburgh's most famous pooch is still a watchable, if somewhat saccharine, children's movie.
- *The Prime of Miss Jean Brodie* (1969) In this classic evocation of 1930s Edinburgh, a charismatic school teacher (Maggie Smith) attempts to mould her young 'gerls' in her own image, with tragic results.
- *Restless Natives* (1985) A whimsical comedy that follows two disillusioned Edinburgh lads as they embark on a highwaymen's spree of nonviolent robberies of tourist coaches, becoming folk heroes in the process.
- *Trainspotting* (1996) A gritty and ground-breaking look at life among Edinburgh's heroin addicts, filled with memorable scenes, sharp dialogue and a pounding soundtrack.

CINEMA

Scotland has never really had its own film industry, but in recent years the government-funded agency **Scottish Screen** (☎ 0141-302 1700; www.scottishscreen.com) has been created to nurture native talent and promote and develop all aspects of film and TV throughout Scotland.

Probably the classic Edinburgh film is Ronald Neame's 1969 screen version of Muriel Spark's classic Edinburgh novel *The Prime of Miss Jean Brodie*. Set in the 1930s, it presents the two contrasting aspects of the city in the juxtaposition of the upper-middle-class Marcia Blane School for Girls (actually Donaldson's School for the Deaf on Henderson Row, now part of Edinburgh Academy, in Stockbridge) with the grim, grey tenements of the Old Town (Greyfriars Kirkyard and the Vennel, Grassmarket).

Screenwriter John Hodge, who wrote the scripts for *Shallow Grave* (1994), *Trainspotting* (1996) and *A Life Less Ordinary* (1997) in collaboration with director Danny Boyle and producer Andrew Macdonald, is actually a qualified doctor who studied medicine at Edinburgh University from 1982 to 1987. The gorgeous apartment in *Shallow Grave* was a studio set but its exterior was played by a Georgian New Town terrace. The unforgettable opening scenes of *Trainspotting* follow Renton as he sprints along Princes St before being spreadeagled across the bonnet of a car in Calton Rd.

Edinburgh's most famous son – in or out of the cinema – is of course the actor Sir Sean Connery, the original and best James Bond, and star of countless hit movies since, including *Highlander* (1986), *The Name of the Rose* (1986), *Indiana Jones and the Last Crusade* (1989), *The Hunt for Red October* (1990), *Just Cause* (1995) and *The League of Extraordinary Gentlemen* (2003). Connery started his working life as 'Big Tam' Connery, sometime milkman and brickie, born in a tenement in Fountainbridge.

Edinburgh hosts a highly regarded international film festival, based at the Filmhouse in Lothian Rd (see p23). The Edinburgh International TV Festival (www.mgeitf.co.uk), held during the August bank holiday weekend, is primarily an industry event, with 1700 delegates attending various discussions, lectures, previews and masterclasses.

MUSIC

When it comes to new bands, Edinburgh tends to be eclipsed by the hipper metropolis of Glasgow – which produced Belle & Sebastian and Franz Ferdinand, to name but two. The city's contribution to the contemporary music scene includes indie rock band Idlewild as well as the now-defunct experimental rockers the Beta Band; reggae-soul-pop singer Finlay Quaye; Shirley Manson, lead singer of Garbage; and jazz saxophonist Tommy Smith.

The airwaves have been awash with female singer-songwriters in recent years, but

TOP FIVE EDINBURGH CDS

- *100 Broken Windows* Idlewild
- *Maverick A Strike* Finlay Quaye
- *Rollin'* Bay City Rollers
- *Sunshine on Leith* Proclaimers
- *The Three EP's* Beta Band

few are as gutsy and versatile as Edinburgh-born, St Andrews–raised KT Tunstall. Although she's been writing and singing for the last 10 years, it was her 2005 debut album *Eye to the Telescope* that introduced her to a wider audience. The bespectacled twin brothers Craig and Charlie Reid, better known as the Proclaimers, live just across the water in Fife; they also released a new album in 2005 *(Restless)* which is as passionate and invigorating as the songs that first made them famous back in the late 1980s: 'Letter from America' and 'I'm Gonna Be (500 Miles)'.

Edinburgh rock musicians who made their names in the 1970s and '80s include Ian Anderson, front man for Jethro Tull, and Mike Scott of the Waterboys. Fish, the lead singer in Marillion, now produces solo albums and runs a successful recording studio in East Lothian. Other Edinburgh acts include the Bay City Rollers, Ballboy, Bert Jansch, Pilot and EMF; Barbara Dickson, Nazareth and the Rezillos hail from Dunfermline, at the far end of the Forth Rd Bridge.

Scotland has always had a strong folk tradition, which underwent an Edinburgh-based revival in the 1960s and '70s. Robin Hall and Jimmy MacGregor, the Corries and the hugely talented Ewan McColl worked the pubs and clubs in the capital and up and down the country. During this time the Incredible String Band and the Boys of the Lough successfully combined folk and rock and have been followed by Runrig (who write songs in Gaelic), the Battlefield Band, Alba, Capercaillie and others. Though folk music rarely hits the headlines these days, the Edinburgh folk scene is alive and kicking; performers to look out for include the Mick West Band, Jock Tamson's Bairns and Tony McManus.

See p143 for details on the live-music scene in Edinburgh.

VISUAL ARTS

Scottish portraiture reached its peak during the Scottish Enlightenment in the second half of the 18th century with the paintings of Sir Henry Raeburn (1756–1823) and his contemporary Allan Ramsay (1713–84; son of the previously mentioned poet Allan Ramsay). You can see many fine examples of their work in the Scottish National Portrait Gallery (p70). Scotland's most famous painting is probably Raeburn's portrait of the *Reverend Robert Walker Skating on Duddingston Loch*, which hangs in the National Gallery of Scotland (p68). This image of a Presbyterian minister at play beneath Arthur's Seat, with all the poise of a ballerina and the hint of a smile on his lips, is perhaps the ultimate symbol of Enlightenment Edinburgh, the triumph of reason over wild nature.

In the early 20th century the Scottish painters most widely acclaimed outside the country were the group known as the Scottish Colourists – SJ Peploe, Francis Cadell, Leslie Hunter and JD Ferguson (all except Hunter were Edinburgh-born) – whose striking paintings drew on French postimpressionist and Fauvist influences. Peploe and Cadell, active in the 1920s and '30s, often spent the summer painting together on the Isle of Iona, and reproductions of their beautiful land- and seascapes appear on many a print and postcard. You can see examples of their work at the Scottish National Gallery of Modern Art (p74).

The painters of the so-called Edinburgh School of the 1930s were modernist landscape artists. Chief among them were William Gillies (1898–1978), Sir William MacTaggart (1903–81) and Anne Redpath (1895–1965). Following WWII, artists such as Alan Davie (b 1920) and Sir Eduardo Paolozzi (1924–2005) gained international reputations in abstract expressionism and pop art. The Dean Gallery (p73) in Edinburgh has a large collection of Paolozzi's work.

TOP FIVE ART GALLERIES

- **City Art Centre** (p62) Populist and popular, mixing a permanent collection of 17th- to 20th-century Scottish art with blockbusting temporary exhibitions.
- **Fruitmarket Gallery** (p63) Minimalist, modern, art-student hang-out.
- **National Gallery of Scotland** (p68) The country's main collection of both Scottish and international pre-20th-century art.
- **Royal Scottish Academy** (p69) Greek temple on Princes St hosting crowd-pulling travelling exhibitions from around the world.
- **Scottish National Gallery of Modern Art** (p74) Grand mansion in beautiful grounds makes a great setting for 20th-century art.

History

History

THE RECENT PAST

The biggest event of recent years has been the long-awaited completion of the new Scottish Parliament Building at Holyrood (p61), which was officially opened by the Queen on 9 October 2004. A minor scandal arose in the wake of the opening when it was revealed that hasty, last-minute landscaping to prepare for the Queen's visit had involved the planting of many mature trees. These were planted at such an advanced age that they were unable to take root, and had died by the following summer. Not to worry; a week after the official opening, the cranes were back on site. Despite the pomp and ceremony, the building wasn't *quite* finished; in fact it was another year before it was finally signed off.

The initial public reaction to the building was mostly negative, ranging from baffled incredulity to downright hostility, but the opinion of architectural experts was much more positive. In fact, the building won a slew of awards in the year following its official opening, culminating in October 2005 with the prestigious Stirling Prize, the 'Oscars of the architectural world', awarded by the Royal Institute of British Architects for the building that has made the greatest contribution to British architecture.

Whatever. There are at least two groups of Edinburghers who are delighted with the new complex. Local skateboarders and BMXers have discovered that the ramps and embankments of the Parliament's landscaped grounds make a most excellent skatepark, dude. And the local pigeons have started roosting and nesting in the abundant nooks and crannies provided by the intricate architectural detailing.

FROM THE BEGINNING

Diners tucking into steaming bowls of mussels or sucking juicy oysters from the shell in seafood restaurants along the Shore in Leith are enjoying a feast whose traditions date back more than 10,000 years. Archaeologists at Cramond, on the northwestern edge of Edinburgh, have recently uncovered huge piles of discarded shells (known as middens, a Scots word meaning 'rubbish heap') which prove that Scotland's earliest inhabitants made good use of the oyster and mussel beds of the Firth of Forth. These primitive encampments have been dated to 8500 BC – the earliest known traces of human activity in Scotland.

As the glaciers retreated in the wake of the last Ice Age, the climate gradually improved (yes, it actually used to be worse than it is now), encouraging people to make this place their permanent home rather than a mere foraging camp. Edinburgh's Castle Rock, a volcanic crag with three vertical sides, was a natural defensive position that must have attracted the first settlers; the earliest signs of habitation on the rock date back to around 900 BC. There is also evidence that people grew crops on the slopes of Arthur's Seat, where traces of ancient cultivation terraces have been found.

HERE COME THE ROMANS

The Roman invasion of Britain began in 55 BC, when Julius Caesar's legions first crossed the English Channel, but the Roman onslaught ground to a halt in the north. Between AD 78 and 84 the Roman governor Agricola marched northwards and spent several years trying to subdue the wild tribes he found there. The Romans called these tribes

TIMELINE

8500 BC	900 BC
Evidence of habitation at Cramond is the earliest known sign of human activity in Scotland	Earliest signs of human habitation at Edinburgh's Castle Rock and Arthur's Seat

TOP FIVE BOOKS ON EDINBURGH'S HISTORY

- *Capital of the Mind: How Edinburgh Changed the World* (2003) by James Buchan – A vivid and engrossing account of the Scottish Enlightenment (1745–1820) in Edinburgh, which saw the capital's transformation from a squalid slum into the Athens of the North.
- *Edinburgh: The Making of a Capital City* (2005) by Brian Edwards and Paul Jenkins (eds) – An academic but profusely illustrated study of the city's development over the last 1000 years.
- *Edinburgh: Picturesque Notes* (1879, republished in 2001) by Robert Louis Stevenson – A fascinating sketch of the city in Victorian times by one of Edinburgh's most famous sons.
- *The Making of Classical Edinburgh* (1993) by AJ Youngson – A detailed, scholarly and well-illustrated history of the building and architecture of Edinburgh's Georgian New Town.
- *She Was Aye Workin': Memories of Tenement Women in Edinburgh and Glasgow* (2003) by Helen Clark and Elizabeth Carnegie – A lively and colourful oral history that brings alive the everyday lives of families living in Edinburgh (and Glasgow) tenements in the early 20th century.

Picts (painted people), probably because they painted their faces or bodies with woad. Agricola's son-in-law, Tacitus, named the northern part of Scotland Caledonia after the Caledones – the first tribe he came across.

By the 2nd century Emperor Hadrian had decided that this inhospitable land of mist, bogs, midges and warring tribes had little to offer the Roman Empire, and between AD 122 and 128 he built the wall that took his name (close to the modern border between Scotland and England). Two decades later Hadrian's successor, Antoninus Pius, invaded Scotland again and built another rampart, the Antonine Wall, between the Firth of Forth and the River Clyde. An important Roman fort and supply station were built at Cramond, with other garrisons at Inveresk and Dalkeith, but they were only manned for about 40 years before the Romans once again withdrew. Cramond's Roman remains are uninspiring, but the village has provided one of Britain's most impressive Roman sculptures (see The Cramond Lioness, p78).

HOW EDINBURGH GOT ITS NAME

When the Romans first arrived in the Lothian region, the chief tribe they encountered was the Votadini, who had settlements on Castle Rock, Arthur's Seat and Blackford Hill. Little is known about these ancient Britons but it seems likely they were the ancestors of the Gododdin, who are mentioned by the Welsh bard Aneirin in a 7th-century manuscript. Aneirin relates how Mynyddog Mwynfawr, king of the Gododdin, feasted with his warriors in the 'halls of Eidyn' before going into battle against the Angles (the tribe who gave their name to Angle-land, or England) at Catraeth (Catterick, in Yorkshire).

The 'capital' of the Gododdin was called Dun Eiden, which meant 'Fort on the Hill Slope', and almost certainly referred to Castle Rock. The Angles, from the kingdom of Northumbria in northeastern England, defeated the Gododdin and captured Dun Eiden in 638. It is thought that the Angles took the existing Celtic name 'Eiden' and tacked it onto their own Old English word for fort, 'burh', to create the forerunner of the name Edinburgh.

THE MACALPIN KINGS

Scotland is thought to have taken its name from the Scotti, or Scots, a Gaelic-speaking Irish tribe that colonised the west of Scotland in the 6th century. The Scots and Picts were eventually united by the threat of invasion by the Norsemen (Vikings) and by their common Christianity.

55 BC
Roman invasion of Britain

AD 122–28
Emperor Hadrian builds a wall close to the modern border between Scotland and England

Coat of arms above the entrance to the Palace of Holyroodhouse (p60)

In 843 Kenneth MacAlpin, the king of Dalriada (modern-day Kintyre and Argyll) and son of a Pictish princess, took advantage of the custom of matrilineal succession to take over the Pictish throne, uniting Scotland north of the Firth of Forth into a single kingdom. He made Scone (near Perth) his capital and brought to it the sacred Stone of Destiny (see p53) used in the coronation ceremonies of Scottish kings.

Nearly 200 years later, Kenneth MacAlpin's great-great-great-grandson, Malcolm II (r 1005–18), defeated the Northumbrian Angles led by King Canute at the Battle of Carham (1018) near Roxburgh on the River Tweed. This victory brought Edinburgh and the Lothian region under Scottish control and extended Scottish territory as far south as the Tweed.

THE CANMORE DYNASTY

Malcolm II's grandson was Malcolm III Canmore (r 1057–93). Malcolm III's father, Duncan, was murdered by Macbeth (as described in Shakespeare's play), and Macbeth himself was killed by Malcolm at Lumphanan in 1057. With his Saxon queen, Margaret, Malcolm Canmore founded a solid dynasty of able Scottish rulers. They introduced new Anglo-Norman systems of government and religious foundations to Scotland. Malcolm and Margaret had their main home in Dunfermline but regularly visited the castle at Edinburgh.

Until this period there was no record of a town at Edinburgh – just the castle – but from the 11th century a settlement grew along the ridge to the east of Castle Rock. It had been made into a royal burgh (a self-governing town with commercial privileges) by 1124, when Malcolm's son, David I (r 1124–53), held court at the castle and founded the abbey at Holyrood.

David's mother, Margaret, had been a deeply religious woman and either he or his brother, Alexander I (r 1107–24), built a church in her honour on Castle Rock; today St Margaret's Chapel is the city's oldest surviving building. David I increased his power by adopting the Norman feudal system, granting land to noble Norman families in return for their acting as what amounted to a royal police force.

The royal burghs – which included Edinburgh and its suburb, Canongate – were permitted to conduct foreign trade, for which purpose Edinburgh created a port at nearby Leith. Edinburgh at the beginning of the 12th century was still something of a backwater, playing second fiddle to the wealthy burghs of Stirling, Perth and Berwick. That all changed

4th century	638
Romans leave Britain	Angles defeat Gododdin and capture Dun Eiden

when David I's successor Malcolm IV (r 1153–65) made the castle in Edinburgh his chief residence and royal treasury.

WARS OF INDEPENDENCE

Two centuries of the Canmore dynasty came to an end in 1286 when Alexander III fell to his death over a cliff at Kinghorn in Fife. He was succeeded by his four-year-old granddaughter, Margaret (the Maid of Norway), who was engaged to the son of King Edward I of England.

Sadly, Margaret died in 1290 during the sea voyage to Scotland from her home in Norway, and there followed a dispute over the succession to the throne. There were no fewer than 13 claimants, but in the end it came down to two: Robert de Brus, lord of Annandale, and John Balliol, lord of Galloway. As the greatest feudal lord in Britain, Edward I of England was asked to arbitrate – he chose Balliol, whom he thought he could manipulate more easily. But instead of withdrawing, as the Scots nobles had expected, Edward tightened his feudal grip on Scotland, treating the Scots king as his vassal rather than his equal. The humiliated Balliol finally turned against Edward and made a treaty with France in 1295 – the so-called 'Auld Alliance'.

EXPLORING YOUR SCOTTISH ROOTS

Genealogy is a hugely popular pastime, and many visitors to Edinburgh take the opportunity to do some detective work on their Scottish ancestry.

The main records used in Scottish genealogical research – the Statutory Registers of births, marriages and deaths (1855 to the present), the Old Parish Registers (1533–1854), and the 10-yearly census returns from 1841 to 1901 – are held at the **General Register Office** (GRO; Map pp218-19; ☎ 314 4433; www.gro-scotland.gov.uk; New Register House, 3 W Register St; admission per half-/full day £10/17; 🕑 9am-4.30pm Mon-Fri), where you can do your own research (half-day passes are for afternoons only, 1pm to 4.30pm). The registration of births, marriages and deaths became compulsory in Scotland on 1 January 1855; before that date the ministers of the Church of Scotland kept registers of baptisms and marriages. The oldest surviving parish registers date back to 1553, but these records are far from complete, and many births and marriages before 1855 went unrecorded.

Nearby, the **National Archives of Scotland** (NAS; Map pp218-19; ☎ 535 1334; www.nas.gov.uk; Register House, 2 Princes St; admission free; 🕑 9am-4.45pm Mon-Fri) holds records of wills, property transactions and many other items of interest to genealogists. On your first visit to the NAS you will need to ask for a reader's ticket (free): bring some form of ID bearing your name and signature (eg passport, driving licence, bank card). Use of the Historical Search Room is free, and is first-come, first-served – you can't book a seat here.

You can consult all these records yourself, but make sure you do some research before leaving home: gather as much information as possible from birth, marriage and death certificates and other family papers in your possession, and interview elderly relatives. You will need full names, dates and places of birth, marriage or death in Scotland. One of the best guides is the book *Tracing Your Scottish Ancestry* by Kathleen B Cory, and there are many useful websites too – GenUKI (www.genuki.org.uk) is a good starting point.

At the ScotlandsPeople website (www.scotlandspeople.gov.uk) you can search the indexes to the Old Parish Registers and Statutory Registers (up to 100 years ago for births, 75 years ago for marriages and 50 years ago for deaths) and the indexes to the 1861, 1871, 1881, 1891 and 1901 census returns; you can view entries on a pay-per-view basis. The International Genealogical Index (www.familysearch.com), compiled by the Mormon Church, includes freely searchable records of Scottish baptisms and marriages from 1553 to 1875.

Another useful resource is the **Scottish Genealogy Society Library & Family History Centre** (Map p222; ☎ 220 3677; www.scotsgenealogy.com; 15 Victoria Tce; 🕑 10.30am-5.30pm Mon, Tue & Thu, 10.30am-8.30pm Wed, 10am-5pm Sat), which maintains the world's largest library of Scottish gravestone inscriptions. Entry is free to society members and £5 for nonmembers.

843 Kenneth MacAlpin unites Scotland north of the Firth of Forth

1018 Battle of Carham: Edinburgh and the Lothian region brought under Scottish control

The first recorded treaty for mutual self-defence between European nations, the agreement declared that if either member was attacked by England, the other would invade. It also gave all Scots dual French citizenship (a right that was not officially revoked until 1903), provided Scotland with a choice of fine French wines and introduced many French words into the Scots language.

The English king responded to the French treaty with a bloody attack. In 1296 he marched on Scotland with an army of 30,000 men, razed the ports of Berwick and Dunbar and butchered the citizens, and captured the castles of Berwick, Edinburgh, Roxburgh and Stirling. Balliol was incarcerated in the Tower of London, oaths of allegiance were demanded from Scottish nobles and, in a final blow to Scottish pride, Edward I removed the Stone of Destiny, the coronation stone of the kings of Scotland, from Scone and took it back to London.

BRAVEHEART

Bands of rebels led by local warlords attacked and harried the English occupiers. One such band, led by William Wallace (whose life was romanticised in the popular 1995 film *Braveheart*), defeated the English army at the Battle of Stirling Bridge in 1297, but Wallace was later captured and executed in London in 1305 (Wallace's giant broadsword can be seen at the Wallace Monument in Stirling, see p187). Inspired by Wallace's example, the Scots nobles looked around for a new leader and turned to Robert the Bruce, grandson of the lord of Annandale who had been rejected by Edward in 1292. Bruce murdered his rival, John Comyn, in February 1306 and had himself crowned king of Scotland at Scone the following month.

Bruce mounted a campaign to drive the English out of Scotland but suffered repeated defeats. According to legend, while Bruce was on the run he was inspired by a spider's persistence in spinning its web to 'try, try, and try again'. He went on to win a famous victory over the English, led by Edward II, at the Battle of Bannockburn in 1314 (see p187). Continued raids on the north of England forced Edward II to sue for peace, and in 1328 the Treaty of Northampton (also known as the Treaty of Edinburgh) gave Scotland its independence, with Robert I, the Bruce, as its king.

One of Robert's last acts before his death in 1329 was to grant Edinburgh a charter giving it control over the port of Leith, the mills on the Water of Leith and much of the surrounding countryside, effectively making it Scotland's most important royal burgh.

A MEDIEVAL MANHATTAN

Bannockburn and the Treaty of Northampton had no lasting effect. After the death of Robert I, the country was ravaged by civil disputes and continuing wars with England. Edinburgh was occupied several times by English armies, and in 1385 the Kirk of St Giles was burnt to the ground. Robert was succeeded by his five-year-old son, David II (r 1329–71), who returned from exile in France in 1341 and made Edinburgh his main residence, building a tower house on the site of what is now the Half Moon Battery in Edinburgh Castle. When David II died without a son, the crown passed to his nephew, Robert II (r 1371–90), the child of his sister Marjory and her husband Walter, the third high steward of Scotland. Thus was born the Stewart dynasty, which would rule Scotland and Britain for the next 300 years.

By the mid-15th century Edinburgh was the de facto royal capital and political centre of Scotland. The coronation of James II (r 1437–60) was held in the abbey at Holyrood and the Scottish Parliament met in the Tolbooth on High St or in the castle. The city's first effective town wall was constructed at about this time, enclosing the Old Town as far east as the Netherbow, and the Grassmarket. This overcrowded area – by then the most populous town in Scotland – became a medieval Manhattan, forcing its densely packed

1295

Scots form the Auld Alliance with France

1296

King Edward I invades Scotland and moves the Stone of Destiny from Perth to London

inhabitants to build upwards instead of outwards, creating tenements that towered up to 12 storeys high.

RENAISSANCE KING

James IV (r 1488–1513) married the daughter of Henry VII of England, the first of the Tudor monarchs, thereby linking the two royal families through 'the Marriage of the Thistle and the Rose'.

James was a true Renaissance man, interested in science, technology and the arts. He commissioned the *Great Michael,* the largest ship in Europe, encouraged the establishment of Edinburgh's first printing press and oversaw the foundation of Edinburgh's Royal College of Surgeons. He was fluent in several languages, wrote his own poetry, and was an enthusiastic amateur dentist, going so far as paying local people to allow him to pull their teeth.

His reign was a golden era that saw Edinburgh Castle become one of Britain's biggest gun foundries, the establishment of a supreme law court and the creation of a Scottish navy. Much graceful Scottish architecture dates from this time, and the Renaissance style can be seen in the alterations and additions made to the royal palaces at Holyrood, Stirling, Linlithgow and Falkland.

Renaissance ideas flourished throughout James IV's reign. Scottish poetry thrived, created by makars (makers of verses) such as William Dunbar, the court poet of James IV, and Gavin Douglas. The intellectual climate provided fertile ground for the rise of Protestantism, a reaction against the perceived wealth and corruption of the medieval Roman Catholic Church that would eventually lead to the Reformation.

However, James' marriage to an English princess didn't prevent the French from persuading him to go to war against his in-laws, and he was killed at the Battle of Flodden in 1513, along with 10,000 of his subjects. To protect Edinburgh from a feared English reprisal its citizens hurriedly built another wall, the Flodden Wall, around the city. The wall, which took more than 40 years to build, was over 1.25 miles long, 25ft (7.5m) high and 5ft (1.5m) thick.

QUEEN OF SCOTS

In 1542 King James V lay on his deathbed in Falkland Palace in Fife – broken-hearted, it is said, after his defeat by the English at Solway Moss. His French wife, Mary of Guise, had borne him two sons but both had died in infancy. On 8 December a messenger brought word that his wife had given birth to a baby girl at the Palace of Linlithgow. Fearing the end of the Stewart dynasty and recalling its origin through Robert the Bruce's daughter, James sighed, 'It cam' wi' a lass, and it will gang wi' a lass.' He died a few days later, leaving his week-old daughter Mary to inherit the throne as Queen of the Scots.

In 1548 Mary (r 1542–67) was sent to France, leaving the country to be ruled by regents. Henry VIII of England wanted the infant queen to be married to his son, but the Scots rejected him. Henry was furious and sent his armies to take vengeance. Parts of Edinburgh were razed, Holyrood Abbey was sacked and the Border abbeys of Melrose, Dryburgh and Jedburgh were burnt down. The 'Rough Wooing', as it was called, failed to persuade the Scots to see the error of their ways, and in 1558 Mary was married to the French dauphin, becoming queen of France as well as Scotland.

WHEN MARY MET JOHN

While Mary was in France being raised as a Roman Catholic, the Reformation tore through Scotland. The hell-fire preachings of John Knox, a pupil of the Swiss reformer Calvin, found sympathetic ears in Edinburgh – Knox was the minister at the kirk of St Giles – and in 1560 the Scottish Parliament created a Protestant church that was independent of Rome

1314
Battle of Bannockburn: Robert the Bruce defeats Edward II

1328
Treaty of Northampton (Treaty of Edinburgh) makes Robert I, the Bruce, king of Scotland

and of the monarchy. The Church of Scotland abolished the Latin Mass and denied the authority of the pope.

Following the death of her sickly husband, the 18-year-old Queen Mary returned to Scotland, arriving at Leith on 19 August 1561. A week later she was formally welcomed to her capital city, and dined in Edinburgh Castle before proceeding down the Royal Mile to the Palace of Holyroodhouse, where she held a famous audience with John Knox.

Knox's views were extreme: he believed that the people had a right to depose their monarch, and saw this Catholic queen as a threat to the Protestant cause. He also believed that there was no middle ground when it came to religion, that one was either of God or of the Devil – and he was in no doubt that Mary was not of God. Mary in turn described Knox as the most dangerous man in her kingdom, and feared a church that denied both royal and papal authority. At their meeting at Holyroodhouse the great reformer harangued the young queen ceaselessly and challenged her Catholic faith; she later agreed to give royal protection to the Protestant Church in Scotland, but for her own part continued to hear Mass in private.

IN MY END IS MY BEGINNING

Mary married Henry Stewart, Lord Darnley, in the Chapel Royal at Holyrood and gave birth to a son (later to become James VI) in Edinburgh Castle in 1566 – you can still visit the tiny room where he was born. Any domestic bliss was short-lived and, in a dramatic train of events, Darnley was involved in the murder of Mary's Italian secretary Rizzio (rumoured to be her lover), shortly before he himself was murdered at his Edinburgh home, probably by Mary's new lover and second-husband-to-be, the Earl of Bothwell.

Mary's enemies – led by her bastard half-brother Lord James Stewart, the Earl of Moray – finally confronted her at Carberry Hill, just east of Edinburgh, and Mary was forced to abdicate in 1567. She fled to England for safety, while her supporters occupied Edinburgh Castle, and a state of near civil war descended on the capital and continued for the next five years. Knox himself fled to St Andrews in 1570, returning in 1572 to live in the famous house (p56) on the Royal Mile that still bears his name before dying later that year.

Meanwhile, having appealed to her cousin, Elizabeth I of England, for protection, Mary found herself a prisoner instead. Elizabeth, a Protestant, feared a Catholic uprising in England and suspected Mary of treason. After 20 years spent pining and plotting in various prisons, the Queen of Scots was beheaded in 1587. Her motto, embroidered on her Cloth of State, had been 'In my end is my beginning', a prescient phrase for a woman whose gruesome end is still remembered in books, plays, poems and songs.

When Elizabeth died childless in 1603 Mary's son, James VI of Scotland, inherited the English throne in the so-called Union of the Crowns, thus becoming James I of England (usually written as James VI/I). James moved his court to London and, for the most part, the Stewarts ignored Edinburgh from then on. Indeed, when Charles I (r 1625–49) succeeded James in 1625, he couldn't be bothered to come north to Edinburgh to be formally crowned as king of Scotland until 1633.

THE KILLING TIME

The 17th century was a time of civil war in Scotland and England. The arrogant attempts by Charles I to impose episcopacy (the rule of bishops) and an English liturgy on the Scottish Church ignited public riots in Edinburgh, most famously the one set off by the chair-tossing talents of Jenny Geddes (see p57) that resulted in the creation of the National Covenant.

The Presbyterian Scottish Church believed in a personal bond with God that had no need of mediation through priests, popes and kings. On 28 February 1638 hundreds gathered in

1371	1560s
Stewart dynasty established	Reformation; Mary Queen of Scots abdicates

St Giles Cathedral (p57) on the Royal Mile

Greyfriars Kirkyard to sign the National Covenant, a declaration affirming their rights and beliefs; you can see an original copy of the Covenant in the Museum of Edinburgh and read the full text online at www.covenanter.org/Westminster/nationalcovenant.htm. Scotland became divided between the Covenanters and those who supported the king.

Edinburgh remained mostly unaffected by the civil wars of the 1640s but was laid low by the plague that raged between 1644 and 1645, when a fifth of the population died. Although the Scots opposed Charles I's religious beliefs and autocratic rule, they were appalled when Oliver Cromwell's parliamentarians executed the king in 1649. They offered his son the Scottish crown as long as he signed the Covenant, which he did. Charles II (r 1649–85) was crowned at Scone on 1 January 1651 but was soon forced into exile by Cromwell, who invaded Scotland and captured Edinburgh; Citadel St in Leith commemorates the site of the fortress he built there.

Following the restoration of Charles II in 1660, the king reneged on the Covenant; episcopacy was reinstated and hard-line Presbyterian ministers were deprived of their churches. Even so, many clergymen continued to reject the bishops' authority and started holding outdoor services, or conventicles. Charles' brother and successor, James VII/II (r 1685–89), was a Catholic who made worshipping as a Covenanter a capital offence. This period came to be known as 'the killing time', during which the Covenanters endured relentless persecution, notably at the hands of 'Bloody MacKenzie' (see boxed text, p64).

With the arrival in England of the Protestant William of Orange in 1688, the Catholic Stuart monarchy was doomed (the spelling 'Stuart' was preferred to 'Stewart' after 1603, in deference to their French allies, whose alphabet has no 'w'). Scottish royalists held on to Edinburgh Castle in the name of King James during the Long Siege of 1689, during which their leader, the Duke of Gordon, held a famous conference with John Graham of Claverhouse (known as 'Bonnie Dundee') at the western postern of the castle (a plaque in the Princes St Gardens marks the spot). Dundee then rode off to raise a Jacobite army and began five more months of civil war that ended with his death at the Battle of Killiecrankie.

1603

Union of the Crowns; Scotland and England joined under a single monarch

1638

National Covenant signed in Edinburgh to protect the Protestant religion in Scotland

UNION WITH ENGLAND

By the end of the 17th century, Edinburgh was indisputably Scotland's most important city. It had been made a cathedral city by Charles I in 1633; the Parliament Hall was built next to St Giles in 1639; and the Bank of Scotland was founded there in 1695. Civil war had left the country and its economy ruined, however, and in the 1690s famine killed up to a third of the population in some areas. The situation was made worse by the failure of an investment venture in Panama (the so-called Darien Scheme, set up by the Bank of England to boost the economy), which resulted in widespread bankruptcy.

The failure of the Darien Scheme made it clear to wealthy Scottish merchants and stockholders that the only way to make money in the lucrative markets of developing colonies was through union with England. The English also favoured union, but for different reasons – fear of their French enemies exploiting Jacobite sympathies in Scotland. To make the choice even starker, the English Parliament threatened to end the Scots' right to English citizenship and ban the duty-free export of Scottish goods to England; it also offered a financial incentive to those who lost money in the Darien Scheme. Despite public opposition, the Act of Union – which brought the two countries under one parliament, one sovereign and one flag, but preserved the independence of the Scottish Church and legal system – took effect on 1 May 1707.

On receiving the Act in Edinburgh, the chancellor of Scotland, Lord Seafield – the leader of the parliament that the Act abolished – is said to have murmured: 'Now there's an end to an auld sang.' Robert Burns later castigated the wealthy politicians who engineered the Union in characteristically stronger language: 'We're bought and sold for English gold – such a parcel of rogues in a nation!'

THE BONNIE PRINCE

One of the most over-romanticised episodes of Scottish history is the tale of Prince Charles Edward Stuart – better known as Bonnie Prince Charlie – and his ill-fated campaign to regain the British crown for his father and restore a Catholic king to the throne.

A series of Jacobite rebellions rocked Scotland in the first half of the 18th century (Jacobite derives from Jacob, the Latin form of James; the Jacobites were originally supporters of the exiled King James VII/II, Prince Charlie's grandfather.) In 1708 Charlie's father, James Edward Stuart, caused panic in Edinburgh when he arrived in the Firth of Forth with a fleet of French ships, but they were seen off by English men o' war. Another attempt in 1715 fizzled out after the inconclusive Battle of Sheriffmuir, which prompted the building of stronger defences at Edinburgh Castle.

The final showdown began in 1745 when Bonnie Prince Charlie himself landed in Scotland. Supported by an army of Highlanders, he captured Edinburgh (except for the castle) in September, holding court at the Palace of Holyroodhouse before defeating the Hanoverian forces of Sir John Cope at Prestonpans (near Musselburgh, just east of the capital). He got as far south as Derby in England but success was short-lived; a Hanoverian army led by the Duke of Cumberland harried him all the way back to the Highlands, where Jacobite dreams were finally crushed at Culloden in 1746. Jacobite prisoners were incarcerated in the vaults of Edinburgh Castle, which became an important military garrison.

NEW TOWN

Increasing stability in the second half of the 18th century allowed Edinburgh to expand. Desperate to relieve the pressure on the overcrowded and insanitary Old Town, the city council proposed to 'boldly enlarge Edinburgh to the utmost'. The council sponsored an architectural competition to design a 'New Town'; the winner was the unknown 23-year-old James Craig. Over the next 50 years elegant Georgian terraces spread across the low ridge to

1707
Act of Union passed; Scottish Parliament dissolved

1740s–1830s
Scottish Enlightenment

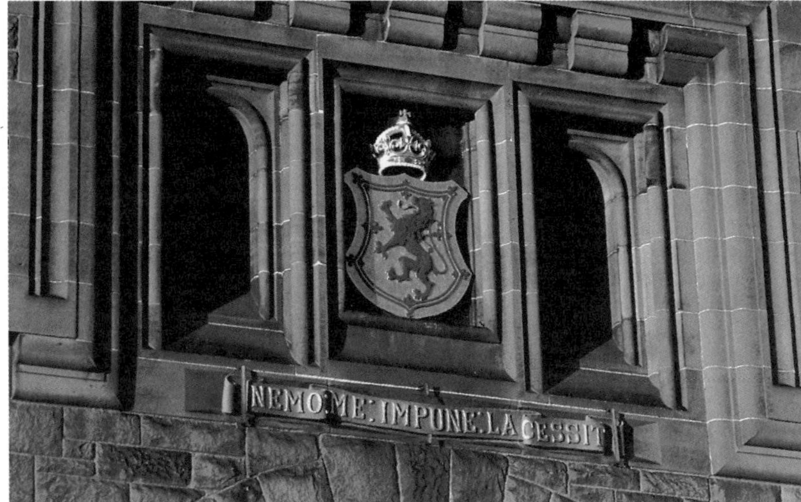

The Scottish royal motto on the Entrance Gateway at Edinburgh Castle (p52)

the north of the castle. Many of the finest houses were designed by architect Robert Adam, whose neoclassical style – a revival of Greek and Roman forms – swept through Europe in the late 18th and early 19th centuries.

A HOTBED OF GENIUS

During a visit to Edinburgh in the late 18th century an English visitor is said to have remarked while standing at the Mercat Cross: 'Here I stand at what is called the Cross of Edinburgh, and can, in a few minutes, take 50 men of genius and learning by the hand.'

Although Edinburgh declined in political importance following the removal of the Scottish Parliament in 1707, its cultural and intellectual life flourished. During the period that came to be called the Scottish Enlightenment (roughly 1740–1830) Edinburgh was known as 'a hotbed of genius', famed throughout Europe for its great philosophers, scientists and artists. In 1762 no less a figure than Voltaire declared that 'today it is from Scotland that we get rules of taste in all the arts, from epic poetry to gardening'.

Edinburgh was home to philosopher David Hume, author of the influential *Treatise on Human Nature,* and political economist Adam Smith, who wrote *The Wealth of Nations.* Adam Ferguson, the founder of sociology, and historian William Robertson emerged as influential thinkers, nourished on generations of theological debate. Medic William Cullen produced the first modern pharmacopoeia, chemist Joseph Black advanced the science of thermodynamics, and geologist James Hutton challenged long-held beliefs about the age of the Earth. Publisher William Smellie established the Encyclopedia Britannica, and architect Robert Adam emerged as Britain's greatest exponent of neoclassicism.

After centuries of bloodshed and religious fanaticism, people applied themselves with the same energy to the making of money and the enjoyment of leisure. There was a revival of interest in Scottish history and vernacular literature, reflected in Robert Fergusson's satires and Alexander MacDonald's Gaelic poetry. The poetry of Robert Burns, a man of the people, achieved lasting popularity. Sir Walter Scott, the prolific novelist and ardent

1843

The Disruption marks the founding of the Free Church of Scotland

1940s

Edinburgh University established as a teaching and research centre of international importance patriot, unearthed the Scottish crown jewels and had them put on public display in Edinburgh Castle.

EDINBURGH MAKES AN IMPRESSION

The renaissance of Scottish culture brought about by the Enlightenment awakened interest in Scotland elsewhere. In 1822 King George IV (r 1820–30) made the first state visit to Scotland by a reigning monarch since Charles II's coronation in January 1651. George IV's procession through Edinburgh, clad in Highland dress, was stage-managed by Sir Walter Scott and marked the beginnings of Edinburgh's tourist industry. The royal association was cemented by Queen Victoria (r 1837–1901), who was famously besotted with all things Scottish and wrote, 'The impression Edinburgh has made on me is very great; it is quite beautiful, totally unlike anything else I have ever seen.'

THE RESURRECTION MEN

In 1505 Edinburgh's newly founded Royal College of Surgeons was officially allocated the corpse of one executed criminal per year for the purposes of dissection. But this was not nearly enough to satisfy the curiosity of the city's anatomists, and in the following centuries an illegal trade in dead bodies emerged, reaching its culmination in the early 19th century when the anatomy classes of famous surgeons such as Professor Robert Knox drew audiences of up to 500 people.

The readiest supply of corpses was to be found in the city's graveyards, especially Greyfriars. Grave robbers – who came to be known as 'resurrection men' – plundered newly interred coffins and sold the cadavers to the anatomists, who turned a blind eye to the source of their research material.

This gruesome trade led to a series of countermeasures, including the mort-safe – a metal cage that was placed over a coffin until the corpse had begun to decompose; you can see examples in Greyfriars Kirkyard (p64) and on Level 5 of the Museum of Scotland (p65). A sexton or relatives of the deceased would keep watch over new graves from watch towers, which can still be seen in St Cuthbert's (p68) and Duddingston (p80) kirkyards.

The notorious William Burke and William Hare, who kept a lodging house in Tanner's Close at the western end of the Grassmarket, took the body-snatching business a step further. When an elderly lodger died without paying his rent, Burke and Hare stole his body from the coffin and sold it to the famous Professor Knox. Seeing a lucrative business opportunity, they figured that, rather than waiting for someone else to die, they could create their own supply of fresh cadavers by resorting to murder.

Burke and Hare preyed on the poor and weak of Edinburgh's Grassmarket, luring them back to Hare's lodging house, plying them with drink and then suffocating their victims. Between December 1827 and October 1828 they murdered at least 16 people, selling their bodies to Professor Knox. When the law finally caught up with them, Hare turned King's evidence and testified against Burke.

Burke was hanged outside St Giles Kirk in High St in January 1829 and, in an ironic twist, his body was given to the anatomy school for public dissection. His skeleton and a wallet made from his skin are still on display in the museum in Surgeon's Hall (p66). Although he was never charged with any crime, Knox's reputation was blackened, and he took to carrying a loaded pistol and a dagger for protection from the public. A rhyme that became popular in the city at the time ran:

Doon the close and up the stair,
But and ben with Burke and Hare;
Burke's the butcher, Hare's the thief,
And Knox the boy that buys the beef!

It was as a result of the Burke and Hare case that the Anatomy Act of 1832 – regulating the supply of cadavers for dissection, and still in force today – was passed.

1947	1979
Edinburgh International Festival and the Fringe both held for the first time	Referendum held on whether to elect a Scottish Assembly: rejected

Religious tensions, never far from the surface, broke out once again in the 19th century over who had the right to appoint Church of Scotland ministers. Since 1712 the civil authorities had held that power; the dissenters supported the right of the congregation to appoint their own minister. It all came to a head in Edinburgh in 1843 when 190 clergymen walked out of the General Assembly, then being held in the Church of St Andrew & St George on George St. The Disruption, as it came to be known, marked the founding of the Free Church of Scotland.

Although the Industrial Revolution affected Edinburgh on a much smaller scale than Glasgow, it brought many changes. Ironworks, potteries, glass factories and light engineering were added to the traditional industries of baking, brewing, distilling and publishing. Edinburgh's population increased rapidly, quadrupling in size to 400,000 – not much less than it is today. The Union Canal was completed in 1822, allowing coal from the Midlothian mines to be transported by barge to the Forth and Clyde Canal and on to Glasgow. No sooner had the canal gone into operation than it was rendered obsolete by the arrival of the railways. New suburbs of Victorian tenement blocks spread over the country estates around the Old and New Towns as the city expanded, swallowing up nearby villages such as Stockbridge and Dean.

WORLD HERITAGE SITE

In the 1920s the city's borders expanded again to encompass Leith in the north, Cramond in the west and the Pentland Hills in the south. Following the reorganisation of Scottish local government in 1975, the city expanded westwards to absorb Queensferry, Ratho and Kirkliston.

Following WWII the city's cultural life blossomed, stimulated by the Edinburgh International Festival and its fellow traveller the Fringe, both held for the first time in 1947 and now recognised as world-class arts festivals. The University of Edinburgh established itself as a teaching and research centre of international importance in areas such as medicine, electronics and artificial intelligence.

Ill-conceived development plans in the 1960s and '70s resulted in the demolition of large parts of Greenside (at the top of Leith Walk), St Leonards, Dalry and Tollcross, and the construction of various concrete monstrosities in and around the city centre, notably the St James Centre at the eastern end of Princes St. Fortunately, not all of the plans were realised, and Edinburgh was spared the horror of a motorway running the length of Princes St Gardens. In reaction, a strong conservation movement emerged to preserve and restore the city's old buildings and to control the impact of any new developments on the city's character. In 1995 both the Old and New Towns were declared Unesco World Heritage Sites.

THERE SHALL BE A SCOTTISH PARLIAMENT

Both Labour and Conservative governments had toyed with the idea of offering Scotland devolution or a degree of self-government, and in 1979 a referendum was held on whether to set up a directly elected Scottish Assembly. Fifty-two percent of those who voted said 'yes' to devolution but the Labour Prime Minister, James Callaghan, decided that everyone who didn't vote should be counted as a 'no'. By this devious reasoning, only 33% of the electorate had voted 'yes', so the Scottish Assembly was rejected.

From 1979 to 1997 Scotland was ruled by a Conservative government in London for which the majority of Scots hadn't voted. Separatist feelings, always present, grew stronger. Following the landslide victory of the Labour Party in May 1997, another referendum was held over the creation of a Scottish Parliament. This time the result was overwhelmingly and unambiguously in favour.

The opening clause of the *Scotland Act 1998* declared, 'There shall be a Scottish Parliament', and the Labour government was true to its word. Elections took place on

1995
Edinburgh's Old and New Towns declared Unesco World Heritage Sites

1996
Stone of Destiny returned to Edinburgh

6 May 1999 and the Scottish Parliament convened for the first time on 12 May in the Assembly Rooms of the Church of Scotland at the top of the Royal Mile. Donald Dewar (1937–2000), formerly the Secretary of State for Scotland, was nominated as first minister (the Scottish Parliament's equivalent of prime minister), and the Parliament was officially opened by Queen Elizabeth II on 1 July 1999.

However, it was not until October 2004 that the Parliament was able to move into its controversial new home in Holyrood at the foot of the Royal Mile.

1997	1999
Referendum held on the creation of a Scottish Parliament: accepted	Scottish Parliament convenes on 12 May; officially opened on 1 July by Queen Elizabeth

Sights

Sights

Modern Edinburgh sprawls over an area of 100 sq miles (259 sq km), from the shores of the Firth of Forth in the north to the foothills of the Pentlands in the south, and from the riverside cottages of Cramond in the west to the seaside suburb of Portobello in the east. Even the separate village of Queensferry, 8 miles to the west of the city centre, now falls within the city's jurisdiction.

Fortunately, most places of interest are concentrated within the city centre – in the medieval core of the Old Town, clustered around Edinburgh Castle and the Royal Mile, and in the orderly grid of the 18th-century New Town immediately to its north. We have grouped the rest of the city's attractions under the convenient headings of four further neighbourhoods: West End and Stockbridge, and Dalry and Morningside, to the northwest, west and southwest of the city centre; Tollcross and Bruntsfield, and Southside and Newington, to the south of the centre; Waterfront Edinburgh, stretching along the Forth from Cramond to Portobello; and Greater Edinburgh, which takes in the outlying areas of Queensferry,

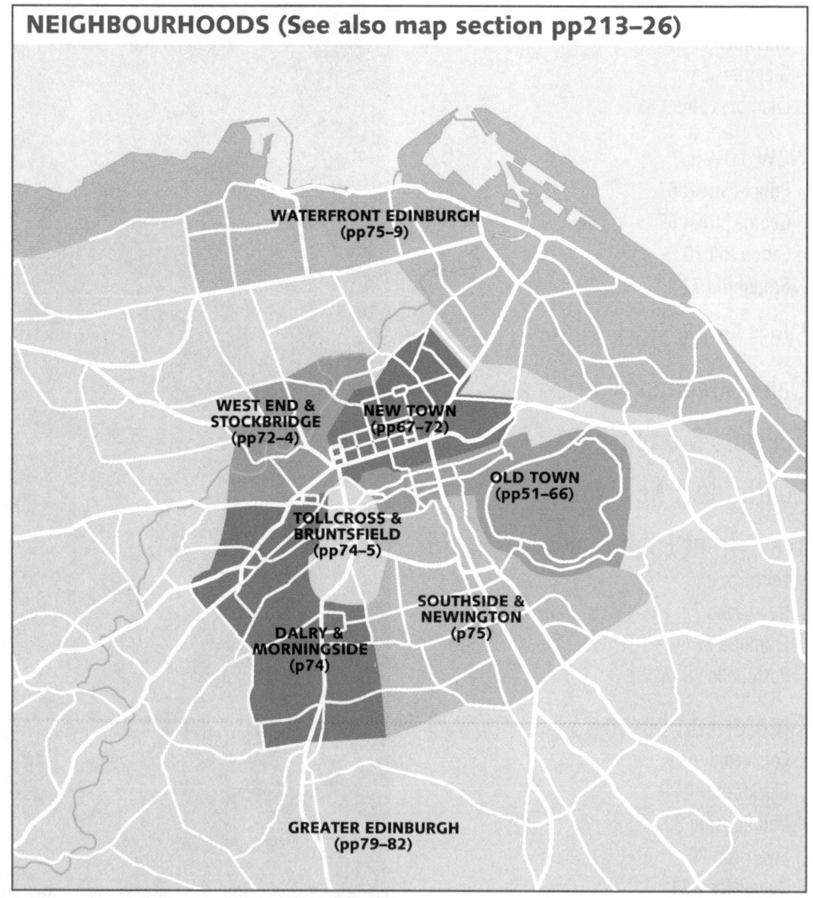

UNDERGROUND EDINBURGH

As Edinburgh expanded in the late 18th and early 19th centuries many old tenements were demolished and new bridges were built to link the Old Town to the newly built areas to its north and south. South Bridge (built between 1785 and 1788) and George IV Bridge (built between 1829 and 1834) lead southwards from the Royal Mile over the deep valley of the Cowgate, but since their construction so many buildings have clustered around them that you can hardly tell they are bridges: George IV Bridge has a total of nine arches but only two are visible; South Bridge has no less than 18 hidden arches.

The subterranean vaults were originally used as storerooms, workshops and drinking dens. But as early-19th-century Edinburgh's population swelled with an influx of penniless Highlanders cleared from their lands and Irish refugees from the Potato Famine, the dark, dripping chambers were given over to slum accommodation and abandoned to poverty, filth and crime.

The vaults were eventually cleared in the late 19th century, then lay forgotten until 1994 when the South Bridge vaults were opened to guided tours (see p50). Certain chambers are said to be haunted and one particular vault was investigated by paranormal researchers in 2001 (see p64).

However, the most notorious tale of underground Edinburgh dates from much earlier – from the plague that struck the city in 1645. Legend has it that the disease-ridden inhabitants of Mary King's Close (a lane on the northern side of the Royal Mile on the site of the City Chambers) were walled up in their houses and left to perish. When the lifeless bodies were eventually cleared from the houses, they were so stiff that workmen had to hack off limbs to get them through the small doorways and narrow, twisting stairs.

Satisfyingly gruesome though the story is, it isn't true – plague did strike, but no-one was walled in, and no hacking off of limbs took place – but, from that day on, the close was said to be haunted by the spirits of the plague victims. The few people who were prepared to live there reported seeing apparitions of severed heads and limbs, and the largely abandoned close fell into ruin. When the Royal Exchange (now the City Chambers) was constructed between 1753 and 1761, it was built over the lower levels of Mary King's Close, which were left intact beneath the building.

Interest in the buried close revived in the 20th century when Edinburgh's city council began to allow occasional guided tours to enter. Since then visitors have reported many supernatural experiences; the most famous ghost is 'Sarah', a little girl whose sad tale has prompted people to leave gifts of dolls in a corner of one of the rooms. In 2003 the close was opened to the public as the **Real Mary King's Close** (p57).

Corstorphine, Swanston, Blackford Hill and Duddingston. See the transport boxed texts in this chapter and p190 for advice about transport to and around Edinburgh.

ITINERARIES

One Day

Edinburgh Castle (p52) is Scotland's number one tourist sight so, if you only have a day to spare, visit here first thing then take a leisurely stroll down the **Royal Mile** (p55), stopping off at any of the museums or attractions that take your fancy. At the bottom of the hill, visit the new **Scottish Parliament Building** (p61) or the **Palace of Holyroodhouse** (p60). Nip into the **Museum of Scotland** (p65) in the afternoon and then, if the weather's fine, take an evening stroll up **Calton Hill** (p70). Round off the day with dinner at a restaurant with a view such as the **Tower** (p107) or **Oloroso** (p110).

Two Days

Follow the 'One Day' itinerary for your first then, on day two, spend the morning soaking up some culture in the **National Gallery of Scotland** (p68)and the **Royal Scottish Academy** (p69), and in the afternoon catch the bus to Leith for a visit to the **Royal Yacht Britannia** (p76). In the evening try to catch a play at the **Traverse Theatre** (p148) or scare yourself silly on a guided ghost tour with **Black Hart Storytellers** (p51).

One Week

If you're lucky enough to have a week in Edinburgh, follow the 'Two Days' itinerary, then spend your third morning exploring the **New Town** (p67) – Walk 2 (p93) would be ideal – and have a lazy lunch at **Circus Café** (p112) in Stockbridge before heading to the **Royal Botanic**

Garden (p73) or the **Scottish National Gallery of Modern Art** (p74). On day four, take it easy with a pampering treatment at **One Spa** (p146), a spot of self-indulgent shopping in **Stockbridge** (p156) and a romantic dinner at **Stac Polly** (p111).

Day five could be a day at the seaside – take the bus to **Queensferry** (p81) for a seafront stroll and have lunch at **Orocco Pier** (p120), then in the afternoon take a boat trip to **Inchcolm Island** (p82) or walk out to magnificent **Hopetoun House** (p81). On day six, take an excursion out of the city to the mysterious **Rosslyn Chapel** (p185) for a spot of Da Vinci Code detective work. Day seven should be saved for a shopping spree from the **West End** (p156) along George St to **Harvey Nichols** (p153). Cap the week with an unforgettable dinner at the sumptuous **Rhubarb restaurant** (p117) in the Prestonfield House Hotel.

ORGANISED TOURS

Bus Tours

Open-topped buses leave from Waverley Bridge outside the main train station and offer hop-on/hop-off tours of the main sights, taking in New Town, Grassmarket and the Royal Mile. They're a good way of getting your bearings, although with a bus map and a Day Saver bus ticket (£2.30) you could do much the same thing but without the commentary. Tours run daily year-round (except for 24 and 25 December), every 10 to 30 minutes from 9.45am to 4.45pm; tickets for all three tours listed here remain valid for 24 hours.

EDINBURGH TOUR

☎ 555 6363; adult/child £8.50/2.50

Lothian Buses' bright-red open-top buses depart every 10 minutes from Waverley Bridge; the one-hour tour covers Old Town, New Town, Calton Hill, Grassmarket, Greyfriars and Holyrood.

TOP FIVE VIEWPOINTS

One of Edinburgh's most appealing features is its many hills, which offer a range of stunning views across the city.

- **Arthur's Seat** (p59) The panorama from the city's highest point stretches from the Forth Bridges to North Berwick.
- **Calton Hill** (p70) Views along Princes St and over the Forth; beautiful sunsets.
- **Edinburgh Castle** (p52) Great views north from Mills Mount Battery, and south from the Esplanade.
- **Museum of Scotland** (p65) The rooftop terrace gives great views of the castle.
- **Scott Monument** (p69) City-centre vantage point with good views of the castle, National Gallery and Old Town.

MAC TOURS

☎ 220 0770; adult/child £8.50/2.50

Offers similar tours every 20 minutes, but in a vintage open-top bus.

MAJESTIC TOUR

☎ 220 0770; adult/child £8.50/2.50

The Britannia tour bus runs every 30 minutes (every 15 minutes in July and August) from Waverley Bridge to the **Royal Yacht Britannia** (p76) at Ocean Terminal via the Royal Botanic Garden and Newhaven, returning via Leith Walk, Holyrood and the Royal Mile.

Cycling Tours

ADRIAN'S EDINBURGH CITY CYCLE TOUR

☎ 07966447206; www.edinburghcycletour.com; adult/child £15/5; 🕑 10am & 2.30pm May-Sep, 10am Oct-Apr

This 5-mile guided cycle tour makes use of back streets and short cuts to avoid steep hills and the worst of the traffic. Tours, which last three hours, begin at the gates of the **Palace of Holyroodhouse** (p60). Bikes are provided, though you can bring your own if you prefer.

Helicopter Tours

LOTHIAN HELICOPTERS

☎ 01875-320032; www.lothianhelicopters.co.uk; Ste 1, Vineyard Business Centre, Tynehead, Pathhead; tours per person £60-235; 🕑 by arrangement

This company offers sightseeing flights over Edinburgh and the Forth Bridges in a seven-seat Bell 206L-4. Prices range from £60 per person for a 15-minute flight to £235 for one hour.

Walking Tours

There are lots of organised walks around Edinburgh, many of them related to ghosts, murders and witches. For starting times, phone or check the websites listed here; booking is recommended.

AULD REEKIE TOURS Map p222

☎ 557 4700; www.auldreekietours.co.uk; 45-47 Niddry St; adult/child £6/4; hourly 7-10pm

More interested in the blood-and-guts aspects of medieval torture than in real history, Auld Reekie can boast a 'working pagan temple' complete with witches' coven. Tours start from the **Tron Kirk** (p58).

BLACK HART STORYTELLERS

☎ 225 9044; www.blackhart.uk.com; adult/concession £8.50/6.50; 7.30pm & 8.30pm

Not suitable for children. The 'City of the Dead' tour of Greyfriars Kirkyard is probably the best of Edinburgh's numerous 'ghost' tours. Many people have reported encounters with the 'MacKenzie Poltergeist' (see p64). Tours depart from the **Mercat Cross** (p58).

CADIES & WITCHERY TOURS Map p222

☎ 225 6745; www.witcherytours.com; 84 West Bow; adult/child £7.50/5; 9pm & 9.30pm

The becloaked and pasty-faced Adam Lyal (deceased) leads a 'Murder & Mystery' tour of the Old Town's darker corners. These tours are famous for their 'jumper- ooters' – costumed actors who 'jump oot' when you least expect it – great fun. Tours begin outside the **Witchery by the Castle** (p107).

CELTIC TRAILS

☎ 448 2869; www.celtictrails.co.uk; tours £25-43; by arrangement

A refreshing alternative to mainstream walking tours is offered by Jackie Queally, who leads guided tours of Edinburgh's ancient and sacred sites, covering subjects such as Celtic mythology, geomancy, sacred geometry, Rosslyn Chapel and the Knights Templar. Tours must be booked in advance.

EDINBURGH LITERARY PUB TOUR

☎ 226 6665; www.edinburghliterarypubtour.co.uk; adult/student £8/6; 7.30pm daily Jun-Sep, Thu-Sun Apr, May & Oct, Fri Nov-Mar

An enlightening two-hour trawl through Edinburgh's literary history – and its associated howffs (pubs) – in the entertaining company of Messrs Clart and McBrain. One of the best of Edinburgh's walking tours. Tours begin at the **Beehive Inn** (p123).

GEOWALKS

☎ 555 5488; www.geowalks.demon.co.uk; tours per person £7-10

For those who are interested in history that goes back for millions, rather than just hundreds, of years, geologist Dr Angus Miller leads walks that explore the geological history of Edinburgh's very own extinct volcano, Arthur's Seat, and the surrounding countryside. See the website for walk times.

MERCAT TOURS Map p222

☎ 557 6464; www.mercattours.com; Mercat House, 28 Blair St; adult/child £7.50/4; 11am-8pm

Mercat Tours offers a wide range of fascinating tours including informative history walks in the Old Town and Leith, 'Ghosts & Ghouls' tours, and visits to haunted underground vaults. Tours begin from the **Mercat Cross** (p58).

OLD TOWN

Drinking p122; Eating p103; Shopping p150; Sleeping p161

Edinburgh's Old Town stretches along a ridge between the castle and Holyrood, and tumbles southward down Victoria St and West Bow to the broad expanse of the Grassmarket and the mossy stones of Greyfriars Kirkyard. It's a jagged, jumbled maze of masonry riddled with closes, wynds (narrow alleys), stairs and vaults, and is cleft along its spine by the cobbled ravine of the Royal Mile.

Before the founding of the New Town in the 18th century, old Edinburgh was an overcrowded and insanitary hive of humanity. Constrained between the boggy ground of the Nor' Loch (now drained and

TRANSPORT

Bus Lothian bus 35 runs along the lower part of the Royal Mile from George IV Bridge to the Palace of Holyroodhouse. Buses 23, 27, 41 and 42 run along the Mound and George IV Bridge, giving access to the Royal Mile and Grassmarket (via Victoria St or Candlemaker Row).

Parking Cars are not allowed on the central part of the Royal Mile between George IV Bridge and North Bridge. There are large car parks at Castle Tce and on New St; outside the Festival period, there is also parking on the Castle Esplanade.

occupied by Princes St Gardens) to the north and the city walls to the south and east, the only way for the town to expand was upwards. The five- to eight-storey tenements that were raised along the Royal Mile in the 16th and 17th centuries were the skyscrapers of their day, remarked upon with wonder by visiting writers such as Daniel Defoe. All classes of society, from beggars to magistrates, lived cheek by jowl in these urban ants' nests, the wealthy occupying the middle floors – high enough to be above the noise and stink of the streets, but not so high that climbing the stairs would be too tiring – while the poor squeezed into attics, basements, cellars and vaults amid the rats, rubbish and raw sewage.

The renovated Old Town tenements still support a thriving city-centre community, but today the street level is crammed with cafés, restaurants, bars, backpacker hostels and tacky souvenir shops. Few visitors wander beyond the main drag of the Royal Mile, but it's worth taking time to explore the countless closes and wynds that lead off the street into quiet courtyards, often with unexpected views of cityscape, sea and hills.

CASTLEHILL

Lined with tall buildings, this narrow street at the top of the Royal Mile is a bustling bottleneck through which tides of tourists ebb and flow on their way to and from the castle.

EDINBURGH CASTLE Map pp218-19

☎ 225 9846; Castlehill; adult/child/concession incl audioguide £9.80/3.50/7.50; 🕐 9.30am-6pm Apr-Sep, 9.30am-5pm Oct-Mar, 11am-5pm 1 Jan, closed 25 & 26 Dec, last ticket sold 45min before closing; 🚌 2, 23, 27, 41, 42 or 45

The brooding, black crags of the Castle Rock, shouldering above Princes St Gardens, are the very reason for Edinburgh's existence. This rocky hill – the glacier-worn stump of an ancient volcano – was the most easily defended hilltop on the invasion route between England and central Scotland, a route followed by countless armies from the Roman legions of the 1st and 2nd centuries AD to the Jacobite troops of Bonnie Prince Charlie in 1745. No-one knows when the rock was first fortified but archaeological excavations have uncovered evidence of habitation from as early as 900 BC.

The castle has played a pivotal role in Scottish history, both as a royal residence – King Malcolm Canmore (r 1057–93) and Queen Margaret made their home here in the 11th century – and as a military stronghold. From the 16th century the royal family favoured more comfortable domestic accommodation at Holyrood and Linlithgow, and the castle became a seat of government and military power. However, in 1566 Mary Queen of Scots underlined its continuing symbolic importance when she chose to give birth to her son, King James VI, in the castle.

The castle suffered extensive damage during the Lang Siege, between 1571 and 1573, when supporters of Mary Queen of Scots held out against the forces of James Douglas, Earl of Morton. It was occupied by English soldiers from 1650 to 1660 during Oliver Cromwell's invasion of Scotland and by Jacobites during the siege of 1689, when the Duke of Gordon faced off against William of Orange.

But when the army of Bonnie Prince Charlie passed through Edinburgh in 1745 it made only a cursory attempt to take the castle before moving quickly on. That was the last time the castle saw military action, and from then until the 1920s it served as the British army's main base in Scotland.

Edinburgh Castle is now Scotland's most popular pay-to-enter tourist attraction, pulling in over 1.2 million visitors in 2004. The **Esplanade**, a parade ground dating from 1820, is now a car park with superb views south over the city towards the Pentland Hills. On the northern side is an equestrian **statue of Field Marshall Earl Haig** (1861–1928). Haig was commander-in-chief of British forces during WWI and was responsible for the policy of attrition and trench warfare that killed thousands of troops.

The **Entrance Gateway** dates from between 1886 and 1888, and is flanked by statues of Robert the Bruce and William Wallace. Above the gate is the Royal Standard of Scotland – a red lion rampant on a gold field – and the Scottish Royal motto in Latin, '*nemo me impune lacessit*'. This translates into Scots as 'wha daur meddle wi' me', and into English as 'watch it, pal' (OK, it literally means 'no one provokes me with impunity'). Inside, a cobbled lane leads up beneath the 16th-century **Portcullis Gate**, topped by the 19th-century **Argyle Tower**, and past the cannon of the **Argyle** and **Mills Mount Batter-**

ies. The battlements here have great views over the New Town to the Firth of Forth.

At the far end of Mills Mount Battery, to the right of the **Cart Shed** (which houses a café and restaurant), is the **One O'Clock Gun** (p67), a gleaming WWII 25-pounder that fires an ear-splitting time signal at 1pm every day (except Sunday, Christmas Day and Good Friday). Beyond lies the **Western Ramparts**, a battlement walk with views over Edinburgh's West End. To the left of the Cart Shed, a road leads down to the **National War Museum of Scotland** (p54).

South of Mills Mount the road curls up leftwards through **Foog's Gate** to the highest part of the Castle Rock, crowned by the tiny **St Margaret's Chapel**, the oldest surviving building in Edinburgh. It's a simple Romanesque structure that was probably built by David I or Alexander I in memory of their mother Queen Margaret sometime around 1130 (she was canonised in 1250). Following Cromwell's capture of the castle in 1650 it was used to store ammunition until it was restored at the order of Queen Victoria; it was rededicated in 1934. The tiny stained-glass windows – depicting Margaret, St Andrew, St Columba, St Ninian and William Wallace – date from the 1920s. Immediately north of the chapel is **Mons Meg**, a giant 15th-century siege gun built at Mons in Belgium in 1449. The gun was last fired in 1681, as a birthday salute for the future King James VII/II, when its barrel burst. Take a peek over the wall to the north of the chapel and you'll see a charming little garden that was used as a **pet cemetery** for officers' dogs.

Beyond is the **Half Moon Battery**, which was built around and over the ruins of **David's Tower** – the royal residence of David II (1329–71) – after it was destroyed in the Lang Siege of 1571–73; you can visit the ruined vaults of the tower via a stairway beneath the battery.

The main group of buildings on the summit of the castle rock is arranged around **Crown Square**, dominated by the hushed shrine of the **Scottish National War Memorial**. Opposite is the **Great Hall**, built for James IV (r 1488–1513) as a ceremonial hall and used as a meeting place for the Scottish Parliament until 1639. Its most remarkable feature is the original 16th-century hammer-beam roof.

On the eastern side of the square is the **Royal Palace**, built during the 15th and 16th centuries, where a series of historical tableaux leads to a strongroom housing the **Honours of Scotland** (the Scottish crown jewels), the oldest surviving crown jewels in Europe. Locked away in a chest following the Act of Union in 1707, the crown (made in 1540 from the gold of Robert the Bruce's 14th-century coronet), sword and sceptre lay forgotten until they were unearthed at the instigation of the novelist Walter Scott in 1818. Also on display here is the **Stone of Destiny** (see below).

Among the neighbouring **Royal Apartments** is the bedchamber where Mary Queen of Scots gave birth to her son James VI, who

THE STONE OF DESTINY

On St Andrew's Day 1996, with much pomp and ceremony, a block of sandstone measuring 26½ by 16½ by 11 inches, with rusted iron hoops at either end, was installed in Edinburgh Castle. For the previous 700 years it had lain beneath the Coronation Chair in London's Westminster Abbey, where almost every English, and later British, monarch from Edward II in 1307 to Elizabeth II in 1953 had parked their backside firmly over it during their coronation ceremony.

This is the legendary Stone of Destiny – said to have originated in the Holy Land, and on which Scottish kings placed their feet during their coronation (not their bums; the English got that bit wrong) – which was stolen from Scone Abbey near Perth by King Edward I of England in 1296. It was taken to London and there it remained for seven centuries – except for a brief removal to Gloucester during WWII air raids, and a three-month sojourn in Scotland after it was stolen by Scottish students at Christmas in 1950 – an enduring symbol of Scotland's subjugation by England.

The Stone of Destiny returned to the political limelight in 1996, when the then Scottish Secretary and Conservative Party MP, Michael Forsyth, arranged for the return of the sandstone block to Scotland. A blatant attempt to boost the flagging popularity of the Conservative Party in Scotland prior to a general election, Forsyth's publicity stunt failed miserably. The Scots said thanks very much for the stone and then, in May 1997, voted every Conservative MP in Scotland into oblivion.

However, many people believe that Edward I was fobbed off with a shoddy imitation in 1296 and that the true Stone of Destiny remains safely hidden somewhere in Scotland. This is not impossible – some descriptions of the original state that it was made of black marble and decorated with elaborate carvings. You can read more in *Stone of Destiny* (Canongate Publishing, 1997) by Pat Gerber, which details the history of Scotland's most famous lump of rock.

TRUNK & DISORDERLY

One of the strangest exhibits in the National War Museum of Scotland is a set of sawn-off elephant's toenails. They belonged to a beast that was adopted as a regimental mascot by the 78th Regiment of Foot (the Ross-shire Buffs) while they were serving in Ceylon (now Sri Lanka) in the 1830s, and travelled back to Edinburgh with them on their return to Scotland. The elephant lived in stables at Edinburgh Castle and was trained to march at the head of the regiment during parades. It was looked after by Private James McIntosh, a bibulous Highlander who regularly retired to the canteen in the evenings to partake of alcoholic refreshment.

The elephant, no doubt feeling lonely and a little disoriented, would follow him to the canteen and loiter with intent, regularly extending its trunk through the window where the amused clientele would serve it large quantities of beer. Legend has it that both McIntosh and the elephant would then retire to the stable and sleep it off together.

was to unite the crowns of Scotland and England in 1603.

The **Castle Vaults** beneath the Great Hall (entered on the west side of Crown Sq via the **Prisons of War** exhibit) were used variously as storerooms, bakeries and prisons. The vaults have been restored as 18th- and early-19th-century prisons, where original graffiti carved by French and American prisoners can be seen on the ancient wooden doors.

HIGHLAND TOLBOOTH KIRK Map p222

Castlehill; 🚌 2, 23, 27, 41, 42 or 45

With Edinburgh's tallest spire (71.7m), this church is a prominent feature of the Old Town skyline. It was built in the 1840s by James Graham and Augustus Pugin (architect of London's Houses of Parliament) and takes its name from the Gaelic services that were held here in the 19th century for Edinburgh's Highland congregations. The interior has been refurbished and it now houses the **Hub** (☎ 473 2000; www.thehub-edinburgh.com; admission free; 🕑 ticket centre 10am-5pm Mon-Sat), the ticket office and information centre for the Edinburgh Festival. There's also a good **café** (see p104).

NATIONAL WAR MUSEUM OF SCOTLAND Map pp218-19

☎ 225 7534; admission incl in Edinburgh Castle ticket; 🕑 9.45am-5.30pm Apr-Nov, 9.45am-4.30pm Dec-Mar; 🚌 2, 23, 27, 41, 42 or 45

The exhibits here, from uniforms, weapons and medals to paintings, photographs and personal diaries, concentrate on individual stories of courage, determination and heartbreak rather than broad historical narratives, making it easier to empathise with the experiences of war than any dry display of dusty weaponry ever could. Various sections cover the history of the Scottish regiments, the unique role of the Highland soldier, and the effects of war on the civilian population, and include unusual exhibits such as a varnished set of elephant's toenails (see above) and the story of Bob the Dog, regimental mascot of the 1st Battalion Scots Fusilier Guards, who chased cannonballs at the Battle of Inkerman and was awarded his own medal.

OUTLOOK TOWER & CAMERA OBSCURA Map p222

☎ 226 3709; Castlehill; adult/child £6.45/4.15; 🕑 9.30am-7pm Jul & Aug, 9.30am-6pm Apr-Jun, Sep & Oct, 10am-5pm Nov-Mar; 🚌 2, 23, 27, 41, 42 or 45

The 'camera obscura' itself is a curious 19th-century device – in constant use since 1853 – that uses lenses and mirrors to throw a live image of the city onto a large horizontal screen. The accompanying commentary is entertaining, and the whole experience has a quirky charm. Stairs lead up through various displays on optics to the Outlook Tower, which offers great views over the city.

SCOTCH WHISKY HERITAGE CENTRE Map p222

☎ 220 0441; 354 Castlehill; adult/child incl tour & tasting £8.50/6.40; 🕑 9.30am-6.30pm May-Sep, 10am-5pm Oct-Apr; 🚌 2, 23, 27, 41, 42 or 45

Housed in a former school, the centre explains the making of whisky from barley to bottle, in a series of exhibits that combine sight, sound and smell. The first, and more interesting, part is led by a guide, while the second part consists of riding a 'barrel car' past several tableaux depicting the history of the 'water of life' – Johnnie Walker meets

Walt Disney. As a reward, you get a wee taste of the real thing, before being channelled into a shop full of whisky. There's also a restaurant, **Amber** (p103), that serves traditional Scottish dishes with, where possible, a dash of whisky thrown in.

ROYAL MILE

The Royal Mile, Edinburgh's oldest street, connects the castle to the Palace of Holyroodhouse. Hemmed in for much of its gently snaking length with tall, 17th- to 19th-century tenement buildings, it retains a grand, baronial atmosphere, heightened in festival time when the pedestrianised central section is crowded with tourists and performers.

The Royal Mile is split into four named sections: Castlehill, the Lawnmarket, High St and Canongate. A corruption of 'Landmarket', **Lawnmarket** takes its name from the large cloth market (selling goods from the land outside the city) that flourished here until the 18th century; this was the poshest part of the Old Town, where many of its most distinguished citizens made their homes.

High Street, which stretches from George IV Bridge down to St Mary's St, is the heart and soul of the Old Town, home to the city's main church, the Law Courts, the City Chambers and – until 1707 – the Scottish Parliament. High St ends at the intersection with St Mary's and Jeffrey Sts, where the Old Town's eastern gate, the **Netherbow Port** (Map p222; part of the Flodden Wall) once stood. Though it no longer exists, its former outline is marked by brass strips set in the road.

Victoria St and the spire of the Highland Tolbooth Kirk (opposite)

Canongate – the section between the Netherbow and Holyrood – takes its name from the Augustinian canons (monks) of Holyrood Abbey. From the 16th century it was home to aristocrats attracted to the Palace of Holyroodhouse. Originally governed by the monks, Canongate remained an independent burgh until 1856.

BRASS RUBBING CENTRE Map p222

☎ 556 4364; Trinity Apse, Chalmers Close; admission free; 🕑 10am-5pm Mon-Sat Apr-Sep, noon-5pm Sun Aug; 🚌 35

Across the street from the Museum of Childhood, Chalmers Close leads down to Trinity Apse, the only surviving part of the 15th-century Trinity College Church. The Gothic apse now houses a Brass Rubbing Centre where you can learn how to take rubbings from the centre's collection of medieval brasses and replicas of Pictish and Celtic stones. Though admission is free, rubbings cost from £1.50.

CANONGATE KIRK Map pp218-19

☎ 226 5138; Canongate; admission free; 🕑 9am-6pm; 🚌 35

A short distance downhill from the Canongate Tolbooth (following) is the attractive curved gable of Canongate Kirk, built in 1688. The surrounding kirkyard contains the graves of several famous characters, including economist Adam Smith (1723–90), author of *The Wealth of Nations*, who lived nearby in Panmure Close, and Mrs Agnes MacLehose (the 'Clarinda' of Robert Burns' love poems). Walk down the left-hand side of the church to a tree and turn left: the grave with the low iron railing belongs to the 18th-century poet Robert Fergusson (1750–74). He was much admired by Robert Burns, who paid for the gravestone and penned the epitaph – take a look at the inscription on the back. A modern statue of Fergusson stands outside the church gate.

CANONGATE TOLBOOTH Map pp218-19

☎ 529 4057; 163 Canongate; admission free; 🕑 10am-5pm Mon-Sat year-round, plus 2-5pm Sun during the Edinburgh Festival; 🚌 35

The Tolbooth is one of the surviving symbols of Canongate's former independence. Built in 1591, it served successively as a collection point for tolls (taxes), a council house, a courtroom and a jail. With its picturesque turrets and projecting clock, it's a splendid example of 16th-century architecture. It now houses a fascinating museum, the **People's Story**, recording the life, work and pastimes of ordinary Edinburgh folk from the 18th century to the present day.

CITY CHAMBERS Map p222

High St; not open to the public; 🚌 35

The imposing Georgian City Chambers, home to the City of Edinburgh Council, was originally built by John Adam (brother of Robert) between 1753 and 1761 to serve as the Royal Exchange – a covered meeting place for city merchants – replacing the traditional meeting place of the Mercat Cross. However, the merchants continued to prefer their old stamping grounds in the street and the building became the offices of the city council in 1811. Though only four storeys high on the Royal Mile side, the building plummets 12 storeys on the northern side, overlooking Cockburn St.

It was built over the sealed-off remains of three Old Town closes; the spooky remains of these can be explored on a guided tour of the **Real Mary King's Close** (see opposite).

GLADSTONE'S LAND Map p222

☎ 226 5856; 477 Lawnmarket; adult/child £5/4; 🕑 10am-7pm Jul & Aug, 10am-5pm Easter-Jun, Sep & Oct; 🚌 2, 23, 27, 41, 42 or 45

In 1617 Thomas Gledstanes, a 17th-century merchant – and ancestor of the 19th-century British prime minister William Gladstone – bought the tenement later known as Gladstone's Land. Built in the mid-16th century and extended in the 17th, it gives a fascinating glimpse of the Old Town's past. The comfortable interior contains fine painted ceilings, walls and beams and some splendid furniture from the 17th and 18th centuries. The volunteer guides provide a wealth of stories and detailed history.

JOHN KNOX HOUSE Map p222

☎ 556 9579; 43-45 High St; adult/child £3/2; 🕑 10am-6pm Mon-Sat; 🚌 35

The Royal Mile narrows at the foot of High St beside the jutting façade of John Knox House. It is the oldest surviving tenement in Edinburgh, dating from around 1490, and the outside staircase, overhanging upper floors and crowstepped gables are all typical of a 15th-century town house. John Knox is thought to have occupied the second floor from 1561 to 1572. The labyrinthine interior has some beautiful painted timber ceilings and interesting displays on Knox' life and work.

LOCH NESS DISCOVERY CENTRE Map p222

☎ 225 2290; 1 Parliament Sq; adult/child £5.95/4; 🕑 9am-10pm Jul & Aug, 9am-8pm Apr-Jun, Sep & Oct, 10am-5pm Nov-Mar; 🚌 2, 23, 27, 41, 42 or 45

This new attraction explores the legend of the Loch Ness monster by means of photographic displays and a 3D movie. Plus, of course, a gift shop crammed with cheekily priced cuddly toys in the form of Nessie…

MUSEUM OF CHILDHOOD Map p222

☎ 529 4142; 42 High St; admission free; 🕑 10am-5pm Mon-Sat, noon-5pm Sun; 🚌 35

Halfway down High St is 'the noisiest museum in the world' – the Museum of Childhood. Often overrun with screaming kids, it covers serious issues related to childhood – health, education, upbringing and so on – but also has an enormous collection of toys, games and books: everything from Victorian dolls to a video history of the 1960s Gerry Anderson TV puppet series *Thunderbirds*.

MUSEUM OF EDINBURGH Map pp218-19

☎ 529 4143; 142 Canongate; admission free; 🕑 10am-5pm Mon-Sat year-round, plus noon-5pm Sun Aug; 🚌 35

Across the street from the Canongate Tolbooth is **Huntly House**. Built in 1570, it is a good example of the accommodation that aristocrats built for themselves along Canongate – the projecting upper floors of plastered timber are typical of the period. It now houses the Museum of Edinburgh, whose exhibits cover the history of the city from prehistory to the present.

The labyrinth of oak-panelled rooms with creaky, polished wooden floors houses a lot of less-than-riveting displays of weights and measures, shop signs and silverware. There are some gems worth seeking out, however, most notably an original copy of the **National Covenant** signed in Greyfriars Kirkyard in 1638, and tasselled with the seals of countless Scottish noblemen. There is also an interesting display on the history of the **One O'Clock Gun** (see p67), but the big crowd-pleaser is the case containing the **dog collar and feeding bowl** that belonged to Greyfriars Bobby, the city's most famous canine citizen (see p64).

MUSEUM ON THE MOUND Map p222

☎ 529 1732; the Mound; admission free; ⏲ 10am-4.45pm Mon-Fri mid-Jun–Aug; 🚌 2, 23, 27, 41, 42 or 45

Housed in the Bank of Scotland's splendid Georgian HQ, this little museum is a treasure trove of gold coins, bullion chests, safes, banknotes, forgeries, cartoons and lots of fascinating old documents and photographs charting the history of Scotland's oldest bank. It was closed for refurbishment at the time of research, re-opening in September 2006.

PARLIAMENT HALL Map p222

☎ 348 5355; 11 Parliament Sq; admission free; ⏲ 10am-4pm Mon-Fri; 🚌 35

Around St Giles Cathedral is the cobbled expanse of **Parliament Square**, flanked to the south by **Parliament House**, the meeting place of the Scottish Parliament from 1639 to 1707 (the neoclassical façade was added in the early 19th century). After the Act of Union the building became the centre of the Scottish legal system, housing the Court of Session and the High Court, a function which it still serves today. The most interesting feature is the 17th-century **Parliament Hall** (dating from 1639), where the Parliament actually met. Now used by lawyers and their clients as a meeting place, it boasts its original oak hammer-beam roof and magnificent 19th-century stained-glass windows depicting the inauguration of the Court of Session by King James V in 1532.

As you enter 11 Parliament Sq (there's a sign outside saying 'Parliament Hall; Court of Session') you'll see the reception desk in front of you; the hall is through the double doors immediately on your right.

REAL MARY KING'S CLOSE Map p222

☎ 0870 243 0160; 2 Warriston's Close, Writers Court, High St; adult/child £8/6; ⏲ 9am-9pm daily Apr-Oct, 10am-4pm Sun-Fri & 10am-9pm Sat Nov-Mar; 🚌 35

The City Chambers were built over the sealed-off remains of Mary King's Close, and the lower levels of this medieval Old Town alley have survived almost unchanged amid the foundations for 250 years. Now open to the public, this spooky, subterranean labyrinth gives a fascinating insight into the everyday life of 17th-century Edinburgh. A drama student in period costume will take you on a guided tour through the vaults, while practising his or her dramatic enunciation.

The scripted tour, with its ghostly tales and gruesome tableaux, can seem a little naff, milking the scary and scatological aspects of the close's history for all they're worth, but there are things of genuine interest to see: there's something about the crumbling 17th-century tenement room, with tufts of horsehair poking from the collapsing lath-and-plaster walls, the ghost of a pattern on the walls, and the ancient smell of stone and dust thick in your nostrils, that makes the hairs rise on the back of your neck.

Then there's wee Annie's room, where a psychic once claimed to have been approached by the ghost of a little girl. It's hard to tell what's more frightening, the story of the ghostly girl or the bizarre heap of tiny dolls and teddies left in a corner by sympathetic visitors.

ST GILES CATHEDRAL Map p222

☎ 225 9442; High St; admission free but donations welcome; ⏲ 9am-7pm Mon-Fri, 9am-5pm Sat & 1-5pm Sun May-Sep, 9am-5pm Mon-Sat & 1-5pm Sun Oct-Apr; 🚌 35

The great grey bulk of St Giles Cathedral dominates High St. Properly called the High Kirk of Edinburgh (it was only a true cathedral – ie the seat of a bishop – from 1633 to 1638 and from 1661 to 1689), St Giles was named after the patron saint of cripples and beggars. There has been a church on this site since the 9th century. A Norman-style church was built in 1126 but was destroyed by English invaders in 1385; the only substantial remains are the central piers that support the tower. The present church dates largely from the 15th century – the beautiful crown spire was completed in 1495 – but much of it was restored in the 19th century.

St Giles Cathedral was at the heart of the Scottish Reformation. John Knox served as minister here from 1559 to 1572, preaching his uncompromising Calvinist message; when Charles I attempted to re-establish episcopacy in Scotland in

1637 by imposing a new liturgy, he only hardened the Scots' attitude against him. As the service from Charles I's *Book of Common Prayer* was read out for the first time in St Giles, a local woman called Jenny Geddes hurled her stool at the dean and called out, 'De'il colic the wame o' thee – wouldst thou say Mass at ma lug?' (The devil buckle your belly – would you say Mass in my ear?) and ignited a riot whose aftermath led to the signing of the National Covenant at Greyfriars the following year. A plaque marks the spot where Geddes launched her protest and a copy of the National Covenant is displayed on the wall.

There are several ornate monuments in the church, including the tombs of James Graham, Marquis of Montrose, who led Charles I's forces in Scotland and was hanged in 1650 at the Mercat Cross, and his Covenanter opponent Archibald Campbell, Marquis of Argyll, who was decapitated in 1661 after the Restoration of Charles II. One of the most interesting corners of the church is the **Thistle Chapel**, built between 1909 and 1911 for the Knights of the Most Ancient & Most Noble Order of the Thistle. The elaborately carved Gothic-style stalls have canopies topped with the helms and arms of the 16 knights – look out for the bagpipe-playing angel amid the vaulting.

By the side of the street outside the western door of St Giles, a cobblestone **Heart of Midlothian** is set in the paving. Passers-by traditionally spit on it for luck (don't stand downwind!). This was the site of the Tolbooth, originally built to collect tolls but subsequently a meeting place for Parliament, the town council and the General Assembly of the Reformed Kirk, then law courts and, finally, a notorious prison and place of execution. The Tolbooth was immortalised in Sir Walter Scott's novel *The Heart of Midlothian*.

At the other end of St Giles is the **Mercat Cross**, a 19th-century copy of the 1365 original, where merchants and traders met to transact business and Royal Proclamations were read. In a revival of this ancient tradition, the coronation of Queen Elizabeth II was proclaimed here by costumed officials in 1952, as was the dissolution of the Westminster Parliament prior to the 2001 general election, much to the bemusement of tourists and locals alike. When (and if) Princes Charles becomes king, his accession will also be proclaimed at the Mercat Cross.

TRON KIRK Map p222

☎ 225 8408; cnr High St & South Bridge; admission free; 🕑 10am-5.30pm Apr-Oct, noon-5pm Nov-Mar; 🚌 35 & all South Bridge buses

At the southwestern corner of the intersection of High St with South Bridge is the Tron Kirk, which takes its name from the *tron*, or public weighbridge, that once stood on the site. It was built in 1637 by John Mylne, the king's master mason, but remodelled in the late 18th century during the construction of South Bridge. The original wooden spire was lost in the great fire of 1824 – you can still see scorch marks around the arch inside the doorway – and was replaced with a much taller stone spire in 1828.

The interior has been gutted, except for the magnificent oak hammer-beam roof, which rivals that in the Great Hall at Edinburgh Castle, and the floor has been excavated by archaeologists to reveal the cobbled surface of **Marlin's Wynd**, a late-16th-century alley with the remains of cellars, staircases and medieval drains on either side.

WRITERS' MUSEUM Map p222

☎ 529 4901; Lady Stair's Close, Lawnmarket; admission free; 🕑 10am-5pm Mon-Sat year-round, noon-5pm Sun Aug; 🚌 2, 23, 27, 41, 42 or 45

Tucked down a close to the east of Gladstone's Land is this little museum dedicated to Robert Burns, Sir Walter Scott and Robert Louis Stevenson. The building alone is worth a visit: Lady Stair's House was built in 1622 and the interior has been restored in grand Jacobean style, with a huge original fireplace, an ornate gallery and panelled ceiling, and an intriguing staircase hidden in a wall, with steps of uneven height designed to trip up intruders. The museum contains portraits, letters and a varied collection of memorabilia, including Burns' diminutive writing desk and Scott's dining-room table. Head downstairs to the Stevenson display for a look at the tall mahogany cabinet that was built by none other than the notorious Deacon Brodie (see p10). It sat in Robert Louis Stevenson's bedroom when he was a child, and no doubt its history played a part in the author's inspiration for *The Strange Tale of Dr Jekyll and Mr Hyde*.

HOLYROOD

The once near-derelict district at the foot of the Royal Mile (formerly the site of a brewery) has been transformed by the construction of the new Scottish Parliament Building, the Our Dynamic Earth tourist attraction, modern offices for the *Scotsman* newspaper, and TV and radio studios for BBC Scotland.

HOLYROOD PARK pp218–19

In Holyrood Park, Edinburgh is blessed with a little bit of wilderness in the heart of the city. The former hunting ground of Scottish monarchs, the park covers 650 acres of varied landscape, including crags, moorland and lochs. The highest point is the summit of **Arthur's Seat** (251m), the deeply eroded remnant of a long-extinct volcano, but the most dramatic feature is the long, curving sweep of **Salisbury Crags**, a russet curtain of columnar basaltic cliffs that rises to the southeast of the Old Town.

The stony path along the foot of the crags is known as the **Radical Road** – it was built in 1820 at the suggestion of Sir Walter Scott, to give work to unemployed weavers (from whose politics it took its name). The path makes a good short walk from Holyrood, with fine views over the Old Town.

At the southern end of Salisbury Crags is the most famous rock outcrop in Edinburgh. Known as **Hutton's Section**, it was used by the pioneering Scottish geologist James Hutton in 1788 to bolster his theory that the basaltic rocks of Salisbury Crags were formed by the cooling of molten lava.

Dug into the hillside near the northern end of the crags is **St Margaret's Well**, a beautiful late-15th-century Gothic well-house. It was moved, stone by stone, to this location in 1860 when its original site in Meadowbank was taken over by a railway depot. You can't get into the chamber, all you can do is peek at the ornate vaulting through the metal grille at the entrance.

About 300m to the east, on a small hill overlooking St Margaret's Loch, are the ruins of **St Anthony's Chapel**. Nearby is a rough stone basin under a large boulder, known as **St Anthony's Well**, whose waters are said to have a curative effect. According to another (and probably related) legend, if you wash your face in the dew on Arthur's Seat on the morning of 1 May, you will be made beautiful.

Holyrood Park can be circumnavigated by car or bike along Queen's Dr – note that the western half of the drive is a major traffic route between the southern and eastern parts of the city, and the eastern half is closed to motorised traffic on Sunday. The parking area beside Dunsapie Loch is only a 15-minute hike away from the summit of Arthur's Seat. See p95 for details of a walk through the park via Arthur's Seat.

OUR DYNAMIC EARTH Map pp218-19

☎ 550 7800; www.dynamicearth.co.uk; Holyrood Rd; adult/child £8.95/5.45; ⏲ 10am-6pm Jul & Aug, 10am-5pm Apr-Jun, Sep & Oct, 10am-5pm Wed-Sun Nov-Mar, last admission 70min before closing; 🚌 36

A modernistic white marquee-roof pitched beneath Salisbury Crags marks the site of Our Dynamic Earth. Advertised with the

MYSTERY OF THE MINIATURE COFFINS

In July 1836 five boys were hunting for rabbits on the slopes of Arthur's Seat when they made a gruesome discovery: in a hollow beneath a rock, arranged on a pile of slates, were 17 tiny wooden coffins.

Each coffin was just four inches (10cm) long, and each contained a roughly carved human figure dressed in handmade clothes. Articles in local newspapers at the time denounced the coffins as the work of witches, but from that day to this no-one has ever found out who placed them there, or why.

The most convincing theory, put forward by researchers in 2000, is that the coffins were made in response to the infamous Burke and Hare murders (see p44), which were committed in 1831–32: the number of coffins matches the number of known victims. It was a common belief that people whose bodies had been dissected by anatomists could not enter the Kingdom of Heaven, and it is thought that someone fashioned the tiny figures in order to provide the murder victims with a form of Christian burial.

Eight of the 17 coffins survive, and can be seen in the Museum of Scotland. Ian Rankin makes use of the story of the coffins in his detective novel *The Falls* (see Reading Edinburgh, p27).

Holyrood Park and Arthur's Seat (p59) seen from Edinburgh Castle

slogan 'Live 4500 million years in one day!', it's billed as an interactive, multimedia 'journey of discovery' through Earth's history from the Big Bang to the present day. Hugely popular with kids of all ages, it's a slick extravaganza of whizz-bang special effects cleverly designed to fire up young minds with curiosity about all things geological and environmental. Its true purpose, of course, is to disgorge you into a gift shop where you can buy plastic dinosaurs and souvenir T-shirts.

The highlights include earthquake simulators, a vertigo-inducing giant-screen video fly-past over the glaciers of Norway, and a huge artificial rainforest that gets drenched with an indoor tropical downpour every five minutes or so. There are loads of hands-on exhibits for the kids, and a soft play area for under-10s.

PALACE OF HOLYROODHOUSE & HOLYROOD ABBEY Map pp218-19

☎ 556 5100; www.royalcollection.org.uk; Canongate; adult/child £8.50/4.50, joint ticket incl admission to Queens Gallery £11/5.50; 9.30am-6pm Apr-Oct, 9.30am-4.30pm Nov-Mar, closed 25 & 26 Dec & during royal visits; 35 or 36

Mary Queen of Scots spent six eventful years (1561–67) living in the Palace of Holyroodhouse, which dominates the eastern end of the Royal Mile. During this time she married Lord Darnley (in the neighbouring abbey) and Bothwell (in what is now the Picture Gallery), debated with John Knox, and witnessed the murder of her secretary, Rizzio.

The palace developed from a guesthouse attached to Holyrood Abbey, which was extended by King James IV in 1501 to create more comfortable living quarters than were possible in the exposed and windy hill-top castle. The oldest surviving section of the building, the northwestern tower, was built in 1529 as a royal apartment for James V and his wife, Mary of Guise.

Although Holyrood was never again used as a permanent royal residence after James VI departed for London in 1603, it was further extended during Charles II's reign, completing the great quadrangle you see today. It lay neglected through much of the 18th century – though Bonnie Prince Charlie briefly held court here in 1745 on his way south to Derby – but was gradually renovated as royal interest in Scotland revived following George IV's visit in 1822.

The guided tour leads you through a series of impressive royal apartments, ending in the **Great Gallery**. The 89 portraits of Scottish kings, commissioned by Charles II, supposedly record his unbroken lineage from Scota, the Egyptian pharaoh's daughter who discovered the infant Moses in a reed basket on the banks of the Nile.

The highlight of the tour is **Mary Queen of Scots' Bed Chamber** in the 16th-century tower house. This bedroom, with its low, painted ceilings and secret staircase connecting to her husband Lord Darnley's bedroom, was where her jealous husband restrained the pregnant queen while his henchmen murdered her secretary – and possible lover – David Rizzio. In her own words, they '...dragged David forth with great cruelty from our cabinet and at the entrance of our chamber dealt him 56 dagger blows'. A plaque in the next room marks the spot where he bled to death. The exit from the palace leads into Holyrood Abbey.

King David I founded **Holyrood Abbey** here in the shadow of Salisbury Crags in 1128. It was probably named after a fragment of the True Cross (*rood* is an old Scots word for cross) said to have been brought to Scotland by his mother St Margaret. As the abbey lay outside the city walls it suffered repeated attacks by English invaders, and the great abbey church was demolished in 1570, except for the nave, which remained in use as Canongate parish church until it collapsed in 1768. Most of the surviving ruins date from the 12th and 13th centuries, although a doorway in the far southeastern corner has survived from the original Norman church. The bay on the right, as you look at the huge, arched, eastern window, is the royal burial vault, which holds the remains of Kings David II, James II and James V, and of Mary's husband Lord Darnley.

In the gardens to the north of the palace is the tiny turreted lodge known as **Queen Mary's Bath House**. According to legend, Mary Queen of Scots used to bathe in white wine here. It is more likely to have been a dovecote or summer house.

QUEEN'S GALLERY Map pp218-19

☎ 556 5100; www.royalcollection.org.uk; Horse Wynd; adult/child £5/3, joint ticket incl admission to palace £11/5.50; 9.30am-6pm Apr-Oct, 9.30am-4.30pm Nov-Mar, closed 25 & 26 Dec & during royal visits; 35 or 36

This stunning modern gallery, which occupies the shell of a former church and school, was opened in 2002 as a showcase for exhibitions of art from the Royal Collections. The exhibitions change every six months or so; for details of the latest, check the website.

SCOTTISH PARLIAMENT BUILDING

Map pp218-19

☎ 348 5200; www.scottish.parliament.uk; admission free, guided tours £3.50; 9am-7pm Tue-Thu, 10am-6pm Mon & Fri in session, 10am-6pm Mon-Fri in recess Apr-Oct, 10am-4pm in recess Nov-Mar, closed 24-27 Dec & 1-3 Jan; 35 or 36

The new Scottish Parliament Building, on the site of a former brewery at the foot of the Royal Mile, was officially opened by the Queen in October 2004. Scotland's most spectacular and controversial new building was a flagship architectural project that went way over budget and way over schedule, and was dogged by contention and bad luck at every step.

The original budget for the project was £40 million, and it was meant to be completed by 2001. The competition to design the new building was won in July 1998 by Catalan architect Enric Miralles, who died of a brain tumour in 2000, only a month after construction began. Donald Dewar, the first leader of Scotland's newly devolved parliament, and a man instrumental in choosing the site and the architect, died later that same year. The project spiralled out of control, and eventually came in 10 times over budget and four years late.

The Scottish press, and many Scots themselves, displayed a very Presbyterian obsession with how much the whole thing cost. (At the time of writing, the estimated final cost was £430.5 million.) But as time passes the issue of cost will fade and the only remaining question will be, 'is this a good building?'

No-one now complains about the price of the Sydney Opera House (14 times its original estimated cost). And when tour guides lead visitors around the Houses of Parliament in London, do they proudly proclaim 'and do you know, the project came in on budget and on time?' No, they don't. (And no, it didn't – the Palace of Westminster was 30 years in the making and cost five times its original budget.)

The Main Hall, where there is an exhibition, a shop and café, and the public gallery in the Debating Chamber are open to the public; alternatively, you can pay for a guided tour which includes a visit to the Debating Chamber, a committee room, the Garden Lobby and, if possible, the office of an MSP (Member of the Scottish Parliament). If you want to see the Parliament in

DECODING THE SCOTTISH PARLIAMENT BUILDING

Enric Miralles (1955–2000), the architect who conceived the Scottish Parliament Building, believed that a building could be a work of art. However, the weird concrete confection that has sprouted at the foot of Salisbury Crags has left the good people of Edinburgh staring and scratching their heads in confusion. What does it all mean?

Exterior

First, you have to understand that the site is no less symbolic than the building itself. Holyrood has been a seat of Scottish power, religious and royal, for more than 1000 years – the ruins of Holyrood Abbey, and the Palace of Holyroodhouse lie just across the road.

Second, you have to see the building from above, from a vantage point on Radical Rd at the foot of Salisbury Crags, or looking down from Regent Tce on Calton Hill, to appreciate its setting. Miralles believed that the building should appear to grow out of the land, a flower of democracy rooted in Scottish soil. And indeed, the cluster of leaf-shaped roofs seems to blossom at the end of a series of linear earthworks, clothed in native Scottish plants, that spread out from Arthur's Seat like the branch of a tree.

Next is the exterior aspect of the building, which has echoes of Scottish landscape and architecture in its details. The **public entrance**, on the eastern side opposite the Palace of Holyroodhouse, is a wall of polished grey concrete and glass, partly hidden behind a latticed forest of wooden poles – reminiscent of birch woods, or of fields of barley. The first-floor façade to the right, and the towers around the left, are decorated with unusual, inverted-L-shaped panels. There was much debate about what these were meant to be – cranes? hammers? James Bond's Walther PPK? – until Miralles' widow revealed that they actually represent a curtain being drawn aside.

The southern aspect, dominated by the committee room towers, is perhaps the least appealing, but the western side, overlooking Reid's Close, is easily the most striking. The west wall of the **MSP Building**, which houses the MSPs' individual offices, is covered in quirkily shaped projecting windows, whose outline is said to have been inspired by the silhouette of the *Rev Robert Walker Skating on Duddingston Loch*, one of Scotland's most famous paintings. There is one for each MSP, a very visual reminder to onlookers of their democratic representatives within.

The northern side of the complex – the **Canongate Wall**, which runs alongside the foot of the Royal Mile – is actually a blast protection wall to guard against potential terrorist car-bombings. The curiously attractive design, inlaid with stones from all over Scotland and inscribed with quotations from Scottish literature, was based on a sketch of Edinburgh streets that Miralles made from his hotel window.

Interior

The **Main Hall**, inside the public entrance, has a low, triple-arched ceiling of polished concrete with saltire-shaped inserts, like a cave, cellar, or castle vault. It is a rather dimly lit space, the starting point for a metaphorical journey from this relative darkness up to the **Debating Chamber** (sitting directly above the Main Hall), which is, in contrast, a palace of light – the light of democracy. This magnificent chamber is the centrepiece of the Parliament, designed not to glorify but to humble the politicians who sit within it. The windows face Calton Hill, allowing MSPs to look up to its monuments (reminders of the Scottish Enlightenment), while the massive, pointed oak beams of the roof are suspended by steel threads above the MSPs heads like so many Damoclean swords.

session, check in advance that it will be sitting – business days are normally Tuesday to Thursday year-round.

COCKBURN & MARKET STREETS

Cockburn St, lined with quirky fashion, jewellery and music shops, leads down from the Royal Mile to Waverley Bridge. Cockburn St was opened in 1856, the first road to give direct access by horse-drawn carriage between the Royal Mile and the recently opened train stations on the site now occupied by Waverley station.

CITY ART CENTRE Map p222

☎ 529 3993; www.cac.org.uk; 2 Market St; admission free except for temporary exhibitions; 10am-5pm Mon-Sat year-round, noon-5pm Sun Aug; 36

Across the street from the Fruitmarket Gallery is the City Art Centre, the largest and most populist of Edinburgh's smaller galleries. Owned by Edinburgh City Council and housed in a former newsprint warehouse, its six floors are home to the city's collection of Scottish art, ranging from the 17th century to the 20th, including works by the Scottish Colourists. There are also many fine paintings, engravings and photographs showing views of Edinburgh at various stages of its history. The centre regularly hosts crowd-pleasing touring exhibitions such as the Gold of the Pharaohs and the Art of Star Wars.

COLLECTIVE GALLERY Map p222

☎ 220 1260; www.collectivegallery.net; 22-28 Cockburn St; admission free; ⏲ noon-5pm Tue-Sat; 🚌 36

Halfway down Cockburn St on the left is the Collective Gallery, an artist-run gallery with regularly changing exhibitions by contemporary Scottish and international artists.

EDINBURGH DUNGEON Map p222

☎ 240 1000; 31 Market St; adult/child 5-14yr £10.95/7.95; ⏲ 10am-7pm Jul & Aug, 10am-5pm Apr-Jun, Sep & Oct, 11am-4pm Mon-Fri, 10.30am-4.30pm Sat & Sun Nov-Mar; 🚌 36

Opposite the foot of Cockburn St, this manufactured attraction combines gruesome tableaux of torture and degradation with live actors who perform scary little sketches along the way. There's also a 'horror labyrinth', a creepy mirror maze inhabited by the ghost of a little drummer boy. Mildly amusing in a large group, mildly embarrassing in a small one and genuinely terrifying for small children. Seriously – not recommended for kids under eight; children under 15 must be accompanied by an adult.

FRUITMARKET GALLERY Map p222

☎ 225 2383; www.fruitmarket.co.uk; 45 Market St; admission free; ⏲ 11am-6pm Mon-Sat, noon-5pm Sun; 🚌 36

One of the city's most innovative galleries, the Fruitmarket showcases contemporary Scottish and international artists; it also has an excellent arts bookshop and **café** (see p108). There are around half a dozen exhibitions a year, ranging from paintings to installations to light-based artworks. Recent exhibitions have included sculpture by Louise Bourgeois and works by Turner Prize nominee Simon Patterson.

STILLS GALLERY Map p222

☎ 622 6203; www.stills.org; 23 Cockburn St; admission free; ⏲ 11am-6pm; 🚌 36

Across the street from the Collective Gallery you'll find Scotland's top photographic gallery, which hosts changing exhibitions of the best of international contemporary photography.

GRASSMARKET

The site of a cattle market from the 15th century until the start of the 20th, the Grassmarket has always been a focal point of the Old Town. As well as being a market, this was the main place of execution in the city, and over 100 martyred Covenanters are commemorated by a **monument** at the eastern end, where the gallows used to stand. The notorious murderers Burke and Hare operated from a now-vanished close off the west end. In 1827 they enticed at least 18 victims to their boarding house, suffocated them and sold the bodies to Edinburgh's medical schools (see p44).

Nowadays the broad, open square, lined with tall tenements and dominated by the looming castle, has many lively pubs and restaurants, including the White Hart Inn, which was once patronised by Robert Burns. The **Cowgate** – the long, dark ravine leading eastwards from the Grassmarket – was once the road along which cattle were driven from the pastures around Arthur's Seat to the safety of the city walls. Today it is the heart of Edinburgh's nightlife, with a few dozen clubs and bars within five minutes' walk of each other.

At the western end of the Grassmarket a narrow close called the Vennel leads steeply up to one of the few surviving fragments of the **Flodden Wall** (Map p222), the city wall that was built in the early 16th century as protection against a feared English invasion. Beyond it is the Telfer Wall, a later extension that continues to Lauriston Pl.

GEORGE HERIOT'S SCHOOL Map p222

☎ 229 7263; Lauriston Pl; not usually open to the public; 🚌 23 or 27

East of the Telfer Wall lies George Heriot's School, one of the most impressive buildings in the Old Town. Built in the 17th century with funds bequeathed by George Heriot (goldsmith and banker to King

James VI, and popularly known as Jinglin' Geordie), it was originally a school and home for orphaned children, but became a fee-paying public school in 1886. It is opened to the public on Doors Open Day (www.doorsopendays.org.uk) in September.

GREYFRIARS

Candlemaker Row leads up from the eastern end of the Grassmarket alongside one of Edinburgh's most famous graveyards. Hemmed in by high walls and overlooked by the brooding presence of the castle, **Greyfriars Kirkyard** is one of Edinburgh's most evocative spots, a peaceful green oasis dotted with elaborate funerary monuments. Many famous Edinburgh names are buried here, including poet Allan Ramsay (1686–1758), architect William Adam (1689–1748), and William Smellie (1740–95), editor of the first edition of *Encyclopaedia Britannica*. On the western side, to the left of the gate into George Heriot's School, a small plaque commemorates William Topaz McGonagall (c 1825–1902) – famed as the world's worst poet – who is buried nearby.

However, the memorial that draws the biggest crowds by far is the tiny statue of **Greyfriars Bobby**, directly in front of the pub beside the kirkyard gate. Bobby was a Skye terrier who maintained a vigil over the grave of his master, an Edinburgh police officer, from 1858 to 1872. The story was immortalised (and romanticised) by Eleanor Atkinson in her 1912 novel *Greyfriars Bobby*, which was made into a movie in 1961 by – who else? – Walt Disney (a remake was released in 2005).

GREYFRIARS KIRK Map p222

☎ 226 5429; www.greyfriarskirk.com; Candlemaker Row; admission free; 🕑 10.30am-4.30pm Mon-Fri & 10.30am-2.30pm Sat Apr-Oct, 1.30-3.30pm Thu Nov-Mar; 🚌 2, 23, 27, 41, 42 or 45

The church of Greyfriars was built on the site of a Franciscan friary and opened for worship on Christmas Day 1620. In 1638

THE MACKENZIE POLTERGEIST

Two centuries ago, boys from George Heriot's School would climb over the wall from the school grounds into Greyfriars Kirkyard to dodge lessons. One of their schoolboy dares was to go up to the mausoleum of Sir George MacKenzie and yell through the keyhole, *'Bluidy MacKenzie come out if ye daur, Lift the sneck and draw the bar'*, before running away giggling and screaming. The tomb was described as long ago as 1824 as 'a place of peculiar horror, as it was supposed to be haunted by the spirit of the bloody persecutor'.

Sir George MacKenzie (1636–91) was the King's Advocate (the chief law officer in Scotland) and was responsible for the persecution of the Covenanters, sending many of them to the gallows – hence his popular nickname, 'Bloody MacKenzie'. Just around the corner from his domed tomb is the Covenanters Prison, a long, narrow corner of Greyfriars Kirkyard where around 1200 Covenanters were incarcerated for five months in appalling conditions, while awaiting trial after the Battle of Bothwell Brig (1679).

In 1999 a homeless man, looking for shelter in the kirkyard on a cold and rainy night, wandered into Bloody MacKenzie's mausoleum. Perhaps fortified by some Buckfast tonic wine, he lifted the metal grating in the floor and descended into the vault. There he found a second, smaller grating in the floor and lifted it too…then accidentally tumbled into the dark hole. The story goes that he found himself sprawled in a mossy heap of human bones, grinning skulls and the dust of decayed flesh.

Just at that moment, the Greyfriars caretaker passed by and noticed the door to MacKenzie's tomb was open. He edged inside with his torch, only to be faced with a deranged figure charging up from the vault, wailing and screaming like a madman. Paranormal investigators have theorised that it was the incredible bolt of fear given off by these two men that awakened what has come to be known as the MacKenzie Poltergeist.

Since 1999 the guides who lead ghost tours around Edinburgh's vaults and graveyards have logged around 350 cases of high-level poltergeist activity, including punching, bruising, scratching, hair-pulling and ankle-grabbing, both in the South Bridge vaults (near the former home of Sir George MacKenzie) and in the Covenanters Prison. There have been around 170 incidents where people have actually collapsed.

The MacKenzie Poltergeist is now the best-documented case of poltergeist activity ever studied. Whether the phenomenon is truly paranormal or just some sort of psychological effect remains to be seen. Meanwhile, ghost-tour customers are queuing up to scare themselves silly by repeating that ancient schoolboy dare. Bloody MacKenzie come out if ye daur…

Gravestones in Greyfriars Kirkyard (opposite)

the National Covenant was signed here, rejecting Charles I's attempts to impose episcopacy and a new English prayer book, and affirming the independence of the Scottish Church. Many who signed it were later executed in the Grassmarket and, in 1679, 1200 Covenanters were held prisoner in terrible conditions in an enclosure in the far corner of the kirkyard.

Inside the church is a small exhibition on the National Covenant, and an original portrait of Greyfriars Bobby dating from 1867. In the kirk you can buy *Greyfriars Bobby – The Real Story at Last*, Forbes MacGregor's debunking of some of the myths. Bobby's grave – marked by a small, pink granite stone – is just inside the entrance to the kirkyard. His original collar and bowl are in the Museum of Edinburgh. At 12.30pm on Sundays there are church services in Gaelic, at which visitors are welcome.

CHAMBERS STREET

Broad and elegant Chambers St stretches from Greyfriars Kirk to the South Bridge, bordered on its southern side by the twin façades, modern and Victorian, of the Museum of Scotland and the Royal Museum, respectively.

At the eastern end of Chambers St is Edinburgh University's **Old College** (Map p222; also called the Old Quad; it now houses the Law Faculty), a neoclassical masterpiece designed by Robert Adam in 1789 but not completed till 1834. Inside the Old College, at the College Wynd end, is the Talbot Rice Gallery.

ROYAL MUSEUM & MUSEUM OF SCOTLAND Map p222

☎ 247 4219; www.nms.ac.uk; Chambers St; admission free except for special exhibitions; 🕑 10am-5pm Mon & Wed-Sat, 10am-8pm Tue, noon-5pm Sun, closed 25 Dec; 🚌 2, 23, 27, 41, 42 or 45

The 19th-century Royal Museum and the late-20th-century Museum of Scotland sit next to each other in Chambers St, one the epitome of Victorian elegance, the other a striking modern edifice in glowing, golden stone.

The **Museum of Scotland** – opened in 1998 – is one of the city's most distinctive landmarks, and the imaginative interior design is an attraction in itself. The five floors of the museum trace the history of Scotland from its geological beginnings to the 1990s, with many stimulating exhibits – it would take several visits to do it justice. Audioguides are available in several languages.

Highlights of the **Early Peoples** galleries on Level 0, in the basement, include a Roman sculpture of a lioness clutching a human head in her jaws, the 20kg of 5th-century silver that makes up the Traprain Treasure, and heavy silver chains dating from the 5th to 9th centuries that could out-bling a gangsta rapper. Also well worth checking out are the beautiful installations by sculptor Andy Goldsworthy, from the huge stacks of old roofing slates to a sphere made entirely of stacked whale bones.

The treasures in the **Kingdom of the Scots** galleries on Levels 1 and 2 include the famous Monymusk Reliquary, a tiny silver casket dating from AD 750, which is said to have been carried into battle with Robert the Bruce at Bannockburn in 1314; a set of charming, 12th-century chess pieces made from walrus ivory; and the ornate crosier that once belonged to the 8th-century St Fillan.

Levels 3 and 4 follow Scotland's progress through the Industrial Revolution, potently symbolised by the towering Newcomen atmospheric engine that once pumped water from flooded Ayrshire coalmines. The **Ways of Death** exhibit on Level 5 – a Goth's paradise of jet jewellery and mourning bracelets made from human hair – contains several fascinating objects, including eight of the 17 tiny coffins that were discovered on the slopes of Arthur's Seat in 1836 (see p59).

Level 6 is given over to the **20th Century**, with a gallery of objects that were chosen by celebrities and members of the general public as representing their lives. These range from footballer Jim Baxter's shirt, worn when Scotland beat newly crowned world champions England at Wembley in 1967 (nominated by Irvine Welsh) and mountaineer Hamish McInnes' innovative all-metal ice axes, to TV presenter Kirsty Wark's Saab convertible and Prime Minister Tony Blair's Fender Stratocaster electric guitar – make of that what you will. And if you want to feel old, there's nothing like seeing familiar objects that you grew up with confined to museum display cases – everything from a 1970s Trimphone to the original PlayStation is on show here. Don't forget to take the lift to the roof terrace for a fantastic view of the castle.

The Museum of Scotland connects with the original **Royal Museum**, dating from 1861, whose stolid grey exterior gives way to a bright and airy glass-roofed atrium. The museum houses an eclectic collection covering the natural world (evolution, natural history, minerals, fossils and so on), archaeology, scientific and industrial technology, and the decorative arts of ancient Egypt, Islam, China, Japan, Korea and the West. Volunteers give free 45-minute guided tours of the Royal Museum (at 3pm daily except Tuesday and Thursday) and the Museum of Scotland (at 2pm daily and also at 6pm on Tuesday).

SURGEONS' HALL MUSEUMS Map p222

☎ 527 1649; www.edinburgh.surgeonshall.museum; 9 Hill Sq; admission adult/child £5/3; 🕒 10am-4pm daily Aug & Sep, noon-4pm Mon-Fri Oct-Jul; 🚌 all South Bridge buses

Surgeons' Hall, a grand Ionic temple designed by William Playfair, was built in 1832 to house the Royal College of Surgeons of Edinburgh, founded in 1505, one of the oldest surgical corporations in the world. The building's massive portico dominates Nicolson St opposite the Festival Theatre, but the entrance to the museums is around the back in Hill Sq, reached via Hill Pl.

The **History of Surgery** is a fascinating exposition on surgery in Scotland from the 15th century, when barbers supplemented their income by performing blood-letting, dental extractions, amputations and other surgical procedures, to the present day. Its most famous exhibit is a wallet fashioned from the skin of the murderer William Burke (of Burke and Hare; see p44), part of a display about Burke and Hare. The adjacent **Menzies Campbell Dental Museum**, with its collections of wince-inducing extraction tools and inventive dentures, covers the same ground for dentistry.

The more famous **Pathology Museum** (in the same building), once accessible only by guided tour, is now open to the public. Housed in the magnificent Playfair Hall, the museum displays a gruesome but compelling 19th-century teaching collection of diseased organs, tumours and battlefield injuries pickled in formaldehyde. It is closed for exams on certain days; check the website.

TALBOT RICE GALLERY Map p222

☎ 650 2210; www.trg.ed.ac.uk; Old College, South Bridge; admission free; 🕒 10am-5pm Tue-Sat, daily during Edinburgh Festival; 🚌 all South Bridge buses

Established by Edinburgh University in 1975, this small art gallery has two exhibition spaces. The neoclassical **Georgian Gallery** was designed by William Playfair and houses a permanent collection of works by old masters, including Dutch landscapes by Van der Velde and Van der Meulen, and a striking bronze anatomical figure of a horse, created in Florence in 1598.

The **White Gallery** is a more modern space that is used to exhibit the works of contemporary Scottish painters and sculptors.

NEW TOWN

Drinking p124; Eating p107; Shopping p153; Sleeping p163

Edinburgh's New Town lies north of the Old, on a ridge running parallel to the Royal Mile and separated from it by the valley of Princes St Gardens. Its regular grid of elegant Georgian terraces is a complete contrast to the chaotic tangle of tenements and wynds that characterises the Old Town.

Between the end of the 14th century and the start of the 18th, the population of Edinburgh – still confined within the walls of the Old Town – increased from 2000 to 50,000. The tottering tenements were unsafe and occasionally collapsed, fire was an ever-present danger and the overcrowding and squalor became unbearable. There was no sewer system and household waste was disposed of by flinging it from the window into the street with a euphemistic shout of 'Gardy-loo!' (from the French '*gardez l'eau*' – beware of the water). Passers-by replied with 'Haud yer haun'!' (hold your hand) but were often too late. The stink that rose from the streets was ironically referred to as 'the floo'rs o' Edinburgh' (the flowers of Edinburgh).

So, when the Act of Union in 1707 brought the prospect of long-term stability, the upper classes wanted healthier, more spacious living quarters, and in 1766 the Lord Provost of Edinburgh announced a competition to design an extension to the city. It was won by an unknown 23-year-old, James Craig, a self-taught architect whose elegant plan envisaged the New Town's main axis, George St, following the crest of a ridge to the north of the Old Town, with grand squares at each end. Building would be restricted to just one side of Princes St and Queen St, so that the houses had views over the Firth of Forth to the north and to the castle and Old Town to the south.

During the 18th and 19th centuries the New Town continued to sprout squares, circuses, parks and terraces, with some of its finest neoclassical architecture designed by Robert Adam. Today the New Town remains the world's most complete and unspoilt example of Georgian architecture and town planning; along with the Old Town, it was declared a Unesco World Heritage Site in 1995.

TRANSPORT

Bus Just about every bus service in Edinburgh runs along Princes St at some point in its journey. But note that not all buses stop at every bus stop: if you're looking for a particular bus, check the route numbers listed on the bus-stop sign.

Parking There are multistorey car parks on Castle Tce, just off Lothian Rd at the west end of Princes St, and in the St James Shopping Centre at the east end. There is metered on-street parking in George St, but don't bet on finding a place easily. Princes St itself is closed to private vehicles.

PRINCES STREET

Princes St (Map pp218–19) is one of the world's most spectacular streets. Built up on one side only – the northern side – it catches the sun in summer and allows expansive

THE DAILY BANG

On Princes St you can tell locals and visitors apart by their reaction to the sudden explosion that rips through the air each day at one o'clock. Locals check their watches, while visitors shy like startled ponies. It's the One O'Clock Gun, fired from Mills Mount Battery on the castle battlements at 1pm sharp every day except Sunday.

The gun's origins date from the mid-19th century, when the accurate setting of a ship's chronometer was essential for safe navigation (finding your longitude at sea depended on knowing the exact time in your home port). The city authorities installed a time-signal on top of the Nelson Monument on Calton Hill – a ball that was hoisted to the top of a flagstaff and dropped exactly on the stroke of one o'clock – that was visible to ships anchored in the Firth of Forth. The gun was added as an audible signal that could be used when rain or mist obscured the ball.

Of course, the ship-bound navigators – and the Edinburgh public – had to make an allowance for the time it took for the sound of the gun (travelling at 330m/s) to reach them. The Edinburgh Post Office Directory used to publish maps showing the time delay for various places – two seconds for New Town, 11 seconds for Leith and up to 15 seconds for vessels anchored offshore. An interesting little exhibition in the Museum of Edinburgh details the history and workings of the One O'Clock Gun.

views across Princes St Gardens to the castle and the crowded skyline of the Old Town. Sadly, much of its original Georgian elegance was destroyed in the 1960s and '70s with the building of concrete façades and modern shop fronts; today it is lined with the gaudy colours of all the big players in UK high-street shopping, from Marks & Spencer to McDonald's. But what a view…

The western end of Princes St is dominated by the red-sandstone edifice of the Caledonian Hilton Hotel and the tower of **St John's Church**, worth visiting for its fine Gothic Revival interior. It overlooks **St Cuthbert's Parish Church**, built in the 1890s on a site of great antiquity – there has been a church here since at least the 12th century, and perhaps since the 7th century. There is a circular **watch tower** in the graveyard – a reminder of the days when graves had to be guarded against body snatchers.

At the eastern end is the prominent clock tower – traditionally three minutes fast so that you don't miss your train – of the Balmoral Hotel, overlooking Waverley train station, and the beautiful **Register House** (1788), designed by Robert Adam, with a statue of the Duke of Wellington on horseback in front. It houses the National Archives of Scotland.

NATIONAL GALLERY OF SCOTLAND

Map p222

☎ 624 6200; www.natgalscot.ac.uk; the Mound; admission free except for special exhibitions; 🕑 10am-5pm Fri-Wed, 10am-7pm Thu, noon-5pm 1 Jan, closed 25 & 26 Dec; 🚍 all Princes St buses

The National Gallery of Scotland is an imposing neoclassical building with Ionic porticoes, designed by William Playfair and dating from the 1850s. Its octagonal rooms, lit by skylights, have been restored to their original Victorian décor of deep-green carpets and dark-red walls, and occasionally experience a deep rumble from trains passing through the tunnel underneath the building. Once a year, in January, the gallery exhibits its collection of Turner watercolours, bequeathed by Henry Vaughan in 1900.

Highlights of the main galleries include Titian's *Three Ages of Man* (Room I), a meditation on the nature of love with some rather suggestive flute-playing from the shepherdess on the left, and his impressive renderings of *Diana and Actaeon* and *Diana and Callisto* (Room II).

Allegory of the Sense of Smell by 17th-century Dutch artist Jan Weenix is of interest in having once been owned by US press magnate William Randolph Hearst; it also appeared briefly as a backdrop in *Monsieur Beaucaire*, a 1946 movie starring Bob Hope. Rubens' *Salome* and Gainsborough's exquisite portrait of *The Honourable Mrs Graham* are in Room X, while Room XI contains Constable's classic landscape the *Vale of Dedham,* and a glowing picture of *Niagara Falls* – you can almost hear the thunder of the water – by Frederic Edwin Church. Room XII is graced by Antonio Canova's white marble sculpture of the *Three Graces,* owned jointly with London's Victoria & Albert Museum.

The upstairs galleries house portraits by Sir Joshua Reynolds and Sir Henry Raeburn, and a clutch of Impressionists including Monet's luminous *Haystacks,* van Gogh's demonic *Olive Trees* and Gauguin's hallucinatory *Vision After the Sermon*. But the painting that really catches your eye is the gorgeous portrait of *Lady Agnew of Lochnaw* by John Singer Sargent, with its barely repressed erotic charge – that ever-so-slightly raised right eyebrow speaks volumes.

The basement galleries dedicated to Scottish art include glowing portraits by Allan Ramsay and Sir Henry Raeburn, rural scenes by Sir David Wilkie and impressionistic landscapes by William MacTaggart. Look out for Raeburn's iconic *Revd Dr Robert Walker Skating on Duddingston Loch* and Sir George Harvey's hugely entertaining *A Schule Skailin* (A School Emptying): a stern dominie (teacher) looks on as the boys stampede for the classroom door, one reaching for a spinning top confiscated earlier. Kids will love the fantasy paintings of Sir Joseph Noel Paton in Room B5, incredibly detailed canvases crammed with hundreds of tiny fairies, goblins and elves.

The National Gallery of Scotland and the Royal Scottish Academy are now linked via a new underground mall – the **Weston Link** – which gives them twice the temporary exhibition space of the Prado in Madrid and three times that of the Royal Academy in London, as well as housing cloakrooms, a lecture theatre and a restaurant. The two galleries have become famous in recent years for 'blockbuster' exhibitions such as Monet: The Seine and the Sea, and The Age of Titian.

PRINCES STREET GARDENS

Map pp218-19

Princes St; admission free; dawn-dusk; all Princes St buses

These beautiful gardens lie in a valley that was once occupied by the Nor' Loch (North Loch), a boggy depression that was drained in the early 19th century. They are split in the middle by the **Mound** – around two million cart-loads of earth dug out from foundations during the construction of the New Town and dumped here to provide a road link across the valley to the Old Town. It was completed in 1830.

In the middle of the western part of the gardens is the **Ross Bandstand**, a venue for open-air concerts in summer and during the Hogmanay celebrations, and the stage for the famous Fireworks Concert during the Edinburgh Festival. At the gate beside the Mound is the **Floral Clock**, a working clock laid out in flowers; it was first created in 1903 and the design changes every year.

ROYAL SCOTTISH ACADEMY

Map pp218-19

RSA; ☎ 225 6671; www.royalscottishacademy.org; the Mound; admission free except for special exhibitions; 10am-5pm Mon-Sat, 2-5pm Sun; all Princes St buses

The distinguished Greek Doric temple at the corner of the Mound and Princes St, its northern pediment crowned by a seated figure of Queen Victoria, is the home of the Royal Scottish Academy (RSA). Designed by William Playfair and built between 1823 and 1836, it was originally called the Royal Institution; the RSA took over the building in 1910. The galleries display a collection of paintings, sculptures and architectural drawings by academy members dating from 1831, and also hosts temporary exhibitions throughout the year – details are posted on the website.

SCOTT MONUMENT Map pp218-19

☎ 529 4068; E Princes St Gardens; admission £3; 9am-6pm Mon-Sat & 10am-6pm Sun Apr-Sep, 9am-3pm Mon-Sat & 10am-3pm Sun Oct-Mar; all Princes St buses

The eastern half of Princes St Gardens is dominated by the massive Gothic spire of the Scott Monument. Built by public subscription in memory of novelist Sir Walter Scott after his death in 1832, it testifies to a popularity largely inspired by his role in rebuilding pride in Scottish identity. You can climb the 287 steps to the top for a superb view of the city; the stone figures that decorate the niches on the monument represent characters from Scott's novels. The statue of Scott, with his favourite deerhound Maida, at the base of the monument was carved from a single 30-tonne block of white Italian marble.

GEORGE STREET

Until recently George St (Map pp218–19) – the major axis of the New Town – was the centre of Edinburgh's financial district and Scotland's equivalent of Wall St. Now many of the big financial firms have relocated to

EDINBURGH FOR CHILDREN

The **Edinburgh and Scotland Information Centre** (p200) has lots of info on children's events, and the handy guidebook *Edinburgh for Under Fives* can be found in most bookshops. The *List* magazine (www.list.co.uk) has a special kids' section listing children's activities and events in and around Edinburgh. The week-long **Children's International Theatre Festival** (☎ 225 8050; www.imaginate.org.uk) takes place each year in late May/early June.

There are good, safe **playgrounds** in most Edinburgh parks, including W Princes St Gardens, Inverleith Park (opposite the Royal Botanic Garden), King George V Park (New Town), the Meadows and Bruntsfield Links.

Ideas for outdoor activities include: going to see the animals at **Edinburgh Zoo** (p79); exploring the **Royal Botanic Garden** (p73); visiting **Greyfriars Bobby's statue** (p64); and feeding the swans or playing on the beach at **Cramond** (p77). During the Festival and Fringe there's lots of **street theatre** for kids, especially on High St and at the foot of the Mound, and in December there's an **open-air ice rink** and **fairground rides** in Princes St Gardens.

If it's raining you can visit the **Museum of Scotland** (p65), which offers the Discovery Centre, a hands-on activity zone on Level 3, and the dioramas of ancient forests on Level 0, where you can play 'spot the animals'; play on the flumes at the **Royal Commonwealth Pool** (p147); try out the earthquake simulator at **Our Dynamic Earth** (p59); or take a tour of the haunted **Real Mary King's Close** (p57).

See also Children, p194.

premises in the new Exchange district west of Lothian Rd, and George St's banks and office buildings have been taken over by designer boutiques, trendy bars and upmarket restaurants.

At the western end of George St is **Charlotte Square**, the architectural jewel of the New Town, which was designed by Robert Adam shortly before his death in 1791. The northern side of the square is Adam's masterpiece and one of the finest examples of Georgian architecture anywhere. **Bute House**, in the centre at No 6, is the official residence of Scotland's first minister. Just off the southeastern corner of the square, at 16 S Charlotte St, a plaque marks the house where Alexander Graham Bell, the inventor of the telephone, was born in 1847.

On the western side of Charlotte Sq, the former St George's Church (1811) is now **West Register House** (Map p217), an annexe to Register House in Princes St. It houses maps and plans owned by the National Archives of Scotland and mounts occasional exhibitions in the entrance hall.

St Andrew Square is not as distinguished architecturally as its sister at the opposite end of George St. This is where the first houses in the New Town were built – compare the rubble walls (originally covered in stucco) of Nos 23 to 26 on the northern side of the square (built in 1772) with the smooth, ashlar masonry and unified façades of Charlotte Sq.

Dominating St Andrew Sq is the fluted column of the **Melville Monument**, commemorating Henry Dundas, First Viscount Melville (1742–1811), who was the most powerful Scottish politician of his time, often referred to when alive as 'Harry IX, the Uncrowned King of Scotland'. The impressive Palladian mansion of **Dundas House** (built between 1772 and 1774) on the eastern side of the square was built for Sir Laurence Dundas (1712–81) – no relation to Viscount Melville. It has been the head office of the Royal Bank of Scotland since 1825 and has a spectacular domed banking hall dating from 1857 (you can nip inside for a look).

A short distance along George St is the **Church of St Andrew & St George**, built in 1784, with an unusual oval nave. It was the scene of the Disruption of 1843, when 451 dissenting ministers left the Church of Scotland to form the Free Church.

GEORGIAN HOUSE Map pp218-19

☎ 226 2160; 7 Charlotte Sq; adult/child £6/4; 10am-7pm Jul & Aug, 10am-5pm Apr-Jun, Sep & Oct, 11am-3pm Mar & Nov; 13, 19, 36, 37 or 41

Owned by the National Trust for Scotland (NTS), Georgian House (dating from 1796) has been beautifully restored to show how Edinburgh's wealthy elite lived at the end of the 18th century. The rooms are furnished with the finest period furniture and the walls are decorated with paintings by Allan Ramsay, Henry Raeburn and Sir Joshua Reynolds. There are costumed guides on hand to add a bit of character, and a 35-minute video presentation helps to bring the place to life.

NATIONAL TRUST FOR SCOTLAND Map pp218-19

NTS; ☎ 243 9300; www.nts.org.uk; 28 Charlotte Sq; admission free; 10am-5pm Mon-Sat; 13, 19, 36, 37 or 41

The headquarters of the NTS is on the southern side of Charlotte Sq. As well as a shop, café and information desk, the building contains a restored 1820s **drawing room** (11am-3pm Mon-Fri) with Regency furniture and a collection of 20th-century Scottish paintings.

SCOTTISH NATIONAL PORTRAIT GALLERY Map pp218-19

☎ 624 6200; 1 Queen St; admission free; 10am-5pm Mon-Sat & noon-5pm Sun, extended hr during Edinburgh Festival; all York Pl buses

Just north of St Andrew Sq, at the junction of Andrew St with Queen St, is the Venetian Gothic palace of the Scottish National Portrait Gallery. Its galleries depict Scottish history through portraits and sculptures of famous Scottish personalities, from Robert Burns and Bonnie Prince Charlie to Sean Connery and Billy Connolly. It also houses the National Photography Collection, which includes works by David Octavius Hill and Robert Adamson, the 19th-century Scottish pioneers of portrait photography.

CALTON HILL

Calton Hill (Map pp218–19; 100m), which rises dramatically above the eastern end of Princes St, is Edinburgh's acropolis, its summit scattered with grandiose monuments dating mostly from the first half of

Old Calton Burying Ground and the Governor's House (below) on Calton Hill

the 19th century. It is also one of the best viewpoints in Edinburgh, with a panorama that takes in the castle, Holyrood, Arthur's Seat, the Firth of Forth, New Town and the full length of Princes St.

Approaching from Princes St along Waterloo Pl you pass over **Regent Bridge**, built across the chasm of Calton Rd between 1816 and 1819 to give access to Calton Hill and allowing the development of the exclusive Georgian terraces on its northern and southeastern sides.

Old Calton Burying Ground, on the southern side of Waterloo Pl, is one of Edinburgh's many atmospheric old cemeteries. It is dominated by the tall black obelisk of the Political Martyrs' Monument, which commemorates those who suffered in the fight for electoral reform in the 1790s. In the southern corner is the massive cylindrical grey stone tomb of David Hume (1711–76), Scotland's most famous philosopher. Hume was a noted atheist, prompting rumours that he had made a Faustian pact with the devil; after his death his friends held a vigil at the tomb for eight nights, burning candles and firing pistols into the darkness lest evil spirits should come to bear away his soul. Near the tomb is a statue of Abraham Lincoln, commemorating Scots-Americans who died in the American Civil War.

Beyond Waterloo Pl, on Regent Rd, is the modernist façade of **St Andrew's House** (built between 1936 and 1939), which housed the civil servants of the Westminster government's Scottish Office until they were moved to the new Scottish Executive building in Leith in 1996. It was built on the site of Calton Gaol, the successor to the much-despised Tolbooth in High St, and once the biggest prison in Scotland. All that remains is the distinctive turreted building just west of St Andrew's House, and best seen from North Bridge – this was the **Governor's House**, built in 1817.

Just beyond St Andrew's House, on the opposite side of the road, is the imposing **Royal High School** building, dating from 1829 and modelled on the Temple of Theseus in Athens. Former pupils include 18th-century architect Robert Adam, Alexander Graham Bell and novelist Sir Walter Scott. The building was at one time lined up as a potential home for the new Scottish Parliament, but it now stands empty; at the time of writing there were plans for it to house a new national centre for photography. To its east, on the other side of Regent Rd, is the **Burns Monument** (1830), a Greek-style memorial to Robert Burns. It was designed by Thomas Hamilton, another former pupil of the school.

You can reach the summit of Calton Hill by the road that runs behind the Royal High School or via the stairs at the eastern end of Waterloo Pl. The largest structure on the summit is the **National Monument**, a rather over-ambitious attempt to replicate the Parthenon and intended to honour Scotland's dead in the Napoleonic Wars. Construction – paid for by public subscription – began in 1822 but funds ran dry when only 12 columns had been erected. It became known locally as 'Edinburgh's Disgrace'.

The design of the **City Observatory**, built in 1818, was based on the ancient Greek Temple of the Winds in Athens. Its original function was to provide a precise, astronomical time-keeping service for marine navigators.

Smoke from Waverley train station forced the astronomers to move to Blackford Hill (see p80) in 1895, and since 1953 the City Observatory has been home to the **Astronomical Society of Edinburgh** (☎ 556 4365; www.astronomyedinburgh.org). Visitors with an interest in astronomy are welcome to attend open evenings when the telescopes are in operation (most Friday evenings when the sky is clear, between 8pm and 10pm).

Just downhill from the observatory is the small circular **Monument to Dugald Stewart** (1753–1828), who was Professor of Mathematics and of Moral Philosophy at Edinburgh University.

NELSON MONUMENT Map pp218-19

☎ 556 2716; Calton Hill; admission £3; 1-6pm Mon & 10am-6pm Tue-Sat Apr-Sep, 10am-3pm Mon-Sat Oct-Mar; all Leith St buses

Looking a bit like an upturned telescope – the similarity is intentional – and offering superb views, the Nelson Monument was built to commemorate Admiral Lord Nelson's victory at Trafalgar in 1805. In 1852 a time-ball was added as a time signal for ships anchored in the Firth of Forth (see p67) – it still drops from the cross-bars of the mast at the top of the monument at 1pm every day.

BROUGHTON

The bohemian neighbourhood of Broughton, centred on Broughton St at the northeastern corner of the New Town, is the focus of Edinburgh's gay nightlife and home to many good bars and restaurants.

EDINBURGH PRINTMAKERS' WORKSHOP & GALLERY Map pp218-19

☎ 557 2479; 23 Union St; 10am-6pm Tue-Sat, closed 24 Dec-9 Jan; 8 or 17

Founded in 1967, this was the UK's first 'open-access' printmaking studio, providing studio space and equipment for professional artists and beginners alike. You can watch printmakers at work in the ground floor studio, while the first floor gallery hosts exhibitions of lithographs and screen prints by local artists. If you fancy having a go yourself, the workshop offers two-day weekend courses (£130) in screen printing, lithography, etching and relief printing.

TRANSPORT

Bus Buses 8 and 17, from Princes St and South Bridge respectively, go along Broughton St.

Parking There is limited, metered on-street parking, but it's better to use the multistorey car parks in the St James Centre and Omni Centre.

MANSFIELD PLACE CHURCH

Map pp218-19

☎ 474 8033; www.mansfieldtraquair.org.uk; Mansfield Pl; 1-4pm 2nd Sun of month May, Jun & Sep-Dec, 10-11.45am Mon-Sat during Edinburgh Festival; 8, 13 or 17

In complete contrast to the austerity of most of Edinburgh's religious buildings, the 19th-century, neo-Romanesque Mansfield Place Church at the foot of Broughton St contains a remarkable series of Renaissance-style frescoes painted in the 1890s by Irish-born artist Phoebe Anna Traquair (1852–1936). Part of the church has been converted for use as office space, but the murals – now restored to their former glory – are on view to the public at certain times (check the website for the latest details).

WEST END & STOCKBRIDGE

Drinking p127; Eating p112; Shopping p156; Sleeping p165

This neighbourhood stretches from the western edge of the New Town south to Tollcross, west to Dalry and north to Stockbridge, taking in the new financial district called the Exchange, the shopping streets of the West End, and Haymarket, home to Edinburgh's other train station. There are few tourist attractions here, but you'll find some good places to stay and some excellent places to eat.

The West End is an extension of the New Town, all Georgian elegance and upmarket shops, but the shiny new Exchange district to its south is a maze of chrome, glass and sandstone modernity, with people in suits striding purposefully between office blocks. This area is now the city's financial powerhouse, home to many banks and insurance company headquarters.

TRANSPORT

Bus Lothian buses 3, 4, 12, 25, 26, 31, 33 and 44 head west from Princes St, along Shandwick Pl to Haymarket. Buses 3, 4, 25, 33 and 44 continue southwest on Dalry Rd, while 12, 26 and 31 head west towards Murrayfield Stadium and Corstorphine. Buses 24, 29 and 42 run from Frederick St in the city centre to Raeburn Pl in Stockbridge. For Dean Village, take bus 13, 19, 37 or 41 from George St to Dean Bridge and walk down Bell's Brae.

Parking There is metered on-street parking in Stockbridge and Dean Village, but spaces are very limited; it's better not to bring a car.

The New Town's Georgian architecture extends north into Stockbridge (Map p217), a trendy district with its own distinct identity, some interesting shops and a good choice of pubs and restaurants. Originally a milling community, Stockbridge was developed in the early 19th century on lands owned largely by painter Sir Henry Raeburn. The garden villas along **Ann Street**, named after Raeburn's wife and dating from 1817, are among the most beautiful and desirable houses in Edinburgh, while the giant Doric columns that line **St Bernard's Crescent** are the most grandiose decoration on any private residence in the city.

If you follow Queensferry St northwards from the western end of Princes St, you come to the **Dean Bridge**, designed by Thomas Telford and built between 1829 and 1832. Vaulting gracefully over the narrow, steep-sided valley of the Water of Leith, it was built to allow the New Town to expand to the northwest. It became notorious as a suicide spot – it soars 27m above the river – and in 1912 the parapets were raised to deter jumpers.

Down in the valley, just west of the bridge, is **Dean Village** (dene is a Scots word for valley); to get there, descend the steep, cobbled lane of Bell's Brae at the southern end of Dean Bridge. The village was founded as a milling community by the canons of Holyrood Abbey in the 12th century and by 1700 there were 11 water mills here, which were operated by the Incorporation of Baxters (the bakers' trade guild). One of the old mill buildings has been converted into flats, and the village is now an attractive residential area.

Several 17th-century houses and carved stones remain. On the parapet of the **old bridge** (18th century) at the foot of Bell's Brae, there is a carving showing crossed 'peels' – long shovels for putting loaves into ovens – and the inscription 'Blesit be God for al His giftis'. On the door lintel of the house opposite is another carving of crossed peels with three loaves of bread, and the words 'God bless the Baxters of Edinbrugh uho bult this hous 1675'.

From the old bridge, you can follow the Water of Leith Walkway downstream to Stockbridge (10 minutes – see p93), or follow the signs upstream to the Scottish National Gallery of Modern Art (15 minutes).

DEAN GALLERY Map p217

☎ 624 6200; 73 Belford Rd; admission free except for special exhibitions; 10am-5pm; 13

Directly across Belford Rd from the Scottish National Gallery of Modern Art, another neoclassical mansion topped with monumental towers (originally an orphans' home) houses its adjunct, the Dean Gallery. The Dean holds the Gallery of Modern Art's collection of Dada and surrealist art, including works by Dali, Giacometti and Picasso, and a large collection of sculpture and graphic art created by the Edinburgh-born sculptor Sir Eduardo Paolozzi. A smaller version of Paolozzi's statue of Newton (which stands outside the British Library in London) is in the garden, while his massive figure of Vulcan is crammed uncomfortably into the Great Hall.

ROYAL BOTANIC GARDEN Map pp214-15

☎ 552 7171; www.rbge.org.uk; 20a Inverleith Row; admission free; 10am-7pm Apr-Sep, 10am-6pm Mar & Oct, 10am-4pm Nov-Feb; 8, 17, 23, 27 or 37

A 10-minute walk northwards from Stockbridge along St Bernard's Row, Arboretum Ave and Arboretum Pl leads to the Royal Botanic Garden. Founded near Holyrood in 1670 and moved to its present location in 1823, Edinburgh's Botanic Garden is the second oldest institution of its kind in Britain (after Oxford), and one of the most respected in the world. Seventy beautifully landscaped acres include splendid Victorian palm houses, colourful swathes of rhododendron and azalea, and a world-famous rock garden. The Terrace Cafe offers good views towards the city centre.

SCOTTISH NATIONAL GALLERY OF MODERN ART Map p217

☎ 624 6200; 75 Belford Rd; admission free except for special exhibitions; 🕑 10am-5pm daily, noon-5pm 1 Jan, closed 25 & 26 Dec; 🚌 13

Set in a neoclassical building surrounded by a leafy sculpture park, 500m west of Dean Village, is the Scottish National Gallery of Modern Art. The collection – housed in bright, modern galleries that belie the building's austere façade – concentrates on 20th-century art, with various European art movements represented by the likes of Matisse, Picasso, Kokoschka, Magritte, Miro, Mondrian and Giacometti. American and English artists are also represented, but most space is given to Scottish painters – from the Scottish Colourists of the early 20th century to contemporary artists such as Peter Howson and Ken Currie. The post-Impressionist works of the Scottish Colourists (Peploe, Hunter, Caddell and Fergusson) are especially popular; in *Reflections, Balloch*, Hunter pulls off the improbable trick of making Scotland look like the south of France.

There's an excellent **café** (p108) downstairs and the surrounding park features sculptures by Henry Moore and Barbara Hepworth, as well as *Landform*, a seductive piece of landscape art by Charles Jencks.

DALRY & MORNINGSIDE

Drinking p128; Eating p114; Shopping p157

Dalry was once a working-class industrial area – there is still one working brewery located in the area – but the opening of new restaurants on Dalry Rd and the building of luxury apartments in Dalry and Port Hamilton – the Edinburgh terminus of the Union Canal – seem to point the way to the neighbourhood's future gentrification.

Morningside, in contrast, has always been a middle- and upper-class suburb; indeed, 'Morningside' is now often used as an adjective describing traditional Edinburgh middle-class respectability. Today this part of Edinburgh is still affluent but much more laid-back, its spacious villas and apartments much sought after by Edinburgh's urban professionals.

CALEDONIAN BREWERY Map p226

☎ 337 1286; wwww.caledonian-brewery.co.uk; 42 Slateford Rd; guided tour per person £7.50; 🕑 tours by arrangement only; 🚌 4, 34, 35 or 44

When the Caledonian Brewery was established in 1869, it was one of more than 40 breweries operating in Edinburgh; today, it is the only survivor. Although the brewery itself was purchased by Scottish & Newcastle in 2004, the Caledonian Brewing Company remains independently owned, and produces excellent real ales such as Deuchar's IPA and Caledonian 80/- (80 shilling). You can arrange a tour for groups of four to 20 people, but they must be booked at least a week in advance; groups of fewer than four may be able to join an existing tour.

TOLLCROSS & BRUNTSFIELD

Drinking p129; Eating p114; Shopping p157; Sleeping p167

Tollcross and Bruntsfield are 19th-century suburbs of mostly tenement flats, close enough to the city centre to be within easy walking distance. Bruntsfield in particular is a popular place to live, with large areas of parkland, spacious tenement apartments and lots of good restaurants and pubs.

THE MEADOWS Map pp224-5

Melville Dr; admission free; 🕑 24 hr; 🚌 5, 24 or 41

This mile-long stretch of lush grass, criss-crossed with tree-lined walks, was once a shallow lake known as the Borough Loch. It was drained in the 1740s and converted into parkland for the newly emerging middle classes to enjoy – Melville Dr (now a main road) and Middle Meadow Walk were laid out as carriage drives and footpaths.

TRANSPORT

Bus The main bus routes south from the city centre are 10, 11, 15, 16, 17, 23, 27 and 45 from the west end of Princes St to Tollcross (all except 10 and 27 continue south to Bruntsfield and Morningside); and 3, 5, 7, 8, 29, 31, 37 and 49 from North Bridge to Newington. Buses 24 and 41 run from Princes St and Hanover St, respectively, to Melville Dr on the south side of the Meadows.

The park is a great place for a picnic or a quiet walk, away from the city bustle – in spring its walks lie ankle-deep in drifts of pink cherry blossom, and there are great views of Arthur's Seat. There are amateur cricket matches in summer and impromptu football games in winter, and you can practice your golf strokes on the pitch-and-putt course on neighbouring Bruntsfield Links. Each year, on the first weekend in June, the park hosts the two-day **Meadows Festival** (☎ 620 9108; www.meadowsfestival.co.uk), with fun-fair and live music.

SOUTHSIDE & NEWINGTON

Drinking p130; Eating p116; Shopping p157; Sleeping p168

This neighbourhood extends from the southern edge of the Old Town from Tollcross and Bruntsfield to Holyrood Park, taking in the 19th-century tenement districts of Marchmont and Sciennes (pronounced 'sheens') and the elegant villa quarters of Grange and Newington. Away from the main thoroughfares of Dalkeith Rd, Clerk St/S Clerk St/Newington Rd and Causewayside/Mayfield Rd, it's a peaceful residential neighbourhood of smart Victorian tenement flats and spacious garden villas. There's not much to see in the way of tourist attractions here, but there are many good restaurants, pubs and places to stay.

The northern and eastern parts of the neighbourhood, which include Edinburgh University's main campus (centred on George Sq) and Pollock Halls of Residence, has a sizable student population and the bookshops, bars, cafés and good-value restaurants that go along with it. The southwestern part, around Grange and Newington, is characterised by garden villas built in the 19th century for Edinburgh's middle and upper classes.

WATERFRONT EDINBURGH

Drinking p133; Eating p117; Sleeping p170

Edinburgh's waterfront stretches for 10 miles along the southern shore of the Firth of Forth, from the pretty riverside village of Cramond in the west to the seaside suburb of Portobello in the east, taking in the former fishing village of Newhaven and the redeveloped industrial docklands of Leith. The western part, from Cramond to Granton, is pleasantly rural, with a quiet, traffic-free promenade walk; the central part, from Granton to Leith, is lined up for a major redevelopment to take place over the next 10 years or so (see p18).

TRANSPORT

Bus Lothian buses 10, 12, 16, and 22 run from Princes St down Leith Walk to the junction of Constitution and Great Junction Sts; from here 10 and 16 go west to Newhaven; 12 goes along Constitution St then east to Portobello; 22 goes north to the Shore and Ocean Terminal. Bus 35 runs from the Royal Mile (eastbound) to Ocean Terminal. Buses 1, 11, 34 and 36 also go from the city centre to terminate at Ocean Terminal; 11 goes via Newhaven. Bus 7 goes from Newington to Newhaven via South Bridge, while Bus 32 links Newhaven and Portobello.

Parking There are large multistorey car parks at Ocean Terminal and Newkirkgate shopping centre. On-street parking is limited; your best bet is on Commercial St.

LEITH

Leith (Map p216), 2 miles northeast of the city centre, has been Edinburgh's seaport since the 14th century, and remained an independent burgh with its own town council until it was incorporated by the city during the 1920s. Like many of Britain's dockland areas, it fell into decay in the decades following WWII but has been undergoing a steady revival since the late 1980s. Old warehouses have been turned into luxury flats and a lush crop of trendy bars and restaurants has sprouted up along the waterfront. The area was given an additional boost in the late 1990s when the Scottish Office (a government department, now renamed the Scottish Executive) relocated to a new building on Leith docks.

The city council has now formulated a major redevelopment plan for the entire Edinburgh waterfront from Leith to Granton, the first phase of which is **Ocean Terminal**, a shopping and leisure complex that includes the former Royal Yacht *Britannia*

The Shore (below) in Leith

and a berth for visiting cruise liners. Parts of Leith are still a bit rough – Salamander St, for example, is a notorious red-light district – but it's a distinctive corner of the city and well worth exploring.

The most attractive part of Leith is the **Shore**, where the Water of Leith runs into Leith Docks. Before the docks were built in the 19th century, this was Leith's original wharf. An iron plaque set into the quay in front of No 30 the Shore marks the **King's Landing** – the spot where King George IV (the first reigning British monarch to visit Scotland since Charles II in 1650) stepped ashore in 1822.

Located north of the bridge across the river is the circular **Signal Tower**, built in 1686 and originally a windmill; it now houses the excellent Fishers seafood restaurant (see p118). Beyond is the 19th-century baronial façade and clock tower of the old Sailor's Home, now the Malmaison Hotel (see p171).

Leith Links, a public park located in the eastern part of Leith, was originally common grazing land, but is more famous as the home of the game of golf. Although golf has not been played on the links since the 19th century, the game has a very long history in Leith. The kirk Session Records of 1610 for the parish church of South Leith note that the Session agreed that there should be no 'public playing suffered on the Sabbath dayes. As playing at the valley bowles, at the penny stane, archery, gowfe etc'.

ROYAL YACHT BRITANNIA Map p216

☎ 555 5566; www.royalyachtbritannia.co.uk; Ocean Terminal, Leith; adult/child £9/5; 9.30am-6pm Apr-Sep, 10am-5pm Oct-Mar, 10am-4pm 24 & 31 Dec, closed 1 Jan & 25 Dec, last admission 1½hr before closing; 1, 11, 22, 34, 35 or 36

One of Edinburgh's biggest tourist attractions is the former Royal Yacht *Britannia*. She was the royal family's floating home during their foreign travels from her launch in 1953 until her decommissioning in 1997, and is now moored permanently in front of Ocean Terminal.

The tour, which you take at your own pace with an audioguide (also available in French, German, Italian and Spanish), gives an intriguing insight into the Queen's private tastes – *Britannia* was one of the few places where the royal family could enjoy true privacy. The entire ship is a monument to 1950s' décor and technology, and the accommodation reveals Her Majesty's preference for simple, unfussy surroundings – the Queen's own bed is surprisingly tiny and plain. In fact, the initial interior design was rejected by the Queen for being too flashy.

There was nothing simple or unfussy about the running of the ship, though. When the Queen travelled, along with her went 45 members of the royal household, five tonnes of luggage and a Rolls-Royce

GOLF ON THE LINKS

Although St Andrews claims seniority in having the oldest golf course in the world, it was at Leith Links in 1744 that the first official rules of the game were formulated by the Honorable Company of Edinburgh Golfers; these 13 rules formed the basis of the modern game. Rule 9 gives some insight into the 18th-century game – 'If a ball be stop'd by any person, Horse, Dog or anything else, the Ball so stop'd must be played where it lyes'. The original document is in the **National Library of Scotland** (Map p222) and the Honorable Company is now the famous Muirfield Golf Club. A stone cairn on the western side of the links bears a plaque that describes how the game was played over five holes, each being around 400 yards.

that was carefully squeezed into a specially built garage on the deck. The ship's company consisted of an admiral, 20 officers and 220 yachtsmen. The decks (of Burmese teak) were scrubbed daily, but all work near the royal accommodation was carried out in complete silence and had to be finished by 8am. A thermometer was kept in the Queen's bathroom to make sure that the water was the correct temperature, and when in harbour one yachtsman was charged with ensuring that the angle of the gangway never exceeded 12 degrees. And note the mahogany windbreak that was added to the balcony deck in front of the bridge – it was put there to stop wayward breezes from blowing up skirts and inadvertently revealing the Royal Undies.

The Majestic Tour bus (see p50) runs from Waverley Bridge to *Britannia*.

TRINITY HOUSE Map p216

☎ 554 3289; 99 Kirkgate; adult/child £3/1.20; all Leith buses

Four hundred yards (364m) south of the Shore, hidden away on a pedestrian mall behind the modern Newkirkgate shopping centre, is a neoclassical building dating from 1816. It was the headquarters of the Incorporation of Masters and Mariners (founded in 1380), the nautical equivalent of a tradesmen's guild, and is a treasure house of old ship models, navigation instruments and nautical memorabilia relating to Leith's maritime history. Trinity House is available to visit by guided tour only; phone to book in advance. A £2.65-million scheme to regenerate the Kirkgate area of Leith was approved in 2003, and the building may eventually be opened to the public.

NEWHAVEN

Immediately to the west of Leith, Newhaven was once a distinctive fishing community whose fishwives tramped the streets of Edinburgh's New Town selling 'caller herrin' (fresh herring) from wicker creels on their backs. Sadly, modern development has dispelled the fishing-village atmosphere, with ugly flats mixed in among the old cottages and terraces. The old fish-market building beside the little harbour now houses the Newhaven Heritage Museum, and the former church is now home to an indoor climbing centre.

NEWHAVEN HERITAGE MUSEUM

Map pp214-15

☎ 551 4165; 24 Pier Pl; admission free; noon-4.45pm; 7, 10, 11 or 16

The former fish market on the eastern side of the harbour now houses a small museum decked out with tableaux celebrating the lives of Newhaven fishers and the origins of Newhaven as a naval dockyard. A 15-minute video illustrates the hard-working lifestyle that survived here until the 1950s, when overfishing put paid to the traditional source of income.

CRAMOND

With its moored yachts, stately swans and whitewashed houses spilling down a hillside at the mouth of the River Almond, Cramond is Edinburgh's most picturesque village. It is also rich in history – it has long been known that the Romans built a fort here in the 2nd century AD (the village's name comes from *Caer Amon*, 'the fort on the River Almond'), but archaeological excavations have revealed evidence of a Bronze Age settlement as long ago as 8500 BC, the oldest known site in the whole of Scotland.

Cramond, which was originally a mill village, has a historic 17th-century church, a 15th-century tower house and some rather unimpressive Roman remains, but most visitors come to enjoy a walk along the river to the ruined mills or to enjoy a meal or a drink at the **Cramond Inn** (p118).

About a mile from the mouth of the river lies **Cramond Island**, uninhabited except for nesting seabirds. The gap between the island and the shore is spiked with a row of concrete teeth, a WWII barrier designed to prevent miniature submarines from creeping upstream to Rosyth naval base.

TRANSPORT

Bus Lothian buses 24 and 41 run to Cramond, the former from Lothian Rd and Princes St, the latter from George IV Bridge, the Mound and George St. From the Cramond bus stop it's a 400m walk north along Cramond Glebe Rd to the village.

Parking There is a large car park off Cramond Glebe Rd, signposted on the right just as the road narrows. Do not continue past this turn-off – parking is not allowed beyond this point.

THE CRAMOND LIONESS

In November 1996 ferryman Robert Graham, who then operated the rowing-boat ferry across the River Almond at Cramond, noticed part of a carved stone sticking out of the mud at low tide. He started to dig it out, thinking it might make a nice ornament for his garden, but when he realised that he was uncovering a 1.5m Roman sculpture of a lioness gripping a man's head in its teeth, he decided he'd better let the experts take over. When the value of his find was realised, Mr Graham received a £50,000 reward for his efforts.

Archaeologists have dated the white sandstone sculpture to the late 2nd or early 3rd century AD, and have conjectured that it was a funerary monument – the 1800-year-old lioness is the only Roman statue of its kind ever found in Britain. At the time of writing it was on display in the Museum of Scotland, but it may eventually be moved to a new interpretation centre that is planned for Cramond.

You can walk out to the island at low tide – there are some small sandy beaches that make pleasant summer picnic sites. The walk takes about 20 minutes and the safe period for crossing lasts from two hours before to two hours after the time of low water.

To check on tide times call **Forth Coastguard** (☎ 01333-450666). Do *not* cross unless you are sure of the tides – every year dozens of people get caught out and have to be rescued.

At the time of writing the **Cramond Ferry**, a rowing boat ferry that provides access to Dalmeny House and a footpath to Queensferry, had been closed since 2000, and was the subject of a bureaucratic wrangle. It may reopen, it may not.

DALMENY HOUSE

☎ 331 1888; www.dalmeny.co.uk; Dalmeny Estate; adult/child £5/3; 🕑 2-5.30pm Sun-Tue Jul & Aug

Dalmeny House, located on the far bank of the river from Cramond, is the seat of the Earls of Rosebery, and a guided tour of the house – often conducted by the present Lord and Lady Rosebery themselves – takes in beautiful 18th-century furniture, tapestries, porcelain and paintings by Millais, Gainsborough, Reynolds and Raeburn. There is also a fascinating collection of Napoleon Bonaparte memorabilia assembled by the fifth Earl of Rosebery.

You can reach Dalmeny House by car from Edinburgh – head west on the A90, following the signs for the Forth Rd Bridge, then leave the main road on the B924 to Dalmeny and Queensferry. The entrance to the house is signposted on the right, half a mile after leaving the A90. If the Cramond Ferry ever reopens (see above), the house is a pleasant 30-minute walk from the far side of the river.

THE MALTINGS

☎ 312 6034; Cramond Village; admission free; 🕑 2-5pm Sat & Sun Jun-Sep, daily during Edinburgh Festival

Located on the riverside in Cramond, a short distance downstream from the ferry landing stairs, you will find the Maltings, which hosts a small exhibition on the history of Cramond.

PORTOBELLO

The northeastern suburb of Portobello is fringed by a mile-long strand of clean golden sand with expansive views along the Firth of Forth to the conical hill of North Berwick Law and across to the rolling fields of Fife. Located 4 miles east of the city centre, Portobello was named after a cottage built there in the 1740s by a veteran of the Battle of Puerto Bello (a naval battle between the British and Spanish in 1739). It saw its first recreational bathers in 1795, when a local entrepreneur introduced bathing machines to the beach, and rapidly grew into a fashionable 19th-century seaside resort known as 'the Brighton of the North'. It was absorbed into Edinburgh in 1896.

Portobello once boasted a quarter-mile-long steamer pier (demolished in 1917) and a huge outdoor swimming pool with wave machine (closed in 1980), but its fortunes fell into decline after the 1960s.

TRANSPORT

Bus Lothian bus 15 or 26 (eastbound) from Princes St, or 46 from St Andrew Sq, will take you to Portobello.

GILMERTON COVE

The latest addition to Edinburgh's historical underground attractions is **Gilmerton Cove** (☎ 557 6464; www.gilmertoncove.org.uk; 16 Drum St, Gilmerton; guided tours adult/child £5/3; ⏲ tours 7pm Wed & Sun, 2pm & 7pm Sat; 🚌 3 or 29), a collection of subterranean passages and chambers hewn out of solid sandstone on the southeastern fringes of the city. Its origins are uncertain, but tradition maintains that it was created by a local blacksmith in the early 18th century, and used as a forge, workshop and illegal drinking den. The cove is more than 12m long, has six chambers with rock benches, and a rock-cut table with a 'punch bowl' carved into it.

To visit Gilmerton Cove, you have to book a one-hour guided tour through **Mercat Tours** (see p51).

In recent years, however, there has been much redevelopment and Porty's popularity is on the rise again. The mile-long **promenade** provides a pleasant seaside walk (go west to east for the best views), the beach swarms with kids on warm summer days, and there are old-fashioned amusement arcades offering slot machines and bingo games. If it's too cold to swim in the sea, there's a restored Victorian **swimming pool** complete with old-fashioned Turkish baths (see p147).

A bronze **plaque** on a cream-coloured cottage at 3 Bridge St commemorates the birthplace of Sir Harry Lauder, the famous music-hall entertainer. An attempt has been made to lure performers back to the seaside through the community arts project Portobello Open Door (www.the-pod.org); during the second week of August it brings a programme of children's events, music gigs and Festival Fringe acts to Portobello. Golden Days (second Saturday in June) is another event that harks back to the 1930s heyday of the seaside holiday, with pony rides on the beach, a sandcastle competition and jazz and swing bands playing in local pubs. And if the New Year's Eve party in the city centre seems too big to handle, Portobello has its own Hogmanay celebrations with plenty of fireworks and live music.

GREATER EDINBURGH

Drinking p134; Eating p120; Sleeping p172

As the city of Edinburgh expanded during the 19th and 20th centuries, it swallowed up several of the outlying villages and rural areas, many of which still preserve a distinct identity within the city today.

The Greater Edinburgh area is a suburban sprawl of villas, bungalows, gardens, parks and the occasional tower block, that encloses the odd hidden corner of history – from leafy Corstorphine to medieval Duddingston, and bucolic Swanston to picturesque Queensferry.

CORSTORPHINE

Corstorphine, on the main road west out of the city, is a douce (respectable) middle-class suburb that takes its name from a medieval village: the early-15th-century parish church still survives on Kirk Loan. Its main feature is Corstorphine Hill, a low, wooded lump which is crisscrossed with footpaths, and much frequented by local dog-walkers. Its sunny southern slopes are home to Edinburgh Zoo, the main reason for visiting.

EDINBURGH ZOO Map pp214-15

☎ 334 9171; www.edinburghzoo.org.uk; 134 Corstorphine Rd; adult/child £9/6; ⏲ 9am-6pm Apr-Sep, 9am-5pm Oct & Mar, 9am-4.30pm Nov-Feb; 🚌 12, 26, 31 or 100

Opened in 1913, located 2½ miles west of the city centre, Edinburgh Zoo is one of the world's leading conservation zoos. Edinburgh's captive breeding programme has saved many endangered species, including Siberian tigers, pygmy hippos and red pandas. The main attractions are the four species of penguin, kept in the world's biggest penguin pool, the sea lion and red panda feeding times, the animal handling sessions, and the Lifelinks 'hands on' zoology centre.

TRANSPORT

Bus Lothian buses 12, 26, 31 or 100 (westbound) from Princes St or Shandwick Pl, or Lothian bus 1 from Princes St or Lothian Rd, pass through Corstorphine.

BLACKFORD HILL

Lying 1½ miles directly south of the city centre, Blackford Hill (164m) offers pleasant walking (see p96) and a splendid panorama of the castle, Old Town and Arthur's Seat. It is also home to the Royal Observatory.

TRANSPORT

Bus Lothian bus 41 (southbound) from Hanover St, the Mound or George IV Bridge stops on Blackford Ave.

ROYAL OBSERVATORY OF EDINBURGH Map pp224-5

☎ 668 8404; www.roe.ac.uk; Blackford Hill; adult/child £3.50/2.50; 7-8.45pm Fri Oct-Mar; 24, 38 or 41

The Royal Observatory was built here in 1896 to replace the City Observatory on Calton Hill, whose view of the night sky had been obscured by smoke from Waverley train station. The original dome still houses a 36-inch reflecting telescope, the largest in the UK. Today the observatory is principally an academic institution, but it opens to members of the public with an interest in astronomy on Friday evenings in winter. If the weather is bad, there is a multimedia gallery with computers and CD-ROMs on astronomy, and a shop selling books and gifts.

DUDDINGSTON

Nestling directly beneath the southeastern slopes of Arthur's Seat, the picturesque little village of Duddingston (Map pp214–15) is a place of great antiquity; archaeologists have unearthed Bronze Age remains here. The village itself dates from the 12th century, though all that remains from that date are parts of **Duddingston Parish Church**, which sits on a promontory overlooking Duddingston Loch. The western door of the church is Norman, decorated with chevron patterns and carvings of Christ on the Cross and a soldier with a sword and axe. There are some interesting medieval relics at the kirkyard gate: the **Joug**, a metal collar that was used, like the stocks, to tether criminals and sinners; and the **Loupin-On Stane**, a stone step to help gouty and corpulent parishioners mount their horses. The early-19th-century **watch tower** inside the gate was built to deter body snatchers.

The village itself consists of only two streets: Old Church Lane and the Causeway. At the western end of the latter stands an 18th-century pub, the Sheep Heid (see p134), and at the eastern end is **Prince Charlie's Cottage**, where the Young Pretender held a council of war before the Battle of Prestonpans in 1745.

To climb Arthur's Seat (251m) from Duddingston, head westwards from the church to the parking area just inside the gate to Holyrood Park, then turn right and climb up the steep stairs known as Jacob's Ladder to another road. Turn right and when you reach another parking area (200m) leave the road and take the path on the left to the summit (20 to 30 minutes total). See also p95.

TRANSPORT

Bus Lothian bus 42 (southbound) from Hanover St, the Mound or George IV Bridge stops on nearby Duddingston Ave.

SWANSTON

Huddled in the shadow of the Pentland Hills on the southern fringe of the city, the tiny hamlet of Swanston is an unlikely survivor – a village green, an old schoolhouse and a square of whitewashed cottages with reed-thatched roofs barely 500m from the roaring traffic of Edinburgh's ring-road. This picturesque spot is a favourite starting point for walks into the Pentland Hills, but is most famous as the childhood summer retreat of Robert Louis Stevenson. Stevenson's father leased the nearby 18th-century villa, **Swanston Cottage**, as a summer home from 1867 to 1880, hoping that the clean air would improve the health of his sickly son.

TRANSPORT

Bus Take bus 4 (westbound) from Princes St and get off at Oxgangs Rd, just past Hunter's Tryst, then walk 750m southwards on Swanston Rd.

WATER OF LEITH

Edinburgh's river is a modest stream, flowing only 20 miles from the northwestern slopes of the Pentland Hills through western and northern Edinburgh to enter the Firth of Forth at Leith. Rarely more than 9m across, it cuts a surprisingly rural swathe through the city, offering the chance to stroll along wooded riverbanks only 500m from Princes St.

Throughout history the river has served as a source of power for water mills and a convenient waste-disposal system, but it has now been cleaned up and provides an important wildlife habitat (you can occasionally see otters and kingfishers) and recreation resource for walkers and anglers. The **Water of Leith Walkway**, a project that started in the 1970s and was only recently completed, now offers an almost uninterrupted 12-mile walking and cycling route along the river from Leith to the village of Balerno, on the southwestern edge of the city. There are access points and signposts throughout its length.

The **Water of Leith Visitor Centre** (Map pp214–15; ☎ 455 7367; www.waterofleith.org.uk; 24 Lanark Rd; adult/child £1.90/1.20; 🕑 10am-4pm daily, closed 24 Dec-3 Jan; 🚌 28, 35, 44 or 66) has interactive displays on the river's wildlife and ecology, and underwater video cameras that allow you to watch aquatic creatures live.

QUEENSFERRY

Although Queensferry lies 8 miles west of the city centre, on the southern bank of the Firth of Forth, it falls within the official boundaries of the city of Edinburgh. Located at the narrowest part of the firth, it served as a port for the ferries that plied across the water to Fife from the earliest times, ceasing only in 1964 when the graceful **Forth Road Bridge** – now the fifth longest in Europe – was opened. The rail-carrying Forth Bridge pre-dates the Forth Road Bridge by 74 years.

Queensferry is a lively and attractive village, with cobbled lanes, 17th- and 18th-century terraced houses and a picturesque little harbour. There are several good pubs and restaurants along High St. One of them is the Hawes Inn (p134), famously mentioned in Robert Louis Stevenson's novel *Kidnapped* and in Sir Walter Scott's *The Antiquary*; it's opposite the Inchcolm ferry, beneath the railway bridge.

TRANSPORT

Bus Take First Edinburgh bus 43 (£2, 30 minutes) westbound from Princes St (eastern end) or Charlotte Sq; there's a bus every 20 minutes. It's a 10-minute walk eastwards from the bus stop to the Hawes Inn and the Inchcolm ferry.

Parking There is plenty of free parking along the seafront west of the Hawes Inn.

Train There are frequent trains (£3.20, 15 minutes) from Waverley and Haymarket to Dalmeny station. From the station exit, the Hawes Inn is a five-minute walk away, along a footpath (across the road from the station, behind the bus stop) that leads north beside the railway and under the bridge.

FORTH BRIDGE

The magnificent Forth Bridge – only outsiders ever call it the Forth Rail Bridge – is one of the finest engineering achievements of the 19th century. Completed in 1890 after seven years' work, its three huge cantilevers span 1447m and its construction took 59,000 tonnes of steel, eight million rivets, 254 tonnes of paint and the lives of at least 58 men. It has become an icon of Scottish engineering excellence, and has appeared in several films, most famously in the 1959 version of *The Thirty-Nine Steps*.

Maintaining the structure is a monumental undertaking – 'it's like painting the Forth Bridge' is a local phrase often used to describe a seemingly never-ending task. There was a furore in the Scottish Parliament in 2003 when one member suggested that, in view of the huge costs of maintenance, the bridge's demolition should be considered. In the same year an £11-million project began, with the intention of sand-blasting the structure back to bare steel and coating it with a modern glass-flake/epoxy paint that is expected to last at least 20 years.

HOPETOUN HOUSE

☎ 331 2451; adult/child £7/4; 🕑 10am-5.30pm Easter-Sep, last admission 4.30pm

Two miles west of Queensferry lies one of Scotland's finest stately homes, in a superb location in lovely grounds beside the Firth of Forth. There are two parts, the older built to Sir William Bruce's plans between 1699 and 1702 and dominated by

THE BURRY MAN

If you happen to be visiting Edinburgh on the first Friday in August, head west to the village of Queensferry to see the Burry Man. As part of the village's gala day festivities, a local man spends nine hours roaming the streets wearing a woolly suit which has been laboriously covered from head to toe in big, green, prickly burrs, and carrying two staves that are decorated with flowers. One glance at his costume – he looks like a child's drawing of a Martian, with added prickles – would make you think that he's suffering some form of bizarre medieval punishment. But the Burry Man is descended from an ancient fertility rite, and it is actually an honour to be selected. If you can't visit in August, there's a Burry Man costume on show in the Queensferry Museum.

a splendid stairwell, the newer designed between 1720 and 1750 by three members of the Adam family, William and sons Robert and John. The highlights are the red-and-yellow Adam drawing rooms, lined in silk damask, and the view from the roof terrace.

The Hope family supplied a viceroy of India and a governor-general of Australia so the upstairs museum displays interesting reminders of the colonial life of the ruling class.

Britain's most elegant equine accommodation – where the marquis once housed his pampered racehorses – is now the stylish **Stables Tearoom** (mains £4-8; ⌚ same as house), a delightful spot for lunch.

Hopetoun House is located 2 miles west of Queensferry along the coast road. Driving from Edinburgh, turn off the A90 onto the A904 just before the Forth Bridge and follow the signs.

INCHCOLM ABBEY

☎ 01383-823332; Inchcolm, Fife; adult/child £3.30/1.30; ⌚ 9.30am-6pm Easter-Sep

The island of Inchcolm lies directly to the east of the Forth bridges, less than a mile off the coast of Fife. Only 800m in length, it is home to the ruins of Inchcolm Abbey, one of Scotland's best-preserved medieval abbeys, founded by Augustinian priors in 1123. In the well-tended grounds stand the remains of a 13th-century church as well as a remarkably well-preserved octagonal chapter house with a stone roof.

The ferry boat **Maid of the Forth** (☎ 331 4857; wwwmaidoftheforth.co.uk) sails to Inchcolm from Hawes Pier in Queensferry. There are two or three sailings daily in July and August, and at weekends only from April to June and in September and October. The return fare costs £13/4.50 per adult/child, including admission to Inchcolm Abbey. It's a half-hour sail to Inchcolm and you get 1½ hours ashore. As well as the abbey, the trip gives you the chance to see the island's grey seals, puffins and other seabirds.

QUEENSFERRY MUSEUM

☎ 331 5545; 53 High St; admission free; ⌚ 10am-1pm & 2.15-5pm Mon & Thu-Sat, noon-5pm Sun; 🚌 First Edinburgh 43

This small town-hall museum on Queensferry's pretty, terraced High St contains some really interesting information on the building of the Forth bridges, along with some fascinating photographs of the railway bridge in various stages of construction. There is also a glass case containing a preserved Burry Man costume (see above).

1 *Hibs supporters at a home match, Easter Road Stadium (p145)* **2** *Entertainment along the Royal Mile during the Edinburgh Festival Fringe (p22)* **3** *Skating in Princes Street Gardens (p69)* **4** *Jazz night at the Fairmile Inn (p1431)*

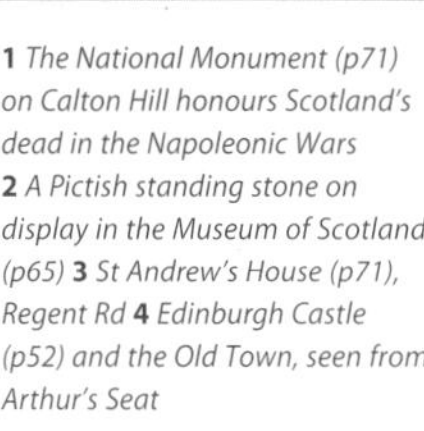

1 *The National Monument (p71) on Calton Hill honours Scotland's dead in the Napoleonic Wars* **2** *A Pictish standing stone on display in the Museum of Scotland (p65)* **3** *St Andrew's House (p71), Regent Rd* **4** *Edinburgh Castle (p52) and the Old Town, seen from Arthur's Seat*

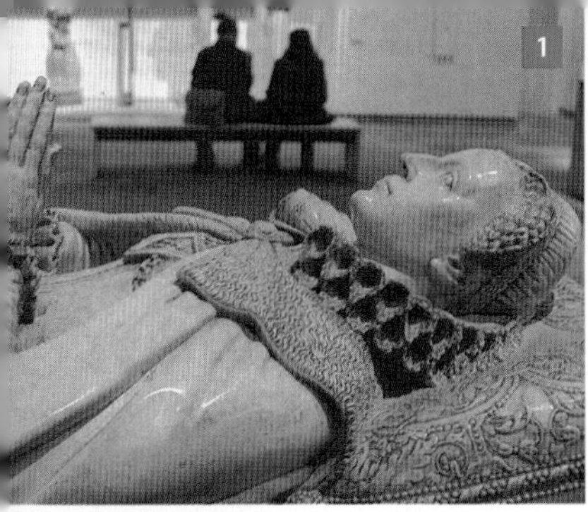

1 *The tomb of Mary Queen of Scots (p39) in the Museum of Scotland* **2** *The icy Polar Room, Our Dynamic Earth (p59)* **3** *The grand Hopetoun House (p81), Queensferry* **4** *A tombstone incorporated into the façade of Greyfriars Kirk (p64)*

1 *A performance at the Edinburgh International Festival (p22)* **2** *Beltane (p20), a pagan fire festival*
3 *The Royal Scottish Academy (p69), Princes St*

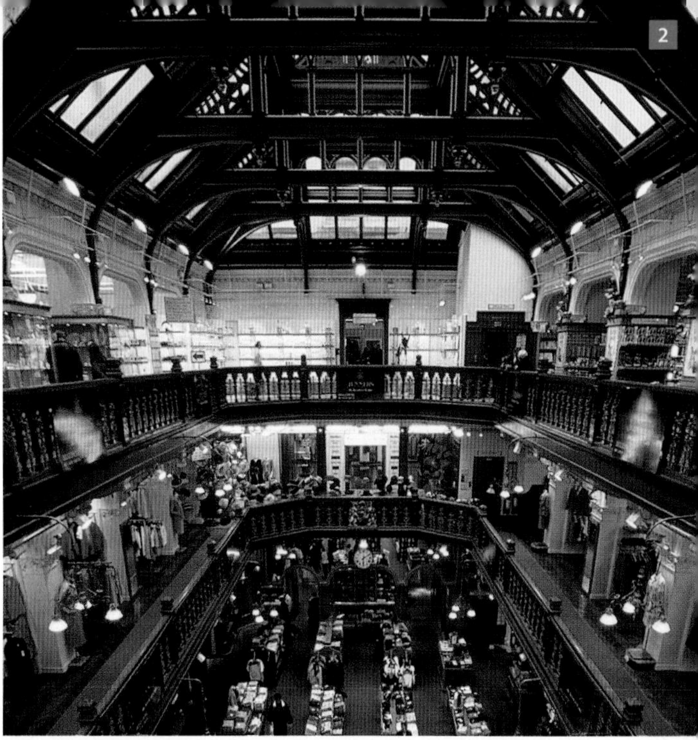

1 The Ocean Terminal
hopping centre (p75) on
dinburgh's waterfront
2 Jenners (p153), Britain's
oldest department store
3 Antique maps and globes
at Carson Clark Gallery
p151)

1 *The stylish Malmaison Hotel (p171) in the heart of Edinburgh's docklands* **2** *Breakfast at Always Sunday (p103), Royal Mile* **3** *Stained-glass window, Café Royal Oyster Bar (p108), New Town* **4** *The Old Chain Pier (p133), a traditional, real-ale pub on Edinburgh's waterfront*

1 *Edinburgh's famous Valvona & Crolla delicatessen (p155)*
2 *The 'Inner Sanctum' suite, Witchery by the Castle (p162)*
3 *Secondhand designer fashions at Greensleeves (p157), Morningside* **4** *Honeycomb (p138), in the underground South Bridge vaults*

1

2

1 *Edinburgh University's New College (p92)* **2** *Canongate Kirk (p55)* **3** *The summit of Arthur's Seat (p59), the highest point in Holyrood Park*

3

Walking Tours

Walking Tours

Edinburgh's compact centre, with its winding streets and steep narrow closes, hidden corners and unexpected views, just begs to be explored on foot. Our selection of walking tours will lead you into many of those hidden corners, many of them – surprisingly – right in the middle of the busiest, most touristy parts of town.

If you'd prefer to take a guided walking tour, there's a broad range of choices listed in the Sights chapter (see p50). Remember that Edinburgh is, in the words of Robert Louis Stevenson, 'a precipitous city' – wear good walking shoes and be prepared for a few steep climbs.

WALK 1: THE OLD TOWN

Edinburgh's Old Town spreads down the Royal Mile to the east of the castle and southwards to the Grassmarket and Greyfriars. This walk explores a few of the Old Town's many interesting nooks and crannies, and involves a fair bit of climbing up and down steep stairs and closes.

WALK FACTS

Start Castle Esplanade

End Greyfriars Kirkyard or Museum of Scotland

Distance 1½ miles

Duration One to two hours

Transport 🚌 2, 23, 27, 41 or 42 (start and end)

Begin on the **Castle Esplanade** 1 (p52), which provides a grandstand view southwards over the Grassmarket; the prominent quadrangular building with all the turrets is George Heriot's School, which you'll be passing later on. Head towards Castlehill and the start of the Royal Mile. The 17th-century house on the right, above the steps of N Castle Wynd, is known as **Cannonball House** 2 because of the iron ball lodged in the wall (look between, and slightly below, the two largest windows). It was not fired in anger, but instead marks the maximum height to which water could flow under gravity alone from the city's first piped water supply.

The low, rectangular building situated across the street (now a touristy tartan-weaving mill) was originally the reservoir that held the Old Town's water supply. On its western wall is the **Witches Well** 3, where a modern bronze fountain commemorates around 4000 people (mostly women) who were burnt or strangled in Edinburgh between 1479 and 1722 on suspicion of witchcraft.

Go past the reservoir and turn left down Ramsay Lane, and take a look at **Ramsay Garden** 4, one of Edinburgh's most desirable addresses, where late-19th-century apartments were built around the octagonal Ramsay Lodge, once home to poet Allan Ramsay. The cobbled street continues around to the right below student residences, to the towers of the **New College** 5, home to Edinburgh University's Faculty of Divinity. Nip into the courtyard to see the statue of John Knox.

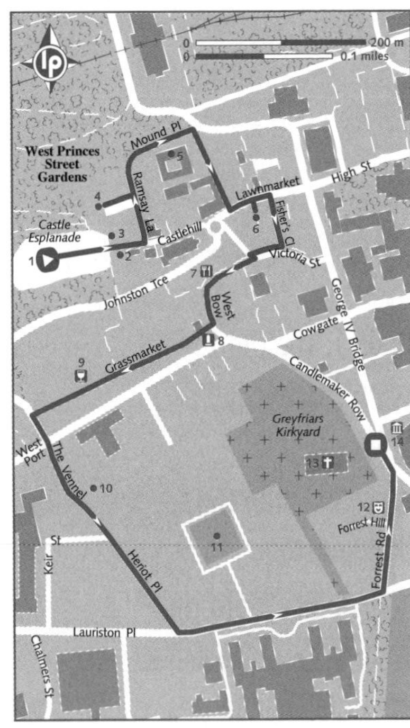

Just past New College turn right and climb up the stairs into Milne's Court, a student residence belonging to Edinburgh University. Exit into the Lawnmarket, cross the street (bearing slightly left) and duck into **Riddell's Court 6** at Nos 322–328, a typical Old Town close. You'll find yourself in a small courtyard but the house in front of you (built in 1590) was originally the edge of the street (the building you just walked under was added in 1726 – check the inscription in the doorway on the right). The arch (with the inscription *'vivendo discimus'*, 'we live and learn') leads into the original 16th-century courtyard.

Go back into the street, turn right, and then right again down Fisher's Close, which leads you onto the delightful Victoria Tce, strung above the cobbled curve of shop-lined Victoria St. Wander right, enjoying the view – **Maxie's Bistro 7** (p105), at the far end of the terrace, is a great place to stop for a drink – then descend the stairs at the foot of Upper Bow and continue downhill to the Grassmarket. At the east end, outside Maggie Dickson's pub, is the **Covenanters' Monument 8** (p63); if you're feeling peckish, there are several good places to eat (p103) and a couple of good pubs – Robert Burns once stayed at the **White Hart Inn 9** (p124).

At the west end of the Grassmarket, turn left up the flight of stairs known as the Vennel. At the top of the steps on the left you'll find the **Flodden Wall 10** (p63). Follow its extension, the Telfer Wall, to Lauriston Pl and turn left along the impressive façade of **George Heriot's School 11** (p63). Note that this is the back of the building – the front was designed to face the castle, and impress the inhabitants of the Grassmarket.

Turn left again at Forrest Rd, and if it's a Sunday afternoon pop into **Sandy Bell's 12** (p142) for a pint and some Scottish folk music. Finish off your walk with a stroll through **Greyfriars Kirkyard 13** (p64) or a visit to the **Museum of Scotland 14** (p65).

WALK 2: NEW TOWN & STOCKBRIDGE

This perambulation probes the more interesting parts of the New Town and ends with a pleasant stroll along the wooded valley of the Water of Leith.

Begin on the east side of St Andrew Sq. Looking westwards along George St, you can see the dome of West Register House – formerly a church – at the far end. The original plans for the New Town envisaged a matching Church of St Andrew on the eastern side of St Andrew Sq, but the rich and ambitious Sir Lawrence Dundas had

WALK FACTS

Start St Andrew Sq

End Deanhaugh St

Distance 2½ miles

Duration 1½ to 2½ hours

Transport 🚌 8, 10, 11, 15, 16, 17, 24, 28 or 45 (start); 🚌 24, 29 or 42 (end)

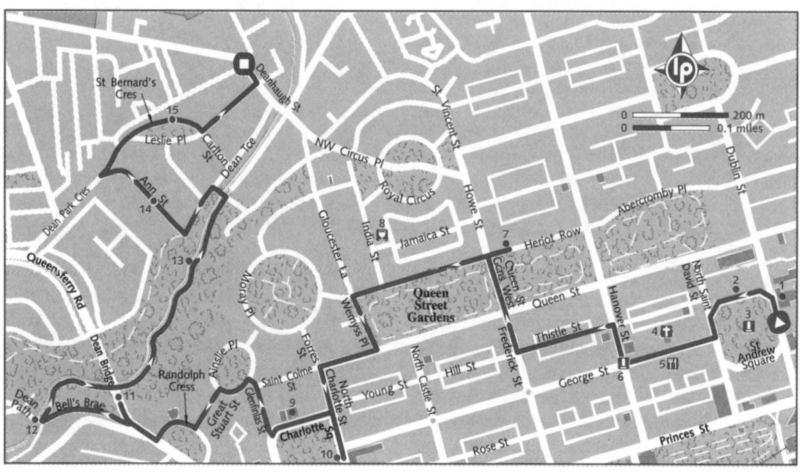

other plans: he bought up the land, and had his own elaborate mansion, **Dundas House** 1 (p70), built on the site.

Go around the north side of the square, passing **23-26 St Andrew Sq** 2 (p70) – the oldest houses in the New Town – and pause to look up at the **Melville Monument** 3 (p70). Walk westwards along George St, past the **Church of St Andrew & St George** 4 (p70). Note the ostentatious temple to Mammon on your left that was once a bank and is now an impressive restaurant (the **Dome** 5; see p109). Turn right at Hanover St, where a **statue of George IV** 6 commemorates his royal visit in 1822, and then left along Thistle St. This and its companion Rose St were built to house the servants, tradesmen and stables that catered to the needs of the New Town gentry; today it still serves a similar purpose, but with restaurants, galleries and shops catering to the wealthy professionals who now inhabit the Georgian town houses.

Turn right on Frederick St and continue downhill past Queen St and its gardens, and turn right into Heriot Row. A few doors along at **17 Heriot Row** 7 an inscription marks the house where Robert Louis Stevenson lived from 1857 to 1880. Retrace your steps and continue westwards along Heriot Row, a typical New Town Georgian terrace. If you're feeling thirsty, the delightful **Kay's Bar** 8 (p125) is just around the corner off India Pl.

Turn left at Wemyss Pl (pronounced 'weems'), then go right and take the first left into N Charlotte St, which leads to **Charlotte Square** (p70). On the north side is the beautiful neoclassical façade of **Bute House** 9 (p70), while off the southeast corner is **16 S Charlotte St** 10, birthplace of Alexander Graham Bell.

After looking around the square, exit via Glenfinlas St in the northwestern corner, and bear left into Ainslie Pl. This elegant oval space, with its octagonal neighbour Moray Pl on one side and semicircular Randolph Cres on the other, constitute the Moray Estate (built between 1822 and 1850), perhaps the most beautiful part of the New Town.

Go left along Great Stuart St, bear right through Randolph Cres and cross busy Queensferry St, before turning right towards **Dean Bridge** 11 (p73). Go out into the middle of the bridge for a view over Dean Village, then return and descend the steep cobbled lane of Bell's Brae –before Dean Bridge was built, this was the main road from Edinburgh to Queensferry. Just before the **old bridge** 12 (p73), turn right along Miller Row and follow the footpath along the Water of Leith. The buildings high up on the cliff above the private gardens on the right are the backs of the ones you saw earlier on Ainslie Pl. Five minutes' walk brings you to **St Bernard's Well** 13, a circular temple with a statue of Hygeia, the goddess of health, built

Bute House (p70), designed by Robert Adam, on Charlotte Sq

in 1789. The sulphurous spring, similar to the ones in Harrogate (in Yorkshire, England), was discovered by schoolboys from George Heriot's School in 1760, and became hugely popular during the late-18th-century fad for 'taking the waters' – one visitor compared the taste to 'the washings of foul gun barrels'.

Where the footpath passes under an arch, climb the steps and cross the bridge over the Water of Leith. Turn left on Dean Tce, then right along **Ann Street** 14 (p73). Having lusted after some of Edinburgh's most beautiful (and expensive) properties, turn right on Dean Park Cres and continue through the tree-lined splendour of **St Bernard's Crescent** 15 (p73). At the far end, a left turn along Leslie Pl will deposit you in Deanhaugh St in the heart of Stockbridge, where various bars, cafés, shops and restaurants await.

WALK 3: CALTON HILL TO DUDDINGSTON

Edinburgh's city-centre hills provide superb views over the city and surrounding countryside. This walk is fairly strenuous, taking in the summits of both Calton Hill and Arthur's Seat.

Start at the eastern end of Princes St, at **Register House** 1 (p68). Walk east along Waterloo Pl, pausing to explore the **Old Calton Burying Ground** 2 (p71), and climb the stairs on the left (after Howie's restaurant). At the top of the steps, on the left, is an iron gate marked **Rock House** 3. This was once the home of David Octavius Hill, an early pioneer of portrait photography. Beyond the gate, turn right up another flight of steps and continue up the path to the top of Calton Hill.

WALK FACTS

Start Register House

End Prince Charlie's Cottage

Distance 4 miles

Duration Two to three hours

Transport 🚌 1, 3, 8, 19, 29, 30, 31, 33, 34 or 37 (start); 🚌 42 (end)

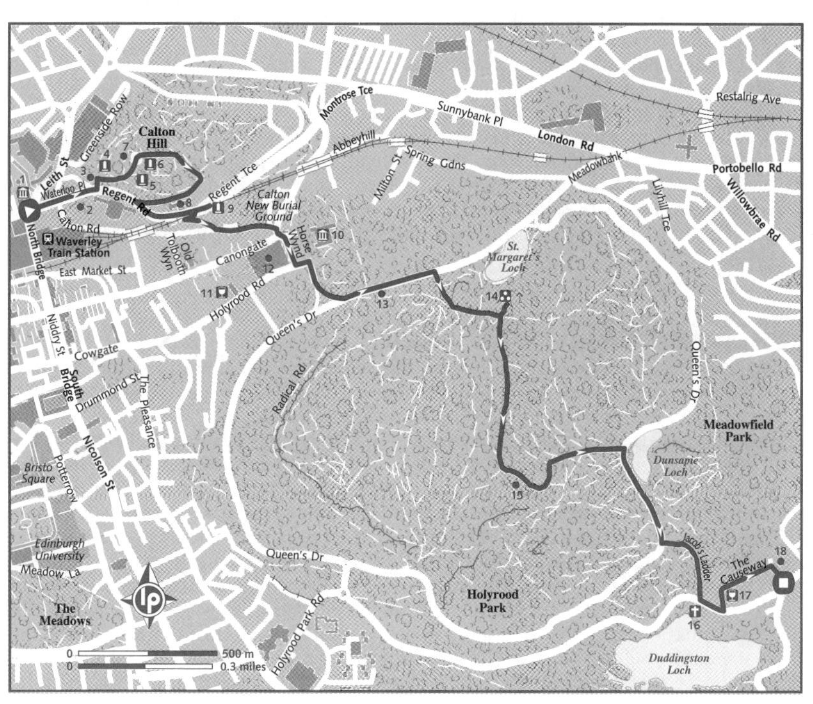

The summit is scattered with the monuments that gave Edinburgh its nickname, Athens of the North – the **Monument to Dugald Stewart** 4 (p72), the **Nelson Monument** 5 (p72), the **National Monument** 6 (p71) and the **City Observatory** 7 (p71). On the northern side, the view extends from the Forth Bridges in the west to the distant conical hill of North Berwick Law in the east.

Walk eastwards from the summit and follow the road curving right and dropping down to Regent Rd. Cross the road and go left until you're opposite the Greek temple of the old **Royal High School** 8 (p71).

Take a quick look at the nearby **Burns Monument** 9, then descend the footpath that drops down on the southern side of Regent Rd; halfway down, double back to the left to reach Calton Rd. Follow Calton Rd east to the **Palace of Holyroodhouse** 10 (p60), and finish the walk here if you're tired. If you need a refreshing drink, head for the **Tun** 11 (p123).

Monument to Dugald Stewart (p72) on Calton Hill

Follow Horse Wynd past the site of the new **Scottish Parliament Building** 12 (p61). Go left at the roundabout and cross the road to **St Margaret's Well** 13 (p59). Follow the path leftwards up the hillside towards the ruins of **St Anthony's Chapel** 14, then head south on the path that follows the floor of a shallow dip just east of Long Row crags. This eventually curves around to the left and climbs more steeply up some steps to a saddle; turn right here and make the final short climb to the rocky summit of **Arthur's Seat** 15 (p59).

After taking in the view, descend eastwards to Queen's Dr at Dunsapie Loch. Turn right and follow the road for about 200m then descend to the left on the steep stairs known as Jacob's Ladder, and turn left along Old Church Lane into Duddingston village. Take a look around **Duddingston Parish Church** 16 (p80) before downing a pint at the **Sheep Heid** 17 (p134). On the way to the bus stop on Duddingston Rd, you'll pass **Prince Charlie's Cottage** 18 (p80).

WALK 4: BLACKFORD HILL

A countryside walk in the heart of the city, this route takes you along a peaceful, wooded valley beside a gurgling stream, then climbs to one of the city's best viewpoints.

Start at the southerly junction of Braid and Comiston Rds, near Buckstone Gardens at the southern edge of the city. From the Buckstone Gardens bus stop on Comiston Rd, walk north along Braid Rd. Just past Buckstone Dr, on the right-hand side of the road you will see a cobbled alcove in the wall, which has a small sandstone pillar, about a metre high, at the back with a plaque above it. This is the **Buck Stane** 1, an ancient boundary marker that once stood 250m to the north; the long, straight stretch of Braid Rd and its continuation south on Comiston Rd follow the line of the old Roman road to the fort at Cramond. Legend has it that in medieval times the king's hunting parties would unleash their buckhounds (ie deerhounds) at this marker as they rode out to hunt in the woods that once clothed the lower slopes of the Pentland Hills; a pole bearing the royal standard would be stuck in the hole on top of the stone to warn that the king was hunting in the area.

Continue north on Braid Rd, down past the Braid Hills Hotel and up again on the far side of the bridge over the Braid Burn. About 600m beyond the bridge, just past the junction with Comiston Tce and opposite 66 Braid Rd, you will see two square slabs of sandstone set into the road, outlined in red brick; these are the **Hanging Stones** 2. These stone sockets once held the posts of a gallows, where the last execution for highway robbery in Scotland took place in 1812.

WALK FACTS

Start Junction of Braid and Comiston Rds

End Royal Observatory

Distance 2½ miles

Duration One to two hours

Transport 🚌 11 or 15 (start); 🚌 24 or 41 (end)

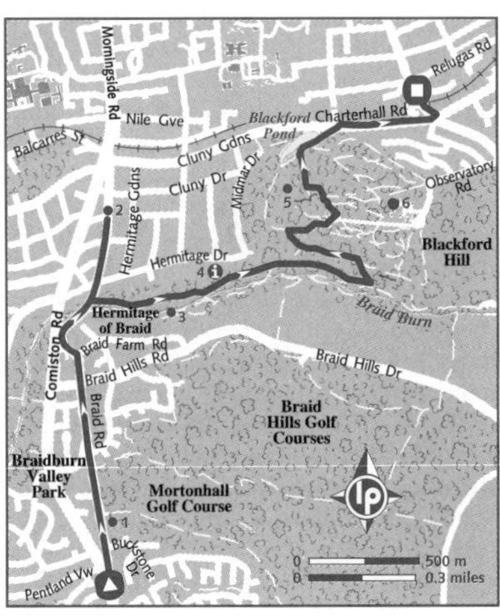

Retrace your step towards the bridge and, just before you reach it, turn left through the gate to the footpath that leads through the **Hermitage of Braid nature reserve** 3. The path meanders through a glen for three-quarters of a mile (with sunlight filtering through the leaves and the sound of birdsongs all around, you'll feel miles from the city), crisscrossing the stream and passing an 18th-century mansion that now houses a visitor centre, **Hermitage House** (4 ☎ 447 7145; admission free; 🕒 2-5pm Mon-Thu & Sat, 2-4pm Fri, noon-5pm Sun). The centre explains the history and wildlife of the glen, and has details of nearby nature trails.

At the eastern end of the reserve you emerge from the trees and pass through a gate beside a bridge; turn left here and head uphill on a broad path that curves back to the left, following the upper edge of the woodland. As the path levels off and curves around to the right, with a stone wall and open fields on the left, look out for a hollow in the slope on your right. A steep path with a flight of wood and turf steps leads up to a radio mast; go around the far end of the fenced enclosure and back left to reach the trig point on the **summit of Blackford Hill** 5 (164m).

The view north from the summit offers a splendid panorama of the city. Straight ahead, beyond the villa gardens, parks and tenements of Morningside and Marchmont, you can see the castle atop its rock with the bristling spine of the Old Town straggling to its right. This view, seen at dawn, was described by Sir Walter Scott in his poem *Marmion*:

> Such dusky grandeur clothed the height
> Where the huge castle holds its state,
> And all the steep slope down,
> Whose ridgy back heaves to the sky,
> Piled deep and massy, close and high,
> Mine own romantic town!

To the right of the Old Town are the monuments on Calton Hill, the bold wedge of Salisbury Crags, and the 'sleeping lion' of Arthur's Seat (the summit lump is supposed to be its head, with the 'body' stretching to its right). On a clear day you'll see the Ochil Hills to the northwest, and even the Highland hills of Ben Vorlich and Stuc a'Chroin; and, far to the east, the conical hump of North Berwick Law. The red-sandstone building with the domes on the hilltop to the east is the **Royal Observatory** 6 (p80).

Descend the north slope of the hill below the trig point by one of several winding paths through the gorse to Blackford Pond, and pause to feed the ducks before heading for the gate at its eastern end. Turn right along Charterhall Rd, and then first left on Blackford Av; a bus stop here (on the left hand side of the road) will take you back into the city centre.

WALK 5: COLINTON DELL & THE UNION CANAL

This walk also treads a rural path through the midst of the city, past a pretty parish church, along a wooded river gorge, and then back towards the city centre via a canal towpath.

Start in Colinton, at the junction of Colinton Rd/Bridge Rd with Dreghorn Loan. Head west on the north side of Bridge Rd, and look out for the newsagent on the right, just before the Colinton Inn; turn right and descend the stairs (signpost for Colinton Parish Church) to Spylaw St. Uphill to your left is a terrace of picturesque cottages dating from 1900, but turn right and cross the bridge over the Water of Leith, then climb up Dell Rd to pretty little **Colinton Parish Church** 1. Although there has been a church here since 1095, it has been destroyed and rebuilt several times; the present building was originally 18th-century, but the Italian-style campanile (bell tower) dates from 1837, and much of the exterior was remodelled in 1907. Robert Louis Stevenson's grandfather was the minister here from 1823 to 1860 and is buried in the kirkyard, which has many interesting stones.

Follow Dell Rd past the church to where it ends, and descend a steep flight of stairs into the wooded ravine of **Colinton Dell** 2. The path follows the riverbank beside a mossy wall, with the scent of wild garlic wafting down from the slope above. This is one of Edinburgh's many rural retreats where the city feels very far away, although there's traffic whizzing past on Lanark Rd less than 200m to the west. When you reach a wooden footbridge over the river, don't cross it; instead, climb up the steep staircase to the left to join the **Water of Leith Walkway** 3, which follows the line of a disused railway. Follow this path for half a mile until it forks, then take the right-hand branch, which descends to the riverbank again. Cross the first bridge you come to and turn left along the far bank of the river. The path here winds up and down through a delightful stretch of woodland, before emerging onto Lanark Rd. Across the road and to the left is the **Water of Leith Visitor Centre** 4 (see p81), with the **Slateford Aqueduct** 5 rising behind it.

You can cut short your walk here (2 miles), and catch bus 28, 34 or 44 from Lanark Rd back into town. Otherwise, follow the walkway past the visitor centre and, once you have passed beneath the aqueduct, turn right up the stairs to reach the bank of the Union Canal.

The Shore (p76) in Leith

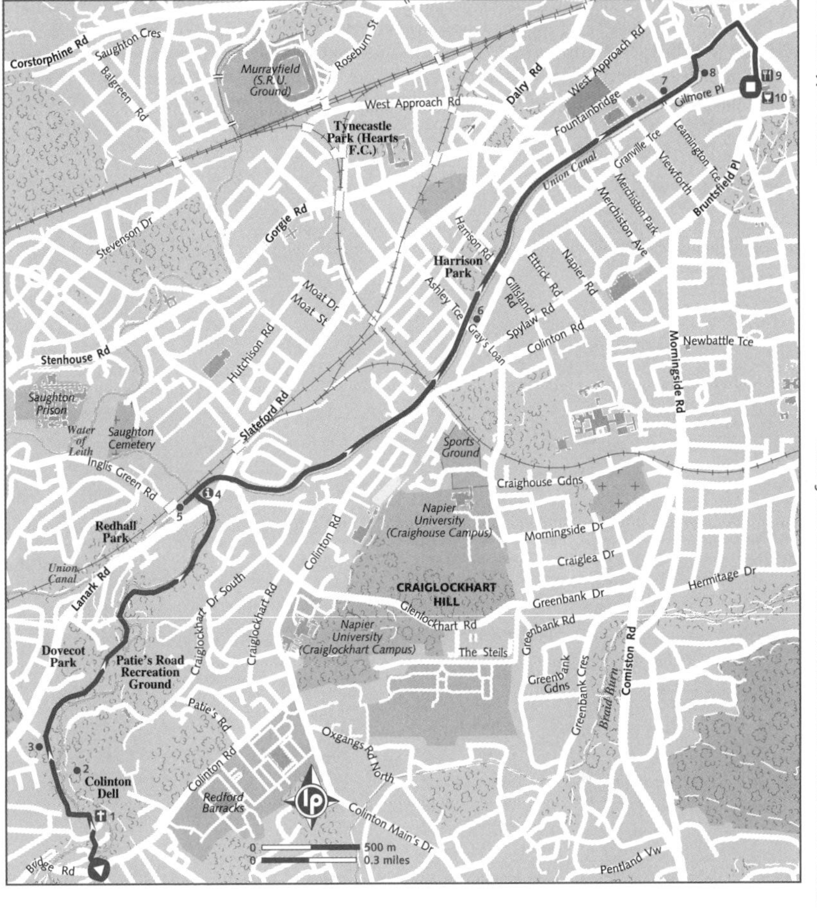

The 31½-mile Union Canal opened in 1822 to take passengers and cargo between Edinburgh and Falkirk, where it linked up with the Forth and Clyde Canal (see p179). It was dug almost entirely by hand; among the thousands of navvies who laboured on its construction were the murderers Burke and Hare (see p44). The eight-arched, 153m-long Slateford Aqueduct carries the canal across the Water of Leith, and is the second-longest in Scotland (the longest is the Avon Aqueduct, near Linlithgow).

WALK FACTS

Start Junction of Colinton and Bridge Rds

End Ndebele or Bennet's Bar

Distance 4½ miles

Duration Two to three hours

Transport 10, 16, 18 or 45 (start); all Tollcross buses (end)

Continue along the canal towpath towards the city centre; keep an eye out for the milestones beside the path. This section of the canal is used by university rowing clubs, and in term time you will often see sculls and fours zipping along. After passing under the Gray's Loan bridge there's a pretty little **basin 6** with rowing boats belonging to the Union Canal Society, whose pavilion lies on the far bank; here, too, is the canal boat restaurant **Zazou** (p116).

The final reach of the canal cuts a peaceful swathe between the backs of residential flats and tenements before reaching the **Leamington Lift Bridge** 7. The bridge was built in 1896, and restored to full working order in 2002; beyond lies **Port Hamilton** 8, the end of the canal, now surrounded by modern offices, flats and restaurants. Go through the passageway to the side of the bar called Cargo, to Fountainbridge; a right turn leads to Lothian Rd in Tollcross, where **Ndebele** 9 (p115) or **Bennet's Bar** 10 (p129) can provide a revitalising refreshment.

Eating

Eating

In the last decade there has been a boom in the number of restaurants in Edinburgh – the city now has more restaurants per head of population than London. Eating out has become a commonplace event rather than something reserved for special occasions, and the choice of eateries ranges from stylish but inexpensive bistros and cafés to gourmet restaurants.

In addition, most pubs serve food, offering either bar meals or a more formal restaurant or both, but be aware that pubs without a Children's Certificate are not allowed to serve children under the age of 14. See p194 for further information.

If you want even more listings than we can provide here, the excellent *Edinburgh & Glasgow Eating & Drinking Guide* (£5.95; www.list.co.uk/ead), published annually by the *List* magazine, contains reviews of around 800 restaurants, cafés and bars.

Opening Hours

In general, lunch is served from noon to 3pm, and dinner from 6pm to 9pm or 10pm. Office workers generally break for lunch between 1pm and 2pm, and city-centre restaurants are often very busy then.

Many places remain open in the afternoon, and a few (especially Indian, Italian and Chinese places) stay open till 11pm or midnight. Cafés generally open from 8am or 9am to 6pm.

The opening hours given in reviews in this chapter are the times during which orders are taken, so if a listing says dinner is available from 7pm to 10pm, then as long as you're seated before 10pm you'll get a meal – it doesn't mean that you have to be out by 10pm!

How Much?

In an average, midrange restaurant you can expect to pay around £10 to £15 a head for lunch, not including drinks, and £20 to £30 a head for dinner, including a bottle of wine between two. At Edinburgh's top tables, you can easily double that. Many places, including the more expensive restaurants, offer good lunch deals. Look out also for pre-theatre or 'early bird' specials (usually available between 5pm and 7pm).

The prices ranges for main courses ('mains') listed in the reviews are for dinner menus, unless otherwise indicated; prices for main courses at lunch are often considerably cheaper.

PRICE GUIDE

Cost of a main course at dinner

£££	£16 and over
££	£8 to £15
£	£7 and less

Booking Tables

Eating out in Edinburgh is popular and booking a table is strongly recommended, especially in August (the Festival) and in December (lots of office parties and Christmas dinners).

The www.5pm.co.uk website lists last-minute offers from restaurants with tables to spare that evening. Using this service you can find a three-course dinner at one of Edinburgh's better restaurants for as little as £12 if you're prepared to eat early or late.

Tipping

Normal practice in Edinburgh is to leave a tip of around 10% unless the service was unsatisfactory. If the bill already includes a service charge (usually 10%), you needn't add a further tip. Note that some restaurants add a compulsory 10% service charge on large groups (usually eight or more people); if this is the case, it should be mentioned on the menu and on the bill.

MODERN SCOTTISH CUISINE

Although Scotland has never been celebrated for its national cuisine – in fact, from haggis to deep-fried Mars Bars, it has more often been an object of ridicule – a new culinary style known as Modern Scottish has emerged in the last 20 years or so.

Most Scottish food writers agree that Ronnie Clydesdale, owner of Glasgow's **Ubiquitous Chip** (see p179), should be credited with 'inventing' Modern Scottish cuisine. As long ago as the 1970s he began championing fresh Scottish produce in his restaurant, in the hope of opening people's eyes to the wealth of top-quality food that the country produced. Back then, most of Scotland's best produce went abroad, and fine dining in Edinburgh was confined to French restaurants.

Despite Clydesdale's pioneering lead (and he's still going strong), Modern Scottish didn't really take off nationwide until the 1990s. But there are now hundreds of restaurants, not just in Edinburgh and Glasgow, but across the length and breadth of Scotland, that proudly claim to serve Modern Scottish cuisine.

It's a style that should be familiar to fans of Californian Cuisine and Mod Oz. Chefs take top-quality Scottish produce – from Highland venison, Aberdeen Angus beef and freshly landed seafood, to root vegetables, raspberries and Ayrshire cheeses – and prepare it simply, in a way that enhances the natural flavours, often adding a French, Italian or Asian twist.

Top Five Modern Scottish Restaurants

- **Atrium** (p115)
- **Number One** (p110)
- **Restaurant Martin Wishart** (p119)
- **Rhubarb** (p117)
- **Tower** (p107)

Self-Catering

There are grocery stores and food shops all over the city, many of them open from 9am to 10pm daily, while many petrol stations also have shops that sell groceries. There are several supermarkets spread throughout the city centre too. The most convenient are: **Marks & Spencer** (Map pp218-19; ☎ 225 2301; 54 Princes St; ⌚ 9am-7pm Mon-Fri, 9am-8pm Thu, 8.30am-6pm Sat, 9am-10pm Sun); **Sainsbury's** (Map pp218-19; ☎ 225 8400; 9-10 St Andrew Sq; ⌚ 7am-10pm Mon-Sat, 9am-8pm Sun); and **Tesco Metro** (Map pp218-19; ☎ 456 2400; 94 Nicolson St; ⌚ 7am-midnight Mon-Sat, 9am-10pm Sun). There are also many excellent delicatessens where you can buy fresh produce from all over the world (see the Shopping chapter, p150).

OLD TOWN

From cosy vaulted cellars to stylish rooftop restaurants, the Old Town offers a wide range of appealing eateries.

ALWAYS SUNDAY Map p222 — Café £

☎ 622 0667; 170 High St, Royal Mile; mains £3-7; ⌚ 8am-6pm Mon-Fri, 9am-6pm Sat & Sun; 🚌 35

If the thought of a greasy fry-up is enough to put you off your breakfast, head instead for this bright and breezy café which dishes up hearty but healthy grub such as fresh fruit smoothies, crisp salads, homemade soups and speciality sandwiches, washed down with Fairtrade coffee or herbal tea. You can sit in the big picture windows and watch the world go by along the Royal Mile, or hide away with the newspapers in the cosy nook up the stairs in the corner opposite the door.

AMBER Map p222 — Scottish ££

☎ 477 8477; 354 Castlehill; mains £12-15; ⌚ noon-4pm daily, plus 7-9pm Fri & Sat; 🚌 2, 35, 41 or 42

Located in the **Scotch Whisky Heritage Centre** (p54), this whisky-themed restaurant manages to avoid the tourist clichés and create genuinely interesting and flavoursome dishes such as salmon cooked with pearl barley, seaweed and Islay malt whisky, or spiced apple crumble with whisky custard.

BLACK BO'S Map p222 — Vegetarian ££

☎ 557 6136; 57-61 Blackfriars St; mains £11-13; ⌚ 6-10.30pm daily, plus noon-2pm Fri & Sat; 🚌 35

You can't accuse the chef at Black Bo's, a very popular vegetarian and vegan eatery located just off the Royal Mile, of being unadventurous. The menu is always

TOP FIVE EATING STREETS

- **Victoria Street/Grassmarket** (p103) Concentration of good restaurants in the shadow of the castle.
- **Lothian Road** (p114) Lots of eateries in the side streets off this main thoroughfare through the theatre district.
- **Thistle Street** (p107) Cobbled New Town back street lined with antique shops and intimate restaurants.
- **Broughton Street** (p107) An eclectic selection of laid-back eating places in the heart of Edinburgh's gay community and close to the Playhouse theatre and Omni Centre cinemas.
- The **Shore** (p117) Atmospheric, cobbled street on the riverside lined with quality restaurants.

interesting – chilli, cashew and carrot crêpe with red pepper salsa, for example – and there are a couple of meat and fish options that might take your fancy too. There's a lively bar next door, which often has live music.

CAFÉ HUB Map p222 Bistro ££

☎ 473 2067; Castlehill, Royal Mile; mains £9-15, 2-course lunch £10, 3-course dinner £18; 🕑 9.30am-10pm Tue-Sat, 9.30am-6pm Sun & Mon; 🚌 2, 23, 27, 41 or 42

A Gothic hall beneath the Tolbooth Kirk – now home to the Edinburgh Festival offices – has been transformed into this bright and breezy bistro with some zingy yellow paint, cobalt-blue furniture and lots of imagination. Drop in for cake and cappuccino, or try something more filling – curried salmon kebab with potato and spinach, or spinach and thyme risotto with roasted courgette.

CAFÉ MARLAYNE Map p222 French ££

☎ 225 3838; 7 Old Fishmarket Close, High St; mains £7-15; 🕑 noon-2pm & 6-10pm Tue-Sat; 🚌 35

This second branch of the New Town French bistro is a hidden gem, stashed away down a steep cobbled alley off the Royal Mile. The maze-like, vaulted dining area sports beech tables and pastel-coloured chairs, with contemporary paintings on cream walls, with a daily menu of fresh market produce and a lovely little lunchtime suntrap of an outdoor terrace.

DAVID BANN Map p222 Vegetarian ££

☎ 556 5888; 56-58 St Mary's St; mains £10-11; 🕑 11am-1am; 🚌 35

If you want to convince a carnivorous friend that cuisine à la veg can be every bit as tasty and inventive as a meat-muncher's menu, take them to David Bann's stylish restaurant, just off the Royal Mile. Dishes such as walnut, mushroom and parsnip kebabs with mashed potato and a rich red-wine gravy are guaranteed to win converts. They also do a tasty brunch – eggs, veggie sausage, mushrooms and potato scone with toasted muffins – from 11am to 5pm at weekends.

DORIC WINE BAR & BISTRO

Map p222 Scottish ££

☎ 225 1084; 15-16 Market St; mains £13; 🕑 11.30am-1am Mon-Sat, noon-1am Sun; 🚌 35

One of Edinburgh's favourite eateries, this 1st-floor bistro (entrance stairs to the right of the Doric Bar) is handy for both Princes St and the Royal Mile. Wooden floors, warm ochre walls and window tables with views of the Scott Monument and Balmoral Hotel complement a menu of fresh Scottish produce, with dishes such as grilled lamb cutlets with spring onion mash and crispy fried leeks, and goat's cheese and rosemary crêpe with caramelised onion and apple.

FAVORIT Map p222 Café £

☎ 220 6880; 19-20 Teviot Pl; sandwiches £4-5, salads £4-6; 🕑 8am-2.30am; 🚌 2, 23, 27, 41 or 42

A stylish café-bar with a slightly retro feel, Favorit caters for everyone – workers grabbing breakfast on the way to the office, coffee-slurping students skiving off afternoon lectures, and late-night clubbers with an attack of the munchies. It also serves the best bacon butties in town – a soft, lightly toasted bap loaded with lots of crispy, streaky bacon, with a choice of HP sauce or tomato ketchup. Yum. There's a second **Favorit** (Map pp224-5; ☎ 221 1800; 30 Leven St; 🕑 8am-1am) in Tollcross.

GORDON'S TRATTORIA

Map p222 Italian ££

☎ 225 7992; 231 High St; mains £8-17; 🕑 noon-midnight Sun-Thu, noon-3am Fri & Sat; 🚌 35

The aroma of garlic bread wafting into the street will guide you into this snug haven of chattering diners, wisecracking waiters and hearty Italian comfort food. In summer you can chomp pizza and slurp wine at a pavement table on the Royal Mile, and the late-night opening means that Gordon's often develops something of a party atmosphere after midnight on Friday and Saturday.

HEIGHTS Map p222 Modern Scottish ££

☎ 473 7156; Apex International Hotel, 31-35 Grassmarket; 3-course dinner £19; 🕑 7-9.30pm Mon-Sat; 🚌 2

Starkly elegant in white, red and grey, Heights' dining room is perched high above the Grassmarket – an entire wall of picture windows allows an uninterrupted view of Edinburgh Castle (during the Edinburgh Festival you'll get a grandstand view of the Military Tattoo fireworks if you're still there around 10.30pm). Typical dishes include herb-filled fillet of sea bass with hazelnut butter, and fillet of beef with creamed potato and wild Scottish mushrooms.

IGG'S Map p222 Spanish £££

☎ 557 8184; 15 Jeffrey St; mains £15-21; 🕑 noon-2.30pm & 6-10.30pm Mon-Sat; 🚌 35

A sumptuous dining room with dark-wood furniture, crisp white linen and rich, mustard-yellow walls make Igg's a good choice for a special night out. The menu is mostly Spanish, with tapas-style starters and interesting main courses such as salmon tartare with a shot of gazpacho, and Manchego (Spanish cheese) gnocchi with wild mushroom and spinach cream sauce.

KEBAB MAHAL Map p222 South Asian £

☎ 667 5214; 7 Nicolson Sq; kebabs £4-6; 🕑 noon-midnight Sun-Thu, noon-2am Fri & Sat; 🚌 all South Bridge buses

Sophisticated it ain't, but this is the Holy Grail of kebab shops – quality shish kebab and tandoori dishes washed down with chilled lassi for less than a fiver. It's a basic cafeteria-style place with a stainless-steel counter and glaring fluorescent lights, but the menu is 100% halal (the Edinburgh Mosque is just 100m along the road) and the kebabs and curries are authentic and delicious. Kebab Mahal? Kebab nirvana.

Metro Brasserie & Café Bar (right)

MAISON BLEUE

Map p222 International £-££

☎ 226 1900; 36-38 Victoria St; mains £5-13; 🕑 noon-3pm & 5-10.15pm; 🚌 2, 23, 27, 41 or 42

Eating at Maison Bleue is a comfortably laid-back affair, like having dinner at an old friend's house – albeit a rather stylish old friend. The intimate ground-floor dining room has woven straw chairs, chunky wooden tables, modern art on bare stone walls, candlelight and cool tunes; upstairs is brighter and more café-like. The menu lists *bouchées* (French for 'mouthfuls') – starter-size helpings of which you can have as many or as few as you wish. The food is an eclectic mix of European, North African and Far Eastern influences, from haggis balls in crispy batter and Vietnamese *nems* (crispy rice pancakes filled with crab and shrimp) to coriander-crusted salmon and Moroccan-style chicken brochettes.

MAXIE'S BISTRO & WINE BAR

Map p222 International ££

☎ 226 7770; 5b Johnston Tce; mains £8-13; 🕑 bistro 11am-11pm, wine bar 11am-1am; 🚌 2, 23, 27, 41 or 42

Maxie's candle-lit cellar bistro, with its cushion-lined nooks set amid stone walls, cream plaster and wooden beams, is a pleasant enough setting for a cosy dinner, but at summer lunch times people queue for the outdoor tables on Victoria Tce, with great views over Victoria St. The food is dependable – Maxie's has been in the food business for more than 20 years – ranging from pastas, steaks and stir-fries to superb seafood platters and daily specials, and there's an excellent selection of wines.

METRO BRASSERIE & CAFÉ BAR

Map p222 International ££

☎ 474 3466; 31-35 Grassmarket; mains £8-12, 3-course dinner £17; 🕑 11am-11pm; 🚌 2

Depending on your tastes, minimalist Metro is either desperately stylish or just looks a little bit like a school canteen.

LATE-NIGHT MUNCHIES

Edinburgh has more than a few places where it's possible to chow down after 10pm. Many of them are Italian, Indian and Chinese restaurants that accept sit-down customers until 11pm on weekdays and midnight on Friday and Saturday. The following places stay open until midnight or even later.

- **David Bann** (p104)
- **Favorit** (p104)
- **Gordon's Trattoria** (p104)
- **Kebab Mahal** (p105)
- **Negociants** (right)

Either way, the international menu is way better than anything you had at school – try teriyaki chicken with bok choi and noodles, or grilled sea bass with Jerusalem artichoke and chorizo aioli – and there's a view of the castle from the window tables.

MONSTER MASH Map p222 Scottish/Café £

☎ 225 7069; 4a Forrest Rd; mains £5-7; 8am-10pm Mon-Fri, 9am-10pm Sat, 10am-10pm Sun; 35 or 41

Classic British grub of the 1950s – bangers and mash, shepherd's pie, fish and chips, deep-fried ice cream – is the mainstay of the menu at this nostalgia-fuelled café. But there's a twist – the food is all top-quality nosh freshly prepared from local produce, including Crombie's gourmet sausages, mustard-flavoured mash, and red wine and onion gravy. Informality is the watchword – don't be surprised if the waiter takes a seat at your table while taking your order.

NAMASTE Map p222 Indian ££

☎ 225 2000; 15 Bristo Pl; mains £6-11; 5.30-11pm year-round, plus noon-2.30pm Mon-Fri Jul & Aug; 2, 41 or 42

The food at this cosy little place is from the North Indian frontier, and the atmosphere has a chilled, hippie-trail-to-Kathmandu feel with incense, candlelight and scattered cushions. Dishes range from curried dhal and *bhindi* (okra) to butter chicken and prawn *jhalfrezie* (cooked with herbs, green pepper and chillis), but our favourite is the fantastically flavoursome *malai kofta*: little cutlets of paneer (cheese), potato and nuts in a rich, creamy, spice-laden sauce. The restaurant serves beer and soft drinks – if you prefer wine, then BYOB (no corkage charge).

NEGOCIANTS Map p222 International ££

☎ 225 6313; 45-47 Lothian St; mains £8-13; 9am-3am Mon-Sat, 10am-3am Sun; 2, 41 or 42

A student stalwart that's been around for 20 years – Edinburgh University's main campus is right across the street – Negociants is a café-bar-bistro that keeps the food coming till well into the wee hours of the morning (last orders for food 2.15am). It's pleasantly quiet during the day, but as the evening wears on it fills up with pre- and post-clubbers fuelling up on mountainous nachos, juicy burgers and sizzling fajitas.

NORTH BRIDGE BRASSERIE

Map p222 Scottish/International ££

☎ 622 2900; 20 North Bridge; mains £12-16; noon-2.30pm & 6.15-10pm Mon-Thu, noon-2.30pm & 6.15-10.30pm Fri & Sat, 12.15-2.30pm & 6.15-10pm Sun; all North Bridge buses

This stylish brasserie inhabits the former lobby of the *Scotsman* newspaper building (now the Scotsman Hotel), a huge airy hall two storeys high, with four massive marble columns supporting the ceiling. There are tables around the cocktail bar on the oak-panelled ground floor, but book a romantic table for two up on the balcony, where you can admire the gilded capitals or gaze down on the street from the arched windows. The service is impeccable and the food beautifully prepared, with dishes such as tender pink rump of lamb with clapshot and haggis, and seared scallops with black pudding and buttery crushed potato.

PANCHO VILLA'S Map p222 Mexican ££

☎ 557 4416; 240 Canongate, Royal Mile; mains £8-13; noon-11pm Mon-Sat, 5-11pm Sun; 35

With homemade salsa and guacamole, plenty of Latin American staff, and bright colours inspired by the manager's home town of Valle de Bravo, it's not surprising that Pancho's is one of the most authentic-feeling Mexican restaurants in town. It's also the city's best-value Mexican, with a two-course set lunch for £7. The menu includes tender steak fajitas, enchiladas *mole poblano* (chicken in a classic Mexican sauce containing hot chillis and bitter chocolate), and spicy vegetarian spinach enchiladas.

POINT RESTAURANT

Map pp218-19 Modern Scottish ££

☎ 221 5555; Point Hotel, 34 Bread St; 2-course lunch £9, 3-course dinner £17; ⌚ noon-2pm & 6-10pm Mon-Thu, noon-2pm & 6-11pm Fri & Sat, noon-2pm & 6-9pm Sun; 🚌 2 or 35

The Point Restaurant's now legendary lunch and dinner menus offer exceptional value – delicious Scottish/international cuisine served by attentive, smartly clad staff in an elegant room with dark-wood furniture, proper linen napkins and Art Deco chandeliers based on a design for Prague's Municipal House. With house wine at only £13.95 per bottle, reservations are strongly recommended.

TOWER Map p222 Modern Scottish £££

☎ 225 3003; Museum of Scotland, Chambers St; mains £15-21; ⌚ noon-11pm; 🚌 2, 35, 41 or 42

A doorman guides you to a private elevator that whisks you up four floors to this sleek restaurant, perched atop the Museum of Scotland building. Decked out in black leather, purple suede, oak and brushed aluminium, the Tower has played host to countless celebrities, from Joanna Lumley to Catherine Zeta-Jones, attracted by the grand views of the castle, a superb wine list, and a menu of top-quality Scottish produce, simply prepared – try half a dozen Scottish rock oysters followed by a chargrilled Aberdeen Angus fillet steak. The pre-theatre menu, available from 5pm to 6.30pm daily, costs £12.50 for two courses.

WITCHERY BY THE CASTLE

Map p222 Scottish/French £££

☎ 225 5613; Castlehill, Royal Mile; mains £20-30; ⌚ noon-4pm & 5.30-11.30pm; 🚌 2, 23, 27, 41 or 42

Edinburgh's most atmospheric restaurant has been a 25-year labour of love for owner and founder James Thomson. Set in a merchant's town house dating from 1595, the Witchery is a candlelit treasury of antique splendour, with oak-panelled walls, low ceilings, opulent wall hangings and red-leather upholstery. Stairs lead down to a second, even more romantic, dining room called the Secret Garden. But décor isn't everything; the menu – which ranges from terrine of foie gras with quince jelly to fillet of well-hung Aberdeen Angus steak with braised puy lentils and *rosti* potatoes – and the wine list (there are almost 1000 bins) are an epicurean's delight. The two-course light lunch (noon to 4pm) and pre- or post-theatre dinners (5.30pm to 6.30pm and 10.30pm to 11.30pm) cost £12.50. Book well in advance.

NEW TOWN

You can barely walk 20 paces along a New Town street without passing a restaurant. The elegant Georgian terraces to the north of Princes St are the epicentre of Edinburgh's fine dining scene, with lots of stylish restaurants offering a wide range of cuisines. The abundance of office workers means that there are lots of weekday lunch specials to look out for too.

BLUE MOON CAFÉ

Map pp218-19 Café £

☎ 557 0911; 1 Barony St; mains £6-8; ⌚ 11am-10pm Mon-Fri, 10am-10pm Sat & Sun; 🚌 8 or 17

The Blue Moon is the focus of Broughton St's gay social life – always busy, always friendly, and serving up tasty nachos, salads, sandwiches and baked potatoes. It's famous for its brilliant homemade hamburgers, which come plain or topped with cheese or chilli sauce, and delicious daily specials.

JAMES THOMSON

When James Thomson founded the **Witchery** (above) in 1979, at the tender age of 20, he became Scotland's youngest licensee. Today the Witchery is still renowned as one of Edinburgh's finest restaurants, and Mr Thomson is now Edinburgh's best-known restaurateur. He began to expand his empire in 1998 when he opened the sleek, modern **Tower restaurant** (above), atop the Museum of Scotland building, and has since added the **Prestonfield House Hotel** (p169) to his portfolio.

As a penniless student chef in Edinburgh in the 1970s, Thomson eked out his grant by working as a waiter at the prestigious Prestonfield House Hotel. In 2003 he bought his former workplace for several million pounds, and endowed it with a magnificently over-the-top restaurant, **Rhubarb** (p117), which is now one of the hottest tables in town.

SOME CULTURE WITH YOUR QUICHE?

You can enjoy some of Edinburgh's best bistro food in the cafés that you'll find in many art galleries and museums. Most of these places offer a freshly prepared lunchtime special – soup and a main course, often with a vegetarian choice – that changes daily, allowing you to combine a spot of cultural browsing with a lunch break. Here's our top five:

Café Delos (Map p222; ☎ 247 4114; 2 Chambers St; mains £6; 🕑 10am-4pm Mon & Wed-Sat, 10am-7pm Tue, noon-4.30pm Sun; 🚌 2, 23, 27, 41 or 42) This little café occupies one end of the magnificent Victorian glass-roofed atrium in the **Royal Museum** (p65), and dishes up delicious deli sandwiches, quiches and cakes, with ingredients provided by **Valvona & Crolla** (see p155).

Café Newton (Map p217; ☎ 624 6273; 72 Belford Rd; mains £6; 🕑 10am-4.30pm; 🚌 13) The elegant café in the **Dean Gallery** (p73) is decked out in smart black-and-white décor, dominated by a gleaming Victoria Arduino espresso machine, and a plaster model of Eduardo Paolozzi's statue of Isaac Newton. The lunch menu (noon to 2.30pm) is Mediterranean, offering tasty soups and platters of grilled goat's cheese, smoked chicken, roast peppers etc.

caféteria@thefruitmarket (Map p222; ☎ 226 1843; 45 Market St; mains £4-6; 🕑 11am-5pm Mon-Sat, noon-5pm Sun; 🚌 35) After checking out the art in the **Fruitmarket Gallery** (see p63), check out the menu in its stylish café – fresh sandwiches, big crunchy salads and hot ciabatta melts – or settle down with a cappuccino to browse the book you just bought in the adjacent art bookshop.

Gallery Café (Map p217; ☎ 332 8600; 74 Belford Rd; mains £5; 🕑 10am-4.30pm; bus 13) Modern design, with curvy Wedgewood-blue chairs and pale-yellow walls, is to be expected in the café at the **Scottish National Gallery of Modern Art** (p74), but more of a surprise is the lovely outdoor seating area, a lunchtime suntrap complete with lawn for the kids to run around on. The menu is hearty comfort food, from parsnip and sage soup to sweet-potato bake.

Gallery Restaurant (Map pp218-19; ☎ 624 6580; Weston Link, National Gallery of Scotland, the Mound; mains £13-18; 🕑 11.45am-3.30pm Mon-Wed, 11.45am-3.30pm & 5.30-10.30pm Thu-Sat, 11am-5pm Sun; 🚌 all Princes St buses) The grandest of Edinburgh's arty eateries, the Gallery is tucked beneath the **Royal Scottish Academy** (p69) building, with a wall of picture windows giving a view of the Princes St Gardens. The menu ranges from posh fish and chips to Mediterranean dishes, and the two-course set lunch costs £11.95.

CAFÉ MARLAYNE

Map pp218-19 French ££

☎ 226 2230; 76 Thistle St; mains £11-15; 🕑 noon-2pm & 6-10pm Tue-Sat; 🚌 13, 24, 29 or 42

All scrubbed, weathered wood and warm yellow walls, little Café Marlayne is a cosy nook offering satisfying French farmhouse cooking – *escargot* with garlic and parsley, oysters with lemon and Tabasco, *boudin noir* (black pudding) with sautéed apples, peppered duck breast with balsamic vinegar – at very reasonable prices. It's only little, so book a table well in advance. There is now a second branch near the Royal Mile.

CAFÉ ROYAL OYSTER BAR

Map pp218-19 French/Seafood £££

☎ 556 4124; 17a W Register St; mains £16-20; 🕑 noon-2pm & 7-10pm; 🚌 all Princes St buses

Pass through the revolving doors on the corner of W Register St and you're transported back to Victorian times – a palace of glinting mahogany, polished brass, marble floors, stained glass, Doulton tiles, gilded cornices and table linen so thick that it creaks when you fold it. The menu is mostly classic seafood, from oysters on ice to succulent *Coquilles St Jacques Parisienne* (scallops in a cream and mushroom sauce) and lobster thermidor, augmented by a handful of beef and game dishes.

CENTOTRE Map pp218-19 Italian ££-£££

☎ 225 1550; 103 George St; pasta dishes £8-12, mains £14-18; 🕑 8am-10pm Mon-Thu, 9am-10.30pm Fri & Sat, 11am-5pm Sun; 🚌 all Princes St buses

A palatial Georgian banking hall, painted plain white and enlivened with fuchsia-pink banners and aubergine booths, is home to this lively, child-friendly Italian bar and restaurant, where the emphasis is on fresh, authentic ingredients (produce imported weekly from Milan, homemade bread and pasta), and uncomplicated enjoyment of food. The signature dish is *contadino* (pasta with a creamy sauce of Italian sausage, wild mushrooms, Parmesan and rocket), but the menu also includes specials such as *polpettone* (a succulent hamburger on sourdough bread), and roast sea bass with tomatoes, capers and olives.

DOME Map pp218-19 International ££-£££

☎ 624 8624; 14 George St; mains £11-18; noon-10pm Sun-Wed, noon-11pm Thu-Sat; 24, 28 or 45

Housed in the magnificent former headquarters of a bank, with a lofty glass-domed ceiling, pillared arches and mosaic-tiled floor, the Dome boasts one of the city's most impressive dining rooms. The menu holds few surprises – from boeuf bourguignon to char-grilled chicken to tortellini in broccoli and blue-cheese sauce – but although the food is well prepared and well presented it's really the setting that sells the place; it's hard to keep your eyes on your plate with all the finery that surrounds you. Dress code is smart: no jeans, trainers or sportswear.

FISHERS IN THE CITY

Map pp218-19 Seafood ££-£££

☎ 225 5109; 58 Thistle St; mains £13-19; noon-10.30pm; 13, 19, 37 or 41

A sleeker, more sophisticated version of the famous Leith restaurant (**Fishers Bistro**, p118), with granite-topped tables and warm yellow and dark-wood décor, Fishers in the City is a busy, modern bar-restaurant with a nautical theme, serving up superior Scottish seafood. The oysters are plump and succulent, the scallops meltingly sweet, the sea bass grilled to perfection, and the staff are knowledgeable and efficient.

FORTH FLOOR RESTAURANT & BRASSERIE

Map pp218-19 Modern Scottish ££-£££

☎ 524 8350; 30-34 St Andrew Sq; mains £15-20; noon-3pm Mon-Fri, noon-3.30pm Sat & Sun, 6-10pm Tue-Sat; all St Andrew Sq buses

The in-store restaurant at Harvey Nichols has west-facing floor-to-ceiling windows overlooking St Andrew Sq, making it a great place to enjoy sunset views. The food has as much designer chic as the surroundings, with dishes such as leek cannelloni with grilled goat's cheese, cherry tomatoes and truffles, and pan-fried honey-glazed salmon with cauliflower linguini and roasted pak choi. The less formal brasserie (on the same floor; 3-course lunch or dinner £17) offers simpler dishes, and also serves a Sunday brunch (11am to 4pm).

GARDEN CAFÉ Map pp218-19 Café £

☎ 624 8624; 17 Rose St; sandwiches £5-6; 9am-5.30pm Mon-Sat; all Princes St buses

This attractive outdoor café is in a sunken courtyard at the back of the Dome. Littered with potted palms strewn beneath the towering stained-glass windows of the Dome's dining room, it becomes a lunchtime suntrap in summer. Soups, salads and sandwiches are on offer, along with excellent coffee and tea.

HADRIAN'S BRASSERIE

Map pp218-19 Scottish/French ££-£££

☎ 557 5000; Balmoral Hotel, 1 Princes St; mains £13-20; 7-10.30am, noon-2.30pm & 6-10.30pm Mon-Sat, 7.30-11am, 12.30-3pm & 6-10.30pm Sun; all Princes St buses

The Balmoral Hotel's brasserie has a 1930s Art Deco feel, with a décor of pale green walls and dark-wood furniture, and white-aproned, black-waistcoated waiters. The menu includes posh versions of popular dishes such as salt-and-pepper prawns (with chips and mayonnaise), confit of pork belly with apple sauce, and duck-filled spring rolls with hoisin sauce and pickled cucumber. There's a three-course set lunch for £12.

HENDERSON'S SALAD TABLE

Map pp218-19 Vegetarian £

☎ 225 2131; 94 Hanover St; mains £5-7; 8am-10.45pm Mon-Sat (plus Sun during the Edinburgh Festival); 23 or 27

Established in 1962, Henderson's is the grandmother of Edinburgh's vegetarian restaurants. The food is mostly organic, guaranteed GM-free, and special dietary requirements can be catered for. The self-service restaurant still has something of a 1970s cafeteria feel to it (but in a nice way), and the daily salads (£1.85 a portion, or £5 for three) and hot dishes are as popular as ever. A two-course lunch/dinner with coffee costs £8.50/9.50.

HOWIE'S

Map pp218-19 Modern Scottish/Fusion ££

☎ 556 5766; 29 Waterloo Pl; 3-course dinner £19; 🕑 12.30-2.30pm & 6-10.30pm; 🚌 1, 5, 7, 14, 19, 22, 25, 34 or 49

A bright and airy Georgian corner-house provides the elegant setting for this, the most central of Howie's four hugely popular Edinbugh restaurants. Their recipe for success includes fresh Scottish produce, good-value, fixed price menus, and eminently quaffable house wines from £8.95 a bottle.

LA P'TITE FOLIE Map pp218-19 French ££

☎ 225 7983; 61 Frederick St; mains £12-15; 🕑 noon-3pm & 6-11pm Mon-Sat, 6-11pm Sun; 🚌 13, 24, 29 or 42

Breton-owned la P'tite Folie is a delightful little wood-panelled bistro whose menu takes in the French classics – *soupe à l'oignon* (French onion soup), *moules marinières* (mussels), *coq au vin* (chicken casserole with red wine and mushrooms) – as well as steaks, seafood and a range of *plats du jour*. The two-course lunch is a bargain at £7.50. There is a second branch in the West End (p112).

MUSSEL INN Map pp218-19 Seafood £-££

☎ 225 5979; 61-65 Rose St; mains £6-16; 🕑 noon-10pm Mon-Sat, 1.30-10pm Sun; 🚌 all Princes St buses

Owned by shellfish farmers on the west coast, the Mussel Inn provides a direct outlet for fresh Scottish seafood. The busy restaurant is decorated with bright beech-wood indoors, but tables spill out onto the pavement in summer. A kilogram pot of mussels with a choice of sauces – try leek, bacon, white wine and cream – costs £10, while a smaller platter of queen scallops costs £7.

NARGILE Map pp218-19 Turkish ££

☎ 225 5755; 73 Hanover St; mains £9-14; 🕑 noon-2pm & 5.30-10.30pm Mon-Thu, noon-2pm & 5.30-11pm Fri & Sat; 🚌 23 or 27

Throw away any preconceptions about doner kebabs: this glitzy Turkish restaurant is a class act. Enjoy a spread of delicious *mezeler* (think Turkish tapas) followed by meltingly sweet, marinated lamb chargrilled to crispy perfection. Finish off with *baklava* (nut-filled pastry soaked in honey) and a Turkish coffee. If it weren't for the prices, you could almost be in Turkey.

NIJI Map pp218-19 Japanese £££

☎ 226 7657; 64 Thistle St; mains £15-20; 🕑 noon-2.30pm & 7-10pm Mon-Sat; 🚌 13, 24, 29 or 42

This stylishly minimalist Japanese restaurant – calm white walls, and dark lacquered tables – offers a menu that ranges from sea-fresh sushi to authentic Japanese classics such as *yakitori* (marinated and grilled kebab), *teriyaki* (marinated beef or fish, pan-fried) and *tempura* (battered and deep-fried pieces of meat, seafood or vegetable with a dipping sauce); probably best to avoid the Rabbie Burns tempura, though – haggis with battered, deep-fried slices of potato and turnip is more reminiscent of a Scottish chip shop than Japan! Finish off with a poached pear with sake sorbet.

NUMBER ONE

Map pp218-19 Modern Scottish £££

☎ 557 6727; Balmoral Hotel, 1 Princes St; mains £25-27; 🕑 noon-2pm & 7-10pm Mon-Thu, noon-2pm & 7-10.30pm Fri, 7-10.30pm Sat, 7-10pm Sun; 🚌 3, 8, 25, 31 or 33

Number One is the stylish and sophisticated queen of Edinburgh's city-centre restaurants, all gold-and-velvet elegance, with a Michelin star sparkling on her crown. The food is top-notch Modern Scottish – choose from à la carte, a three-course lunch for £35, or a six-course tasting menu for £65 – and the service is just on the right side of fawning; you'll need two of the waiters to pull you out of the opulent sofas that you sink into as you peruse the menu. Best to book ahead, and dress up a bit for dinner.

OLOROSO

Map pp218-19 Modern Scottish £££

☎ 226 7614; 33 Castle St; mains £15-22; 🕑 noon-2.30pm & 7-10.30pm; 🚌 13, 19, 37 or 41

Oloroso is one of Edinburgh's most stylish restaurants, perched on a glass-encased New Town rooftop with views across a Mary Poppins chimneyscape to the Firth of Forth and the Fife hills. Swathed in sophisticated cream linen and charcoal upholstery enlivened with splashes of deep yellow, the dining room serves top-notch Scottish produce with Asian and Mediterranean touches. On a fine afternoon you can savour a snack and a drink on the outdoor

The stylish Oloroso restaurant (opposite)

roof terrace while soaking up the sun and a view of the castle.

ROTI Map pp218-19 Indian ££

☎ 225 1233; 70 Rose St Lane N; mains £12-15; 6pm-midnight Tue-Sat; 13, 19, 37 or 41

No ordinary Indian restaurant this, but an intimate, minimalist space with low lighting, coffee-and-cream décor, crisp white table linen and framed jewellery on the walls. The menu is intriguing, offering dishes that lie well off the beaten curry trail, such as chargrilled quail with Indian spices, Goan fish curry (sour, salt and sweet all at the same time), and *achari macchali* (roast pickled salmon that melts in the mouth).

STAC POLLY

Map pp218-19 Modern Scottish ££-£££

☎ 556 2231; 29-33 Dublin St; mains £12-18; 6-11pm daily, plus noon-2.30pm Mon-Fri; 10, 11, 16 or 17

Named after a mountain in northwestern Scotland, Stac Polly's kitchen adds sophisticated twists to fresh Highland produce. Meals such as smoked salmon, lime and avocado mousse, followed by roast saddle of venison with a thyme and red wine reduction, keep the punters coming back for more. The restaurant's famous signature dish – baked filo pastry parcels of haggis, served with plum sauce – is so popular it's almost become a national dish. What would Burns think? The dining room, a cosy maze of stone-walled cellars, is formal but intimate; the original branch of **Stac Polly** (Map pp218-19; ☎ 229 5405; 8-10 Grindlay St) is less formal and easier to get a table at.

VALVONA & CROLLA CAFFÈ BAR

Map pp218-19 Italian/Café ££

☎ 556 6066; 19 Elm Row, Leith Walk; mains £9-15; 8am-6pm Mon-Sat, 10.30am-4.30pm Sun; all Leith Walk buses

The menu at this bright and cheerful café, tucked upstairs at the back of the famous **deli** (see p155), is based on the owners' family recipes from central and southern Italy, such as *spaghetti alla vongole* (pasta with clams, garlic, chilli and parsley) and *ravioli con ricotta e rucola* (ravioli filled with rocket and cream cheese in a butter and sage sauce). Fancy some wine with that? Choose a bottle from the deli on your way in and have it served at your table (£4 corkage). Breakfast is served from 8am to 11.30am Monday to Saturday, and lunch from noon to 3pm. During the Edinburgh Festival the café is open for dinner too, from Thursday to Saturday.

VALVONA & CROLLA VINCAFFÈ

Map pp218-19 Italian ££-£££

☎ 557 0088; 11 Multrees Walk, St Andrew Sq; mains £9-17; 8am-late Mon-Sat, 11am-5.30pm Sun; all St Andrew Sq buses

Foodie colours dominate the décor at this delightful Italian wine bar and bistro (head upstairs from the deli counter): bottle-green pillars and banquettes, chocolate- and cream-coloured walls, espresso-black tables. The food is straightforward but made with the finest-quality ingredients, ranging from superb antipasto (a wooden platter spread with cured meats, sausage, mozzarella, olives and tomatoes) to a *fritto misto* (mixed fry) of Scottish seafood and

TOP FIVE TABLES WITH A VIEW

- **Forth Floor Restaurant** (p109)
- **Heights** (p105)
- **Old Chain Pier** (p119)
- **Oloroso** (opposite)
- **Tower** (p107)

TOP FIVE BREAKFASTS

- **Always Sunday** (p103) From smoked salmon and scrambled eggs to fruit and cereal, washed down with Fairtrade coffee, this bright and breezy caff offers a healthy alternative.
- **Blue Moon Café** (p107) For £6 the Blue Moon will ply you with a full Scottish breakfast, or its tasty vegetarian equivalent.
- **Forth Floor Brasserie** (p109) Harvey Nichols' stylish brasserie offers a tasty Sunday brunch (£13.50), including a Bloody Mary, accompanied by live jazz from 12.30pm till 3.30pm.
- **Montpeliers** (p115) Breakfast offerings (£3 to £7) – served from 9am all the way through to 6pm – include pancakes and maple syrup, French toast, eggs Benedict and yoghurt with fruit.
- **Valvona & Crolla Caffè Bar** (p111) Brekkie with an Italian flavour: full *paesano* (meat) or *verdure* (veggie) fry-ups, or deliciously light and crisp *panettone* in *carrozza* (sweet brioche dipped in egg and fried). There are also almond croissants, muesli, yoghurt and fruit, freshly squeezed orange juice and perfect Italian coffee.

courgette. Most of the extensive wine list is available by the glass, but it's worth splashing out on a bottle of the slightly sparkling pink pinot grigio.

WEST END & STOCKBRIDGE

The well-heeled West End and Stockbridge districts are well supplied with quality eating places, ranging from upmarket cafés to boutique hotel restaurants to cosy candlelit bistros.

BUFFALO GRILL Map p217 American ££

☎ 332 3864; Raeburn Pl; mains £8-15; 6-10.30pm Mon-Thu, 6-11pm Fri, 5-11pm Sat, 5-10.30pm Sun; 24, 49 or 32

This Stockbridge incarnation is a bit more spacious than the original branch, but has the same Wild West décor and beefy, all-American menu. Unlike the original branch, this place is fully licensed, but they still allow you to BYOB if you prefer (£1 corkage charge per bottle).

CHANNINGS RESTAURANT

Map p217 Scottish/Mediterranean ££

☎ 315 2225; 12-16 S Learmonth Gardens; mains £10-17, 2-/3-course lunch £12/15; noon-3pm & 6-10pm Mon-Fri, 12.30-3pm & 6-10pm Sat & Sun; 19, 37 or 41

The restaurant at Channings Hotel is a relaxing modern space in subdued shades of brown, cream and pale green, bright and lively at lunch time, low-lit and intimate in the evenings. The menu offers fresh Scottish produce served with a Mediterranean twist – braised lamb shank with Spanish black beans and chorizo, or baked coley (white fish) with a parsley crust, with potato purée and langoustine jus.

CIRCUS CAFÉ Map pp218-19 Café ££

☎ 220 0333; 15 Northwest Circus Pl; mains £10-13; 10am-11pm; 24, 29 or 42

This upmarket café is set in a former bank that has been given a designer makeover (think mahogany, mirrors, dark-chocolate suedette, and shimmering opalescent chandeliers). More silver spoon than greasy spoon, it's a place where the battered cod and chips is served with truffle-scented garden peas, the hamburger is made of meltingly tender beef laced with chopped coriander, and a humble cheese-and-ham sandwich is transmogrified into 'Joselito Gran Reserva ham and brie on a sourdough ficelle'. There is also an excellent deli downstairs where, between 4pm and 7pm, you can choose a bottle of wine and drink it in the café for no extra charge.

LA P'TITE FOLIE Map p217 French ££

☎ 225 8678; 9 Randolph Pl; mains £12-15, 2-course lunch £7.50; noon-3pm Mon-Sat, 6-11pm daily; 13, 19, 37 or 41

La P'tite Folie's second branch, housed in an unusual, Tudor-lookalike building tucked behind West Register House is completely different in character to the Frederick St original. The upstairs dining room has a pleasantly clubbish feel, with green walls and dark-stained wood – try to grab the table in the little corner turret, with a view along Melville St to the spires of St Mary's Cathedral.

NEW EDINBURGH RENDEZVOUS
Map p217 Chinese ££
☎ 225 2023; 10a Queensferry St; mains £7-9; 11.45am-11.30pm Mon-Sat, 1-11.30pm Sun; 13, 19, 36, 37 or 41

Edinburgh's oldest Chinese restaurant – it first opened its doors in 1956 – is still one of its best, a no-frills, no-nonsense dining room offering an extensive menu of expertly prepared Cantonese and Peking dishes, not only classic favourites such as deep-fried shredded beef with chilli sauce and aromatic crispy duck with pancakes, but also more adventurous dishes such as shredded sea blubber, boneless duck's feet with mustard sauce, and pickled cabbage with chilli sauce.

PETIT PARIS Map p217 French ££
☎ 226 1890; 17 Queensferry St; mains £12-15; noon-3pm & 5.30-10pm Mon-Thu, noon-3pm & 5.30-11pm Fri & Sat; 13, 19, 36, 37 or 41

Like the name says, this is a little piece of Paris complete with gingham tablecloths in red, blue and green, French posters and ads on the walls, friendly (often French) staff and French music in the background. You can indulge in an *apéro* (Dubonnet, Ricard or absinthe) while you choose from a menu of classics such as *escargots* in Pernod and garlic, *coq au vin* and *bouillabaisse*. There's a lunch and early evening special that offers a *plat du jour* and a coffee for £5.90, available from noon to 3pm and 5.30pm to 7pm. There's another branch (same menu, but with the advantage of outdoor tables in summer) in the **Old Town** (Map p222; ☎ 226 2442; 38-40 Grassmarket; noon-3pm & 5.30-10.30pm, closed Sun Oct-Mar).

PIZZA EXPRESS Map p217 Italian £-££
☎ 332 7229; 1 Deanhaugh St; mains £6-8; 11.30am-11.30pm; 24, 29 or 42

Trust Stockbridge to have a designer pizza restaurant. Housed in a former bank beneath a Baronial clock tower, it has a stylish interior on two levels overlooking the Water of Leith, and a decked outdoor terrace right on the riverbank. The thin and crisp-crusted gourmet pizzas include such delights as the Veneziana (onions, capers, olives, pine kernels, sultanas) and the Prince Carlo (leeks, rosemary, Parmesan).

SONGKRAN Map p217 Thai ££
☎ 225 7889; 24a Stafford St; mains £8-11; noon-2.30pm & 5.30-11pm Mon-Sat; all West End buses

You'd better book a table and be prepared for a squeeze to get into this tiny basement restaurant. The reason for the crush is some of the best Thai food in Edinburgh: try the tender *yang* (marinated and barbecued beef, chicken or prawn), the crisp and tart orange chicken, or the chilli-loaded warm beef salad. There are two branches – choose here for lunch, the **Stockbridge branch** (below) for dinner.

SONGKRAN II Map pp218-19 Thai ££
☎ 225 4804; 8 Gloucester St; mains £8-11; noon-2.30pm & 6-10.45pm Mon-Sat, 6-10.45pm Sun; 24, 29 or 42

Songkran II dishes up the same menu of excellent Thai food as the West End branch, but in the more romantic atmosphere of a 17th-century town house, decorated with Thai paintings, statues and wood-carvings.

THE RESTAURANT
Map pp214-15 Modern Scottish ££
☎ 476 7209; 29 Roseburn Tce; mains £12-16; noon-2pm & 6-10pm Tue-Sat, 11am-2pm & 5-9pm Sun; 12, 26, 31 or 38

It's worth heading west that extra mile to visit the Restaurant, a buzzing little bistro whose décor mixes bare brick, wood panelling and contemporary art with champagne tablecloths, chocolate napkins and bentwood chairs. The atmosphere is laid back, and the menu takes Scottish produce and gives it a French, Mediterranean or Asian twist with dishes such as rich risotto of wild mushrooms, pesto and Parmesan, hot-smoked salmon with gazpacho sauce,

TOP FIVE VEGETARIAN RESTAURANTS

Many Edinburgh restaurants, of all descriptions, offer vegetarian options on the menu – some good, some bad, some indifferent. The places listed below are all 100% veggie (with vegan options), and all fall into the 'very good' category.

- **Ann Purna** (p116)
- **David Bann** (p104)
- **Henderson's Salad Table** (p109)
- **Kalpna** (p117)
- **Susie's Diner** (p117)

and the signature dish of seared scallops with black pudding and mashed potato (a surprisingly successful combination).

DALRY & MORNINGSIDE

The gradual 'gentrification' of Haymarket and Dalry Rd has seen the area's long-established Indian and Chinese restaurants challenged by a rash of stylish new eateries. Restaurants here are widely spaced, but the ones below are worth seeking out.

FIRST COAST

Map p217 Scottish/International ££

☎ 313 4404; 99-101 Dalry Rd; mains £8-14; noon-2pm & 5-11pm Mon-Sat; 2, 3, 4, 25, 33 or 44

Our favourite neighbourhood bistro, First Coast has a striking main dining area with pale-grey wood panelling, white-painted walls, stripped stone and Victorian cornices, and a short and simple menu offering hearty comfort food such as slow-cooked ham hough with mustard mash, fillet of hake with pea and chorizo stew, and Sussex pond pudding with orange and thyme ice cream. At lunch, and from 5pm to 6.30pm, you can have any main course for £6.50, or a main and a sweet for £8.95.

MCKIRDY'S STEAKHOUSE

Map p217 Scottish ££

☎ 229 6660; 151 Morrison St; mains £10-15; 5.30-10pm Sun-Thu, 5-10.30pm Fri & Sat; 2

In 1999 the McKirdy brothers – owners of a butcher's business that was established in 1895 – decided to cut out the middleman and open their own restaurant. The result is one of Edinburgh's best steakhouses, with friendly staff serving starters such as haggis with Drambuie sauce, and juicy, perfectly cooked steaks from rump to T-bone (£22), accompanied by mustard mash or crispy fries. There's a kids' menu, and you can get a two-course early dinner for £12.95 before 6.30pm.

OMAR KHAYYAM Map p217 Indian ££

☎ 220 0024; 1 Grosvenor St; mains £8-12; noon-2pm & 5-11pm Mon-Fri, noon-11pm Sat, 4.30-11pm Sun; all Haymarket buses

A mainstay of Edinburgh's curry-house scene, the Omar Khayyam is an old-fashioned Punjabi restaurant with attentive, waistcoated waiters, plush décor and an ornate fountain trickling away in the middle of the dining room. The food is always fresh and flavourful, ranging from old favourites such as chicken tikka masala to more unusual dishes like Kabul chicken (with chick peas, cumin and coriander). If you enjoy curried seafood, try the Handi Fish Dopiaza – rich and spicy without overwhelming the flavour of the fish.

SUSHIYA Map p217 Japanese ££

☎ 313 3222; 19 Dalry Rd; mains £7-11, sushi servings £3-7; noon-10pm Mon-Thu, noon-11pm Fri & Sat; 2, 3, 4, 25, 33 or 44

The neat, geometric décor in this smart little sushi bar – square hardwood tables with square black-leather stools and square light fittings, set against white walls, wasabi-green doors and brushed steel – is mirrored in the neat, geometric portions of market-fresh tuna, salmon, scallop and octopus prepared to order by the smiling Mr Yuen, along with teriyaki beef and chicken, udon noodles and ramen soup. A touch of authentic background noise is added by a couple of small video screens playing non-stop Japanese game shows.

TOLLCROSS & BRUNTSFIELD

Tollcross and Bruntsfield eating options range from the mixed bag of upmarket restaurants and Italian and Chinese places in the theatre district of Lothian Rd to the laid-back bistros of Bruntsfield.

APARTMENT Map pp224-5 International ££

☎ 228 6456; 7-13 Barclay Pl; mains £7-12; 5.45-11pm Mon-Fri, noon-11pm Sat & Sun; all Bruntsfield buses

Effortlessly cool and almost always busy, the Apartment is just too popular – fantastic bistro food and a buzzy, youthful atmosphere make it hard to get a table. Book in advance – by at least three weeks, preferably – and don't be surprised if you still have to wait. But it's worth being patient for treats such as marinated lamb meatballs with merguez and basil-wrapped goat's cheese, or roasted monkfish marinated in yoghurt with sweet red chilli, served up by the friendly and all-too-gorgeous waiting staff.

ATRIUM

Map pp218-19 Modern Scottish £££

☎ 228 8882; 10 Cambridge St; mains £17-23; noon-2pm & 6-10pm Mon-Fri, 6-10pm Sat; all Lothian Rd buses

Elegantly draped in cream linen and candlelight, the Atrium is one of Edinburgh's most fashionable restaurants, counting Mick Jagger and Jack Nicholson among its past guests. The cuisine is Modern Scottish with a Mediterranean twist, with the emphasis on the finest of fresh seasonal produce – halibut poached in red wine, or wild mushroom and rabbit terrine with endive marmalade. The entrance is to the left of the foyer in the Traverse Theatre.

BLUE BAR CAFÉ

Map pp218-19 Modern Scottish ££

☎ 221 1222; 10 Cambridge St; mains £9-15; noon-2.30pm & 5.30-10.30pm Mon-Sat; all Lothian Rd buses

Set above the foyer of the Traverse Theatre, this cool white minimalist space is a lighter and less formal alternative to the Atrium. The food is simple but skilfully cooked and presented – from Crombie's sausages with mash and onion gravy, to braised lamb shank with balsamic lentils – and the atmosphere loud and chatty with all those luvvies from the theatre downstairs.

MARQUE CENTRAL

Map pp218-19 Modern Scottish ££

☎ 229 9859; 30b Grindlay St; mains £12-17; 11.45am-2pm & 5.30-10pm Tue-Thu, 11.45am-2pm & 5.30-11pm Fri, noon-2pm & 5.30-11pm Sat; all Lothian Rd buses

Tucked between the Lyceum Theatre and the Usher Hall, this split-level bistro (go for an upstairs table if you have the choice) is perfectly positioned to catch the theatre-going crowds. The menu is top-notch Modern Scottish, with dishes such as loin of venison with rosti potato, caramelised parsnip and balsamic onion jus, or fillet of halibut and king prawns with red pepper and tomato jam, and there are nice little touches like home-baked bread and a complimentary *amuse-gueule*. The pre- or post-theatre special of two/three courses for £13.50/16 is available from 5.30pm to 7pm and 9pm to 10pm Tuesday to Thursday, and 9.30pm to 11pm Friday and Saturday.

MONTPELIERS Map p226 International ££

☎ 229 3115; 159-161 Bruntsfield Pl; mains £7-15; food served 9am-10pm; all Bruntsfield buses

Montpeliers is a popular and stylish bar (see p130) with a separate restaurant area done up in cheerful chocolate and orange colours, offering good food all day long. It has a pleasant laid-back buzz – the place is rarely empty, at any time of day – and the menu wanders the globe from Thai fishcakes to Greek salad to Cajun chicken to Mexican fajitas.

NDEBELE Map pp224-5 South African £

☎ 221 1141; 57 Home St; mains £5-7; 10am-10pm; all Tollcross buses

This South African café is hidden deep in darkest Tollcross, but is worth seeking out for the changing menu of unusual African dishes (including at least one veggie option) – try a boerewors sandwich (sausage made with pork, beef and coriander) with mielie meal or samp'n'beans. Before you leave, pop downstairs for a look at the gallery of African art.

ORIGINAL KHUSHI'S Map p222 Indian £-££

☎ 667 0888; 30 Potterrow; mains £5-9; noon-11pm Mon-Sat, 5-10pm Sun; 2, 41 or 42

Established in 1947, Khushi's started out as an authentic Punjabi canteen and became something of an Edinburgh institution. In 2003 it moved to shiny new premises next to Edinburgh University's George Sq campus, but retained its original menu of basic Indian dishes, marinated and cooked in the traditional way, served with no frills at reasonable prices – the lamb *bhuna* and fish curry combine real depth of flavour with a sinus-clearing chilli kick. It's not licensed but you can bring your own booze (no corkage), or check out their range of fruit-juice cocktails.

RAINBOW ARCH Map pp218-19 Chinese ££

☎ 221 1288; 8-16 Morrison St; mains £7-11; noon-3am; all Lothian Rd buses

It's always a sign of a good Chinese restaurant when you see members of the local Chinese community eating there, and you'll see plenty of them at the Rainbow Arch; this is the only restaurant in Edinburgh serving authentic dim sum. The menu is more adventurous than most – look out for deep-fried minced octopus cakes – and even the standard dishes, such as lemon chicken, are better than average.

SANTINI Map pp218-19 Italian £££

221 7788; 8 Conference Sq; mains £18-23; noon-2.30pm Mon-Fri, 6.30-10.30pm Mon-Sat; all Lothian Rd buses

Tucked away at the back of the Sheraton Grand Hotel, Santini is one of a small family of select restaurants with branches in London and Milan. This is a cut (two cuts, even) above your average Italian restaurant: the dining area is draped in white muslin and linen, with flagstone floors, mosaic panels and cinnamon-coloured armchair seats, and the waiting staff are dressed just as elegantly in Versace and Gucci. The quality of the food matches the surroundings, from starters such as smoked swordfish with pink peppercorns and *Poire William* to main events such as roast duck with cured bacon, chestnuts and honey.

THAI LEMONGRASS

Map pp224-5 Thai ££

229 2225; 40-41 Bruntsfield Pl; mains £7-12; 5-11.30pm Mon-Thu, noon-11.30pm Fri-Sun; all Bruntsfield buses

From the waiter's prayerlike gesture of greeting to the gold Buddha gazing down on the diners, everything about this restaurant feels authentically Thai. The rustic décor of terracotta tiles, yellow walls, dark-stained wood and cane table-mats makes for a relaxing ambience, enlivened by a constant buzz of conversation, while the rich and varied flavours of the food – fiery chilli, fragrant lemongrass, tangy lime leaves and sweet coconut – will keep you coming back for more.

TOP FIVE ROMANTIC RESTAURANTS

- **Café Marlayne** (p108)
- **Rhubarb** (opposite)
- **Santini** (above)
- **Stac Polly** (p111)
- **Witchery by the Castle** (p107)

The romantic Witchery by the Castle (p107)

ZAZOU Map p226 Scottish/French ££

669 3294; Union Canal, Ogilvie Tce, Polwarth; 3-course dinner £25; by advance booking only; 38

How's this for dinner with a difference – hire a whole canal-boat and cruise along the Union Canal as you dine. The menu varies, but offers a choice of four starters and four main courses, including one fish and one vegetarian option. Book at least seven days in advance; groups of six or more (maximum 12) can have the boat to themselves.

SOUTHSIDE & NEWINGTON

The student stronghold of Southside, between George Sq and Clerk St, is home to many good-value bistros, cafés and vegetarian places. And don't miss Rhubarb at Prestonfield House Hotel, one of Edinburgh's most talked-about restaurants.

ANN PURNA

Map pp218-19 Indian/Vegetarian £-££

662 1807; 45 St Patrick's Sq; mains £5-9; noon-2pm & 5.30-11pm Mon-Fri, 5.30-11pm Sat & Sun; 42

This little gem of a restaurant serves exclusively vegetarian dishes from southern India in a bright, unfussy dining room enlivened by a few homely decorations. If you're new to this kind of food, opt for a thali – a self-contained platter that contains two starters, four different curry dishes, rice, *puri* (puffed bread) and a dessert.

BUFFALO GRILL Map pp218-19 American ££

☎ 667 7427; 12-14 Chapel St; mains £8-15; noon-2pm & 6-10.30pm Mon-Fri, 6-10.30pm Sat, 5-10pm Sun; 42

The Buffalo Grill is cramped, noisy, fun and always busy, so book ahead. An American-style menu offers burgers, steaks and side orders of fries and onion rings, along with fish and chicken dishes, prawn tempura and a vegetarian burger, but steaks are the main event. This place is not licensed, but you can BYOB for a corkage charge of £1 per bottle of wine, or 50p per beer.

KALPNA

Map pp224-5 Indian/Vegetarian £-££

☎ 667 9890; 2-3 St Patrick Sq; mains £5-8; noon-2pm & 5.30-11pm Mon-Sat, 5.30-10pm Sun; all South Bridge buses

A long-standing Edinburgh favourite, Kalpna is one of the best Indian restaurants in the country, vegetarian or otherwise. The cuisine is mostly Gujarati, with a smattering of dishes from other parts of India – try the *khoya kaju* (vegetables, cashew nuts, sultanas and pistachios in a cream sauce with coriander and nutmeg, served with coconut rice and *puri*). Specials include the buffet lunch (£5.50) and the Kalpna thali (£9.50), which includes samosas, two curry dishes, rice, *puri* and a dessert.

RHUBARB

Map pp214-15 Modern Scottish £££

☎ 225 1333; Prestonfield House Hotel, Priestfield Rd; mains £20-30; noon-3pm & 6-11pm

Set in the splendid 17th-century Prestonfield House, Rhubarb is as much a feast for the eyes as for the taste buds. From the floodlit façade, glowing like a ruby in the night, to the striped and swirling scarlets, burgundies and vermilions that deck the walls, curtains, carpets and upholstery, the décor flaunts a full palette of rich reds set off with black and gold. The air of decadence is enhanced by the flicker of scented Diptyque candlelight, and the sensuous surfaces – damask, brocade, marble, gilded leather – make you want to touch everything. The over-the-top décor is matched by the intense flavours and rich textures of the food – sweet garlic-crusted cod on minted pea purée; roast fillet of Angus beef with a brandy and red wine sauce; voluptuous rhubarb *crème brûlée* – and the wine list runs to 500 bins. Don't miss the opportunity to take your postprandial coffee and brandy upstairs to the sumptuous fireside sofas in the Tapestry Room. A set-menu lunch (£16.95) is available from noon to 3pm.

SURUCHI Map p222 Indian ££

☎ 556 6583; 14a Nicolson St; mains £8-14; noon-2pm & 5.30-11pm Mon-Sat, 5.30-11pm Sun; all South Bridge buses

A laid-back Indian eatery characterised by handmade turquoise tiles, lazy ceiling fans and chilled-out jazz guitar, Suruchi offers a range of exotic dishes as well as the traditional tandoori standards. Try *shakuti* from Goa (lamb or chicken with coconut, poppy seeds, nutmeg and chilli), or vegetarian *kumbhi narial* (mushrooms, coconut and coriander). An amusing touch is provided by the menu descriptions – they're translated into broad Scots ('a beezer o' a curry this...gey nippie oan the tongue').

SUSIE'S DINER Map pp218-19 Vegetarian £

☎ 667 8729; 51-53 W Nicolson St; mains £3-6; noon-8pm Mon, noon-9pm Tue-Sat; 2, 41 or 42

Susie's is a down-to-earth self-service veggie restaurant with scrubbed wooden tables, rickety chairs and a friendly atmosphere. The menu changes daily but includes things such as tofu, aubergine and pepper casserole, and Susie's famous falafel plates. Billed as 'the best falafel in the Western world', these crunchy, cumin-laced chick-pea patties are well worth trying.

WATERFRONT EDINBURGH

Edinburgh has not made too much of its waterfront in the past, but the regeneration of Leith has seen the Shore (on the banks of the Water of Leith) and Dock Pl (just to the west of the Shore) develop a sizable enclave of gourmet restaurants, many with appealing historic settings. There is also a handful of long-established waterfront pubs serving excellent bar lunches and suppers.

CRAMOND GALLERY BISTRO Scottish ££

☎ 312 6555; 5 Riverside; 2-course lunch £10; 10am-6pm May-Sep, 10am-5pm Oct-Apr; 24 or 41

Housed in a listed 16th-century building, this snug little bistro doubles as an art gallery and enjoys a delightful setting beside the River Almond (there are outdoor tables in summer). The menu includes good fish dishes as well as excellent home-baked apple tart, cakes and pastries.

CRAMOND INN Scottish £-££

☎ 336 2035; 30 Cramond Glebe Rd; mains £5-10; bar 11am-11pm Mon-Thu, 11am-midnight Fri & Sat, 12.30-11pm Sun; food served noon-2.45pm & 5.30-8.30pm Mon-Thu, noon-2.45pm & 5.30-9.15pm Fri & Sat, 12.30-6pm Sun; 24 or 41

The picturesque Cramond Inn is a welcoming, traditional pub sporting lots of wood-panelled nooks, antique furniture and cosy fireplaces, with regular patrons propping up the bar or wedged in a corner with the newspaper. The menu consists of classic pub grub, carefully prepared – fishcakes with dill mayo, haddock (deep-fried in beer batter) and chips, steak and ale pie, bangers and mash with red wine gravy – and there are daily specials such as tomato and basil soup, and rocket and Parmesan salad.

DANIEL'S BISTRO Map p216 French ££

☎ 553 5933; 88 Commercial St; mains £8-14; 10am-10pm; 16, 22, 35 or 36

The eponymous Daniel is a native of Alsace, and his all-French kitchen staff combine top Scottish and French produce with Gallic know-how. The Provençal fish soup is richly flavoured, and classic main courses range from slow-cooked, Alsatian-style knuckle of pork to hearty Alpine *tartiflette* (potato, onion and bacon baked in cream and topped with cheese). The chic glass-walled dining room is decked out in blonde wood and steel, with picture-window views of the Scottish Executive's modern architecture. There's a business lunch deal for £7.65, and you can nip in here for morning coffee or afternoon cake, too.

FISHERS BISTRO

Map p216 Seafood ££-£££

☎ 554 5666; 1 the Shore; mains £13-21; noon-10.30pm; 16, 22, 35 or 36

This cosy little bar-turned-restaurant, tucked beneath a 17th-century signal tower, is one of the city's best seafood restaurants. The menu changes with the morning's catch, but there are also a few regulars: Fishers' fishcakes are an Edinburgh institution, crisp on the outside, filled with flaky salmon and creamy mashed potato, and served with lemon and chive mayonnaise. Booking is recommended – if you can't get a table here, try their more sophisticated New Town branch, **Fishers in the City** (p109).

KHUBLAI KHAN

Map p216 Mongolian ££

☎ 555 0005; 43 Assembly St; dinner £20; 6-10.30pm daily, plus 12.30-2.30pm Fri & Sun; 12, 16 or 35

How many cities outside Ulan Baator can boast a Mongolian restaurant? OK, the authenticity may be questionable but it certainly makes a change from curry or pizza. Choose from a buffet of raw meat, seafood and vegetables, flavoured with oils, spices and sauces of your choice, and have it cooked to order on a Mongolian-style barbecue (veggies have their own grills). The cost of dinner includes three courses and all you can eat from the buffet – as the menu says: 'You may repeat the experience as often as any tight-fitting clothing you may be wearing will allow'.

MALMAISON BRASSERIE

Map p216 French ££

☎ 468 5000; 1 Tower Pl; mains £11-15; noon-2.30pm & 6-11pm daily, plus 7-10am Mon-Fri & 7-11am Sat & Sun; 16, 22, 35 or 36

Clean-cut, contemporary design and wholesome French cooking are the distinguishing features of the Malmaison Brasserie, set in the hotel of the same

TOP FIVE SEAFOOD RESTAURANTS

- **Café Royal Oyster Bar** (p108)
- **Fishers Bistro** (right)
- **Fishers in the City** (p109)
- **Mussel Inn** (p110)
- **Waterfront Wine Bar & Grill** (p120)

TOP FIVE FISH & CHIPS

Most of Edinburgh's best fish and chip shops are owned by members of the city's sizable Scots-Italian community. In Scotland a takeaway portion of fish and chips is called a 'fish supper'; a piece of fish without the chips is a 'single fish'. The sign of a good fish supper is a light, crispy batter that stays crispy to the end.

Scots chips shops generally sell haddock (rather than cod, the English favourite), and in an Edinburgh chip shop you will be asked if you want 'salt and sauce' on your food. The latter is a runny brown concoction, a bit like diluted, vinegary, HP sauce; if you'd prefer salt and vinegar (or nothing at all), say so.

- **L'Alba D'Oro** (Map pp218-19; ☎ 557 2580; 5-9 Henderson Row, New Town; fish supper £4.80; 🕑 noon-1.30pm & 5-11pm Mon-Fri, 5-11pm Sat & Sun; 🚌 23, 27 or 36) One of the few places where you can pick up a bottle of decent wine along with your fish and chips.
- **L'Aquila Bianca** (Map p217; ☎ 332 8433; 17 Raeburn Pl, Stockbridge; fish supper £4.90; 🕑 4.30pm-12.30am Sun-Thu, 4.30pm-1am Fri & Sat; 🚌 24, 29 or 42) Home-delivery service to central Edinburgh districts, 5pm to midnight.
- **Deep Sea** (Map pp218-19; ☎ 557 0276; 2 Antigua St, New Town; fish supper £4.60; 🕑 noon-2am Sun-Thu, noon-3am Fri & Sat; 🚌 all Leith Walk buses) Long-standing, late-opening, reliably good.
- **Gallery Restaurant** (see p108; fish and chips £10) Excellent, upmarket fish and chips with peas and tartar sauce, for the sit-down crowd only (no takeaways).
- **Rapido** (Map pp218-19; ☎ 556 2041; 79 Broughton St, New Town; fish supper £4.20; 🕑 11.30am-2pm & 4.30pm-1am Sun-Thu, 11.30am-2pm & 4.30pm-2am Fri & Sat; 🚌 8 or 17) Not only fish and chips, but also baked potatoes, pizzas, sandwiches and Ben and Jerry's ice cream.

name. The à la carte menu includes dishes such as *daube de boeuf* (ox cheeks braised in red wine), confit of duck with braised puy lentils, and creamy, caramelly *crème brûlée*. The *prix fixe* three-course lunch menu costs £11.

OLD CHAIN PIER Map pp214-15 Pub Grub £-££

☎ 552 1233; 1 Trinity Cres; mains £5-10; 🕑 food served noon-9pm Mon-Sat, 12.30-8pm Sun; 🚌 16 or 32

Built on the site of a jetty where steamers once set sail for Stirling, the Old Chain Pier is a lovely little pub overlooking – nay, overhanging – the Firth of Forth on the waterfront east of Granton Harbour. Order a pint of real ale, grab a window table and enjoy the view across the water to the hills of Fife while you peruse a menu that includes regulars such as Trinity chowder (a creamy stew of mussels and smoked haddock), rich and meaty lamb casserole, and butternut squash and leek risotto, plus adventurous daily specials such as pan-fried squid.

RESTAURANT MARTIN WISHART

Map p216 French £££

☎ 553 3557; 54 the Shore; mains £23-27; 🕑 noon-2pm & 7-10pm Tue-Fri, 7-10pm Sat; 🚌 16, 22, 35 or 36

In 2001 this restaurant became the first in Edinburgh to win a Michelin star. The eponymous chef has worked with Albert Roux, Marco Pierre White and Nick Nairn, and brings a modern French approach to the finest Scottish produce, from roast fillet of John Dory to braised saddle of lamb. The dining room is crisply elegant, the service professional and discreet, and the food beautifully presented. A set three-course lunch costs £21, and a six-course tasting menu is £60. Book ahead as far as possible.

SHORE Map p216 Seafood ££-£££

☎ 553 5080; 3-4 the Shore; mains £13-17; 🕑 noon-2.30pm & 6.30-10pm Mon-Fri, noon-3pm & 6.30-10pm Sat & Sun; 🚌 16, 22, 35 or 36

The atmospheric dining room next door to the popular Shore bar is a haven of wood-panelled peace, with old photographs, nautical knick-knacks, fresh flowers and an open fire adding to the romantic theme. The menu is small and specialises in Scottish seafood and game.

SMOKE STACK Map p216 American ££

☎ 476 6776; 19 Shore Pl; mains £8-16; 🕑 noon-2.30pm & 6-10.30pm Mon-Thu, noon-2.30pm & 5-10.30pm Fri, noon-10.30pm Sat, 5-10.30pm Sun; 🚌 16, 22, 35 or 36

The kitchen at Smoke Stack concentrates on one thing and manages to do that one thing very well indeed – charcoal grilling.

Not only prime Scottish steaks and meltingly tender burgers, but also tuna, salmon and chicken, all get the smoking, sizzling treatment before being served in a dining area that is more art gallery than steak house: ochre walls hung with modern art, bare wood floors and trendy iron-legged tables.

VINTNERS ROOMS Map p216 French £££

☎ 554 6767; the Vaults, 87 Giles St; mains £16-22; ⌚ noon-2pm & 7-10pm Tue-Sat, noon-2.30pm Sun; 🚌 22

A Georgian wine-merchant's sale-room, beautifully decorated with original 18th-century stucco work (the auctioneer stood in the alcove to the left of the fireplace), forms the beautiful centrepiece of this delightful French restaurant, tucked away on a back street near the Water of Leith. The menu changes with the seasons, offering the likes of warm pigeon salad with roast pumpkin, and fillet of Scottish beef with wild mushroom sauce.

WATERFRONT WINE BAR & GRILL

Map p216 Scottish/Seafood ££-£££

☎ 554 7427; 1c Dock Pl; mains £13-18; ⌚ noon-9.30pm Mon-Thu, noon-10.30pm Fri & Sat, 12.30-9.30pm Sun; 🚌 16, 22, 35 or 36

The Waterfront is a cosy warren of timber-lined nooks and crannies housed in a single-storey red-brick building that was once a waiting room for ferries across the Forth of Firth. There's a bright and airy conservatory dining room at the back, and outdoor tables on a floating terrace in the dock. The menu is dominated by seafood, from fresh Loch Etive oysters and chargrilled squid to monkfish tail wrapped in smoked bacon and sweet-fleshed Scottish lobster.

GREATER EDINBURGH

In recent years Queensferry has produced a couple of excellent restaurants with great views of the Forth bridges.

BOAT HOUSE Seafood ££

☎ 331 5429; 19b High St; mains £13-17; ⌚ noon-2.30pm & 5.30-10pm Tue-Sat, 12.30-8pm Sun; 🚌 First Edinburgh 43

You would be hard put to find a better site for a seafood restaurant – any closer to the sea and you'd reach out the window and pull mussels from the rocks. Perched right on the high-water mark at the foot of the Boat House Steps, this place is a cosy, candle-lit nook filled with pine tables, bric-a-brac and old photos of Queensferry. The menu changes daily, depending on the morning's catch; specialities include a rich seafood bisque and smoked haddock fishcakes. Book early and ask for a window table.

OROCCO PIER Scottish/Mediterranean ££-£££

☎ 331 1298; 17 High St; mains £13-20; ⌚ bar 11am-midnight Sun-Thu, 11am-1am Fri & Sat, food served 9am-10pm; 🚌 First Edinburgh 43

The big selling point here is a wooden balcony overhanging the sea, with stunning views of the Forth road and rail bridges. Picture windows mean that you can still enjoy the view when the weather prevents outdoor dining. The restaurant is stylish and modern, with lots of dark wood, tan upholstery and fairy lights. The menu is strong on seafood, beef and lamb – the spicy cumin-and-coriander–cented salmon fishcakes make a tasty starter, while mains range from roast rack of lamb with tarragon and mustard crust to roast sea bass with herbs and garlic.

Drinking

Drinking

Edinburgh has always been a drinker's city. The 18th-century poets Robert Fergusson and Robert Burns spent much of their time in – and often drew inspiration from – Edinburgh's public houses and, rather than attend his law lectures at Edinburgh University, the young Robert Louis Stevenson preferred to haunt the city's many howffs (drinking dens) – a practice perpetuated by many Edinburgh students to this day.

Although many city-centre pubs have been 'themed' or converted into vast drinking halls catering to office workers unwinding at the end of a day, the neighbourhood bar is still a social centre where you can meet friends, watch football on TV, listen to live music or take part in the weekly quiz night. Edinburgh has over 700 pubs – more per square mile than any other UK city – and they are as varied and full of character as the people who drink in them, from Victorian palaces to stylish pre-club bars, and from real-ale howffs to trendy cocktail bars.

Pubs generally open from 11am to 11pm Monday to Saturday and 12.30pm to 11pm on Sunday. Many open later on Friday and Saturday, staying open till midnight or 1am, while those with a food or music licence can party on until 3am. The bell for last orders rings about 15 minutes before closing time, and you're allowed 15 minutes' drinking-up time after closing.

For more pubs check out the Eating (p102) and Entertainment (p136) chapters.

OLD TOWN

The pubs on the Royal Mile are – not surprisingly – aimed mainly at the tourist market, but there are still some good old-fashioned drinking dens hidden up the closes and along the side streets.

Many Grassmarket pubs have outdoor tables on sunny summer afternoons, but in the evenings they are often favoured by boozed-up lads on the pull. Cowgate – Grassmarket's extension to the east – leads into Edinburgh's club land.

ROYAL MILE & AROUND

CITY CAFÉ Map p222

☎ 220 0125; 19 Blair St; 11am-1am; 35

Though it dates from the late 1980s, this is still one of Edinburgh's most popular pre-club bars, with a 1950s-American-diner look, pool tables, great munchies and convivial bar staff. The downstairs DJ spins hip-hop, R&B, ragga and funk from 9pm Tuesday to Thursday, and happy hour runs from 5pm to 8pm. It's also a place of pilgrimage for Irvine Welsh fans: the bar was mentioned in *Trainspotting*.

ECCO VINO Map p222

☎ 225 1441; 19 Cockburn St; noon-midnight Mon-Thu, noon-1am Fri & Sat, 12.30pm-midnight Sun; all South Bridge buses

With outdoor tables on sunny afternoons, and cosy candle-lit intimacy in the evenings, this comfortably cramped Tuscan-style wine bar offers a tempting range of Italian wines (though only a few are available by the glass – it's best to share a bottle) as well as an all-day menu of tasty antipasti.

ENSIGN EWART Map p222

☎ 225 7440; 225 Lawnmarket; 11am-11.30pm Mon-Thu, 11am-midnight Fri & Sat, 12.30pm-midnight Sun; 2, 23, 27, 41 or 42

The nearest pub to the castle, the Ensign Ewart trades on its historic setting and military associations. A mix of tourists, students from the university residences in Milne's Court and castle personnel drop in to enjoy real ale, a range of 40 malt whiskies and good bar food. There's live folk music on Friday, Saturday and Sunday evenings.

JOLLY JUDGE Map p222

☎ 225 2669; 7a James Court; noon-midnight Mon & Thu-Sat, noon-11pm Tue & Wed, 12.30-11pm Sun; 2, 23, 27, 41 or 42

Tucked away down an Old Town close, the Judge exudes a cosy 17th-century ambience with its low, timber-beamed ceilings and numerous nooks and crannies. The convivial atmosphere is undisturbed by TV, music or gambling machines, and has the added attraction of a cheering log fire in cold weather.

TRAD VS TRENDY

At one end of Edinburgh's broad spectrum of hostelries lies the traditional 19th-century bar, which has preserved much of its original Victorian decoration and generally serves cask-conditioned real ales and a staggering range of malt whiskies. At the other end is the modern 'style bar', with a cool clientele and styling so sharp you could cut yourself on it. The bar staff here are more likely to be serving cocktails. Here are some suggestions from each end of the range:

Top Five Traditional Pubs

- **Abbotsford** (p124)
- **Athletic Arms (The Diggers)** (p128)
- **Bennet's Bar** (p129)
- **Café Royal Circle Bar** (p124)
- **Sheep Heid** (p134)

Top Five Trendy Bars

- **Assembly Bar** (p130)
- **Borough** (p130)
- **Monboddo Bar** (p130)
- **Opal Lounge** (p125)
- **Tonic** (p126)

MALT SHOVEL Map p222

☎ 225 6843; 11-15 Cockburn St; 11am-midnight Mon-Thu, 11-1am Fri & Sat, 12.30pm-midnight Sun; all South Bridge buses

A traditional-looking pub, with dark wood and subdued tartanry, the Malt Shovel offers a good range of real ales and more than 100 malt whiskies, and is famed for its regular Tuesday night jazz and Wednesday night folk-music sessions.

ROYAL MILE TAVERN Map p222

☎ 557 9681; 127 High St; 11am-midnight Mon-Fri, 11-1am Sat, 12.30-11pm Sun; 35

An elegant, traditional Edinburgh bar lined with polished wood, mirrors and brass, the Royal Mile serves real ale, good wines and fine food – *moules marinières* and crusty bread is a lunch-time speciality. Wednesday nights see a lively session of traditional Scottish music.

TUN Map pp218-19

☎ 557 9297; Tun Bldg, Holyrood Rd; 11am-11pm Sun-Thu, 11-1am Fri & Sat; 35

Set among the coloured-glass and steel architecture of the redeveloped Holyrood district next to the Scottish Parliament Building, the Tun is a funky fish tank of a place, with chunky leather sofas, steel bar stools and a sloping back wall that looks like a sample page from a floor-tile catalogue. It's popular with political types and media people from the neighbouring BBC studios and the *Scotsman* newspaper offices just across the road.

VILLAGER Map p222

☎ 226 2781; 49-50 George IV Bridge; noon-1am; 2, 23, 27, 41 or 42

Designed as a cross between a traditional pub and a style bar, Villager has friendly staff, welcoming regulars and a comfortable, laid-back vibe. It can be standing room only in the main bar in the evenings (the cocktails are excellent), but the side room, with its brown leather sofas and sub-tropical pot plants really comes into its own for a lazy Sunday afternoon with the papers.

WORLD'S END Map p222

☎ 556 3628; 4 High St; 11am-1am Mon-Sat, 12.30pm-1am Sun; 35

The World's End is a traditional local pub, with plenty of regulars as well as tourists, named because this part of High St once lay next to the Old Town's eastern limit – part of the 16th-century Flodden Wall can still be seen in the basement. It does good bar food, including excellent fish and chips.

GRASSMARKET

BEEHIVE INN Map p222

☎ 225 7171; 18-20 Grassmarket; 11am-midnight Mon-Thu, 11am-1am Fri & Sat, 11am-10pm Sun; 2

The historic Beehive – a former coaching inn – is a big, buzzing party pub, with a range of real ales, but the main attraction is sitting out the back in the Grassmarket's only beer garden, with views up to the castle. The Beehive is the starting point for the **Edinburgh Literary Pub Tour** (see p51).

BOW BAR Map p222

☎ 226 7667; 80 West Bow; noon-11.30pm Mon-Sat, 12.30-11pm Sun; 2, 23, 27, 41 or 42

A busy, traditional pub, unspoilt by touristy trappings despite its nearness to the Royal Mile, the Bow Bar serves a range of excellent real ales and a vast selection of malt whiskies: this is not the sort of place to go asking for Bacardi Breezers. There are snug window seats and leather benches, but you'll find it's often standing room only on Friday and Saturday evenings.

THREE SISTERS Map p222

☎ 622 6800; 39 Cowgate; 9am-1am; 35

This huge pub is actually three bars – one American, one Irish and one Gothic – with a big cobbled courtyard for outdoor drinking in summer. It's a bit of a mad party place, aimed squarely at the student/sports fan/backpacker market, with large-screen TVs, club nights, and vodka and Red Bull by the pitcher.

WHITE HART INN Map p222

☎ 226 2806; 34 Grassmarket; 11am-1am; 2

A brass plaque outside this pub proclaims: 'In the White Hart Inn Robert Burns stayed during his last visit to Edinburgh, 1791.' Claiming to be the city's oldest pub in continuous use (since 1516), it also hosted William Wordsworth in 1803. Not surprisingly, it's a traditional, cosy, low-raftered place with folk-music sessions on Wednesday, Thursday and Sunday.

NEW TOWN

George St, once the city's most prestigious business street, has changed enormously in the last decade. Many of the offices are now designer boutiques and all the grand old bank buildings have been turned into stylish bars, allowing city wags to make lots of lame jokes about liquid assets and standing orders. Most of the city's most fashionable new bars are on or near George St.

Neighbouring Rose St was once a famous pub crawl, where generations of students, sailors and rugby fans would try to visit every pub on the street (around 17 of them) and down a pint of beer in each one. These days shopping, not boozing, is Rose St's *raison d'être*, but it still has a few pubs worth visiting.

Bohemian Broughton, at the eastern end of the New Town, is the centre of Edinburgh's gay scene, and has an eclectic mixture of traditional real-ale pubs, modern pre-club bars and all-out gay bars.

GEORGE STREET

ABBOTSFORD Map pp218-19

☎ 225 5276; 3 Rose St; 11am-11pm Mon-Sat; all Princes St buses

Dating from 1902 and named after Sir Walter Scott's country house, the Abbotsford is one of the few pubs in Rose St that has retained its Edwardian splendour, with a grand mahogany island bar. It has long been a hang-out for writers, actors, journalists and media people and has many loyal regulars.

CAFÉ ROYAL CIRCLE BAR Map pp218-19

☎ 556 1884; 17 W Register St; 11am-11pm Mon-Wed, 11am-midnight Thu, 11am-1am Fri & Sat, 12.30-11pm Sun; all Princes St buses

Perhaps *the* classic Edinburgh bar, the Café Royal's main claims to fame are its magnificent oval bar and the series of Doulton tile portraits of famous Victorian inventors. Check out the bottles on the gantry – staff line them up so it looks as if there's a mirror there, and many a drink-befuddled customer has been seen squinting and wondering why they can't see their reflection.

CUMBERLAND BAR Map pp218-19

☎ 558 3134; 1-3 Cumberland St; 11am-1am Mon-Sat, 12.30pm-1am Sun; 13

Immortalised as the stereotypical New Town pub in Alexander McCall-Smith's serialised novel *44 Scotland Street*, the Cumberland has an authentic, traditional wood-brass-and-mirrors look (despite it being relatively modern), and it serves well-looked-after, cask-conditioned ales as well as a wide range of malt whiskies. There's also a pleasant little beer garden outside.

FRAZER'S COCKTAIL BAR Map pp218-19

☎ 624 8624; 14 George St; noon-11pm Sun-Wed, noon-midnight Thu, noon-12.30am Fri & Sat; 24 or 28

Frazer's is the bar at the Dome, formerly a temple to Mammon (it was originally a bank's head office) and now a shrine to Dionysus – stand in the foyer for a moment and be impressed. The gleaming bar (to your left) is a beautiful Art Deco masterpiece and serves fine real ales as well as pukka cocktails.

GRAPE Map pp218-19

☎ 557 4522; 13 St Andrew Sq; 11am-11pm Mon-Wed, 11am-midnight Thu,11am-1am Fri & Sat, 12.30-9pm Sun; all Princes St buses

This popular wine bar is yet another bank conversion, its spacious rooms graced with grandiose columns, ornate plasterwork and a sparkling glass dome. It pulls in an upmarket crowd of designer shoppers and office workers, with 25 wines and a range of champagnes available by the glass.

GREAT GROG WINE BAR Map pp218-19

☎ 225 1616; 43 Rose St; 10am-11pm Sun-Thu, 10am-1am Fri & Sat; all Princes St buses

A chilled-out haven in the middle of bustling Rose St, Great Grog is the ideal place to kick back in a leather sofa and choose from a list of more than 30 wines available by the glass (if you want to go for a whole bottle, the choice increases to over 100 varieties).

GUILDFORD ARMS Map pp218-19

☎ 556 4312; 1 W Register St; 11am-11pm Mon-Thu, 11am-midnight Fri & Sat, 12.30pm-midnight Sun; all Princes St buses

Located next door to the Café Royal, the Guildford is another classic Victorian pub full of polished mahogany, brass and ornate cornices. The bar lunches are good; try to get a table in the unusual upstairs gallery, with a view over the sea of drinkers down below.

Opal Lounge (right)

KAY'S BAR Map pp218-19

☎ 225 1858; 39 Jamaica St; 11am-midnight Mon-Thu, 11-1am Fri & Sat, 12.30-11pm Sun; 13, 24, 29 or 42

Housed in a former wine-merchant's office, tiny Kay's Bar is a cosy haven with red leather benches, a gleaming mahogany bar and a fine range of real ales and malt whiskies. Old wine and sherry barrels adorn one wall, and a cast-iron fireplace holds a coal fire in winter. At lunch time food is served in the tiny back room (only two tables, so get in early or book ahead).

KENILWORTH Map pp218-19

☎ 226 4385; 152-154 Rose St; 9.30am-11pm Mon-Thu, 9.30am-12.45pm Fri & Sat, 12.30-11pm Sun; all Princes St buses

A gorgeous Edwardian drinking palace, complete with original fittings – from the tile floors, mahogany circle bar and gantry, to the ornate mirrors and gas lamps – the Kenilworth was Edinburgh's original gay bar back in the 1970s. Today it attracts a mixed crowd of all ages and serves a good range of real ales and malt whiskies.

OLOROSO LOUNGE BAR Map pp218-19

☎ 226 7614; 33 Castle St; 11am-1am Mon-Sat, 12.30pm-1am Sun; 13, 19, 37 or 41

The roof-top lounge at the Oloroso restaurant is one of Edinburgh's hippest hangouts – this bar would be at home in New York, Paris or London. Sleek leather sofas and floor-to-ceiling windows allow comfortable views across the city to Arthur's Seat, and the drinks menu includes gourmet offerings such as a Berry Balsamic Champagne Cocktail (Pommery rosé blended with strawberries and black pepper, topped with balsamic vinegar).

OPAL LOUNGE Map pp218-19

☎ 226 2275; 51 George St; noon-3am; 24, 41 or 42

One of Edinburgh's trendiest bars, the Opal is jammed at weekends with affluent 20-somethings who've spent about £200 and two hours in front of the mirror to achieve that artlessly scruffy look. During the week,

The bar at Tonic (below)

when the air-kissing, cocktail-sipping crowds thin out, it's a good place to relax with a fruit smoothie (or one of those expensive but excellent cocktails) and sample the tasty Asian food on offer. Expect to queue on weekend evenings.

OXFORD BAR Map pp218-19

☎ 539 7119; 8 Young St; 11am-1am Mon-Sat, 12.30pm-1am Sun; 13, 19, 37 or 41

The Oxford is that rarest of things these days, a real pub for real people, with no 'theme', no music, no frills and no pretensions. 'The Ox' was immortalised by Ian Rankin, author of the Inspector Rebus novels, who is a regular here (as is his fictitious detective).

ROBERTSONS 37 Map pp218-19

☎ 225 6185; 37 Rose St; 11am-11pm Mon-Sat; all Princes St buses

No 37 is to malt whisky connoisseurs what the Diggers once was to real-ale fans. Its long gantry sports a choice of more than 100 single malts, and the bar provides a quiet and elegant environment in which to sample them.

STANDING ORDER Map pp218-19

☎ 225 4460; 62-66 George St; 10am-1am; 24, 41 or 42

One of several converted banks situated on George St, the Standing Order is a cavernous beer hall with a fantastic vaulted ceiling and some cosy rooms located off to the right: look for the one containing the original 27-tonne safe. Despite its size, it can be standing room only at the weekend.

TILES BAR-BISTRO Map pp218-19

☎ 558 1507; 1 St Andrew Sq; 8am-midnight Mon-Fri, 11am-midnight Sat & Sun; all Princes St buses

A regular haunt of city lawyers and accountants, Tiles is a smart and stylish bar in yet another converted bank, with live jazz on Sunday evenings at 6.30pm. It takes its name from the lovely Victorian tiles inside.

TONIC Map pp218-19

☎ 225 6431; 34a N Castle St; 3pm-1am Mon-Sat, 5pm-1am Sun; 13, 24, 29 or 42

As cool and classy as a perfectly mixed martini, Tonic prides itself on the quality and authenticity of its cocktails, of which there are more than a hundred to choose from. The bar's décor includes polished wood and limestone as well as Philippe Starck–designed bar stools, and the clientele ranges from local office workers on work-a-day lunch breaks to celebrities during the Edinburgh International Festival.

BROUGHTON

BASEMENT Map pp218-19

☎ 557 0097; 10a-12a Broughton St; ⏲ noon-1am; 🚌 8 or 17

The Basement is a laid-back and pleasantly grungy bar – check out the weird, welded furniture made from tank-tracks, camshafts and motorcycle chains – with staff decked out in Hawaiian shirts that are almost as loud as the blue and orange décor. Background tunes are upbeat but not intrusive and, if you get peckish, excellent Mexican munchies are available.

CASK & BARREL Map pp218-19

☎ 556 3132; 115 Broughton St; ⏲ 11am-12.30am Sun-Thu, 11am-1am Fri & Sat; 🚌 8 or 17

At the foot of Broughton St, the spit-and-sawdust style Cask & Barrel is a beer-drinker's delight, with a selection of up to 10 real ales, as well as Czech and German beers, and a more than adequate array of TV screens for keeping up with the football or rugby.

CLAREMONT BAR Map pp214-15

☎ 556 5662; 133-135 E Claremont St; ⏲ 11am-midnight Mon-Thu, 11am-1am Fri & Sat, 12.30-11pm Sun; 🚌 13

The Claremont is a friendly, gay-owned bar that looks like a fairly traditional Edinburgh pub at first glance, until you spot the sci-fi paraphernalia (check out the *Star Trek* clock and model USS *Enterprise* behind the bar, and the wee red-eyed alien up the stairs) and the flyers for the Absolutely Dragulous club night for cross-dressers. Saturday nights are men only, with themes ranging from Bearscots (hairy faces) on the first Saturday of the month to Gaykilts (speaks for itself!) on the second Saturday.

CLARK'S BAR Map pp218-19

☎ 556 1067; 142 Dundas St; ⏲ 11am-11pm Mon-Wed, 11am-11.30pm Thu-Sat, 12.30-11pm Sun; 🚌 23 or 27

A century old and still going strong, Clark's caters to a clientele of real-ale aficionados, football fans (there are three TVs), local office workers and loyal regulars, who appreciate an old-fashioned, no-frills pub with lots of wood panelling and polished brass, and cosy little back rooms for convivial storytelling.

MATHERS Map pp218-19

☎ 556 6754; 25 Broughton St; ⏲ 11am-midnight Mon-Thu, 11am-12.30am Fri & Sat, 12.30-11pm Sun; 🚌 8 or 17

Mathers is the 40-something generation's equivalent of the 20-something's Basement bar across the street: a friendly, relaxed pub with Edwardian décor serving real ales and good pub grub, with football and rugby matches on the TV.

PIVO Map pp218-19

☎ 557 2925; 2-6 Calton Rd; ⏲ 4pm-3am; 🚌 all Leith St buses

Aiming to add a little taste of Bohemia to Edinburgh's club scene, Pivo (Czech for 'beer') serves bottled and draught Czech beers – the Staropramen is God in a glass – and two-pint cocktails (try a 'longer absinthe', absinthe with lemonade and lime). Edinburgh's up-and-coming DJs are on hand to provide the soundtrack from 9pm till closing.

REGENT Map pp218-19

☎ 661 8198; 2 Montrose Tce; ⏲ 11am-1am Mon-Sat, 12.30pm-1am Sun; 🚌 15 or 35

This is a pleasant, gay local with a relaxed atmosphere (no loud music), serving coffee and croissants plus excellent real ales, including Deuchars IPA and Caledonian 80/-. Meeting place for the Lesbian and Gay Real Ale Drinkers club (first Monday of month, 9pm).

WEST END & STOCKBRIDGE

The West End and Haymarket are home to a handful of good old-fashioned pubs, plus a smattering of newer places. Drinking in Stockbridge is also a relaxed, traditional affair, involving comfy seats, conversation and real ale, wine or whisky – if it's a wild time you're after, look elsewhere.

ANTIQUARY Map pp218-19

☎ 225 2858; 72-78 St Stephen St; ⏲ 11.30am-12.30am Mon-Wed, 11.30am-1am Thu-Sun; 🚌 24, 29 or 42

A dark, downstairs den of traditional beersmanship, with bare wooden floorboards and dark wood tables and chairs, the long-established Antiquary has lively open folk-music sessions on Thursday nights, when all comers are welcome to perform.

BAILIE BAR Map pp218-19

☎ 225 4673; 2 St Stephen St; 🕑 11am-midnight Mon-Thu, 11am-1am Fri & Sat, 12.30-11pm Sun; 🚌 24, 29 or 42

Tucked down in a basement, the Bailie is an old Stockbridge stalwart, a dimly lit, warm and welcoming nook with a large circular island bar, a roaring fire in winter, and TVs screening the live football. Serves good coffee as well as real ales and malt whiskies.

BERT'S BAR Map p217

☎ 225 5748; 29-31 William St; 🕑 11am-11pm Mon-Wed, 11am-1am Thu-Sat; 🚌 all Shandwick Pl buses

A classic re-creation of a 1930s-style pub – a welcoming womb with a warm wood and leather décor, complete with a jar of pickled eggs on the bar – Bert's is a good place to sample real ale and down-to-earth pub grub such as Scotch pies and bangers and mash. There's another branch, under the same management, in **Stockbridge** (Map p217; ☎ 332 6345; 2 Raeburn Pl; 🕑 11am-midnight Mon-Thu, 11am-1am Fri & Sat, 12.30pm-1am Sun; 🚌 24, 29, 42).

CUBA NORTE Map p217

☎ 221 1430; 192 Morrison St; 🕑 noon-midnight Sun-Wed, noon-1am Thu-Sat; 🚌 all Haymarket buses

Swagger in, order a Cuba libre and prepare to salsa. Cuba Norte provides a little touch of Latino levity in the cold northern winters, dishing up good Cuban tapas and Havana cigars as well as hip-swaying salsa beats (dance sessions are held at 10pm Friday and Saturday). You can hone your technique at one of the regular salsa classes, held Monday to Thursday (beginners at 7pm, intermediates at 8pm, advanced at 9pm).

INDIGO YARD Map p217

☎ 220 5603; 7 Charlotte Lane; 🕑 8.30am-1am; 🚌 13, 19, 36, 37 or 41

Set around an airy, stone-floored and glass-roofed courtyard, Indigo Yard is a fashionable West-End watering hole that has been patronised by the likes of Liam Gallagher, Pierce Brosnan and Kylie Minogue. Good food – including open-air barbecues during the summer months – just adds to the attraction.

RYAN'S BAR Map pp218-19

☎ 226 6669; 2 Hope St; 🕑 10.30am-1am Mon-Sat, noon-midnight Sun; 🚌 13, 19, 36, 37 or 41

Housed in a former fruit market, Ryan's retains its original, impressive vaulted ceiling. It's best known as a lively bar where office workers gather at the end of the day (dress code: no jeans or trainers after 7pm), with DJs playing Thursday to Saturday in the main bar, and a pianist in the more intimate cellar bar. In summer there are outdoor tables, and good food is served all day.

DALRY & MORNINGSIDE

Despite their differences, middle-class Morningside and rough-and-ready Dalry are both well supplied with a range of atmospheric real-ale pubs.

ATHLETIC ARMS (THE DIGGERS) Map p226

☎ 337 3822; 1-3 Angle Park Tce; 🕑 noon-midnight Mon-Thu, noon-1am Fri & Sat, 12.30-6pm Sun; 🚌 1, 28 or 34

Named for the cemetery across the street – the grave-diggers used to nip in and slake their thirst after a hard day's interring – the Diggers dates from the 1890s. Its heyday as a real-ale drinker's mecca has gone, but the beer is still good and it's still staunchly traditional – the décor has barely changed in 100 years – and it's packed to the gills with football and rugby fans on match days.

CALEY SAMPLE ROOM Map p226

☎ 337 7204; 58 Angle Pk Tce; 🕑 11am-midnight Mon-Thu, 11am-1am Fri & Sat, 12.30pm-midnight Sun; 🚌 4, 28, 34, 35 or 44

Owned by the nearby **Caledonian Brewery** (p74), the Sample Room is a big, lively pub with a wide range of excellent real ales. It's popular with sports fans too, who gather to watch football and rugby matches on the large-screen TVs.

CANNY MAN'S Map p226

☎ 447 1484; 237 Morningside Rd; 🕑 11.30am-11pm Mon-Wed, 11.30am-midnight Thu-Sat, 12.30-11pm Sun; 🚌 11, 15, 16, 17 or 23

A lovably eccentric pub, the Canny Man's is a crowded warren of tiny rooms crammed

THE OTHER NATIONAL DRINK…

Here's a fascinating piece of trivia: there are only two countries in the world where a locally manufactured soft drink challenges Coca-Cola for the title of biggest selling soft drink: Scotland and Peru. And in both countries the local drink is brightly coloured and tastes of bubble gum. In Peru the challenger is Inca Cola, and in Scotland it's Barr's Irn-Bru (promoted since the 1980s as 'Scotland's other national drink'), which has long outsold Coca-Cola but is currently neck and neck (each has around 25% of the market).

Barr's has been making soft drinks in Scotland since 1880, but it was in 1901 that it launched a new beverage called 'Iron-Brew' (labelling regulations forced a change of spelling to 'Irn-Bru' in 1946). As with Coke, the recipe (32 ingredients, including caffeine and ammonium ferric citrate – the source of the iron in the name) remains a closely guarded secret known by only two people. Scots swear by its efficacy as a cure for hangovers, which may account for its massive sales. You can even get Irn-Bru along with your Big Mac in Scottish branches of McDonald's.

In recent years Barr's has begun to build its brand overseas, exporting its quirky, humorous and award-winning advertising campaigns portraying Irn-Bru drinkers as mischievous and rascally. Irn-Bru is popular in Russia, where it is the third-favourite soft drink after Coke and Pepsi (maybe it's that hangover thing again), and in the Middle East, but it has yet to challenge Coke and Pepsi in the USA. In fact, it is listed by the US Food and Drug Administration as a banned substance, because it contains banned artificial colourings.

Tasting Notes

Colour is a rusty, radioactive orange. Nosing reveals a bouquet of bubble gum, barley sugar and something vaguely citrus, maybe tangerine? Carbonation is medium, and mouth-feel…well, you can almost feel the enamel dissolving on your teeth.

with a bizarre collection of antiques and curiosities (a description that could apply to some of the regulars), where the landlord regularly refuses entry to anyone who looks scruffy, inebriated or vaguely pinko/commie/subversive. If you can get in, you'll find it serves excellent real ale, vintage port and Cuban cigars.

GOLDEN RULE Map p226

☎ 622 7112; 30 Yeaman Pl; 🕑 11am-11.30pm Mon-Sat, 12.30-11pm Sun; 🚌 10 or 27

Hard to find but worth the hunt, the Golden Rule is a great wee boozer with a lively atmosphere and up to eight real ales on tap. The main bar is stuffed with friendly locals (there's a lively and competitive pub quiz on Tuesday evenings), and the smaller side-room down the steps has an excellent jukebox.

TOLLCROSS & BRUNTSFIELD

Tollcross, formerly a working-class industrial district, has a good range of traditional, real-ale pubs, though designer bars are beginning to make inroads, especially in the trendier district of Bruntsfield to the south.

BENNET'S BAR Map pp224-5

☎ 229 5143; 8 Leven St; 🕑 11am-12.30am Mon-Wed, 11am-1am Thu-Sat, 12.30-11.30pm Sun; 🚌 all Tollcross buses

Bennet's has managed to retain almost all of its beautiful Victorian fittings, from the leaded stained-glass windows and ornate mirrors to the wooden gantry and brass water taps on the bar. If whisky is your poison, there are over 100 malts to choose from.

BLUE BLAZER Map pp218-19

☎ 229 5030; 2 Spittal St; 🕑 11am-1am Mon-Sat, 12.30pm-1am Sun; 🚌 2 or 35

With its bare wooden floors, cosy fireplace and efficient bar staff, the Blue Blazer is a down-to-earth antidote to the designer excess of Monboddo across the road, catering to a loyal clientele of real-ale enthusiasts, pie eaters and Saturday horse-racing fans.

CLOISTERS Map pp218-19

☎ 221 9997; 26 Brougham St; 🕑 noon-midnight Sun-Thu, noon-12.30am Fri & Sat; 🚌 24

Housed in a converted manse (minister's house) that once belonged to the next-door church, and furnished with well-worn, mismatched wooden tables and chairs,

The bar at Oxygen (opposite)

Cloisters now ministers to a mixed congregation of students, locals and real-ale connoisseurs. It has decent grub and coffee, and a nice warm fireplace in winter.

MONBODDO BAR Map pp218-19
☎ 221 5555; 34 Bread St; ⌚ 11am-midnight Mon-Thu, 11am-1am Fri & Sat, noon-midnight Sun; 🚌 2 or 35
Tollcross is better known for its traditional pubs than for the sleek designer looks of the Monboddo, part of the Point Hotel. The polished steel bar, spindly chairs, chocolate-leather banquettes and modern artworks are complemented by efficient, friendly staff who know how to mix a superb champagne cocktail.

MONTPELIERS Map p226
☎ 229 3115; 159-161 Bruntsfield Pl; ⌚ 9am-1am; 🚌 all Bruntsfield buses
The 'in' place to down a pint in Bruntsfield, Monty's is packed at weekends with rugby-playing, public-school-educated financial analysts chasing sun-tanned, blonde Emmas and Carolines just back from skiing in St Moritz or villa-hunting in Tuscany. The food (see p115) and the beer are good, though.

SOUTHSIDE & NEWINGTON

Southside's large student population is well served by lots of stylish pre-club bars and café-bars clustered around Edinburgh University's George Sq and Old College buildings.

ASSEMBLY BAR Map p222
☎ 220 4288; 41 Lothian St; ⌚ 9am-1am; 🚌 2, 41 or 42
Assembly originally opened in 1996 (as Iguana), making it positively prehistoric for a style bar, but a combination of timeless décor, cool sounds, big sofas and good-value food has kept it popular. There's a relaxed crowd of mostly students topping up on coffee during the day, but the atmosphere heats up as pre-clubbers pour in during the evening.

BOROUGH Map pp224-5
☎ 668 2255; 72-80 Causewayside; ⌚ 11am-1am; 🚌 42
The Borough Hotel's bar brings a whiff of the *Sex and the City* lifestyle to the Southside, with its broad expanses of timber flooring, deep leather sofas, expertly

assembled cocktails and an extensive menu of carefully chosen wines. The Bloody Borough Mary cocktail has no less than 10 perfectly judged ingredients, and could just as easily create a hangover as cure one.

CENTRAAL Map pp218-19

☎ 667 7355; 32 W Nicolson St; 11am-1am Mon-Sat, 11am-midnight Sun; 42

This relaxing Belgian-themed bar is set in an atmospherically lit underground vault of bare brick, fairy lights, candles and vast voluptuous leather sofas that you can easily lose yourself in. It has an extensive menu of Belgian and other international beers (from around 25 different countries), excellent coffee, and an all-day menu of tasty food.

HUMAN BE-IN Map pp218-19

☎ 662 8860; 2-8 W Crosscauseway; 11am-1am Mon-Fri, noon-1am Sat & Sun; 42

A stylish café-bar with a choice of tables, comfy booths or chill-out sofas (plus outdoor tables in summer), the Be-In is a popular hang-out for moneyed students (Edinburgh University is across the road). It has live jazz on Sunday nights, and DJs playing on Friday and Saturday nights from 9pm. The bar also has an inventive Mediterranean/Asian menu with good vegetarian options.

OXYGEN Map p222

☎ 557 9997; 3 Infirmary St; 10am-1am; all South Bridge buses

Oxygen is a popular pre-club venue with industrial-chic décor, cool tunes, cocktails, a range of imported beers and a tempting food menu. There's a resident DJ pumping out house music from Wednesday to Sunday, and live jazz on Tuesday nights at 9pm.

PEAR TREE HOUSE Map p222

☎ 667 7533; 38 W Nicolson St; 11am-midnight Mon-Thu, 11am-1am Fri & Sat, 12.30pm-midnight Sun; 2, 41 or 42

The Pear Tree is another student favourite, with comfy sofas and board games inside, plus the city centre's biggest beer garden outside. There's live music in the garden on Sunday afternoons in summer.

TOP FIVE COFFEE BREAKS

Elephant House Café (Map p222; ☎ 220 5355; 21 George IV Bridge; 8am-11pm; 2, 23, 27, 41 or 42) Here you'll find counters at the front, tables with views of the castle at the back, and little effigies and images of elephants everywhere. Excellent cappuccino and homemade food – pizzas, quiches, pies, sandwiches and cakes – at reasonable prices make it deservedly popular with students, shoppers and office workers.

Glass & Thompson (Map pp218-19; ☎ 557 0909; 2 Dundas St; 8.30am-6pm Mon-Sat, 10.30am-4.30pm Sun; 23 or 27) Grab a table in this spick and span New Town deli and sip a double espresso as you ogle the cheeses in the cold counter or watch the world go by through the floor-to-ceiling windows. Munchies include tasty platters such as dolmades and falafel, or Parma ham and Parmesan.

Plaisir du Chocolat (Map p222; ☎ 556 9524; 253 Canongate, Royal Mile; 10am-6pm; 35) This elegant Art Nouveau *salon du thé* is a little corner of chocolate heaven: thick, sweet French-style hot chocolate, chocolate espresso, handmade chocolates, chocolate cakes and chocolate pastries are all on the menu.

Starbucks (Map pp218-19; ☎ 226 5881; 120b Princes St; 7.30am-8pm Mon-Sat, 9.30am-6pm Sun; all Princes St buses) You may not approve of its plans for world domination, and the coffee is only so-so, but there's no denying that Starbucks' Princes St flagship – reputedly the largest coffee shop in Scotland – enjoys what is probably the best view in the city. Settle down in an armchair and take in the breathtaking panorama of the castle and gardens across the street.

Valvona & Crolla Caffè Bar (Map pp218-19; ☎ 556 6066; 19 Elm Row, Leith Walk; 8am-6pm Mon-Sat, 11am-4.30pm Sun; all Leith Walk buses) Outside the busy lunch period (noon to 3pm; see Eating p111), this deli café serves up authentic strong Italian coffee accompanied by bitter chocolate cake or genuine Italian lemon tart.

HOW TO BE A MALT WHISKY BUFF

'Love makes the world go round? Not at all! Whisky makes it go round twice as fast.'

From Whisky Galore, *by Compton Mackenzie (1883-1972).*

Whisky tasting today is almost as popular as wine tasting was in the yuppie heyday of the late 1980s. Being able to tell your Ardbeg from your Edradour is *de rigueur* among the whisky-nosing set, so here are some pointers to help you impress your friends.

What's the difference between malt and grain whiskies?

Malts are distilled from malted barley – that is, barley that has been soaked in water, then allowed to germinate for around 10 days until the starch has turned into sugar – while grain whiskies are distilled from other cereals, usually wheat, corn or unmalted barley.

So what is a single malt?

A single malt is a whisky that has been distilled from malted barley and is the product of a single distillery. A pure (vatted) malt is a mixture of single malts from several distilleries, and a blended whisky is a mixture of various grain whiskies (about 60%) and malt whiskies (about 40%) from many different distilleries.

Why are single malts more desirable than blends?

A single malt, like a fine wine, somehow captures the essence of the place where it was made and matured – a combination of the water, the barley, the peat smoke, the oak barrels in which it was aged, and (in the case of certain coastal distilleries) the sea air and salt spray. Each distillation varies from the one before, like different vintages from the same vineyard.

How should a single malt be drunk?

Either neat, or preferably with a little water added. To appreciate the aroma and flavour to the utmost, a measure of malt whisky should be cut (diluted) with one-third to two-thirds as much spring water (still, bottled spring water will do). Ice, tap water – except for Edinburgh's exceptionally clean-tasting tap water – and (God forbid) mixers are for Philistines. Would you add lemonade or ice to a glass of Chablis?

Give me some tasting tips!

Go into a bar and order a Lagavulin (Islay) and a Glenfiddich (Speyside). Taking each one in turn, hold the glass up to the light to check the colour; stick your nose in the glass and take two or three short, sharp sniffs, followed by a sip or two. Then cut each one with half as much again of still, bottled spring water, and repeat the process. By now, everyone in the pub will be giving you funny looks, but never mind.

For the Lagavulin you should be thinking: amber colour, peat-smoke, iodine, seaweed. For the Glenfiddich: pale white-wine colour, malt, pear drops, acetone, citrus. Then try some others. Either you'll be hooked, or you'll wake up next morning with the headache from hell and a tongue like a bar-room carpet and never touch whisky again.

Where's the cheapest place to buy Scotch whisky?

A French supermarket, unfortunately. In the UK, where a bottle of single malt typically costs £25 to £35, taxes account for around 72% of the price, making Scotland one of the most expensive places in Europe to enjoy its own national drink.

If you're serious about spirits, the **Scotch Malt Whisky Society** (Map p216; ☎ 0131-554 3451; www.smws.com) has branches all round the world. Membership of the society costs from £70 per year and includes use of members' rooms in Edinburgh and London.

SOUTHSIDER Map p222

☎ 667 2003; 3-7 W Richmond St; 🕑 11am-midnight Mon-Wed, 11am-1am Thu-Sat, 12.30pm-midnight Sun; 🚌 all Newington buses

Always busy with students and regulars, the Southsider is a big, old-fashioned, slightly rough-around-the-edges pub that pulls in people from further afield with a good selection of real ales, table football, Wednesday night pub quizzes, and live music on Thursday, Saturday and Sunday.

WATERFRONT EDINBURGH

As befits a dockland area, Leith and Newhaven are well supplied with old-fashioned pubs, once the haunts of shore-going sailors but now increasingly gentrified for the district's new upmarket residents.

CAMEO BAR Map p216

☎ 554 9999; 23 Commercial St; ⌚ noon-1am; 🚌 16, 22, 35 or 36

How's this for bar-room games one-upmanship? Forget table football, darts or pool; this pub has its own six-hole putting green out the back! When you're not practising your golfing skills, the bright red Cameo offers a warm, relaxing bar with open fire in winter, good food, live music and a giant-screen TV for sporting occasions.

CARRIERS QUARTERS Map p216

☎ 554 4122; 42 Bernard St; ⌚ 11am-11pm Sun-Wed, 11am-midnight Thu, 11am-1am Fri & Sat; 🚌 16, 22, 35 or 36

With a low wooden ceiling, stone walls and a fine old fireplace, the Carriers has all the historic atmosphere that its 18th-century origins would imply. It serves real ales and malt whiskies, and traditional Scottish bar meals such as stovies and haggis.

OLD CHAIN PIER Map pp214-15

☎ 552 1233; 32 Trinity Cres; ⌚ noon-11pm Mon-Wed, noon-midnight Thu-Sat, 12.30-11pm Sun; 🚌 16 or 32

As well as being a great place to eat (see p119), the Old Chain Pier is an award-winning real ale pub, full of polished wood, brass and nautical paraphernalia: the building was once the 19th-century booking office for steamers across the Firth of Forth. The pier from which it takes its name was washed away in a storm in 1898.

OLD DOCK BAR Map p216

☎ 555 4474; 3-5 Dock Pl; ⌚ 11am-11pm Mon-Thu, 11am-midnight Fri & Sat, 12.30-11pm Sun; 🚌 16, 22, 35 or 36

Although it has been through several incarnations since it opened in 1813, the Old Dock Bar has now returned to its original role of a convivial, traditional Leith pub, with cosy wood-partitioned booths indoors, and outdoor tables overlooking the water in summer. It serves good old-fashioned tavern food such as seafood pie and devilled whitebait, as well as a good range of real ales and quality wines.

PORT O'LEITH Map p216

☎ 554 3568; 58 Constitution St; ⌚ 9am-12.45am Mon-Sat, 12.30pm-12.45am Sun; 🚌 12, 16 or 35

Open from early morning to serve local dock workers, this is a good old-fashioned, friendly local boozer with an anchor above the door and a cosy interior swathed with flags and cap bands left behind by visiting sailors (the harbour is just down the road). Pop in for a pint and you'll end up staying till closing time.

STARBANK INN Map pp214-15

☎ 552 4141; 64 Laverockbank Rd; ⌚ 11am-11pm Mon-Wed, 11am-midnight Thu-Sat, 12.30-11pm Sun; 🚌 16 or 32

Along with the Old Chain Pier, the Starbank is an oasis of fine ales and good homemade food on Edinburgh's windswept waterfront. There's a conservatory and beer garden at the back, in winter a blazing fire to toast your toes in front of, and live folk music on Sunday afternoons.

GREATER EDINBURGH

HAWES INN

☎ 331 1990; Newhalls Rd, Queensferry; 🕑 11am-11pm Mon-Sat, 12.30-10.30pm Sun; 🚌 First Edinburgh 43

This 350-year-old coaching inn, famously mentioned in *The Antiquary* by Sir Walter Scott and in Robert Louis Stevenson's *Kidnapped,* is an atmospheric warren of rustic rooms tucked beneath the southern end of the Forth Bridge. It's a child-friendly place serving excellent pub grub, with a main menu ranging from fresh sandwiches to haggis, steaks and seafood, plus a kids' menu. There are outdoor tables in summer.

SHEEP HEID Map pp214-15

☎ 656 6951; 43-45 the Causeway, Duddingston; 🕑 11am-11pm Mon-Wed, 11am-midnight Thu-Sat, 12.30-11pm Sun; 🚌 42

Possibly the oldest licensed premises in Edinburgh – dating back to 1360 – the Sheep Heid is more like a country pub than a city bar. Set in the semi-rural shadow of Arthur's Seat in Duddingston, it's famous for its 19th-century skittles alley and lovely beer garden. The name comes from an ornamental snuff box in the form of a sheep's head that was presented to the inn by James VI in 1580, commemorated in a carving which sits above the bar.

Entertainment

Entertainment

Glasgow folk have a colourful expression – 'all fur coat and nae knickers' – that they apply to Edinburgh, suggesting that it projects an air of middle-class respectability on the surface but is cheap and dirty underneath. There's an element of truth there – the city that inspired the story of Jekyll and Hyde certainly has its seamier side – and the high culture epitomised in the Edinburgh Festival finds its counterpoint in the city's reputation as a pub-crawler's paradise.

Edinburgh has a number of fine theatres and concert halls, and there are independent art-house cinemas as well as mainstream movie theatres. Many pubs offer entertainment ranging from live Scottish folk music to pop, rock and jazz to karaoke and quiz nights, while the new generation of style bars purvey house, dance and hip-hop to the pre-clubbing crowd (see the Drinking chapter, p122, for more information).

CINEMA

Film buffs will find plenty to keep them happy in Edinburgh's art-house cinemas, the Filmhouse and the Cameo, while popcorn munchers can choose from a range of multiplexes. Most offer concessions for school kids, students, the unemployed and senior citizens, and most have wheelchair access and induction loops for hearing-impaired customers.

You can check cinema listings in the *Edinburgh Evening News* newspaper and the *List*.

CAMEO Map pp224-5

Box office ☎ 228 4141, info ☎ 228 2800; 38 Home St; tickets adult/child £5.90/3.50; 🚌 10, 11, 15, 16 or 17

The independently owned, three-screen Cameo is a good old-fashioned cinema showing an imaginative mix of mainstream as well as art-house movies. There is a good programme of midnight movies, late-night double bills and Sunday matinees, and the seats in Screen 1 are big enough for you to get lost in. At the time of writing, the Cameo was up for sale and its future was uncertain; however, plans to convert it to a pub have been blocked and supporters have launched a campaign to preserve its historic auditorium, which dates from 1914, as an art-house cinema (see www.savethecameo.org).

CINEWORLD Map p226

☎ 0871 200 2000; 130 Dundee St; tickets adult/child £5.80/3.60; 🚌 1, 28, 34 or 35

Cineworld is a massive 12-screen multiplex, complete with café-bar, movie-poster shop and scarily overpriced popcorn.

DOMINION Map p226

Box office ☎ 447 4771, info ☎ 447 2660; 18 Newbattle Tce; tickets adult/child £6.10/3.90; 🚌 11, 15, 16, 17 or 23

The much-loved Dom is a delightful independent, family-run four-screener in a 1938 Art Deco building. The programme is unashamedly mainstream and family-oriented, and popular films often have a good old-fashioned intermission so you can buy an ice cream halfway through.

FILMHOUSE Map pp218-19

Box office ☎ 228 2688, info ☎ 228 2689; 88 Lothian Rd; tickets adult/child £5.80/4.20; 🚌 all Lothian Rd buses

The Filmhouse screens a full programme of art-house, classic, foreign and second-run

Edinburgh Playhouse (p148)

WHAT'S ON

Edinburgh's most comprehensive source of what's-on information is the *List* (www.list.co.uk; £2.20), an excellent fortnightly listings and reviews magazine (also covering Glasgow) available from most newsagents. It now has some competition in the form of the *Skinny* (www.skinnymag.co.uk), another listings mag covering both Edinburgh and Glasgow.

The *Gig Guide* (www.gigguide.co.uk) is a free monthly leaflet that advertises regular music gigs under the headings 'Rock, Pop & Blues', 'Jazz' and 'Folk & World'; you can pick it up in bars, cafés and music venues. The free monthly booklet *What's On Edinburgh & Lothians* (www.whatson-scotland.co.uk) covers a wide range of events and exhibitions, including art galleries and museums. The *Edinburgh Evening News* newspaper has daily reviews and listings of cinema, music, theatre, clubs, comedy and arts events.

Some online ticket agencies that service a range of Edinburgh venues and events, from rock gigs to rugby matches:

See (☎ 0870 264 3333; www.seetickets.com)

Ticketline (☎ 0870 444 5556; www.ticketline.co.uk)

Ticketmaster (☎ 0870 534 4444; www.ticketmaster.co.uk)

Ticketweb (☎ 0870 060 0100; www.ticketweb.co.uk)

films, with lots of themes, retrospectives and 70mm screenings, and is the main venue for the annual International Film Festival. It has wheelchair access to all screens. Matinees and early evening screenings are cheaper, and the bargain Friday matinees (starting before 4pm) cost only £3/1.70 per adult/child.

ODEON Map pp218-19

☎ 0871 224 4007; 118 Lothian Rd; tickets adult/child £6/4.80; 🚌 all Lothian Rd buses

This five-screen multiplex shows mainstream and first-run films and special children's matinees. All screens have wheelchair access.

VUE CINEMA Map pp218-19

☎ 0871 224 0240; Omni Centre, Greenside Pl; tickets adult/child £6/3.80; 🚌 all Leith Walk buses

A 12-screen multiplex, with three 'Gold Class' screens (tickets cost £8.50) where you can watch your movie of choice from the comfort of a luxurious leather reclining seat complete with side table for your drink and complimentary snacks. There's a second Vue multiplex at Ocean Terminal in **Leith** (Map p216).

COMEDY

Stand-up comedy has come to dominate the Fringe in the last decade, and its popularity has spun off a couple of decent comedy clubs and countless comedy nights in various pubs – check the Comedy listings in the *List*.

BEDLAM THEATRE Map p222

☎ 225 9893; www.improverts.com; 11b Bristo Pl; admission £3.50; 🚌 2, 23, 27, 41 or 42

The Bedlam hosts a long-established (more than 10 years) weekly improvisation slot, the Improverts, which is hugely popular with local students. Shows kick off at 10.30pm every Friday, and you're guaranteed a robust and entertaining evening.

JONGLEURS Map pp218-19

☎ 0870 787 0707; www.jongleurs.com; Omni Centre, Greenside Pl; admission £12-20; 🚌 all Leith Walk buses

This branch of the nationwide chain of comedy clubs, housed in the Omni Centre at the top of Leith Walk, stages comedy shows on Friday and Saturday nights all year round, with four in-house stand-ups and occasional gigs by big-name UK comics. The shows end at 11pm, but you can keep on drinking and dancing until 3am.

STAND COMEDY CLUB Map pp218-19

☎ 558 7272; www.thestand.co.uk; 5 York Pl; admission £1-10; 🚌 all York Pl buses

The Stand, founded in 1995, is Edinburgh's main comedy venue. It's a cabaret bar – you can eat and drink as well as laugh – with shows every night (doors open 7.30pm), plenty of big-name appearances, and a free improv show at Sunday lunch time.

CLUBBING

Edinburgh's club scene took a nose dive a few years back, with attendances falling as the huge crowds and huge venues that characterised the late 1990s were deserted in favour of more intimate DJ sessions in late-night style bars. In response, Edinburgh's clubs have become more diverse and stage a wider mix of cultural events, including live gigs, comedy and even art exhibitions.

Most of the venues are concentrated in and around the twin sumps of Cowgate and Calton Rd, to either side of the Royal Mile – so it's downhill all the way…

Club nights are fickle things, coming and going with the seasons; for details check the latest issue of the *List* and look for flyers in pre-club bars and record shops – Underground Solush'n (see p152) in Cockburn St is a good place for information.

BONGO CLUB Map pp218-19

☎ 558 8844; www.thebongoclub.co.uk; Moray House, Paterson's Land, 37 Holyrood Rd; 🚌 35

During the day the weird and wonderful Bongo Club offers a café-bar and exhibition space, and transforms at night into one of the city's coolest club venues; it also hosts live music, theatre, cabaret, and 'any other art form'. It's still famous for the resident hip-hop, funk and breakbeat night **Headspin** (admission £8; 🕒 10.30pm-3am, 2nd Sat of month); also worth checking out is the booming bass of roots-and-dub reggae night **Messenger Sound System** (admission £7; 🕒 11pm-3am, 1st & 3rd Sat of month).

CABARET VOLTAIRE Map p222

☎ 220 6176; www.cabaret-voltaire.co.uk; 36 Blair St; 🚌 35

An atmospheric warren of stone-lined vaults houses Edinburgh's most 'alternative' club, which eschews huge dance floors and egotistical DJ-worship in favour of a 'creative crucible' hosting an eclectic mix of DJs, live acts, comedy, theatre, visual arts and the spoken word. Well worth a look.

CC BLOOMS Map pp218-19

☎ 556 9331; 23 Greenside Pl; 🕒 6pm-3am Mon-Sat, 8pm-3am Sun; 🚌 all Leith St buses

The raddled old queen of the Edinburgh gay scene, CC's offers two floors of deafening dance and disco. It's a bit overpriced and often overcrowded but still worth a visit – if you can get past the bouncers and the crowds of drunks looking for a late drink.

EGO Map pp218-19

☎ 478 7434; 14 Picardy Pl; 🚌 8 or 17

A glitzy two-floor venue in a former casino decked out with huge Renaissance-style wall paintings, gay-friendly Ego dishes up everything from the hard house, trance and techno of **NuklearPuppy** (admission £8; 🕒 10.30pm-3am, 2nd Fri of month) to the dance classics of **Fever** (admission £12; 🕒 11pm-3am, 3rd Sat of month).

EL BARRIO Map pp218-19

☎ 229 8805; www.elbarrio.co.uk; 104 West Port; admission free, after midnight Fri & Sat £5; 🕒 10pm-3am Sun-Thu, 9pm-3am Fri & Sat; 🚌 2 or 35

Edinburgh's sizable Spanish-speaking community congregates at this lively Latino bar to clink Cuba libres, slurp minty *mojitos* and get down to some naughty Latin-American rhythms. There's a club session every night, and if you're not sure of your moves there are pre-club salsa classes too (see p140).

HONEYCOMB Map p222

☎ 556 2442; www.the-honeycomb.com; 15-17 Niddry St; 🚌 35

Tucked away in the underground vaults beneath South Bridge, Honeycomb is one of Edinburgh's hottest clubs. It is home to the long-running **Manga** (admission £9; 🕒 10.30pm-3am, 3rd Sat of month), Edinburgh's unmissable drum'n'bass club, as well as the consistently crowded classics night **Motherfunk** (admission free; 🕒 10.30pm-3am Tue) and new grime and hip-hop club **Mardi Grah** (£10; check website for dates).

LIQUID ROOM Map p222

☎ 225 2564; www.liquidroom.com; 9c Victoria St; 🚌 2, 23, 27, 41 or 42

Set in a subterranean vault deep beneath Victoria St, the Liquid Room is a superb

TOP FIVE PRE-CLUB BARS

- **Assembly Bar** (p130)
- **Borough** (p130)
- **Opal Lounge** (p125)
- **Oxygen** (p131)
- **Pivo** (p127)

club venue with a thundering sound system. There are weekly club nights Wednesday to Friday and Sunday – the long-running **Evol** (admission £5; 10.30pm-3am Fri) is an Edinburgh institution catering to the indie-kid crowd, and is regularly voted as Scotland's top club night out, while the gay-friendly garage and house night **Taste** (admission £8; 11pm-3am Sun) is always packed out.

OPIUM Map p222

225 8382; www.opiumrocks.com; 71 Cowgate; 2 or 35

This traditionally grungy venue in the tunnel-like trench of central Cowgate houses the dark and stylish Opium, the city's top rock club. Friday and Saturday nights are a thrash-fest of alternative rock, metal, nu-metal and indie, while the popular **Toxik** (admission free; 11pm-3am Wed) describes itself as 'the sinister side of all things metal'.

PLANET OUT Map pp218-19

524 0061; 6 Baxter's Pl; 4pm-1am Mon-Fri, 2pm-1am Sat & Sun; all Leith St buses

Planet Out is a stylish gay bar and club that pulls in a younger crowd than CC Blooms and has a better party atmosphere at the weekends – it's a bit quieter through the week, when you can chill out on the sofas and blether.

RED VODKA CLUB Map p222

225 1757; www.redvodkaclub.co.uk; 73 Cowgate; 8pm-3am; 2 or 35

Red is a stylish, dimly lit, cellarlike venue with a bar that specialises in flavoured and frozen vodkas. Pretty much every night is a club night, with drinks promos during the week; Fridays focus on funk, disco and r'n'b, Saturdays are for classic dance and party tunes.

STEREO Map pp218-19

229 9438; www.clubstereo.co.uk; 28 King's Stables Rd; 28

Stereo pulls in a pissed-up, studenty, dance-till-you-puke crowd, who queue up for the weekly **Shagtag** (admission £5; 10pm-3am Tue), a hugely successful student night which involves a complicated snogging-by-numbers event. Weekends are devoted to party nights, with the crowds gamely thrashing away to a soundtrack of pop, funk, disco and house while trying not to barf up the gallon of cheap promo drinks they just downed.

STUDIO 24 Map pp218-19

558 3758; www.studio24edinburgh.co.uk; 24 Calton Rd; 35

Studio 24 has two levels, with an intimate, relaxed drinking area above the main, sweaty dance floor. The programme covers all bases, from house to Goth to nu-metal. The **Mission** (admission £5; 11pm-3am Sat) is the city's classic Goth and metal night (with Junior Mission, for under-18s, running 7pm to 10pm the same evening), while the newer **Orange Street** (admission £2; 11pm-3am, 2nd Fri of month) offers a pounding menu of ska, reggae and dancehall.

SUBWAY Map p222

225 6766; www.subwayclubs.co.uk; 69 Cowgate; admission before midnight free, after midnight £1-2; 7pm-3am; 2 or 35

Set in the darkest and dingiest part of the Cowgate, Subway is famed as a dark and dingy club where you can lose yourself in a heaving mass of sweaty students stomping away to a deafening soundtrack of cheesy chart hits. Recently it has diversified, offering rock, indie and punk from **Misfits** (admission free; 11pm-3am Tue) and a fortnightly Goth night, **Neon** (admission free; 11pm-3am Sun).

VENUE Map pp218-19

557 3073; www.edinvenue.com; 17-23 Calton Rd; 35

Spread over three floors, the Venue is an old-school club of the sticky floors and scuffed furniture variety, a vast, bare-brick and wood-panelled venue with an air of faded grandeur; try the **Tokyo Blu** (admission £5; 10.30pm-3am, 1st Sat of month) club night for laid-back Latin funk, electro and disco. The Venue is also home to

TOP FIVE GAY CLUBS

- **CC Blooms** (opposite)
- **Ego** (opposite)
- **Liquid Room** (opposite)
- **Planet Out** (left)
- **Venue** (above)

GAY & LESBIAN EDINBURGH

Edinburgh has a small – but perfectly formed – gay and lesbian scene, centred on the area around Broughton St (known affectionately as 'The Pink Triangle') at the eastern end of the New Town. Although not as mad, bad and dangerous to know as the Glasgow scene, it has enough pubs and clubs to keep the boozing and cruising crowd happy.

There are several club nights that are gay- or lesbian-only or that attract a large gay contingent. A few of the more permanent fixtures are mentioned in the Clubbing section of this chapter, but as club nights and venues change often, it's best to check *ScotsGay* magazine (www.scotsgay.com) or the *List* for the latest details. For community contacts see p196.

Joy (www.clubjoy.co.uk; admission £8-10; 11pm-3am, last Sat of month), Edinburgh's longest-running and most upfront gay club night.

WEE RED BAR Map pp218-19

229 1442; Edinburgh College of Art, Lauriston Pl; 23, 27, 35 or 45

The Wee Red Bar at the College of Art has been around so long there's a danger the authorities will slap a blue plaque on it and declare it a national monument. Wee, red and frequented, hardly surprisingly, by lots of art students, it's famous for the **Egg** (admission £4.50; 11pm-3am Sat), a weekly smorgasbord of classic punk, ska, northern soul, indie etc that is still one of the best club nights in the city.

WHY NOT? Map pp218-19

624 8633; 14 George St; admission £3-7.50; 10pm-3am Fri & Sat; all St Andrew Sq buses

Located downstairs to the right of the Dome, Why Not? is a sophisticated club playing mainstream chart sounds to a well-heeled 30-something New Town crowd. Dress smart and be sure to raid a cash machine on the way.

DANCE

Whether you prefer to watch a performance or get up and perform yourself, Edinburgh has a varied and invigorating selection of dance venues.

DANCE BASE Map p222

225 5525; www.dancebase.co.uk; 14-16 Grassmarket; 8am-9.30pm Mon-Fri, 10am-5.45pm Sat; 2

Scotland's National Centre for Dance is a complex of dance studios housed in a spectacular modern building in the shadow of the castle; it's worth a visit for the architecture alone. The centre runs courses in all kinds of dance – from ballroom to belly, hip-hop to Highland, tango to tap – as well as hosting workshops and performances.

EDINBURGH FESTIVAL THEATRE Map p222

529 6000; www.eft.co.uk; 13-29 Nicolson St; tickets £8-50; box office 10am-6pm Mon-Sat, till 8pm on show nights; all South Bridge buses

The curving glass-and-steel façade of the Festival Theatre houses the city's main venue for ballet, contemporary dance and opera; it also stages musicals, concerts, drama and children's shows. Performances by the critically acclaimed **Scottish Ballet** (www.scottishballet.co.uk) are a regular feature of the programme. Based in Dundee, the **Scottish Dance Theatre** (www.scottishdancetheatre.com/home) occasionally performs in Edinburgh, usually at the Edinburgh Festival Theatre.

EL BARRIO Map pp218-19

229 8805; www.elbarrio.co.uk; 104 West Port; admission free; 10pm Thu & Sun, 9pm Fri & Sat; 2 or 35

Perfect your dips and hone those merengue moves at El Barrio's salsa classes before burning up the dance floor at the ensuing Latino club night. Beginners are welcome, and there's no need to book or even bring a partner – just turn up and start dancing. **Cuba Norte** (p128) also hosts salsa dance classes and sessions.

THISTLE HOTEL Map pp218-19

556 0111; edinburgh@thistle.co.uk; 107 Leith St; show & dinner £46.50, show only £25; 6.45pm Apr-Oct; all Leith St buses

The Thistle Hotel stages 'Jamie's Scottish Evening', a night of Scottish country dancing, music, songs and comedy accompanied by a four-course dinner (including the chance to try some haggis).

MUSIC

It's not only at Festival time that Edinburgh comes alive with the sound of music – the city has a wide range of venues offering classical, rock, folk and jazz all year round.

CLASSICAL MUSIC & OPERA

Edinburgh is home to the **Scottish Chamber Orchestra** (SCO; www.sco.org.uk), one of Europe's finest and well worth hearing. Its performances are usually held at the Queen's Hall or the Usher Hall.

The **Scottish Opera** (www.scottishopera.org.uk) and the **Royal Scottish National Orchestra** (RSNO; www.rsno.org.uk) are based in Glasgow but regularly perform in Edinburgh, at the Edinburgh Festival Theatre and Usher Hall respectively.

GREYFRIARS KIRK Map p222

☎ 226 5429; Greyfriars Pl; tickets £6-12; 2, 23, 27, 41 or 42

The Edinburgh Symphony Orchestra, established in 1964 and composed of amateur musicians, performs concerts here, usually in March, May and November. There are regular organ recitals and concerts throughout the year – contact the **Edinburgh and Scotland Information Centre** (see p200) for details.

QUEEN'S HALL Map pp224-5

☎ 668 2019; www.queenshalledinburgh.co.uk; Clerk St; tickets £10-24; box office 10am-5.30pm Mon-Sat, or till 15min after show begins; all Newington buses

The Queen's Hall is home to the Scottish Chamber Orchestra, but it also hosts jazz concerts, tribute bands and a whole range of other events.

ST GILES CATHEDRAL Map p222

☎ 225 9442; www.stgiles.net; High St, Royal Mile; tickets free-£7; 35

The big kirk on the Royal Mile hosts a regular and varied programme of classical music, including popular lunch-time and evening concerts as well as organ recitals, notably at 6pm on Sunday; check the website for full details. The cathedral choir sings at the 10am and 11.30am Sunday services.

USHER HALL Map pp218-19

☎ 228 1155; www.usherhall.co.uk; Lothian Rd; tickets £8-27; box office 10.30am-5.30pm Mon-Sat, till 8pm on show nights; all Lothian Rd buses

Built in 1914 with money donated by the brewery magnate Andrew Usher, the architecturally impressive 2900-seat Usher Hall hosts concerts by the RSNO and performances of popular music.

FOLK

The capital is a great place to hear traditional Scottish (and Irish) folk music, offering both regular spots and impromptu sessions. The following bars also have regular folk sessions: the Ensign Ewart (p122), the Malt Shovel (p123), the Antiquary (p127) and the White Hart Inn (p124).

FINNEGAN'S WAKE Map p222

☎ 226 3816; 9b Victoria St; admission free; 5pm-1am Mon-Thu, 1pm-1am Fri-Sun; 2, 23, 27, 41 or 42

Finnegan's is a cavernous – and often raucous – Irish theme pub with a stage where you can catch a live band (mostly Irish and Scottish folk and folk-rock) at 10pm, seven nights a week.

HEBRIDES BAR Map p222

☎ 220 4213; 17 Market St; admission free; 11am-midnight Mon-Thu, 11am-1am Fri & Sat, 12.30pm-midnight Sun; 35

Friendly, welcoming and in a handy location for the Waverley train station, the Hebrides offers a taste of Highland hospitality in the heart of the city. The bar has live Scottish and Irish folk, Celtic and bluegrass music on Wednesday to Saturday evenings at 9pm and on Sunday afternoons at 4pm.

PLEASANCE CABARET BAR Map p222

☎ 650 2349; 60 the Pleasance; admission £6-8; 8-11pm Wed; 35

The Pleasance is home to the **Edinburgh Folk Club** (www.edinburghfolkclub.org.uk), which runs a programme of visiting bands and singers at 8pm on Wednesdays; there's no advance booking, so buy your ticket at the door. The bar is a major Fringe venue, so there are no concerts here during the Festival period.

ROYAL OAK Map p222

☎ 557 2976; www.royal-oak-folk.com; 1 Infirmary St; admission free; 11am-2am Mon-Sat, 12.30pm-2am Sun; all South Bridge buses

The ever-popular Royal Oak rivals Sandy Bell's (see next) as Edinburgh's most popular folk venue, with music every night in both public bar and lounge. Admission to the downstairs lounge, with its tiny bar and space for only 30 punters, is free but by ticket only, so get there early (9.30pm start) if you want to be sure of a place. On Saturday nights there's a gig (6pm) followed by a sing-along session (9.30pm) – bring your own instruments (or a good singing voice). Sunday night gigs (8.30pm), organised by the Wee Folk Club, cost £3.

TOP FIVE LAZY SUNDAY AFTERNOONS

- Sunday matinee double bill at the **Cameo cinema** (p136)
- Jazz brunch at **Forth Floor Restaurant & Brasserie** (p109)
- Hydrotherapy in a rooftop pool at **One Spa** (p146)
- A stroll along the towpath of the **Union Canal** (see p98)
- Sweating in the steam room at **Portobello Turkish Baths** (p147)

SANDY BELL'S Map p222

☎ 225 2751; 25 Forrest Rd; admission free; 11.30am-12.45am Mon-Sat, 12.30-11pm Sun; 2, 23, 27, 41 or 42

This unassuming bar has been a stalwart of the traditional music scene in Edinburgh since The Corrs were in nappies. There's folk music almost every evening at 9pm, from 3pm on Saturday and pretty much all day on Sunday.

SHORE Map p216

☎ 553 5080; 3-4 the Shore; admission free; 11am-midnight Mon-Sat, 12.30-11pm Sun; 16, 22, 35 or 36

This is a snug, traditional, wood-panelled bar on the waterfront in Leith, complete with open fire and upright piano, that hosts lively informal folk sessions on Wednesday nights at 9pm.

TASS Map p222

☎ 556 6338; 1 High St, Royal Mile; admission free; 11am-midnight Mon-Thu, noon-1am Fri & Sat, 12.30pm-midnight Sun; 35

This Royal Mile pub takes Scotland's national bard Robert Burns as its theme, and is a great place for an impromptu song or six – there are regular folk sessions on Wednesday, Friday and Saturday, but musicians are welcome to bring along their instruments any time.

JAZZ

The climax of Edinburgh's jazz calendar is the week-long International Jazz & Blues Festival in late July/early August, but there are plenty of regular gigs throughout

The Royal Oak (above)

the year advertised in the *Gig Guide* and in the free quarterly *Jazz* booklet, both of which can be picked up in jazz venues. Visiting jazz bands often play at the Queen's Hall.

Henderson's (p109), a popular vegetarian restaurant, has live music (mainly jazz and classical guitar) at 7.30pm most evenings.

EIGHTY QUEEN STREET Map pp218-19

☎ 226 5097; 80 Queen St; admission free; ⏲ noon-11pm Mon-Wed, noon-midnight Thu, noon-1am Fri & Sat; 🚌 13, 19, 37 or 41

The clubbish Cellar Bar at Eighty Queen Street, with its stone floor, polished mahogany bar and wicker chairs and sofas, provides a traditional setting for live jazz three times a week. There's a jam session on Monday (from 9pm), a guest band on Saturday afternoons (2pm to 5pm), and the house band on Saturday nights (9pm to midnight).

FAIRMILE INN

☎ 445 2056; 44 Biggar Rd; admission £4-7; ⏲ noon-11pm Mon-Thu, noon-midnight Fri & Sat, 12.30-11pm Sun; 🚌 4, 11, 15 or 18

This Art Deco 1930s-style pub, on the southern edge of the city, is home to the Edinburgh Jazz'n'Jive Club. The Friday night gigs (from 8pm) put the emphasis on traditional jazz, from ragtime to New Orleans to swing.

JAZZ BAR Map p222

☎ 220 4298; www.thejazzbar.co.uk; 1a Chambers St; admission free-£5; ⏲ 4pm-1am Mon-Thu, 4pm-3am Fri, noon-3am Sat & Sun; 🚌 all South Bridge buses

This atmospheric cellar bar, with its polished parquet floors, bare stone walls, candle-lit tables and stylish steel-framed chairs, is owned and operated by jazz musicians. There's live music every night from 9pm (admission free Monday to Wednesday).

JAZZ CENTRE Map p222

☎ 467 5200; www.jazzcentre.co.uk; 4-6 Grassmarket; admission free-£10; ⏲ 11am-1am; 🚌 2

Set on the 1st floor of a converted church, complete with stained-glass windows and soaring ceiling, the Jazz Centre (above the Lot bistro) hosts live gigs from Wednesday to Saturday, with bands kicking off at 7.30pm or 8.30pm.

ROCK, BLUES & POP

In the last decade many of Edinburgh's live-music venues have closed down or been converted into clubs and bars, and the capital's live-music scene today is not a patch on Glasgow's. There are occasional rock gigs at clubs such as the Bongo Club, Cabaret Voltaire and the Venue.

Big-name bands and solo artists tend to play at Glasgow's SECC these days; those who include Edinburgh usually appear at the Edinburgh Playhouse. In summer promoters take advantage of the seating installed for the Military Tattoo to stage a few spectacular concerts on the Castle Esplanade. These are atmospheric but potentially cold and wet.

Tickets to major gigs are usually sold at **Virgin Megastore** (Map pp218-19; ☎ 220 3234; 125 Princes St) and **Ripping Records** (Map p222; ☎ 226 7010; 91 South Bridge), as well as through the online agencies mentioned in What's On (p137).

BANNERMAN'S Map p222

☎ 556 3254; www.bannermansgigs.co.uk; 212 Cowgate; admission £4; ⏲ noon-1am; 🚌 2

A long-established favourite, Bannerman's bar straggles through a warren of old vaults beneath South Bridge, and pulls in a lively crowd of students and backpackers. The beer is good, and there is live music (mostly indie/rock) in a crowded cavernlike space every night except Tuesday.

EDINBURGH CORN EXCHANGE

Map pp214-15

☎ 443 0404; www.ece.uk.com; 10 Newmarket Rd; ticket prices vary; ⏲ gigs only; 🚌 35

Opened by Blur in 1999 and home to the annual 'T on the Fringe' and Blues festivals, the Corn Exchange is a 3000-seat hall in a converted market building in the west of the city that hosts big-name bands from the Proclaimers to the Magic Numbers.

GIG Map pp218-19

☎ 229 7670; www.gigedinburgh.co.uk; 31 Lothian Rd; admission £6; ⏲ gigs only; 🚌 all Lothian Rd buses

A far better use of a prime city-centre venue than its previous incarnation as the cheesy disco club Revolution, Gig is a live music and DJ venue that aims to showcase the best of Britain's up-and-coming bands.

JAM HOUSE Map pp218-19

☎ 226 4380; www.thejamhouse.com; 5 Queen St; admission Sun-Wed free, after 10pm Thu £3, after 10pm Fri & Sat £5; 5pm-3am; all York Pl buses

The brainchild of rhythm'n'blues pianist and TV personality Jools Holland, the Jam House is set in a former BBC TV studio and aims to offer a combination of fine dining and live jazz and blues performances. Admission is for over-21s only, and there's a smart-casual dress code.

LIQUID ROOM Map p222

☎ 225 2564; www.liquidroom.com; 9c Victoria St; tickets £4-14; gigs only; 2, 23, 27, 41 or 42

One of the city's top live-music venues, boasting a superb sound system, the Liquid Room stages all kinds of gigs from local bands to big names like Moby, Coldplay, Clap Your Hands Say Yeah and the Damned, plus tribute bands and blasts from the past such as the Sensational Alex Harvey Band. It's also a great clubbing venue (see p138).

WHISTLE BINKIE'S Map p222

☎ 557 5114; www.whistlebinkies.com; 4-6 South Bridge; admission free; 7pm-3am; all South Bridge buses

This crowded cellar bar just off the Royal Mile has live music, including rock, blues and folk, every night of the week. Open mic night, from 10pm on Mondays, showcases new talent. Check the website for what's on when.

READINGS

The tradition of Edinburgh's many poets and storytellers is kept alive in the following two venues.

SCOTTISH POETRY LIBRARY Map pp218-19

☎ 557 2876; www.spl.org.uk; 5 Crichton's Close, Canongate; tickets free-£3; 11am-6pm Mon-Fri, 11am-4pm Sat; 35

Housed in an award-winning modern building close to the new Scottish Parliament, the Scottish Poetry Library holds a huge collection of contemporary and historic poetry in Scots, Gaelic and English. Check the website for details of regular poetry readings and other events.

SCOTTISH STORYTELLING CENTRE Map p222

☎ 557 5724; www.scottishstorytellingcentre.co.uk; 43-45 High St, Royal Mile; tickets £3-12; 35

The Scottish Storytelling Centre was founded in 1992 to encourage and support the ancient art of storytelling, and to help preserve the oral culture of Scotland. It operates a programme of storytelling performances both at the centre and at other venues throughout Edinburgh.

SPORT

Edinburgh has plenty of places where you can perk up those sagging muscles with a spot of healthy exercise. Football and rugby fans can shout themselves hoarse at one of the city's three major stadiums, and golfers can take their pick from around 90 courses within easy reach of the city.

CLIMBING

Although Edinburgh can boast an impressive, cliff-bound mini-mountain in the form of Arthur's Seat, bylaws make it illegal to climb on Salisbury Crags and other rock outcrops in Holyrood Park. The nearest natural rock climbing is at Traprain Law, near Haddington (20 miles east of Edinburgh) and at Aberdour on the Fife coast (15 miles north). There are, however, two excellent indoor climbing centres.

ADVENTURE CENTRE

☎ 333 6333; www.adventurescotland.com; South Platt Hill, Ratho; climbing arena adult/child per day £11/6.50, beginner's lessons from £20; climbing arena 2-10pm Mon-Fri, 10am-7pm Sat & Sun, fitness centre 6.30am-9pm Mon-Fri, 8am-6pm Sat & Sun

Located in a former quarry on the banks of the Union Canal, 9 miles west of Edinburgh, this impressive centre is the largest covered climbing arena in the world, offering both artificial walls and natural rock crags. Attractions include an aerial adventure course (adult/child £8/6), fitness centre, health spa and sauna. The centre can be reached by car via the M8 motorway, or on foot or bicycle via the Union Canal towpath. Lothian Buses service 67 (£1, 30 minutes, hourly) runs from Waterloo Pl in the city centre to Ratho village, from where it's a 10-minute walk to the centre.

ALIEN ROCK Map pp214-15

☎ 552 7211; www.alienrock.co.uk; 8 Pier Pl, Newhaven; adult/child £6.50/4; ⌚ noon-11pm Mon-Thu, noon-10pm Fri, 10am-9pm Sat & Sun; 🚌 7, 10, 16 or 32

A converted church overlooking Newhaven harbour provides top-notch indoor climbing facilities, with a range of walls up to 20m high, and a separate, extensive bouldering area; boots and harness can be hired for £3.50. A two-hour beginner's course costs £25 per person, including equipment.

CYCLING

Edinburgh and surroundings offer many excellent opportunities for cycling; see p191.

FOOTBALL

Edinburgh has two rival football (soccer) teams playing in the Scottish Premier League: Heart of Midlothian (aka Hearts, nicknamed the Jam Tarts or Jambos), founded in 1874, and Hibernian (aka Hibs, Hibbies or Hi-bees), founded in 1875. The domestic football season lasts from August to May and most matches are played at 3pm on Saturday or 7.30pm on Tuesday or Wednesday.

EASTER ROAD STADIUM

Map pp218-19

☎ 661 2159; www.hibs.co.uk; 12 Albion Pl; tickets £18-25; 🚌 1 or 35

Hibernian's home ground is northeast of the city centre. Hibs has not won the Scottish Cup since 1902, but came close in 2001, making it to the final only to lose 3-0 to Glasgow Celtic. The last trophy it won was the Scottish League Cup in 1991–92.

TYNECASTLE STADIUM Map p226

☎ 200 7200; www.heartsfc.co.uk; Gorgie Rd; tickets £10-35; 🚌 1, 2, 3, 25 or 33

Hearts – winner of the Scottish Cup in 1998 – has its ground southwest of the centre in Gorgie. Purchased by Lithuanian businessman Vladimir Romanov in 2005, Hearts' ageing stadium needs to be extended and redeveloped if it is to remain viable.

GOLF

There are 19 golf courses in Edinburgh itself, and another 70 within 20 miles of the city. For details of other courses in and around Edinburgh, check out www.scotlands-golf-courses.com.

BRAID HILLS GOLF COURSE

Map pp214-15

☎ 447 6666; Braid Hills Approach; weekday/weekend green fees £15/17; 🚌 11 or 15

This challenging public course is 10 minutes' south of the city centre, spread across gorse-clad ridges and heath land with great views of the Old Town and Arthur's Seat.

LOTHIANBURN GOLF COURSE

☎ 445 2206; www.lothianburngolfclub.com; 106a Biggar Rd, Fairmilehead; weekday/weekend green fees £18.50/24.50; 🚌 4 or 15

Historic Lothianburn Golf Course, dating from the 1890s, enjoys a scenic setting at the foot of the Pentland Hills.

MELVILLE GOLF CENTRE

☎ 663 8038; www.melvillegolf.co.uk; Lasswade, Midlothian; 9-hole green fee £10-12, range (50 balls) £3; ⌚ 9am-10pm Mon-Fri & 9am-8pm Sat & Sun; 🚌 3

This golfing centre on the southern edge of the city offers a nine-hole course, floodlit

FAMOUS LINKS COURSES

Some of the most famous links courses in the world lie within an hour's drive of Edinburgh, including **Muirfield** (☎ 01620-842 123; Gullane; green fees per round £110; ⌚ visitors Tue & Thu) and **Gullane No 1** (☎ 01620-842 255; W Links Rd, Gullane; green fees per round £60-75; ⌚ visitors 10.30am-noon & 2.30-4pm Mon-Fri) in East Lothian; and **St Andrews Old Course** (☎ 01334-476 666; www.standrews.org.uk; Pilmour House, St Andrews; green fees in high/low season £85/56; ⌚ visitors Mon-Sat) in Fife, 55 miles north of Edinburgh across the Firth of Forth. The Alfred Dunhill Cup, the world's most prestigious international team tournament, takes place at the Old Course in mid-October; the British Open Championship is also held here regularly. To play on any of these courses you will have to book at least a month in advance.

driving range, putting green, equipment hire, professional tuition and a golf shop.

HORSE RACING

MUSSELBURGH RACECOURSE

☎ 665 2859; www.musselburgh-racecourse.co.uk; Linkfield Rd, Musselburgh; admission £13-20; 🚌 15

Horse-racing enthusiasts should head 6 miles east to Scotland's oldest racecourse (founded 1816), where meetings are held throughout the year.

RUGBY UNION

Each year, from January to March, Scotland's national rugby team takes part in the **Six Nations Rugby Union Championship** (www.6nations.net). The most important fixture is the clash against England for the Calcutta Cup, which takes place in Edinburgh in even-numbered years (and at Twickenham in London in odd-numbered years). At club level, the season runs from September to May.

MURRAYFIELD STADIUM Map pp214-15

☎ 346 5000; www.scottishrugby.org; 112 Roseburn St; tickets from £20; 🚌 2, 12, 26, 31, 36, 63, 69 or 100

Murrayfield Stadium, about 1½ miles west of the centre, is the venue for international rugby matches. Most tickets for Six Nations games are allocated through rugby clubs; any that remain go on sale at the **Ticket Centre** (☎ 346 5100) in Murrayfield Stadium about two weeks before the competition begins, or you can buy online at www.scottishrugby.org.

SKIING & SNOWBOARDING

Skiing in Edinburgh? Yup – Europe's longest dry ski slope lies on the northern slopes of the Pentland Hills at the southern edge of the city.

MIDLOTHIAN SNOWSPORTS CENTRE

☎ 445 4433; Biggar Rd, Hillend; adult/child 1st hr £7.80/5.20, per additional hr £3.20/2.20; 🕑 9.30am-9pm Mon-Fri, 9.30am-7pm Sat & Sun May-Aug, 9.30am-9pm Mon-Sat, 9.30am-7pm Sun Sep-Apr; 🚌 4 or 15

You can punish your thighs in preparation for winter via the two button tows and chairlift that serve the 400m-long artificial slope (100m vertical difference), two nursery areas and fun jump slope, all floodlit in winter. Admission includes skis, boots and poles (snowboard gear costs an extra £2.50 for the first hour, then an extra £1 per additional hour). Beginner's courses cost from £11.40/£7.50 (adult/child) for one hour.

SAUNA, SPA & FITNESS

A TOUCH OF ZEN Map pp218-19

☎ 557 5159; www.atouchofzen.co.uk; 7 Dundonald St; 30min massage from £20; 🕑 2-8pm Mon, noon-5.30pm Tue, 9am-7pm Wed & Thu, 9am-8pm Fri, 10am-2pm Sat; 🚌 13

This New Town clinic specialises in shiatsu massage, but other treatments such as Rossiter System assisted stretching, therapeutic massage and acupuncture are also available.

EDINBURGH FLOATARIUM Map pp218-19

☎ 225 3350; www.edinburghfloatarium.co.uk; 29 NW Circus Pl; floating per hr £25; 🕑 9am-8pm Mon-Fri, 9am-6pm Sat, 9.30am-4pm Sun; 🚌 24, 29 or 42

Escape from the bustle of the city centre in a warm, womblike flotation tank, or take advantage of the many other therapies on offer, including facials, aromatherapy massage, reflexology, shiatsu, reiki, and Indian head massage (appointments necessary). There's a sweet-scented shop, too, where you can buy massage oils, incense, candles, homeopathic remedies, CDs and so on.

MEADOWBANK SPORTS CENTRE Map pp214-15

☎ 661 5351; 139 London Rd; admission price varies; 🕑 7.30am-10pm; 🚌 4, 5, 15, 26, 44 or 45

Public facilities at Scotland's main sports arena include a fitness studio, gym, free weights room, squash courts, martial arts dojo, athletics track and a children's soft play area.

ONE SPA Map pp218-19

☎ 221 7777; www.one-spa.com; Sheraton Grand Hotel, 8 Conference Sq, Lothian Rd; 25min from £30; 🕑 6.30am-10pm Mon-Fri, 7am-9pm Sat & Sun; 🚌 all Lothian Rd buses

This gorgeous rooftop spa offers a wide range of pampering treatments from reflexology and reiki to facials and hot-stone therapy. The setting is unbeatable, with a beautiful oval indoor pool, rooftop hydrotherapy pool, rustic sauna, curvaceous mosaic-tiled 'aroma grotto', and gym. You can book individual treatment sessions or splash out on a half-/full-day package (from £65/190), which combines a programme of treatments with free use of the spa facilities.

PORTOBELLO TURKISH BATHS

Map pp214-15

☎ 669 6888; Portobello Swim Centre, 57 Promenade; admission from £4.40; ⌚ women only 9am-1pm & 3-9pm Wed, men only 9am-9pm Tue, mixed 3-9pm Mon, 9am-9pm Thu & Fri, 9am-3.40pm Sat & Sun; 🚌 12, 15, 19, 32, 42 or 49

The big draw at Portobello's municipal swimming pool is not the pool itself but the beautifully restored 19th-century Turkish baths, with three hot rooms, a steam room and a plunge pool, where you can sweat away the aches and pains of a hard day's sightseeing.

PURE Map p216

☎ 561 1320; www.purespauk.com; 2nd fl, Ocean Terminal, Leith; 10min hand massage from £7; ⌚ 10am-9pm Mon-Sat, 11am-6pm Sun; 🚌 11, 22, 34, 35 or 36

Pure specialises in providing short (10- to 30-minute) beauty treatments – manicure, pedicure, waxing, facials etc – as well as longer massage, aromatherapy and hot-stone treatments and half-day spa packages.

UNION YOGA Map pp218-19

☎ 558 3334; www.unionyoga.co.uk; 25 Rodney St; drop-in class from £8; ⌚ 6.30am-9pm Mon-Fri, 8.30am-noon Sat; 🚌 8, 13 or 17

The bamboo-floored studio here is one of Europe's largest. As well as drop-in sessions and eight-week courses in Astanga yoga, it offers a free 45-minute introductory session at 6.30pm on Wednesday for people who have never tried yoga before.

Walking on Arthur's Seat (p59)

SWIMMING

The Firth of Forth is a bit on the chilly side for enjoyable bathing, but there are several indoor alternatives on offer.

DALRY SWIM CENTRE Map p226

☎ 313 3964; 25-29 Caledonian Cres; admission from £1.50; ⌚ 8am-10pm Mon-Fri, 9am-3.40pm Sat & Sun; 🚌 2, 3, 4, 25, 33 or 44

A refurbished Victorian baths with 25m pool, sauna and gym.

GLENOGLE SWIM CENTRE Map p217

☎ 343 6376; Glenogle Rd; admission from £1.50; ⌚ 7.30am-10pm Mon-Fri, 7.45am-4pm Sat, 9am-4pm Sun; 🚌 36

An atmospheric Victorian swimming baths also with 25m pool, sauna and gym.

ROYAL COMMONWEALTH POOL Map pp224-5

☎ 667 7211; 21 Dalkeith Rd; admission adult/child £3.30/2; ⌚ 9am-9.30pm Mon, Tue, Thu & Fri, 10am-9.30pm Wed, 10am-4.30pm Sat & Sun; 🚌 2, 14, 30 or 33

The city's main facility is the Royal Commonwealth Pool, which was built for the 1970 Commonwealth Games. It has a 50m Olympic pool, diving pool, children's pool, flumes and fitness centre.

WARRENDER SWIM CENTRE Map pp224-5

☎ 447 0052; 55 Thirlestane Rd; admission from £1.50; ⌚ 7.30am-9.30pm Mon-Fri, 9am-3.40pm Sat & Sun; 🚌 24 or 41

A recently refurbished, traditional Victorian pool with modern facilities, including gym, sauna and yoga classes.

WALKING

Edinburgh is lucky to have several good walking areas within the city boundary, including Arthur's Seat, Calton Hill, Blackford Hill, Hermitage of Braid, Corstorphine Hill and the coast and river at Cramond. The Pentland Hills, which rise to over 500m, stretch southwestwards from the city for 15 miles, offering excellent high- and low-level walking.

You can follow the Water of Leith Walkway from the city centre to Balerno (8 miles), and continue across the Pentlands to Silverburn (6½ miles) or Carlops (8 miles), and return to Edinburgh by bus. Another good option is to walk along the towpath of the Union Canal, which begins in Fountainbridge (Map p226) and runs all the way to Falkirk (31 miles). You can return to Edinburgh by bus at Ratho (8½ miles) and Broxburn (12 miles), and by bus or train from Linlithgow (21 miles).

See the Walking Tours chapter for more information (p92).

WATERSPORTS

The Firth of Forth provides sheltered waters for all kinds of sailing and watersports.

PORT EDGAR MARINA & SAILING SCHOOL

☎ 331 3330; www.portedgar.co.uk; Shore Rd, Queensferry; box office boat rental sessions 10am-noon & 2-4pm year-round, plus 7-9pm Mon-Fri Apr-Oct; First Edinburgh 43

Owned and operated by Edinburgh City Council, this yachting marina in the shadow of the Forth Rd Bridge rents out Topper/420/Wayfarer sailing dinghies at £11/20/27 for a two-hour session. It also offers canoeing, power-boating and sailing courses.

THEATRE

Despite the huge international popularity of the Edinburgh Festival and Fringe, theatre audiences during the rest of the year have been falling, prompting much doom and gloom regarding the future funding of Edinburgh's theatres. For more theatres see Dance (p140).

BEDLAM THEATRE Map p222

☎ 225 9893; www.bedlamtheatre.co.uk; 11b Bristo Pl; tickets £3-4; box office open for performances only; 2, 12, 23, 27, 41 or 42

Situated at the southern end of George IV Bridge in a converted church, the much-loved Bedlam is home to the **Edinburgh University Theatre Company** (EUTC; www.eutc.org.uk), and also serves as a popular Fringe venue. As well as staging EUTC productions, it hosts performances by visiting theatre companies.

EDINBURGH PLAYHOUSE Map pp218-19

☎ 524 3301, bookings ☎ 0870 606 3424; 18-22 Greenside Pl; tickets £10-30; box office 10am-6pm Mon-Sat, till 8pm on show nights; all Leith Walk buses

This restored theatre at the top of Leith Walk stages Broadway musicals, dance shows, opera and popular-music concerts.

KING'S THEATRE Map pp224-5

☎ 220 4349; www.eft.co.uk; 2 Leven St; tickets £10-25; box office open 1hr before show; all Tollcross buses

The King's is a traditional family theatre with a programme of musicals, drama, comedy and its famous annual Christmas pantomime.

NETHERBOW THEATRE Map p222

☎ 556 9579; 43-45 High St; tickets £4-6; 35

This small 75-seat theatre on the Royal Mile features modern Scottish and international drama, and is also home to the **Scottish Storytelling Centre** (see p144). At the time of writing it was undergoing a major renovation and expansion, and was due to reopen in spring 2006.

ROYAL LYCEUM THEATRE Map pp218-19

☎ 248 4848; www.lyceum.org.uk; 30b Grindlay St; tickets £10-25; box office 10am-6pm Mon-Sat, till 8pm on show nights; all Lothian Rd buses

A grand Victorian theatre located beside the Usher Hall, the Lyceum stages drama, concerts, musicals and ballet.

TRAVERSE THEATRE Map pp218-19

☎ 228 1404; www.traverse.co.uk; 10 Cambridge St; tickets £5-12; box office 10am-6pm Mon, 10am-8pm Tue-Sat, 4-8pm Sun; all Lothian Rd buses

The Traverse Theatre is the main focus for new Scottish writing and stages an adventurous programme of contemporary drama and dance. The box office is open on Sunday only if there is a performance that evening.

Shopping

Shopping

Shopping in Edinburgh offers everything from muzak-lulled mall-crawling and traditional department stores to browsing in dinky little designer boutiques and rubbing shoulder-bags with fussing fashionistas in Harvey Nicks. And all in a compact city centre that you can cover without blowing the bank on taxis or getting blisters from your Blahniks.

Princes St is Edinburgh's trademark shopping street, lined with all the big high-street stores from Marks & Spencer to Dixons to Debenhams, with more up-market designer shops a block north on George St, and many smaller specialist stores on pedestrianised Rose St. There are also two big city-centre shopping malls – Princes Mall, at the eastern end of Princes St next to the Balmoral Hotel, and the nearby St James Centre, at the top of Leith St – plus a designer shopping complex with a flagship Harvey Nichols store on the eastern side of St Andrew Square. Ocean Terminal in Leith, anchored by Debenhams and BHS department stores, is the biggest shopping centre in Edinburgh.

Other central shopping streets include South Bridge, Nicolson St and Lothian Rd. For more off-beat shopping – including fashion, music, crafts, gifts and jewellery – head for the cobbled lanes of Cockburn, Victoria and St Mary's Sts, all near the Royal Mile in the Old Town; William St in the West End; and Raeburn Pl and St Stephen's St in Stockbridge.

Opening Hours

Most shops are open from 9am to 5.30pm Monday to Wednesday, Friday and Saturday, and till 7pm or 8pm on Thursday. Plenty of shops open on Sunday too, but with shorter hours, generally from noon until 4pm or 5pm.

OLD TOWN

The top end of the Royal Mile, from the castle down to the Lawnmarket, is infested with tacky tartan tourist shops, but there are many good shops further downhill and on nearby Victoria, Cockburn and St Mary's Sts.

AHA HA HA Map p222 Toys & Gifts

☎ 220 5252; 99 West Bow; 10am-6pm Mon-Sat year-round, plus noon-4pm Sun Aug & Dec; 2

The guys at Aha Ha Ha have enough plastic poo, fake vomit, stink bombs and remote-control electronic farting machines to keep your average Dennis the Menace happy for a month or more. It's also a good place to go if you're looking for Halloween masks, costumes, magic tricks and practical jokes.

ARMSTRONG'S Map p222 Fashion

☎ 220 5557; 83 Grassmarket; 10am-6pm Mon-Sat, noon-6pm Sun; 2

Armstrong's is an Edinburgh fashion institution (established in 1840, no less), a quality secondhand clothes emporium offering everything from elegant 1940s dresses to funky 1970s flares. As well as retro fashion, it's a great place to hunt for 'previously owned' kilts and Harris tweed, or to seek inspiration for that fancy-dress party.

AVALANCHE RECORDS Map pp218-19 Music

☎ 228 1939; 28 Lady Lawson St; 9.30am-6pm Mon-Sat, noon-6pm Sun; 2 or 35

Along with Fopp, Avalanche is a sacred place of pilgrimage for music fans in search of good-value CDs – especially indie, rock and punk.

BIG IDEAS Map p222 Fashion

☎ 226 2532; 96 & 116 West Bow; 10am-5.30pm Mon-Sat; 2, 23, 27, 41 or 42

This boutique stocks a wide range of designer fashion for women sized 16 and

TOP FIVE SHOPPING AREAS

- **Cockburn Street** (left)
- **George Street** (p153)
- **Princes Street** (p153)
- **Stockbridge** (p156)
- **Victoria Street/West Bow** (left)

above, with labels including Elena Grunert, Almia, Bittie Kai Rind, Wille, Laurie, Sahara, Head Over Heels and others.

CARSON CLARK GALLERY

Map pp218-19 Antique Maps

☎ 556 4710; 181-183 Canongate; 10.30am-6pm Mon-Sat; 35

This friendly shop has knowledgeable staff who will advise on their interesting range of original and facsimile antique maps, charts and plans of Scotland, Europe and the rest of the world, as well as some gorgeous antique globes.

CASEY'S Map p222 Confectionery

☎ 556 6082; 52 St Mary's St; 9am-5.30pm Mon-Sat; 35 or 64

In the US it's 'candy', in Australia it's 'lollies', but in Scotland it's always been 'sweeties'. Casey's is a good old-fashioned sweetie shop where the shelves are lined with glass jars full of glorious tooth-dissolving delicacies. You can buy Scottish childhood favourites such as soor plooms, kola kubes, butter nuts and Carluke balls (don't ask) by the quarter-pound (OK then, 125g).

CASHMERE STORE

Map p222 Fashion

☎ 226 1577; 2 St Giles St, Royal Mile; 9.30am-6pm Mon-Sat; 35

This shop stocks a wide range of traditional and modern knitwear, in over 30 colours, plus a big choice of cashmere accessories such as scarves and shawls.

CORNICHE Map p222 Fashion

☎ 556 3707; 2 Jeffrey St; 10am-5.30pm Mon-Sat; 35

A major stockist of designer clothes for women, with a selection of big-name labels such as Jean-Paul Gaultier, Vivienne Westwood, Anna Sui, Katharine Hamnett and Alexander McQueen. The next-door branch concentrates on designer menswear.

CRUISE Map p222 Fashion

☎ 556 2532; 14 St Mary's St; 10am-6pm Mon-Fri, 9.30am-6pm Sat, noon-5pm Sun; 35

This branch of Cruise stocks designer casual wear for men. The main outlet is located on **George Street** (see p153).

DESIGNS ON CASHMERE

Map p222 Fashion

☎ 556 6394; 28 High St, Royal Mile; 10am-5.30pm Mon-Sat; 35

A good place to shop for top-quality cashmere clothing for both men and women, along with cashmere scarves, hats, gloves, snoods and capes.

EDINBURGH FARMERS MARKET

Map pp218-19 Food & Drink

☎ 652 5940; Castle Tce; 9am-2pm Sat; 28

This colourful weekly event attracts stallholders selling everything from wild boar, venison and home-cured pedigree bacon to organic bread, free-range eggs, honey and handmade soap.

FOPP Map p222 Music

☎ 220 0133; 55 Cockburn St; 10am-6.30pm Mon-Sat, 11am-6pm Sun; 35

Fopp began as a one-man record stall in Glasgow, but is now the UK's largest independent music store. It's a good place to

CLOTHING SIZES

Measurements approximate only, try before you buy

Women's Clothing						
Aus/UK	8	10	12	14	16	18
Europe	36	38	40	42	44	46
Japan	5	7	9	11	13	15
USA	6	8	10	12	14	16
Women's Shoes						
Aus/USA	5	6	7	8	9	10
Europe	35	36	37	38	39	40
France only	35	36	38	39	40	42
Japan	22	23	24	25	26	27
UK	3½	4½	5½	6½	7½	8½
Men's Clothing						
Aus	92	96	100	104	108	112
Europe	46	48	50	52	54	56
Japan	S		M	M		L
UK/USA	35	36	37	38	39	40
Men's Shirts (Collar Sizes)						
Aus/Japan	38	39	40	41	42	43
Europe	38	39	40	41	42	43
UK/USA	15	15½	16	16½	17	17½
Men's Shoes						
Aus/UK	7	8	9	10	11	12
Europe	41	42	43	44½	46	47
Japan	26	27	27½	28	29	30
USA	7½	8½	9½	10½	11½	12½

hunt for cheap CDs and vinyl – prices are much better than at Virgin – and the friendly staff really know what they're talking about. There's a second branch in the **New Town** (Map pp218-19; ☎ 220 0310; 7 Rose St; 9.30am-7pm Mon-Sat, 11am-6pm Sun).

FUDGE HOUSE OF EDINBURGH

Map pp218-19 Confectionery

☎ 556 4172; 197 Canongate, Royal Mile; 10am-5.30pm; 35

Another monument to the Scots' sweet tooth, this family business offers acres of homemade fudge, including chocolate and peppermint, rum and raisin, hazelnut, and tasty Highland cream. Mmmmm. There's a coffee shop too.

GEOFFREY (TAILOR) INC

Map p222 Scottish

☎ 557 0256; 57-59 High St, Royal Mile; 9am-5.30pm Mon-Wed, Fri & Sat, 9am-7pm Thu, 10am-5pm Sun; 35

Geoffrey can fit you out in traditional Highland dress, run up a kilt in your own clan tartan, or just hire out the gear for a wedding or other special event. Its offshoot, 21st Century Kilts, offers modern fashion kilts in a variety of fabrics; celebrity customers include Robbie Williams and Vin Diesel.

IAN MELLIS Map p222 Food & Drink

☎ 226 6215; 30a Victoria St; 10am-6pm Mon-Fri, 9.30am-6pm Sat; 2, 23, 27, 41 or 42

Mellis is Scotland's finest cheesemonger, purveying the best of British and Irish cheeses. This is the place to purchase traditional Scottish cheeses, from smooth Lanark Blue (the Scottish Roquefort) to sharp Isle of Mull Cheddar. There's another branch in **Stockbridge** (Map pp218-19; ☎ 225 6566; 6 Bakers Pl, Kerr St; 9.30am-6pm Mon-Wed, 9.30am-6.30pm Thu, 9.30am-7pm Fri, 9am-6pm Sat, 11am-5pm Sun).

JOYCE FORSYTH DESIGNER KNITWEAR Map p222 Fashion

☎ 220 4112; 42 Candlemaker Row; 10am-5.30pm Tue-Sat; 2, 23, 27, 41 or 42

The colourful knitwear on show at this intriguing little shop will drag your ideas about woollens firmly into the 21st century. Ms Forsyth's trademark design is a flamboyant flared woollen coat (can be knitted to order in colours of your own choice) but there are also box jackets, jumpers, hats, scarves and shawls.

TOP FIVE DESIGNER KNITWEAR STORES

- **Arkangel** (p156)
- **Cashmere Store** (p151)
- **Designs on Cashmere** (p151)
- **Jenners** (opposite)
- **Joyce Forsyth Designer Knitwear** (left)

MR WOOD'S FOSSILS Map p222 Gifts

☎ 220 1344; 5 Cowgatehead; 10am-5.30pm Mon-Sat; 2

Founded by the famous fossil hunter who discovered 'Lizzie', the oldest fossil reptile yet discovered, this fascinating speciality shop has a wide range of minerals, gems, fossils and other geological gifts.

PALENQUE Map p222 Jewellery

☎ 557 9553; 56 High St, Royal Mile; 10am-5.30pm Mon-Sat; 35

Palenque is a treasure trove of contemporary silver jewellery and hand-crafted accessories made using ceramics, textiles and metalwork. There's a second branch in the **New Town** (Map pp218-19; ☎ 225 7194; 99 Rose St; 10am-5.30pm Mon-Sat).

ROYAL MILE WHISKIES Map p222 Whisky

☎ 225 3383; 379 High St, Royal Mile; 10am-6pm Mon-Sat, 12.30-6pm Sun (till 8pm daily Jul–mid-Sep); 35

If it's a drap of the cratur ye're after, this place stocks a vast selection of single malts, in miniature and full-size bottles. There's also a range of blended whiskies, Irish whisky and bourbon, and you can shop online at www.royalmilewhiskies.com.

UNDERGROUND SOLUSH'N

Map p222 Music

☎ 226 2242; 9 Cockburn St; 10am-6pm Mon-Wed & Sat, 10am-7pm Thu & Fri, 1-5pm Sun; 35

A paradise for those in search of new and secondhand vinyl, this place has thousands of records – techno, house, jungle, hip-hop, R&B, funk, soul and 45s – plus a (smaller) selection of CDs, T-shirts, videos, books and merchandise. It's also a good place to find out what's happening on the local music/clubbing scene.

WEST PORT BOOKS

Map pp218-19 Secondhand Books

☎ 229 4431; 147 West Port; 10.30am-5.30pm Mon, Thu & Fri, noon-5.30pm Tue, Wed & Sat; 2 or 35

A long-established secondhand bookshop, West Port has a good range of material covering Scottish history and has published its own edition of *An Atlas of Old Edinburgh*, a collection of facsimile antique maps of the city from 1544 to the 19th century. It also specialises in titles covering Indian and Himalayan history and art.

NEW TOWN

Princes St, with its department stores and high-street chains, and George St, lined with designer boutiques, are the high-rent heart of Edinburgh's retail trade. The area surrounding Broughton St has good browsing potential, especially if you are into second-hand bookshops; it's also a good place to pick up deli food for a picnic or barbecue.

GEORGE & PRINCES STREETS

BOUDICHE Map pp218-19 Lingerie

☎ 226 5255; 15 Frederick St; 10am-6pm Mon-Wed, Fri & Sat, 10am-8pm Thu, noon-4pm Sun; all Princes St buses

Boudiche is a divinely decadent boudoir designed to make shopping a lush, leisurely experience. Lingerie is the main event, and you can try on basques and bustiers in the opulent changing rooms, each one equipped with a mirrored dressing table and an antique bell to call for a shop attendant.

CRUISE Map pp218-19 Fashion

☎ 226 3524; 94 George St; 10am-6pm Mon-Fri, 9.30am-6pm Sat, noon-5pm Sun; 13, 19, 37 or 41

An ornately corniced and pilastered foyer leads into three floors of white-painted, minimalist art-gallery-like décor showing off the best of mainstream designer labels for men and women, including Paul Smith, Jasper Conran, Hugo Boss, Joseph Tricot, Armani and Dolce & Gabbana. There's another branch of Cruise in the **Old Town** (p151), which stocks men's casual wear.

EDINBURGH WOOLLEN MILL

Map pp218-19 Woollens

☎ 226 3840; 139 Princes St; 9am-7pm Mon-Fri, 9am-6pm Sat, 11am-5pm Sun; all Princes St buses

The Edinburgh Woollen Mill is a stalwart of the tourist trade, with several branches all over Edinburgh offering a good selection of traditional jerseys, cardigans, scarves, shawls and rugs, and Pringle knitwear.

HARVEY NICHOLS

Map pp218-19 Department Store

☎ 524 8388; 32-34 St Andrew Sq; 10am-6pm Mon-Wed, 10am-8pm Thu, 10am-7pm Fri & Sat, 11am-5pm Sun; all St Andrew Sq buses

Harvey Nicks, which dominates the east side of St Andrew Sq, is as famous for its eye-popping price tags as for its range of world-famous brand names. The Edinburgh store offers four floors of designer labels, from Prada shades to Paul Smith suits, via lingerie, luggage, hats and handbags.

JENNERS Map pp218-19 Department Store

☎ 225 2442; 48 Princes St; 9am-6pm Mon & Wed-Sat, 9.30am-6pm Tue, 11am-5pm Sun; all Princes St buses

Founded in 1838, Jenners is the *grande dame* of Edinburgh shopping, and Britain's oldest department store. Its labyrinthine five floors stock a wide range of quality goods, both classic and contemporary – it's especially strong on designer shoes and handbags, hats, knitwear and Oriental rugs – and includes a food hall, a hairdresser, a gift-wrapping service and four cafés.

JO MALONE Map pp218-19 Cosmetics

☎ 478 8555; 93 George St; 10am-6pm Mon-Wed, 10am-7pm Thu, 9.30am-6pm Fri & Sat, noon-5pm Sun; 13, 19, 37 or 41

This sweet-smelling palace of posh cosmetics has in-store experts offering a 'fragrance-combining' consultation that will allow you to choose your perfect perfume, along with a range of other scents to 'layer' over it. Try the original nutmeg and ginger bath oil that made Ms Malone famous, or other intriguing combinations such as lime, basil and mandarin, or amber and lavender.

LIME BLUE Map pp218-19 Jewellery

☎ 220 2164; 107 George St; 10am-6pm Mon-Wed, Fri & Sat, 10am-7pm Thu, 1-5pm Sun; 13, 19, 37 or 41

Put on those shades and tighten your grip on that purse – you'll be dazzled by both the merchandise and the price tags in this elegant and clean-cut jewellery emporium, with diamond-encrusted necklaces and rings by Leo Pizzo, finely crafted brooches by Picchiotti, and watches by Versace. Downstairs you'll find a broad range of silver jewellery, crystalware and other luxury goods.

MAPPIN & WEBB

Map pp218-19 Jewellery

☎ 225 5502; 88 George St; 9.30am-5.30pm Mon-Sat, noon-4pm Sun; 13, 19, 37 or 41

Mappin & Webb are jewellers to HM the Queen, no less, and stock a range of jewellery, watches, gifts and silverware of the highest quality, including silver-plated tableware, crystal and silver whisky decanters, silver hip flasks and diamond rings.

ONE WORLD SHOP

Map pp218-19 Arts & Crafts

☎ 229 4541; St John's Church, Princes St; 10am-5.30pm Mon-Wed, Fri & Sat, 10am-7pm Thu year-round, plus 10am-5.30pm Sun Aug, Nov & Dec; all Princes St buses

The One World Shop sells a wide range of handmade crafts from developing countries, including paper goods, rugs, textiles, jewellery, ceramics, accessories, food and drink, all from accredited Fair Trade suppliers. During the Festival period (when the shop stays open till 6pm) there's a crafts fair in the churchyard outside.

OTTAKAR'S Map pp218-19 Books

☎ 225 4495; 57 George St; 9am-7pm Mon, Wed, Fri & Sat, 9.30am-7pm Tue, 9am-8pm Thu, 11.30am-5.30pm Sun; 13, 19, 37 or 41

Part of a nationwide chain of bookshops, Ottakar's prides itself on its knowledgeable staff and independent approach. This branch offers a good selection of Scottish titles and a large children's department, as well as a decent coffee shop upstairs.

You can even get a shiatsu massage in the Mind, Body and Spirit department (£10, 12.30pm to 5.30pm Saturday)!

SAMARKAND GALLERIES

Map pp218-19 Rugs

☎ 225 2010; 16 Howe St; 10am-5.30pm Mon-Sat; 13, 24, 29 or 42

This clean-lined modern gallery-shop exhibits a colourful display of contemporary and antique rugs, runners, flat-weaves, dowry bags and tribal weavings from Turkey, the Caucasus, Iran, Afghanistan and Central Asia. The owner is extremely knowledgeable, having lived in Iran for five years and travelled extensively in the carpet-weaving areas of Afghanistan, Iran and Turkey.

SCOTTISH GALLERY

Map pp218-19 Art

☎ 558 1200; 16 Dundas St; 10am-6pm Mon-Fri, 10am-4pm Sat; 23 or 27

Home to Edinburgh's leading art dealers, Aitken Dott, this private gallery exhibits and sells paintings by contemporary Scottish artists and by masters of the late 19th and early 20th centuries (including the Scottish Colourists), as well as a wide range of ceramics, glassware, jewellery and textiles.

TISO Map pp218-19 Outdoor Sports

☎ 225 9486; 123-125 Rose St; 9.30am-5.30pm Mon, Wed, Fri & Sat, 10am-5.30pm Tue, 9.30am-7.30pm Thu, noon-5pm Sun; all Princes St buses

Founded by the late Scottish mountaineer Graham Tiso, Edinburgh's biggest outdoor

equipment store offer four floors of camping, hiking, climbing, canoeing, skiing and snowboarding gear.

TROON Map pp218-19 Fashion

☎ 557 4045; 1 York Pl; 🕑 10am-5pm Mon, 10am-5.30pm Tue-Sat; 🚌 all York Pl buses

Troon is a cool little nook crammed with desperately desirable designer gear from lesser-known names like Ally Cappellino, Betty Jackson and Finnish design house Marimekko.

VIRGIN MEGASTORE

Map pp218-19 Music

☎ 220 2230; 125 Princes St; 🕑 9am-6pm Mon-Wed, Fri & Sat, 9am-8pm Thu, 10am-6pm Sun; 🚌 all Princes St buses

The Virgin Megastore is, well, a megastore, with wall-to-wall racks of mostly mainstream CDs, DVDs, cassettes and a bit of vinyl, plus computer games, T-shirts and posters. It also has a Ticketmaster counter where you can buy tickets for major music gigs.

WATERSTONE'S Map pp218-19 Books

☎ 226 2666; 128 Princes St; 🕑 8.30am-8pm Mon-Sat, 10.30am-7pm Sun; 🚌 all Princes St buses

Waterstone's flagship Princes St branch has four floors of books, with a good Scottish section on the ground floor and lots of travel guides and a coffee shop on the 2nd floor; it also hosts frequent book signings and author events. There are three other branches: **East End** (Map pp218-19; ☎ 556 3034; 13 Princes St; 🕑 9am-8pm Mon-Fri, 9am-7pm Sat, 10am-7pm Sun); **George Street** (Map pp218-19; ☎ 225 3436; 83 George St; 🕑 9am-8pm Mon-Fri, 9am-7pm Sat, 11am-6pm Sun); and **Ocean Terminal** (Map p216; ☎ 554 7732; Ocean Terminal, Ocean Dr, Leith; 🕑 10am-8pm Mon-Fri, 10am-7pm Sat, 11am-6pm Sun).

WHISTLES Map pp218-19 Fashion

☎ 226 4398; 97 George St; 🕑 10am-6pm Mon-Wed & Fri, 10am-7.30pm Thu, 9am-6pm Sat, 1-6pm Sun; 🚌 13, 19, 37 or 41

Crisp white and hot pink décor sets off the racks of designer clothes for women in this branch of the well-known London-based store. Lots of little black dresses here – just the place if you're looking for something a little more dressy for that special occasion – as well as quirky and off-beat styles.

BROUGHTON

CROMBIE'S Map pp218-19 Butcher

☎ 557 0111; 97-101 Broughton St; 🕑 8am-6pm Mon-Fri, 8am-5pm Sat; 🚌 8 or 17

Crombie's is a top-quality butcher shop where the good folk of Edinburgh go to stock up on prime Scottish beef and lamb, and superb homemade haggis. It's also famous for its gourmet sausages, with almost three dozen varieties ranging from wild boar and apricot to basil, beef and blackberry.

MCNAUGHTAN'S BOOKSHOP

Map pp218-19 Secondhand Books

☎ 556 5897; 3a-4a Haddington Pl; 🕑 9.30am-5.30pm Tue-Sat; 🚌 all Leith Walk buses

The maze of shelves at McNaughtan's basement bookshop – established in 1957 – houses a broad spectrum of general secondhand and antiquarian books, with good selections of Scottish, history, travel and illustrated titles.

Q-STORE Map pp218-19 Gay & Lesbian

☎ 477 4756; 5 Barony St; 🕑 11am-7pm Mon-Fri, 11am-6pm Sat, 1-5pm Sun; 🚌 8 or 17

Next door to the Blue Moon Café, the Q-Store is a gay and lesbian shop selling books, mags, videos, DVDs, sex toys, naughty underwear and clubbing gear.

SECOND EDITION

Map pp218-19 Secondhand Books

☎ 556 9403; 9 Howard St; 🕑 10am-5.30pm Tue-Sat; 🚌 8, 17, 23 or 27

This is a small bookshop for serious collectors buying and selling rare editions, with a good range of titles on Scottish subjects. The owner goes to buy books on weekday mornings, so wait until after noon if you want to be absolutely sure that the shop will be open.

VALVONA & CROLLA

Map pp218-19 Delicatessen

☎ 556 6066; 19 Elm Row; 🕑 8am-6.30pm Mon-Sat, 10.30am-5.30pm Sun; 🚌 all Leith Walk buses

The acknowledged queen of the Edinburgh delicatessens, established during the 1930s, Valvona & Crolla is packed with Mediterranean goodies, including an excellent choice of fine wines. It also has a good **café** (see p111).

WEST END & STOCKBRIDGE

Edinburgh's West End has a string of high-street chain stores on the main drag of Shandwick Pl, but there's also a hidden enclave of decadent designer shops clustered around the junction of William and Stafford Sts.

Stockbridge is a good place to shop for gifts, crafts and jewellery. The main shopping areas are on Raeburn Pl, Henderson Row and St Stephen St, which has a selection of boutiques selling everything from jewellery to secondhand books to retro furniture.

ADAM POTTERY Map pp218-19 Arts & Crafts

☎ 557 3978; 76 Henderson Row; 🕑 10am-5.30pm Mon-Sat; 🚌 36

This small independent pottery produces its own colourfully glazed ceramics, both decorative and functional, in a wide range of styles, with objects ranging from coffee cups to garden planters. Visitors are welcome to visit the studio to watch potters at work.

ANNIE SMITH Map p217 Jewellery

☎ 332 5749; 20 Raeburn Pl; 🕑 10am-5.30pm Mon-Sat, noon-5pm Sun; 🚌 24, 29 or 42

Annie Smith's back-of-the-shop studio creates beautiful and original jewellery to contemporary designs in silver and 18-carat gold, with beaten and worked surfaces that reflect natural textures such as rock, ice and leaves. If there's nothing in the shop that takes your fancy, you can commission Ms Smith to make something to order.

ARKANGEL Map p217 Fashion

☎ 226 4466; 4 William St; 🕑 10am-5.30pm Mon-Wed, Fri & Sat, 10am-6.30pm Thu; 🚌 all Shandwick Pl buses

Owners Janey and Lulu will help you pick out a glamorous outfit from their carefully selected wardrobe of off-beat European chic and vintage style – look out for the superb cashmere knitwear by Scots designer Hillary Rohde, and fashion brands such as Antoine & Lilli and Stella Cadente.

TOP FIVE FOR SCOTTISH JEWELLERY

- **Annie Smith** (above)
- **Galerie Mirages** (right)
- **Mappin & Webb** (p154)
- **Palenque** (p152)
- **Scottish Gems** (p158)

BLACKADDER GALLERY

Map p217 Gifts

☎ 332 4605; 5 Raeburn Pl; 🕑 10am-5.30pm Mon-Sat, 1-5pm Sun; 🚌 24, 29 or 42

This is a great place for girly gifts, from colourful handmade cards and giftwrap to copper and silver jewellery, scented candles, art prints and accessories.

GALERIE MIRAGES Map p217 Gifts

☎ 315 2603; 46a Raeburn Pl; 🕑 10am-5.30pm Mon-Sat, 1-5pm Sun; 🚌 24, 29 or 42

A narrow lane between two houses (beside Peckham's deli) leads to this Aladdin's Cave packed with jewellery, textiles and handicrafts from all over the world. It's best known for its silver, amber and gemstone jewellery in both ethnic and contemporary designs, but you'll also find things like scented sandalwood boxes, handmade paper goods, colourful cushions and gorgeous throws.

HELEN BATEMAN Map p217 Shoes

☎ 220 4495; 16 William St; 🕑 9.30am-6pm Mon-Sat; 🚌 all Shandwick Pl buses

From sparkly stilettos and sleek satin pumps to 1950s-style open-sided court shoes and soft suede loafers, Helen Bateman's shop has every kind of handmade shoe and boot you could ever wish for. You can even order customised satin shoes – slingbacks, pumps or kitten heels – dyed to any colour and decorated with whatever your heart desires.

SAM THOMAS Map p217 Fashion

☎ 226 1126; 18 Stafford St; 🕑 9.30am-6pm Mon-Sat; 🚌 all Shandwick Pl buses

This William St boutique has a good range of affordable designer gear, from casual to evening wear, as well as reasonably priced accessories including jewellery, bags, belts, boots and shoes.

THE STORE Map p217 Delicatessen

☎ 315 0300; 13 Comely Bank Rd; 🕑 10am-8pm Mon-Thu, 9am-6pm Fri & Sat, 11am-5pm Sun; 🚌 24, 29 or 42

Head down to the Store to load up your shopping basket with the finest foodstuffs from northeast Scotland – Aberdeen Angus beef, grass-fed lamb, venison, smoked salmon and fresh bread, cheese and eggs.

DALRY & MORNINGSIDE

ANOTHER PLANET Map p226 — Toys & Gifts

☎ **337 0072; 34 Ashley Tce; 🕑 10am-6pm Mon-Sat; 🚌 38**

This shop – named so that the owner could answer the phone with 'Hello, this is Tom from Another Planet' – sells things that fly, sail, spin or are otherwise operated by the breeze, from £1.50 plastic boomerangs to £1000 X-Sails (mini land-yachts; the latest, ultracool, big boys' toys). There's also lots of animated toys and kits of the kind that 11-year-olds (of all ages) drool over.

GREENSLEEVES Map p226 — Fashion

☎ **447 8042; 203 Morningside Rd; 🕑 10am-5.30pm Mon-Sat; 🚌 5, 11, 15, 16, 17 or 23**

If you want to buy a designer dress without breaking the bank, have a flick through the rails at Greensleeves, which specialises in high-quality secondhand clothes, handbags and shoes, many with designer labels.

JONATHAN AVERY DESIGN
Map p226 — Kitchen Equipment

☎ **447 1000; 7-9 Church Hill Pl; 🕑 9.30am-5pm Mon-Fri, 10am-5.30pm Sat; 🚌 11, 15, 16, 17 or 23**

Avery is a designer of customised non-fitted kitchen furniture, and this beautifully arranged shop lets you imagine the kitchen of your dreams while browsing the range of highly desirable kitchen accessories, ceramics, books and gifts.

TOLLCROSS & BRUNTSFIELD

BOARDWISE Map pp218-19 — Outdoor Sports

☎ **229 5887; 4 Lady Lawson St; 🕑 10am-6pm Mon-Sat year-round, plus noon-5pm Sun Dec; 🚌 2 or 35**

Boardwise supplies all the gear – and the cool threads – you'll need for any board-based sports, be it snow, skate or surf.

MCALISTER MATHESON MUSIC
Map pp218-19 — Music

☎ **228 3827; 1 Grindlay St; 🕑 9.30am-7pm Mon-Fri, 9am-5.30pm Sat; 🚌 2 or 35**

This is Scotland's biggest and most knowledgeable business dealing in classical music CDs, DVDs and books – just about every staff member seems to have a music degree. It also stocks a selection of Scottish folk and Celtic music.

PECKHAM'S Map p226 — Delicatessen

☎ **229 7054; 155-159 Bruntsfield Pl; 🕑 8am-midnight Mon-Sat, 9am-11pm Sun; 🚌 all Bruntsfield buses**

Peckham's is a busy neighbourhood deli selling all the usual deli stuff: smoked salmon, gravadlax and kippers, all kinds of cheeses, freshly made bread and sandwiches, and organic veggies. There's also a great selection of wines and whiskies, and you can buy booze here until 11pm, seven days a week.

STATIONERY OFFICE BOOKSHOP
Map pp218-19 — Books

☎ **0870 606 5566; 71 Lothian Rd; 🕑 9am-5pm Mon-Wed & Fri, 9.30am-5pm Tue; 🚌 all Lothian Rd buses**

The Stationery Office has a good selection of books on business, Scottish history, law, travel (including travel guides) and computers, and the widest range of Ordnance Survey maps in town.

WONDERLAND Map pp218-19 — Toys

☎ **229 6428; 97-101 Lothian Rd; 🕑 9.30am-6pm Mon-Fri, 9am-6pm Sat year-round, plus noon-5pm Sun 1-24 Dec; 🚌 all Lothian Rd buses**

Wonderland is a classic, kids-with-their-noses-pressed-against-the-window toy shop that is filled with model aircraft, spaceships and radio-controlled cars, but it also caters to the serious train-set and model-making fraternity.

SOUTHSIDE & NEWINGTON

The eclectic Southside offers a broad range of retail therapy, including the crafts and antique shops on Causewayside and the bookshops clustered around the university.

BACKBEAT Map pp218-19 Music

☎ 668 2666; 31 E Crosscauseway; ⏰ 10am-5.30pm Mon-Sat; 🚌 42

If you're hunting for secondhand vinyl from way back, this cramped little shop has a stunning and constantly changing collection of jazz, blues, rock and soul, plus lots of '60s and '70s stuff, though you have to take some time to hunt through the clutter.

BLACKWELL'S BOOKSHOP

Map p222 Books

☎ 622 8222; 53-62 South Bridge; ⏰ 9am-8pm Mon & Wed-Fri, 9.30am-8pm Tue, 9am-6pm Sat, noon-6pm Sun; 🚌 all South Bridge buses

James Thin's, founded in 1848, was the city's principal home-grown bookstore and Edinburgh University's main supplier. Now owned by Blackwell's of Oxford, its four floors still have an admirable selection of reading matter, particularly academic books, foreign languages and Scottish history.

COURTYARD ANTIQUES

Map pp224-5 Antiques

☎ 662 9008; 108a Causewayside; ⏰ 10am-5pm Mon-Sat; 🚌 42

Hidden down a lane, the Courtyard has two crowded floors of wooden furniture (19th century to the 1970s), toys and militaria, including some fascinating bric-a-brac that ranges from 78rpm records to a homemade canvas canoe.

FLIP Map p222 Fashion

☎ 556 4966; 60-62 South Bridge; ⏰ 9.30am-5.30pm Mon-Wed, 9.30am-6pm Thu-Sat; 🚌 all South Bridge buses

Flip is a vast American emporium purveying all things denim, canvas, cowboy and retro to (mainly) students and skaters at marked-down prices.

FORBIDDEN PLANET

Map p222 Fashion

☎ 225 8613; 40-41 South Bridge; ⏰ 10am-5.30pm Mon-Wed, Fri & Sat, 10am-6pm Thu, noon-5pm Sun; all South Bridge buses

This place stocks a wide range of sci-fi comics, graphic novels, DVDs and T-shirts, as well as *Star Trek*, *Simpsons* and *South Park* merchandise. It's also the place for *Alien vs Predator* action figures, Bleeding Edge dolls and Kurt Cobain lunchboxes (if you have to ask, you don't wanna know…).

KILBERRY BAGPIPES

Map pp224-5 Scottish

☎ 668 3303; 93 Causewayside; ⏰ 9am-5pm Mon-Fri, 9am-1pm Sat; 🚌 42

Makers and retailers of traditional Highland bagpipes, Kilberry also sells piping accessories, snare drums, books, CDs and learning materials.

MEADOWS POTTERY

Map pp224-5 Crafts

☎ 662 4064; 11a Summerhall Pl; ⏰ 10.30am-5.30pm Mon-Sat; 🚌 42

This little shop sells a range of colourful, high-fired oxidised stoneware, both domestic and decorative, all hand-thrown on the premises. If you can't find what you want, you can commission custom-made pieces.

SCOTTISH GEMS Map p226 Jewellery

☎ 447 5579; 162 Morningside Rd; ⏰ 9.30am-5.30pm Mon-Sat; 🚌 5, 11, 15, 16, 17 or 23

Scottish Gems sources its jewellery and crafts from top Scottish artisans, specialising in gold and silver jewellery in both traditional – mostly Celtic – and modern designs. Items range from intricate Celtic interlace designs and traditional Scottish thistles to delicate butterflies in silver and enamel, pewter goods and turned wooden bowls in the form of traditional silver quaichs.

WORD POWER Map pp218-19 Books

☎ 662 9112; 43 W Nicolson St; ⏰ 10am-6pm Mon-Fri, 10.30am-6pm Sat, noon-5pm Sun; 🚌 all South Bridge buses

Word Power is a radical independent bookshop that supports both small publishers and local writers. It stocks a wide range of political, gay and feminist literature, as well as non-mainstream fiction and nonfiction.

Sleeping

Sleeping

A boom in hotel building has seen Edinburgh's tourist capacity swell significantly in the last decade, but you can guarantee that the city will still be packed to the gills during the festival period (August and early September) and over Hogmanay (New Year). If you want a room during these periods, book as far in advance as you can – a year ahead if possible. In general, it's best to book ahead for accommodation at Easter and from mid-May to mid-September. Accommodation might also be in short supply during the Royal Highland Show (late June) and over the weekends when international rugby matches are being played at Murrayfield (two or three weekends from January to March).

Accommodation Styles

Edinburgh offers a wide range of accommodation options, from moderately priced guesthouses set in lovely Victorian villas and Georgian town houses to expensive and stylish boutique hotels. There are also plenty of international chain hotels, and a few truly exceptional hotels housed in magnificent historic buildings. At the budget end of the range, there is no shortage of youth hostels and independent backpacker hostels, which often have inexpensive double and twin rooms available.

Price Ranges

Rates at a typical midrange hotel or guesthouse start at around £50 to £60 for a double room. Hotel rates vary with the time of year, and are usually highest during peak season (August and New Year), closely followed by high season (June, July and September). You'll find the lowest rates in February, March and November.

PRICE GUIDE

Cost of a double room per night:

£££	£121 and over
££	£51 to £120
£	£50 and less

Long-term Rentals

The Edinburgh rental market has boomed in recent years and there are plenty of rooms, apartments and houses to let. Rates for a single or double room in a shared flat start at around £250 per calendar month in central districts such as Tollcross and Marchmont, though £280 to £380 is more common. A one-bedroom flat in the highly desirable New Town would cost at least £550 per month, but you can get a flat with two double bedrooms in Bruntsfield for around £800. If you don't mind travelling into the city, it's possible to find a two-bedroom house or cottage within an hour's drive of Edinburgh for £500 per month.

The minimum lease on long-term rental properties is usually six months, but there are also many short-term lettings available (usual minimum three nights), especially during the summer and the festival period. Most landlords will demand a security deposit (normally one month's rent) plus a month's rent in advance; some will also ask for some sort of reference.

If you want to search for long-term accommodation yourself, check out the property section in the Thursday edition of the *Scotsman* newspaper, or the flatshare section in the *List* magazine (see p137), or check the letting agency websites listed in the boxed text, opposite. Hostel noticeboards are also a good place to look.

When you inspect a flat it's wise to take someone else with you, both for safety reasons and for help in spotting any shortcomings. A few things to check before signing a tenancy agreement include: the cost of gas, electricity, phone, TV and council tax and how they're to be paid for; whether there's street parking and/or how convenient is public transport; the arrangements for cleaning the house or flat; and whether the lease allows you to have friends to stay.

APARTMENTS & LETTING AGENCIES

There's plenty of self-catering apartment accommodation in Edinburgh. The minimum stay is usually one week in the summer peak season, three nights or less at other times.

VisitScotland and the **Edinburgh and Scotland Information Centre** (see Tourist Information, p200) can provide listings of self-catering accommodation in Edinburgh and the Lothians. Depending on facilities, location and time of year, prices range from £150 to £850-plus per week. At the more expensive end of the market are serviced apartments, which can be let by the night and include a daily cleaning service and house manager.

The following prices are for a one-bedroom apartment (sleeping two or three):

Edinburgh Central Apartments (Map pp218-19; ☎ 622 7840; www.edinburgh-central-apartments.co.uk; 23-27 Home St; apt per week £250-895) Provides basic but comfortable one- to four-bedroom flats in centrally located Tollcross.

Fountain Court Apartments (Map p217; ☎ 622 6677; www.fountaincourtapartments.com; 123 Grove St; apt per night £90-185; P) These places close to Haymarket come with well-equipped kitchens (microwave, dishwasher, washing machine) and free private parking; the Edinburgh Quay apartments overlook the Union Canal.

Glen House Apartments (Map pp218-19; ☎ 228 4043; www.edinburgh-apartments.co.uk, 101 Lauriston Pl; apt per week £300-1400) This is a large agency that can provide flats of all sizes and categories throughout Edinburgh.

There are also many letting agencies that will find both short- and long-term accommodation for you and act as your agent in dealings with landlords. Most have websites where you can search for available properties by cost, number of bedrooms and location. They include:

Clouds Accommodation Agency (Map pp218-19; ☎ 550 3808; www.clouds.co.uk; 26 Forth St)

Edinburgh Property Management (Map pp224-5 ☎ 623 2100; www.e-p-m.com; 104 Marchmont Cres)

James Gibb Property Management (Map p217; ☎ 229 3481; www.jamesgibb.co.uk; 4 Atholl Pl)

Ryden Lettings (Map pp218-19; ☎ 226 2545; www.rydenlettings.co.uk; 100 Hanover St)

Reservations

If you arrive in the city without a room, there are several agencies that can help. VisitScotland's **booking service** (within the UK ☎ 0845 225 5121, from outside the UK ☎ +44 1506 83212) will try and find a room to suit, and will charge you a £3 fee if successful. You can also search for accommodation on **VisitScotland Edinburgh's** website (www.edinburgh.org).

If you are having trouble finding a vacant room for the Festival period, try **Festival Beds** (☎ 225 1101; www.festivalbeds.co.uk), which specialises in matching visitors with B&Bs during August only.

OLD TOWN

Staying in the Old Town puts you in the heart of Edinburgh's historical heritage, within easy walking distance of the castle and Holyroodhouse. But there's a dearth of decent midrange options – most accommodation here is in hostels or expensive hotels; anything in between is mostly in characterless chain hotels.

APEX INTERNATIONAL HOTEL

Map p222 Hotel ££

☎ 300 3456; www.apexhotels.co.uk; 31-35 Grassmarket; s £80-220, d £80-240; 🚌 2; P

Centrally located and with good business facilities, the modern 175-room Apex is the best of the Old Town's chain hotels, with stylish rooms, stunning views of the castle and an excellent rooftop restaurant (**Heights**, p105).

BANK HOTEL Map p222 Hotel ££

☎ 622 6800; www.festival-inns.co.uk; 1 South Bridge; s £60-100, d £60-140; 🚌 all South Bridge buses

Not so much a hotel as a pub with rooms, the Bank is an imposing neoclassical building on the corner of the Royal Mile and North Bridge, slap bang in the middle of everything. Location-wise you could only do better by camping out in St Giles Cathedral. Formerly a bank (surprise, surprise), the hotel has nine elegant rooms spread over three floors (no elevator), each one themed around famous Scots, including

Robert Burns, Robert Louis Stevenson and Charles Rennie Mackintosh.

BRODIE'S BACKPACKER HOSTEL

Map p222 Hostel £

☎ 556 6770; www.brodieshostels.co.uk; 12 High St, Royal Mile; dm £10-16; 🚌 35; 💻

Brodie's is a small (54 beds), friendly place with four dorms (three mixed and one women-only). The comfortable beds (in quirky custom-made A-frame bunks) are fitted out with tartan flannel covers, and the dorms are ranged around a cosy lounge area with an open fire and no TV, which makes for good socialising. Top location bang in the middle of the Royal Mile.

CASTLE ROCK HOSTEL Map p222 Hostel £

☎ 225 9666; www.scotlands-top-hostels.com; 15 Johnston Tce; dm £12.50-14; 🚌 2, 23, 27, 41 or 42; 💻

With its bright, spacious, single-sex dorms, superb views and helpful staff, this 200-bed hostel prompts plenty of positive feedback from travellers. It has a great location only a minute's walk from the castle (but a fair uphill trek from train and bus stations), a games room, reading lounge, and big-screen video nights; however, the foam mattresses aren't the most comfortable we've tried.

EDINBURGH BACKPACKERS HOSTEL

Map p222 Hostel £

☎ 220 1717; www.hoppo.com; 65 Cockburn St; dm £14-18.50; 🚌 35; 💻

Just a short walk up the hill from Waverley train station, Edinburgh Backpackers is clean, bright and friendly, with a lively bistro-bar on the ground floor. It's right in the heart of Edinburgh's pub culture, which makes it great for partying but not so good for a peaceful night's sleep.

HOLYROOD HOTEL

Map pp218-19 Hotel ££-£££

☎ 550 4500; www.macdonaldhotels.co.uk; 81 Holyrood Rd; s £85-210, d £120-230; 🚌 36

A modern luxury hotel with a traditional feel, the Holyrood sits at the foot of Salisbury Crags, alongside the new Scottish Parliament Building and only minutes from Our Dynamic Earth and the Palace of Holyroodhouse. Facilities include a 14m pool, gym, sauna and steam room. Check the website for special offers.

TOP FIVE HOTELS WITH A HISTORY...

A number of Edinburgh's most atmospheric hotels are housed in interesting historic buildings. Here are our top five:

- **Bank Hotel** (p161)
- **Malmaison Hotel** (p171)
- **Point Hotel** (p168)
- **Prestonfield House Hotel** (p169)
- **Scotsman Hotel** (below)

ROYAL MILE RESIDENCE

Map p222 Apartments £££

☎ 226 5155; www.royalmileresidence.com; 65 Cockburn St; 2-bedroom apt per night £130-225; 🚌 35

You would never guess that the classic Old Town tenement façade just down the hill from the Fringe office conceals some of the most desirable serviced apartments in Edinburgh, complete with décor by Whytock and Reid (interior designers to the aristocracy). There are six two-bedroom flats (each sleeps up to four people); those at the rear have views over the city to the Firth of Forth, while those at the front overlook the Royal Mile.

SCOTSMAN HOTEL Map p222 Hotel £££

☎ 556 5565; www.thescotsmanhotelgroup.co.uk; 20 North Bridge; s from £240, d £250-350, ste £450-750; 🚌 all South Bridge buses; ♿

The grand Scottish Baronial pile that overlooks the North Bridge – opened in 1904 and hailed as 'the most magnificent newspaper building in the world' – is now home to one of Edinburgh's finest luxury hotels. The labyrinthine former offices of the *Scotsman* newspaper house 56 bedrooms and 13 suites, sporting oak-panelled walls, specially commissioned tweed fabrics and acres of veined marble. Standard rooms on the northern side enjoy superb views over the New Town and Calton Hill, while the Penthouse Suite (£1200 a night) has its own private library, sauna, and rooftop terrace complete with barbecue.

WITCHERY BY THE CASTLE

Map p222 Suites £££

☎ 225 5613; www.thewitchery.com; Castlehill, Royal Mile; ste £295; 🚌 28

Set in a 16th-century Old Town house in the shadow of Edinburgh Castle, the Witchery's seven lavish suites are extravagantly furnished with antiques, oak panelling, tapestries, open fires and roll-top baths, and supplied with flowers, chocolates and complimentary champagne. Our favourites are the Gothic Library Suite, overlooking the Royal Mile – the faux-book-lined bathroom has a heated floor, its own log fire and a bath big enough for two – and the Old Rectory, with its gilt Gothic woodcarving, lush red and purple drapery and tartan-clad mannequins. The downsides include the disappointing breakfasts (continental only, served in your room; no hot food available), absence of room service, and the Witchery's overwhelming popularity – you'll have to book several months in advance to be sure of getting a room.

NEW TOWN

The New Town offers a range of accommodation options, from elegant Georgian guesthouses to gleaming boutique hotels, all within easy reach of the city's main shopping and restaurant areas. Many places are also within walking distance of the bus and train stations.

41 HERIOT ROW Map pp218-19 Guesthouse ££

☎ 225 2720; www.wwwonderful.net; 41 Heriot Row; s £70-80, d £95-110; 🚌 13, 24, 29 or 42

This Georgian apartment is an elegant yet relaxing retreat that will delight lovers of books and antiques. There are only two bedrooms – a twin at the back of the house (with views of the Firth of Forth) and a double at the front – both with floors of glowing golden pine, oriental rugs, big brass bedsteads, and antique armchairs just made for reading. Breakfast is served, complete with best crockery and silverware, at a table in the spacious drawing room, beside a window that looks out onto Queen St Gardens.

AILSA CRAIG HOTEL

Map pp218-19 Hotel £-££

☎ 556 1022; www.townhousehotels.co.uk; 24 Royal Tce; s £25-55, d £50-90; 🚌 all London Rd buses

The Ailsa Craig is a grand Georgian town house dating from 1820, set on a peaceful tree-lined terrace overlooking Royal Tce Gardens. The décor is beginning to look a little dated, lying somewhere between chintzy and chain-hotel bland, but many of the 18 comfortably upholstered rooms have grand views, and it enjoys a great location on a quiet street, only 10 minutes' walk from Princes St and close to the Playhouse Theatre and Broughton St nightlife.

ARDENLEE GUEST HOUSE

Map pp218-19 Guesthouse £-££

☎ 556 2838; www.ardenlee.co.uk; 9 Eyre Pl; s £30-50, d £50-90; 🚌 23, 27 or 36

A renovated Victorian town house with nine well-kept rooms, the Ardenlee sports many beautiful period features including a colourful tiled vestibule, cast-iron and ceramic fireplace surrounds, and a lovely oval staircase. The bedrooms are smartly kitted out in modern fabrics and homely colours, and the location is ideal: on a quiet street away from the noise and bustle of the city centre, but only a short walk from Princes St.

BALMORAL HOTEL Map pp218-19 Hotel £££

☎ 556 2414; www.thebalmoralhotel.com; 1 Princes St; s £210-360, d £240-410, ste £495-1325; 🚌 all Princes St buses; ♿

Built in 1902 as the North British Station Hotel for the North British railway company, the Balmoral (renamed in 1990) is a major city landmark rising directly above Waverley train station. Its sumptuous rooms offer some of the most luxurious accommodation in Edinburgh, including suites with 18th-century décor, marble bathrooms and stunning sunset views of Princes St and the Scott Monument. There's also a spa and gym with 20m pool in the basement.

CALEDONIAN HILTON HOTEL

Map pp218-19 Hotel £££

☎ 222 8888; www.hilton.com; 4 Princes St; s £140-270, d £150-375; 🚌 all Princes St buses; ♿

An Edinburgh institution, the 'Caley' is a vast red-sandstone palace of Edwardian pomp and splendour dating from 1903, one of two grandiose hotels at opposite

TOP FIVE ROOMS WITH A VIEW

- **Balmoral Hotel** (above)
- **Glasshouse** (p164)
- **Orocco Pier** (p172)
- **Point Hotel** (p168)
- **Scotsman Hotel** (opposite)

ends of Princes St built by competing railway companies at the turn of the 20th century (the other is the Balmoral). It offers 251 five-star rooms – mostly in bland international style, though the more expensive executive rooms have antique furniture and 'olde-worlde' décor – and has a spa, swimming pool, gym, and full business and conference facilities.

CASTLE GUEST HOUSE

Map pp218-19 Guesthouse ££

☎ 225 1975; www.castleguesthouse.com; 38 N Castle St; s £30-40, d £60-80; 🚌 all Princes St buses

Dark, polished wood and deep-red walls characterise the traditional décor in this lovely Georgian town house in the heart of the New Town. The seven bedrooms (all on the 3rd floor; no elevator) are a little spartan, but at these prices and with this location (Princes St shops, Rose St pubs and Thistle St restaurants are just minutes away, and you can walk to the castle in a quarter of an hour) it seems churlish to moan.

CITY CENTRE TOURIST HOSTEL

Map pp218-19 Hostel £

☎ 556 8070; www.edinburghhostels.com; 3rd fl, 5 W Register St; dm £12-20; 🚌 all Princes St buses; 💻

These days, backpacker hostels in Edinburgh are ten-a-penny, but the City Centre has been around for a while now and knows its market well. Its big selling points are location, location and location – tucked away in an alley between Princes St and St Andrew Sq, and barely a caber's toss from bus and train stations. The atmosphere is more homely than party, and the hostel is generally kept spotless and tidy; if there's one thing to moan about, it's the sorry trickle that passes for a shower.

DENE GUEST HOUSE

Map pp218-19 Guesthouse £

☎ 556 2700; www.deneguesthouse.com; 7 Eyre Pl; s £25-35, d £40-80; 🚌 23, 27 or 36

The Dene is an informal and family-friendly guesthouse set in a charming Georgian town house. Though neatly decorated and kitted out with country pine furniture, some of the rooms might feel a little on the cramped side; if possible, go for a spacious double on the 1st floor. Princes St is just a short walk away and (unusually for Edinburgh guesthouses) dogs are welcome.

DUKES OF WINDSOR STREET

Map pp218-19 Hotel ££

☎ 556 6046; www.dukesofwindsor.com; 17 Windsor St; s £35-80, d £60-140; 🚌 1, 4, 5, 15, 19, 26, 34, 44 or 45

From its Ionic-columned portico to its black, wrought-iron balconies, Dukes of Windsor Street is the epitome of an elegant Georgian town house, a mere 10-minute stroll from Princes St and Waverley train station. The eight luxurious bedrooms are fitted out with crisp white bed linen, soft fluffy towels and posh toiletries, while the chic breakfast room offers a varied menu that includes vegan and wheat-free options.

GLASSHOUSE Map pp218-19 Boutique Hotel £££

☎ 525 8200; www.theetoncollection.com; 2 Greenside Pl; r £130-375, ste £345-450; 🚌 all Leith Walk buses

With floor-to-ceiling windows, stunning artwork and a two-acre roof garden, Edinburgh's newest luxury hotel is a palace of cutting-edge design, entered through the neo-Gothic façade of a preserved mid-19th-century church. All the bedrooms are on the two topmost floors, and all have balconies or terraces – choose between those with views over the city and those opening onto the secluded rooftop garden – and are fitted with Egyptian cotton sheets, leather sofas, and luxurious glass and marble bathrooms with heated stone floors.

HOWARD Map pp218-19 Boutique Hotel £££

☎ 274 7402; www.thehoward.com; 34 Great King St; s £108-145, d £206-275, ste £270-295; 🚌 13; Ⓟ

Pampering is perhaps too weak a word for the service you get at this small (18 rooms) but beautifully turned out Georgian hotel. On arrival, each guest is assigned a personal 'butler' who will do everything from unpacking your bags and polishing your shoes to 'organising your social itinerary' and serving dinner in your room – or even breakfast in bed. Gorgeous period décor, including striped Regency wallpaper and roll-top baths, is complemented by high-tech features such as email-TV and Internet access in all rooms.

MINGALAR GUEST HOUSE

Map pp218-19 Guesthouse £

☎ 556 7000; www.criper.com; 2 E Claremont St; s £28-60, d £45-70; 🚌 8 or 17

Mingalar means 'welcome' in Burmese, and you'll certainly feel right at home in this Georgian-style town house, whose many original features include marble fireplaces and stained-glass front door. There are seven bright, high-ceilinged bedrooms, all with en-suite bathrooms, and each equipped with a fridge containing ice and a jug of fresh milk for your tea and coffee (no vile UHT stuff here). There are two family rooms (each with one double and two single beds, £84 to £120 for four) which makes the Mingalar a bargain if you're travelling with kids.

PARLIAMENT HOUSE HOTEL

Map pp218-19 Hotel £££

☎ 478 4000; www.parliamenthouse-hotel.co.uk; 15 Calton Hill; s/d £120/180; 🚌 all Leith Walk buses

Tucked away in a quiet corner of Calton Hill, the cosily traditional, 53-room Parliament House is only five minutes' walk from Princes St and Waverley train station. There's a welcoming lounge with an open fire and plaid upholstery, friendly and helpful staff, and spacious rooms (though lots of stairs, and no elevator).

A room at Rick's (right)

TOP FIVE ROMANTIC HIDEAWAYS

- **Channings** (p166) Unwind in an Edwardian slipper bath or modern Jacuzzi.
- **Dundas Castle** (p170) Really get away from it all in the secluded Boathouse.
- **Howard** (opposite) Where your personal butler will serve breakfast in bed.
- **Scotsman Hotel** (p162) The hotel's North Bridge Brasserie is perfect for dinner *à deux*.
- **Witchery by the Castle** (p162) Themed Gothic suites let your imagination run riot, and the baths are big enough for two.

RICK'S Map pp218-19 Boutique Hotel ££

☎ 622 7800; www.ricksedinburgh.co.uk; 55a Frederick St; r £95-118; 🚌 13, 24, 29 or 42

Describing itself as 'not a hotel' but a 'restaurant with rooms' (10 of them), Rick's pulls in a young and fashionable crowd with its sharp styling and laid-back atmosphere. The bedrooms boast walnut headboards, designer fabrics and DVD players, along with fluffy bathrobes, well-stocked mini-bars and Molton Brown toiletries.

ROYAL GARDEN APARTMENTS

Map pp218-19 Apartments £££

☎ 625 1234; www.royal-garden.co.uk; York Bldgs, Queen St; 1-bedroom apt per night £135-180, 2-bedroom apt £205-275; 🚌 all York Pl buses

The family-friendly Royal Garden has 30 luxurious, centrally located one- and two-bedroom apartments with daily maid service, business facilities, a private garden (with access to private Queen St Gardens) and use of the Scotsman Hotel's health club and pool. The penthouse apartments (£265 to £385 per night) sleep up to six people, and have rooftop balconies with superb views towards the Firth of Forth and the Fife hills.

WEST END & STOCKBRIDGE

The West End and Stockbridge offer a good selection of midrange and top end hotels, many in spacious Georgian and Victorian villas and town houses. If you're arriving by rail from the direction of Glasgow, you should get off at Haymarket station for hotels in this area.

BELFORD BACKPACKERS HOSTEL

Map p217 Hostel £

☎ 220 2200; www.hoppo.com; 6-8 Douglas Gardens; dm £14-18.50, d £45-55, d with bathroom £50-60; 🚌 13; 💻

The Belford, housed in a converted 19th-century church, must be the only place in Edinburgh where you can bed down beneath magnificent neo-Gothic stained-glass windows. Less than half a mile from Haymarket train station, this is a busy, bustling place with a party vibe; the dorms are separated only by partition walls with no ceilings, so unless you have brought your earplugs they can be a bit noisy. The double rooms are in a separate part of the building and offer more peace and quiet.

BONHAM Map p217 Boutique Hotel £££

☎ 274 7400; www.thebonham.com; 35 Drumsheugh Gardens; s £110-145, d £146-196, ste £262-350; 🚌 19, 36, 37 or 41

The Bonham is one of the few Edinburgh hotels that manages a successful fusion of Victorian interiors with bold modern colours and contemporary design. Cool, crisp bed linen, luxury bathrooms and friendly but unobtrusive service make for a memorable stay. Though set in a quiet West End backstreet, the Bonham is only five minutes' walk from Princes St.

BOTANIC HOUSE HOTEL

Map pp214-15 Hotel £-££

☎ 552 2563; www.botanichousehotel.com; 27 Inverleith Row; s £50-80, d £50-125; 🚌 8, 17, 23 or 27

The six-room Botanic is a stylish little hotel set in a Georgian building on the edge of the Royal Botanic Garden. The room to ask for is 'the double room with view' – a big, bright, 1st-floor bedroom in shades of oatmeal and white, with a huge bow window overlooking the hotel garden and the Palm House.

CHANNINGS Map p217 Boutique Hotel £££

☎ 274 7401; www.channings.co.uk; 12-16 S Learmonth Gardens; s £105-140, d £138-230, ste £206-275; 🚌 19, 36, 37 or 41

Channings is a charming Edwardian-style hotel with the feel of an expensive private club; the reception and lounge areas sport polished wood panelling, leather armchairs, huge, comfy sofas, fine artworks, vases of fresh flowers and open fires. The rooms are tailored in rich fabrics such as silk, velvet and suede, with comfortable mattresses and fluffy towels and bathrobes. If it's a special occasion, lash out on a superior room – ask for the one with the beautiful four-poster bed, which has a black-and-white tiled bathroom with a Victorian roll-top bath big enough for two.

CHRISTOPHER NORTH HOUSE HOTEL

Map pp218-19 Boutique Hotel ££

☎ 225 2720; www.christophernorth.co.uk; 6 Gloucester Pl; s £68-90, d £98-178; 🚌 24, 29 or 42

This is a small and elegant boutique hotel set in a lovely Georgian building, with an appealing blend of contemporary décor and original architectural features. It's handy for shops and restaurants in Stockbridge and walks along the Water of Leith, and the city centre is a short walk uphill. The neighbouring building (same management) houses the luxurious Number 10 apartments, complete with polished wood floors, goose-down duvets and Phillipe Starck bathrooms.

DUNSTANE HOUSE HOTEL

Map p217 Hotel ££

☎ 337 6169; www.dunstanehousehotel.co.uk; 4 West Coates; s £55-85, d £67-98; 🚌 12, 26, 31 or 100; 🅿

The friendly, 16-room Dunstane House Hotel is a large Victorian villa dating from 1850 with many original features including period fireplaces, stained glass and ornate cornices. The rooms are beautifully decorated in warm shades of rose and peach, or chocolate and gold, and the deluxe rooms have four-poster beds.

EDINBURGH RESIDENCE

Map p217 Suites & Apartments £££

☎ 226 3380; www.theedinburghresidence.com; 7 Rothesay Tce; ste £135-280, apt £260-395; 🚌 19, 36, 37 or 41

Nothing more than a discreet brass plaque advertises the presence of the Edinburgh Residence, a collection of 29 luxury suites and apartments housed in a peaceful Georgian terrace. The rooms are vast – the top-end apartments have a floor area the size of a tennis court – and sumptuous, with Zoffany wallpapers, Nina Campbell designer furniture, plush fabrics and spa-

TOP FIVE GAY-FRIENDLY GUESTHOUSES

- Amaryllis Guest House (right)
- Ardmor House (p171)
- Ayden Guest House (p171)
- Fairholme Guest House (p169)
- Six Mary's Place (right)

cious bathrooms, some with a claw-foot bathtub big enough to swim in, others with a Jacuzzi made for two.

MELVIN HOUSE HOTEL Map p217 Hotel £££

☎ 225 5084; www.melvinhouse.co.uk; 3 Rothesay Tce; s £79-120, d £140-180; 🚌 19, 36, 37 or 41

Built in 1883 as a grand home for the founder of the *Scotsman* newspaper, the Melvin House is a Victorian extravaganza of ornately carved oak, parquet floors, Persian rugs, stained glass, coffered ceilings and grandiose fireplaces. The 22 rooms are large and comfortable, decorated in bright modern colours in contrast to the period feel of the public areas.

NUMBER 17 Map p217 Guesthouse ££

☎ 315 4088; www.numberseventeen.co.uk; 17 Learmonth Tce; s £65-80, d £80-130; 🚌 19, 37 or 41

There are not too many B&Bs in Edinburgh where you are treated to breakfast around the kitchen table, sitting in front of a big Aga stove which the owner (a Cordon Bleu chef) uses to produce mouth-watering home baking. Number 17 is a listed Victorian town house with three bedrooms, all en suite. Our favourite is the Green Room on the ground floor, with Persian rugs scattered on a varnished pine floor, a huge sleigh bed, and lots of antique furniture. No kids allowed.

ORIGINAL RAJ Map p217 Hotel £

☎ 346 1333; www.rajempire.com; 6 West Coates; s £40-50, d £50-60; 🚌 12, 26, 31 or 100

Passers-by do a double take when they spot the Bombay bicycle rickshaw and marble elephant in the garden of this otherwise innocuous villa. Edinburgh's only Indian-themed hotel has 17 spacious bedrooms decorated with colourful Indian fabrics, embroidered cushions, handmade wooden furniture and old photos of Indian rajahs. All are comfortable, but the room to ask for is the Bollywood Suite, which has a separate lounge area with sofa and coffee table.

SIX MARY'S PLACE Map p217 Guesthouse ££

☎ 332 8965; www.sixmarysplace.co.uk; 6 Mary's Pl, Raeburn Pl; s £35-55, d £70-100; 🚌 24, 29, 36 or 42

Six Mary's Place is an attractive Georgian town house, fully refurbished with a designer mix of period features, contemporary furniture and modern colours. Breakfasts are vegetarian only, served in an attractive conservatory with a view of the garden. The lounge, with its big comfy sofas, offers free coffee and newspapers, and a computer where you can check your email.

TOLLCROSS & BRUNTSFIELD

The Tollcross and Bruntsfield districts lie just south of the city centre, only 10 minutes away by bus. Accommodation is mostly guesthouses and B&Bs, which are concentrated along Gilmore Pl in Tollcross, and around Viewforth and Hartington Gardens in Bruntsfield.

AMARYLLIS GUEST HOUSE

Map pp224-5 Guesthouse £

☎ 229 3293; www.amaryllisguesthouse.com; 21 Upper Gilmore Pl; s £25-45, d £36-80; 🚌 10 or 27; Ⓟ

The gay-friendly Amaryllis is a cute little Georgian town house with a luxuriant garden, set on a quiet back street. It has five bright and cheerful rooms, all except one with en-suite facilities; the family room can sleep two adults and four children. Princes St is only 15 minutes' walk away.

BRUNTSFIELD YOUTH HOSTEL

Map pp224-5 Hostel £

☎ 0870 155 3255; www.syha.org.uk, www.hibackpacker.com; 7 Bruntsfield Cres; dm £14-16; 🚌 11 or 16

The best of Edinburgh's SYHA (Scottish Youth Hostels Association) hostels enjoys an attractive setting in a Victorian terrace overlooking Bruntsfield Links, a lovely tree-lined park about a mile south of Princes St in a pleasant residential district with a large student population. The 126-bed hostel has spick and span four- to 10-bed dorms, brightly decorated in bold colours and kept scrupulously clean.

EDINBURGH CITY HOTEL

Map pp218-19 Hotel ££

☎ 622 7979; www.bestwesternedinburghcity.co.uk; 79 Lauriston Pl; s £60-120, d £80-190; 🚌 23, 27 or 45

Dating from 1879 and now tastefully restored and redecorated, the Edinburgh City Hotel was originally the Edinburgh Royal Maternity Hospital. The refurbished rooms are spacious, bright and modern – some retain original features such as bay windows and turrets – and the hotel is less than 15 minutes' walk from Edinburgh Castle.

GREENHOUSE Map p226 Guesthouse ££

☎ 622 7634; www.greenhouse-edinburgh.com; 14 Hartington Gardens; s £55-75, d £60-80; 🚌 11, 15, 16, 17, 23 or 45

Edinburgh's most environmentally aware guesthouse is wholly vegetarian and vegan, uses low-energy light bulbs and recycles as much as possible; even the soap and shampoo are free of animal products. Set in a refurbished Victorian terrace, the Greenhouse has six bedrooms enlivened by brightly coloured counterpanes; ask for room 3, a spacious double with large bay window and wing-back armchairs.

KNIGHT RESIDENCE

Map pp218-19 Apartments ££

☎ 622 8120; www.theknightresidence.co.uk; 12 Lauriston St; d apt £110-170, 2-bedroom apt £150-190; 🚌 2 or 35

Works by contemporary artists adorn the modern one- and two-bedroom apartments (available by the night) that make up the Knight Residence. Each has a fully equipped kitchen and a comfortable lounge with cable TV, video and stereo (and an extension speaker in the bathroom). You can even order specific CDs and videos to be waiting in your rooms when you arrive. It has a good central location in a quiet street only a few minutes' walk from the Grassmarket.

POINT HOTEL Map pp218-19 Hotel £££

☎ 221 5555; www.point-hotel.co.uk; 34 Bread St; s £70-140, d £125-170, ste from £350; 🚌 2 or 35

Love it or hate it, there's no denying that the cutting-edge design of the Point Hotel is a talking point. For some, its stark minimalism and bold use of colour epitomise the best of contemporary design; for others, it's just plain garish. The superior bedrooms (known as Executive rooms) and the four Jacuzzi-equipped suites are spacious and stylish, with chic black leather sofas and fantastic views of Edinburgh Castle. But the standard rooms are frankly disappointing for a hotel in this price range.

ROBERTSON GUEST HOUSE

Map p226 Guesthouse ££

☎ 229 2652; www.robertson-guesthouse.com; 5 Hartington Gardens; s £28-50, d £56-100; 🚌 all Bruntsfield buses

Set in a Victorian terrace tucked away down a quiet backstreet, the homely six-room Robertson Guest House has a good range of healthy breakfast offerings including yoghurt, fresh fruit and a vegetarian cooked breakfast.

TOWN HOUSE Map pp224-5 Guesthouse ££

☎ 229 1985; www.thetownhouse.com; 65 Gilmore Pl; s £35-45, d £70-90; 🚌 10 or 27

The five-room Town House is a plush little place, offering the sort of quality and comfort you might expect from a much larger and more expensive hotel. It's an elegant Victorian terraced house with big bay windows, spacious bedrooms (all en suite) and a breakfast menu that includes salmon fishcakes and kippers alongside the more usual offerings.

SOUTHSIDE & NEWINGTON

Southside and Newington have the city's greatest concentration of good midrange guesthouses and B&Bs, as well as several excellent hotels. If you're hunting for vacancies on foot, the best strips are Newington Rd, Minto St, Mayfield Gardens and Craigmillar Park.

45 GILMOUR RD

Map pp224-5 Guesthouse £-££

☎ 667 3536; www.edinburghbedbreakfast.com; 45 Gilmour Rd; s £35-47, d £50-94; 🚌 all Newington buses

A peaceful setting, large garden and friendly owners contribute to the appeal of this Victorian terraced house, which overlooks the local bowling green. The décor is an intriguing blend of 19th- and 20th-century influences, with bold Victorian reds, pine floors and a period fireplace in the lounge, a rocking horse and hanging banners in the hallway, and a 1930s vibe in the three spacious bedrooms.

AONACH MOR GUEST HOUSE

Map pp224-5 Guesthouse £-££

☎ 667 8694; www.aonachmor.com; 14 Kilmaurs Tce; r per person £25-45; 🚌 2, 14, 30 or 33

This elegant Victorian terraced house is located on a quiet backstreet and has seven bedrooms, all beautifully decorated, with many original period features. Our favourite is the 1st-floor bedroom at the front, with the bay window.

ARGYLE BACKPACKERS

Map pp224-5 Hostel £

☎ 667 9991; www.argyle-backpackers.co.uk; 14 Argyle Pl; dm £12-15, d & tw £34-40; 🚌 41; 💻

The Argyle, spread across three adjacent terraced houses, is an upmarket hostel offering double and twin rooms as well as four- to eight-bed dorms (mixed sex). There is a comfortable TV lounge, an attractive little conservatory, and a pleasant walled garden at the back where you can sit outside in summer.

BOROUGH HOTEL

Map pp224-5 Boutique Hotel ££

☎ 668 2255; www.boroughhotel.com; 72-80 Causewayside; r £70-275; 🚌 42

Modern art and minimalist décor characterise this small but appealing hotel, designed by Ben Kelly (best known for designing bars like Manchester's Hacienda). The 12 bedrooms are compact but stylish, with high ceilings, king-size beds with duck-down duvets, and large warehouse-style windows. Paintings by contemporary artists lend a splash of colour to the bare white walls, and Molton Brown toiletries lend a touch of luxury to the chrome and ceramic bathrooms.

FAIRHOLME GUEST HOUSE

Map pp224-5 Guesthouse £-££

☎ 667 8645; www.fairholme.co.uk; 13 Moston Tce; s £25-45, d £50-80; 🚌 42

A pleasant family-run Victorian villa with five rooms (four en suite), the gay- and vegetarian-friendly Fairholme has been recommended by several readers. It's on a quiet street close to a main bus route into the city centre.

GLENALLAN GUEST HOUSE

Map pp224-5 Guesthouse ££

☎ 667 1667; www.glenallan.co.uk; 19 Mayfield Rd; s £45-75, d £70-110; 🚌 42

A bit of old-fashioned luxury is on offer at the Glenallan, a Victorian terraced house with five plush bedrooms, posh toiletries, and home-baked bread on the breakfast table, set in a sunny flower-filled garden on a main bus route into town. Children aged eight and under not accepted.

HOPETOUN Map pp224-5 B&B £-££

☎ 667 7691; www.hopetoun.com; 15 Mayfield Rd; s £25-45, d £50-90; 🚌 42

The Hopetoun is a homely Victorian terrace about 10 minutes by bus from the city centre. There are two bedrooms, both decorated in bright and cheerful modern shades, with colourful paintings on the walls – no tartan kitschery here – and the landlady is a fount of knowledge about local history and traditional Scottish music.

KILDONAN LODGE HOTEL

Map pp224-5 Hotel ££

☎ 667 2793; wwwkildonanlodgehotel.co.uk; 27 Craigmillar Park; s £49-75, d £78-130; 🚌 all Newington buses; P

A grand garden villa, built for a wealthy Victorian businessman, the Kildonan is an elegant small hotel offering 12 spacious, high-ceilinged bedrooms, some with four-poster beds and spa baths. The country-house atmosphere is enhanced by the stag's head in the lobby and the open fireplace in the dining room.

PRESTONFIELD HOUSE HOTEL

Map pp214-15 Boutique Hotel £££

☎ 668 3346; www.prestonfield.com; Priestfield Rd; d from £195, ste from £275; P

If the blonde wood, brown leather and brushed steel of modern boutique hotels leave you cold, then this is the place for you. A 17th-century mansion set in 20 acres of parkland (complete with peacocks and Highland cattle), Prestonfield House is the 'ultimate retort to minimalism'. Draped in

A SCOTSMAN'S HOME IS...

...his castle but a Scottish castle can also be your home – at least for a couple of days. A number of castles around Edinburgh offer accommodation to visitors.

Borthwick Castle (☎ 01875-820514; borthwickcastle@hotmail.com; North Middleton, Gorebridge; s £80-100, d £120-220) Fifteenth-century Borthwick Castle stands foursquare on a hillside overlooking the Gore Water. At 33.5m, it is one of the tallest and most impressive tower-houses in Britain. Mary Queen of Scots sought refuge here in 1567, and the castle walls still bear the scars of cannon fire from the time in 1650 when it was besieged by Oliver Cromwell's forces. Today it is a luxury hotel with 10 'bedchambers', five of them with four-poster beds. Dinner in the vaulted Great Hall, complete with log fire and candlelight, is a memorable experience. Borthwick Castle is 12 miles southeast of Edinburgh, near North Middleton on the A7 road to Galashiels.

Dalhousie Castle (☎ 01875-820153; www.dalhousiecastle.co.uk; Bonnyrigg; s £130-145, d £175-200, ste £290-335) Situated on the bank of the River South Esk just 7 miles southeast of Edinburgh city centre, Dalhousie Castle was built in the 15th century for the Ramsay family; it was converted to a hotel in 1972. The castle's 27 rooms include 14 with historical themes, such as the barrel-vaulted De Ramseia Suite with its 18th-century carved oak bed, a stone alcove containing the 500-year-old castle well, and an oak-panelled bathroom with a (considerably more recent) double Jacuzzi; and the vast Robert the Bruce Suite, decked out in shades of burgundy and blue, with a canopied king-size bed. The hotel also has a luxurious spa.

Dundas Castle (☎ 319 2039; www.dundascastle.co.uk; South Queensferry; r from £330) Built in 1818 to the design of William Burn, and incorporating a 15th-century keep, Dundas Castle was originally the seat of the Dundas family. Now the home of Sir Jack Stewart-Clark and his family, the castle can be rented for a wedding or the ultimate dinner party. There are nine luxurious twin/double rooms with en suite, but you have to take a minimum of four at once – for around £1750 per night all in, including free run of the castle for a day. A gourmet dinner will cost from £45 per guest. Alternatively, you can rent the double room in the Boathouse for a romantic hideaway at £330 per night. Dundas Castle is 8 miles west of Edinburgh city centre, just south of South Queensferry.

damask, packed with antiques and decorated in red, black and gold, the interior is opulent, decadent and extravagant – look out for original tapestries, 17th-century embossed leather panels, £500-a-roll hand-painted wallpaper, and pert-buttocked *putti* twanging arrows from 200-year-old moulded plaster ceilings. Despite the antique splendour, the hotel's 30 rooms are supplied with all mod cons, including Internet access, Bose sound systems, DVD players and flat-screen TVs.

SHERWOOD GUEST HOUSE

Map pp224-5 Guesthouse £

☎ 667 1200; www.sherwood-edinburgh.com; 42 Minto St; s £30-60, d £40-75; 🚌 all Newington buses; P

One of the most attractive guesthouses on Minto St, the Sherwood is a refurbished Georgian terraced house decked out with hanging baskets and shrubs. Inside are six en-suite rooms that combine Regency-style striped wallpaper with modern fabrics and pine furniture. It has TV in all rooms, and there are two private off-road parking spaces.

SOUTHSIDE GUEST HOUSE

Map pp224-5 Guesthouse ££

☎ 668 4422; www.southsideguesthouse.co.uk; 8 Newington Rd; s £45-96, d £64-116; 🚌 all Newington buses

Though set in a typical late-Georgian terrace, the Southside transcends the traditional guesthouse category and feels more like a modern boutique hotel. Its eight stylish rooms just ooze interior design, standing out from other Newington B&Bs through the clever use of bold colours and modern furniture.

WATERFRONT EDINBURGH

Accommodation close to the waterfront is still a bit out of the mainstream, but is handy for the Royal Yacht *Britannia* and Leith's excellent restaurant scene (see p117). Pilrig St, halfway down the western side of Leith Walk, has a concentration of guesthouses, while Portobello, with its sandy beach, is a good place for kids.

ARDMOR HOUSE Map p216 Guesthouse ££

☎ 554 4944; www.ardmorhouse.com; 74 Pilrig St; s £45-70, d £65-110; 🚌 11

The Ardmor is a stylishly renovated Victorian house with five gorgeous en-suite bedrooms. The décor successfully blends period fireplaces, sash windows, panelled doors and cornices with contemporary furniture and mellow modern colours, while the bedrooms deliver all those little touches that make a place special: good reading lights, powerful showers, thick towels, crisp white bed linen, and free newspapers at breakfast.

AYDEN GUEST HOUSE

Map p216 Guesthouse £-££

☎ 554 2187; www.ayden-edinburgh.com; 70 Pilrig St; s £35-80, d £50-90; 🚌 11

Another refurbished Victorian town house with spacious rooms, the Ayden oozes cool contemporary style in shades of coffee and cream, and offers crisp bed linen, fluffy towels, and luxurious breakfasts cooked by a professional chef. The Ayden is also family-friendly (two of the five rooms are family rooms, one of them with a double and three single beds), and can provide a cot and high-chair on request.

BALMORAL GUESTHOUSE

Map p216 Guesthouse £

☎ 554 1857; www.balmoralguesthouse.co.uk; 32 Pilrig St; s £25-35, d £36-66; 🚌 11

This comfortable five-bedroom guesthouse is located in an elegant Victorian terrace off Leith Walk. The house dates from 1856, and the owners have a good eye for antiques (including, unusually, antique radios); period furniture gives the bedrooms here a pleasantly old-fashioned atmosphere.

GLOBETROTTER INN

Map pp214-15 Hostel £

☎ 336 1030; www.globetrotterinns.com; 46 Marine Dr; dm £10-20; d £30-42; 🚌 42; 💻

A large and comfortable hostel with luxury bunks, TV lounges, sauna and gym, the Globetrotter is good value but can occasionally be plagued by noisy stag-party groups. It's close the waterfront, about 20 minutes by free hourly shuttle bus from the city centre (pick-up from Waverley Station).

MALMAISON HOTEL

Map p216 Hotel ££-££

☎ 468 5000; www.malmaison-edinburgh.com; 1 Tower Pl; s £115-165, d £120-185, ste £225-255; 🚌 16, 22, 35 or 36; Ⓟ

The stylish, award-winning Malmaison is housed in a 19th-century former seaman's mission in the heart of Edinburgh's docklands. There are 100 bedrooms, and it seems that no two are decorated alike – some are in shades of black, brown and cream, others in greys, lilacs and blues, but all have king-size beds, rich fabrics, colourful cushions and fluffy bathrobes. Ask for a superior room at the front of the hotel for extra space and a view over the river.

The 'Summer Room' at Dundas Castle (opposite)

ROBERT BURNS GUEST HOUSE

Map pp214-15 Guesthouse £

☎ 669 5678; www.robertburnshotel.co.uk; 41 Abercorn Tce; r £35-90; 🚌 15 or 26

This child-friendly guesthouse is an attractive semi-detached Victorian villa close to Portobello Beach, run by a New York couple. It has six bright, comfortable rooms with modern pine furniture (five en suite), and the Scottish breakfast menu is complemented by American hash browns. The owner is a keen golfer and can help you arrange a round of golf on local courses.

SHERIDAN GUEST HOUSE

Map pp214-15 Guesthouse ££

☎ 554 4107; www.sheridanedinburgh.co.uk; 1 Bonnington Tce, Newhaven Rd; s £35-60, d £56-90; 🚌 11

Fresh flowers are a feature of the Sheridan, from the colourful blooms that frame the doorway to the bouquets in the dining room, which is also dotted with woodcarvings and artworks collected during the owners' travels in Southeast Asia. The eight bedrooms (all en suite) blend crisp colours (Etruscan orange bedspreads and cream walls) with contemporary furniture, stylish modern lighting and colourful paintings, which complement the clean-cut Georgian lines of this spacious town house.

STRAVEN GUEST HOUSE

Map pp214-15 Guesthouse £-££

☎ 669 5580; www.stravenguesthouse.com; 3 Brunstane Rd N; s £28-45, d £50-78; 🚌 15 or 26; Ⓟ

Located well out from the city centre (20 minutes by bus) but only a block from Portobello's long sandy beach, the Straven is a large Victorian villa with seven homely en-suite bedrooms. The guesthouse is eco-friendly, with a commitment to recycling, energy conservation and waste reduction, and uses Fair Trade products where possible. No children under 12 years old.

GREATER EDINBURGH

DOVECOTE HOUSE

Guesthouse £-££

☎ 467 7467; www.dovecotehouse.co.uk; 6 Dovecote Rd; s £25-35, d £50-80; 🚌 12, 26, 31 or 100

Dovecote House is a delightful three-bedroom B&B set in a Victorian garden villa in the posh western suburb of Corstorphine. The décor is beautifully light, clean and modern, blending shades of oatmeal, brown and white with stylish contemporary furniture in oak, beech and pine, and the setting seems a million miles away from the traffic, noise and crowds of the city centre (although in reality, Princes St is only a 10-minute bus ride away).

OROCCO PIER

Boutique Hotel ££

☎ 331 1298; www.oroccopier.co.uk; 17 High St, South Queensferry; s/d/t from £75/100/160; 🚌 First Edinburgh 43

Take one 17th-century coaching inn, transform the interior with the latest in contemporary design, plant it on the shores of the Firth between Scotland's two most famous bridges, and add huge picture windows and outdoor terraces for admiring the panoramic view. *Et voilà* – Orocco Pier. The 12 modern, minimalist bedrooms come in cool shades of cream that complement the polished wood floors; five of them (Nos 2, 3, 4, 11 and 12) have sea views across the Firth of Forth.

boat trip adult/child/family £8/4.25/21.50; ⌚ 9.30am-6pm Apr-Oct, 10.30am-4pm Nov-Mar)

Linlithgow Canal Centre (☎ 01506-671215; www.lucs.org.uk; Manse Rd Canal Basin, Linlithgow; admission free; ⌚ 2-5pm Sat & Sun Easter-Sep, plus 2-5pm Mon-Fri Jul & Aug)

Linlithgow Palace (☎ 01506-842896; Church Peel, Linlithgow; admission adult/child £4/1.60; ⌚ 9.30am-6.30pm Apr-Sep, 9.30am-4.30pm Oct-Mar)

St Michael's Church (☎ 01506-842188; Church Peel, Linlithgow; admission free; ⌚ 10am-4.30pm Mon-Sat, 12.30-4.30pm Sun May-Sep, 10am-3pm Mon-Fri Oct-Apr)

Eating

Bridge Inn (☎ 0131-333 1320; www.bridgeinn.com; 27 Baird Rd, Ratho; mains £8-15; ⌚ bar 11am-11pm Mon-Sat, 12.30-11pm Sun, food served noon-2.30pm & 6.30-9pm) A cosy, 19th-century coaching inn on the banks of the Union Canal, with lots of toys and play equipment to keep the kids amused.

Champany Inn (☎ 01506-834532; Champany; mains £12-22; ⌚ 12.30-2pm & 7-10pm Mon-Fri, 7-10pm Sat) A country restaurant famous for its excellent Aberdeen Angus steak and Scottish lobster. The neighbouring **Chop and Ale House** (mains £6-14) is a less-formal alternative to the main dining room. The inn is 2 miles northeast of Linlithgow on the A803/A904 road towards Bo'ness and Queensferry.

Four Marys (☎ 01506-842171; 65-76 High St, Linlithgow; mains £4-9; ⌚ food served noon-3pm & 5-9pm Mon-Fri, noon-9pm Sat & Sun) An attractive traditional pub (opposite the palace entrance) that serves real ales and excellent pub grub, including haggis, neeps and tatties.

Marynka (☎ 01506-840123; 57 High St, Linlithgow; lunch mains £6-10, 2-course dinner £21.50; ⌚ noon-2pm & 6-11.30pm Tue-Sat) A pleasant little gourmet restaurant.

ST ANDREWS

☎ 01334

The reverence in which golf is held in this pretty, prosperous seaside town is one of Scotland's more endearing eccentricities. St Andrews is the headquarters of golf's governing body, the Royal & Ancient Golf Club, and the location of the world's most famous golf course, the St Andrews Old Course.

Even if belting little white balls with sticks isn't your thing, it's still well worth the trip. St Andrews boasts an impressive collection of medieval ruins and university buildings, and there's some idyllic coastal scenery nearby. Exploring the streets on foot is easy and rewarding, with lots of cobbled lanes and alleys, and an inviting choice of shops, pubs and restaurants.

You'll hear just as many English accents around town as you will Scottish; it's home to an ancient university where wealthy English undergraduates (Prince William studied here) rub shoulders with Scottish theology students.

St Andrews is said to have been founded by St Regulus, who arrived from Greece in the 4th century bringing important relics, including some of the bones of St Andrew, Scotland's patron saint. The town soon grew into a major pilgrimage centre and later became the ecclesiastical capital of the country. The university was founded in 1410, the first in Scotland; King James I received part of his education here, as did James III.

Golf was being played here as long ago as the 15th century, and the Old Course dates from the 16th. The Royal & Ancient Golf Club was founded in 1754 and the imposing clubhouse was built 100 years later. The British Open Championship, which

TRANSPORT

Distance from Edinburgh 62 miles

Direction Northeast

Travel time 1½ hours

Bus Stagecoach Fife operates a bus service from Edinburgh to St Andrews via Kirkcaldy (£6.50, two hours, hourly).

Car From Queensferry St in Edinburgh city centre, follow signs for the Forth Rd Bridge (toll £1, northbound only), then continue north on the M90 motorway. Exit at junction 8 and follow the A91 to St Andrews.

Train There is no train station in St Andrews itself, but you can take a train (one hour) from Edinburgh to Leuchars, 5 miles to the northwest. Ask for a railbus ticket – a standard return fare is £18.60, a cheap day return £13 – which includes travel on bus 94, 94A, 96, 99 or 99A between the station and St Andrews town centre.

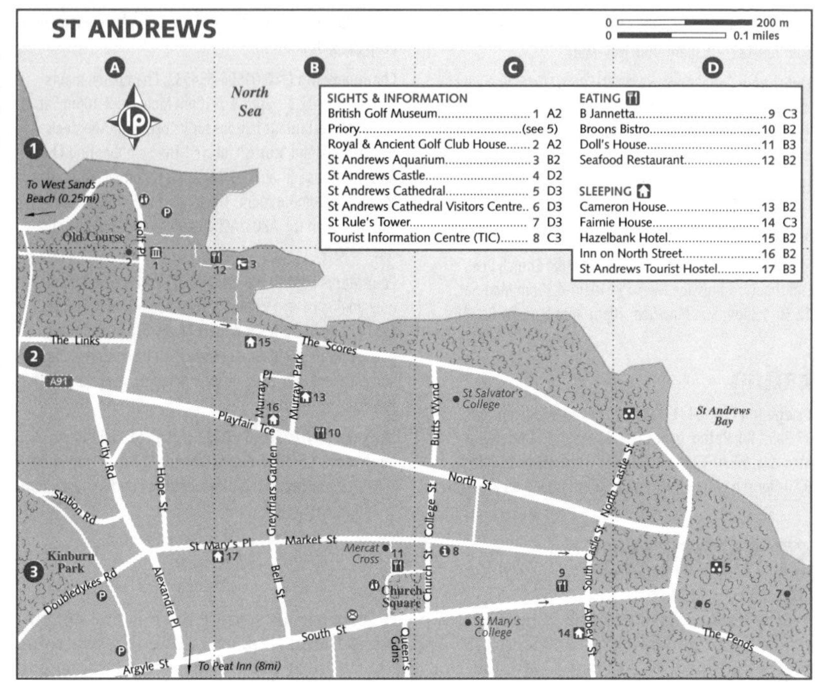

was first held in 1860 in Prestwick, near Glasgow, has taken place regularly at St Andrews since 1873.

At the eastern end of North St is the ruined western façade of what was once the largest and one of the most magnificent cathedrals in the country. Although founded in 1160, **St Andrews Cathedral** wasn't consecrated until 1318 and remained a focus of pilgrimage until it was pillaged in 1559, during the Reformation. Many of the town's buildings were constructed using stones from the ruined cathedral.

The bones of St Andrew lay under the high altar; until the cathedral was built, they had been enshrined in the nearby Church of St Regulus (St Rule). All that remains of the church is **St Rule's Tower** (admission is included in the cathedral ticket), which is well worth the climb for the view over the town. In the same area are parts of the ruined 13th-century priory.

The cathedral's visitor centre includes the calefactory, the only room where the monks could warm themselves by a fire. Masons' marks on the red-sandstone blocks, identifying who shaped each block, can still clearly be seen. There's also a collection of Celtic crosses and gravestones that have been found on the site.

Not far from the cathedral, **St Andrews Castle** is mostly in ruins, but the site itself is evocative with dramatic coastal views. The most intriguing feature is the complex of siege tunnels, said to be the best surviving example of siege engineering in Europe. You can walk along the damp, mossy tunnels, now lit by electric light – but be warned, it helps if you're short! The castle was founded around 1200 as the fortified home of the bishop. A visitor centre gives a good audiovisual introduction and also has a small collection of Pictish stones.

From the castle follow the Scores to the west past St Salvator's College to **St Andrews Aquarium**, where the exhibits include sharks, seals, piranhas and a fascinating sea-horse display. Nearby is the **British Golf Museum**, a surprisingly interesting and modern museum with good audiovisual displays and touch screens as well as golfing memorabilia.

Opposite the museum is the clubhouse of the **Royal & Ancient Golf Club** (not open to the public); beyond stretches the **Old Course** (see p145) and beside it the **West Sands**, the long, long beach made famous by the film *Chariots of Fire*.

Information

St Andrews TIC (☎ 472021; ...rews.co.uk; 70 Market St; 9.30am-8p... ...am-6pm Sun Jul-Aug, 9.30am-7pm Mon-S... ...n Sun Jun, Sep & early Oct, 9.30am-6pm M... ...-4pm Sun Apr & May, 9.30am-5.30pm Mo... ...n-12.30pm Sat mid-Oct–Mar)

Ex

If you... regio... cours...

Sights

British Golf Museum ...ruce Embankment; admission adult/child ....30am-5.30pm Mon-Sat & 10am-5pm ...Oct, 10am-4pm daily Nov-Easter)

CAS... Con... dun... Stirli...

St Andrews Aquar... ...4786; the Scores; admission adult/child £5.95/... ...am-6pm Easter-Oct, 10am-5pm Nov-Easter)

St Andrews Cas... ...7196; N Castle St; admission adult/child £4/1... ....30am-6.30pm Apr-Sep, 9.30am-4.30pm Oct-M...

Fl... Sc... no...

St Andrews C... (☎ 472563; North St; admission incl cast... ...child £5/2, cathedral only £3/1.20; 9.30am-... ...Apr-Sep, 9.30am-4.30pm Oct-Mar)

Eatin...

B Janne... (☎ 473285; 31 South St; 2-dip cone from £1.80; ... 9am-6pm) A St Andrews institution – on a hot weeker... ...here is a constant stream of people outside the place f... ...erishly licking a delicious ice-cream cone before it melts ...a puddle. Choose from 52 flavours.

Broc...ns Bistro (☎ 478479; 119 North St; mains £6-12; lunch & dinner) Housed in part of an old cinema, this is a friendly, humming bar-bistro with a smoky atmosphere, students, busy waiters and kicking cocktails.

Doll's House (☎ 477422; 3 Church Sq; mains £10-13; noon-2.30pm & 5.30-10pm) A relaxed, informal and child-friendly restaurant with a changing menu of French and Scottish cuisine. The £7 two-course lunch is unbeatable value, and the early-evening two-course deal for £13 isn't bad either.

Peat Inn (☎ 840206; Cupar; 3-course lunch/dinner £21/32; 12.30-2.30pm & 7-9.30pm Tue-Sat) This is one of the best restaurants in Scotland, housed in a rustic country inn about 6 miles southwest of St Andrews, with a Michelin rosette–winning menu. To get there, head south for 5 miles on the A915 then turn right on the B940 for another 1½ miles.

Seafood Restaurant (☎ 479475; the Scores; 3-course dinner £35; noon-4pm & 6pm-late) St Andrews' finest restaurant, set in a stylish glass-walled room built out over the sea, with panoramic views of St Andrews Bay. Offers top-class seafood and an excellent wine list.

Sleeping

Cameron House (☎ 472306; www.cameronhouse-sta.co.uk; 11 Murray Park; r per person £34) A soft and cuddly guesthouse that makes you feel right at home, down to the teddy bears hanging off the bed posts.

Fairnie House (☎ 474094; www.fairniehouse.freeserve.co.uk; 10 Abbey St; r per person £22-28) A relaxed and friendly B&B in a Georgian town house, with one double and two twin rooms.

Hazelbank Hotel (☎ 472466; www.hazelbank.com; 28 the Scores; s £80, d £90-120) The elegant Hazelbank is a small (10 rooms) but comfortable family-run hotel in a fine 1898 town house. The rooms have king-size beds and the four sea-view rooms are delightful.

Inn on North Street (☎ 473387; www.theinnonnorthstreet.com; 127 North St; s/d £70/100) A classy guesthouse with traditional décor and crisp white bed linen. Rooms are all the same price but some are much better than others – Nos 1 to 3 come with a Jacuzzi.

St Andrews Tourist Hostel (☎ 479911; www.hostelsaccommodation.com; Inchcape House, St Mary's Pl; dm £12; 7am-11pm;) Only five minutes' walk from the bus station, and the only year-round backpacker accommodation in town, so it fills up quickly.

St Andrews Castle (opposite)

EAST LOTHIAN

The fertile farmland of East Lothian stretches eastward from Edinburgh along the southern shores of the Firth of Forth to the seaside resort of North Berwick and the seabird colonies of the Bass Rock. The region is packed with interesting places to visit, ranging from fascinating industrial and aircraft museums to spectacular castles and sandy beaches, plus lots of great bird-watching opportunities.

At the junction where the A198 leaves the A1 is the village of **Prestonpans**. A simple monument on the eastern edge of the village marks the site of the Battle of Prestonpans, where the Jacobite army of Bonnie Prince Charlie defeated the government forces of Sir John Cope in 1745; a battlefield walk is held each year on 21 September, the anniversary of the encounter. Beside the shore road on the western outskirts is **Prestongrange Industrial Heritage Museum**, on the site of a former coal mine – coal has been dug from this site since monks first exploited the surface seams 800 years ago.

TRANSPORT

Distance from Edinburgh 24 miles (to North Berwick)

Direction East

Travel time One hour

Bus First Edinburgh bus 124 runs every 20 minutes between Edinburgh and North Berwick (1¼ hours), stopping at Prestonpans, Aberlady, Gullane and Dirleton. Buses X6 and X8 run from Edinburgh to Haddington every 30 minutes; a return ticket costs £7.

Car Follow the A1 east from Edinburgh city centre to the junction at Tranent, then take the A198 to North Berwick.

Train There are hourly trains between Edinburgh and North Berwick, stopping at Prestonpans; a return ticket costs £7.60 (cheap day return £4.70), and the journey takes 35 minutes.

Two miles east of Prestonpans is the hidden gem of **Seton Collegiate Church**, dating from the 15th century and, like Rosslyn Chapel (see opposite), with Templar associations. The interior has starkly beautiful Gothic vaulting and window tracery, the tombs of members of the Seton family, and the church's bell, cast in Holland and dating from 1577.

The attractive village of Aberlady sits at the head of the broad expanse of **Aberlady Bay**. When the tide goes out it exposes around 400 hectares of sand and mud flats, part of a nature reserve that provides excellent bird-watching. In autumn and winter vast flocks of up to 10,000 waders, mostly lapwings and golden plovers, and 15,000 pink-footed geese fly in to feed, and in spring there's a good chance of seeing ospreys.

Haddington straddles the River Tyne 5 miles south of Aberlady. **St Mary's Parish Church**, built in 1462, is the largest parish church in Scotland and one of the finest pre-Reformation churches in the country. Nearby **Lennoxlove House**, a lovely country house dating originally from around 1345, contains fine furniture and paintings, and memorabilia relating to Mary Queen of Scots.

North Berwick is an attractive Victorian seaside resort. When the weather is fine there are great views to the spectacular **Bass Rock**, stained white in spring and summer with the guano from thousands of nesting gannets.

It is possible to sail around the Bass Rock on boat trips leaving from North Berwick harbour. Alternatively, just walk to the eastern end of the harbour and visit the **Scottish Seabird Centre**, an ornithologist's paradise that uses remote-controlled video cameras sited on the Bass Rock and other islands to relay live images of nesting gannets and other seabirds.

There are two contrasting castles within easy reach of North Berwick. Two miles to the west is **Dirleton Castle**, an impressive medieval fortress with massive round towers, a drawbridge and a horrific pit dungeon, surrounded rather incongruously by beautiful manicured gardens. Perched on a sea-cliff 3 miles to the east is the spectacular ruin of **Tantallon Castle**. Built around 1350, it was the fortress residence of the Douglas Earls of Angus, defended on one side by a series of ditches and on the other by an almost sheer drop into the sea.

In the countryside a few miles to the south of North Berwick (take the B1347) is the former RAF airfield at East Fortune that is now home to the superb **National Museum of Flight**. The huge collection of aircraft ranges from Percy Pilcher's 'Hawk' glider – dating from 1896 – to classic fighters such as the Spitfire and English Electric Lightning, and the more recent Phantom and Harrier; the prize exhibit is one of the seven Concordes remaining when the supersonic plane went out of service. Each July the museum hosts Scotland's biggest air show.

Information

North Berwick TIC (☎ 01620-892197; Quality St; ⏰ 9am-6pm Mon-Sat, 11am-4pm Sun)

Sights

Dirleton Castle (☎ 01620-850330; Dirleton; admission adult/child £3.30/1.30; ⏰ 9.30am-6.30pm Apr-Sep, 9.30am-4pm Oct-Mar)

Lennoxlove House (☎ 01620-823720; Lennoxlove Estate; admission adult/child £4.50/2.50; guided tours 1.30-4pm Wed, Thu & Sun Easter-Oct)

National Museum of Flight (☎ 01620-880308; East Fortune Airfield; admission adult/child £5/free; ⏰ 10am-5pm Apr-Oct, 10am-4pm Sat & Sun Nov-Mar)

Prestongrange Industrial Heritage Museum (☎ 0131-653 2904; www.prestongrange.org; Morrison's Haven, Prestonpans; admission free; ⏰ 11am-4pm Apr-Oct)

St Mary's Parish Church (☎ 01620-823109; Sidegate, Haddington; admission free; ⏰ 11am-4pm Mon-Sat, 2-4.30pm Sun Apr-Sep)

Scottish Seabird Centre (☎ 01620-890202; www.seabird.org; the Harbour, North Berwick; admission adult/child £6.95/4.50; ⏰ 10am-6pm Apr-Oct, 10am-4pm Mon-Fri & 10am-5.30pm Sat & Sun Nov-Mar)

Seton Collegiate Church (☎ 01875-813334; Port Seton; admission adult/child £2/80p; ⏰ 9.30am-6.30pm Apr-Sep)

Tantallon Castle (☎ 01620-892727; admission adult/child £3.30/1.30; ⏰ 9.30am-6.30pm Apr-Sep, 9.30am-4pm Sat-Wed Oct-Mar)

Eating & Sleeping

Beach Lodge (☎ 01620-892257; 5 Beach Rd, North Berwick; r per person £27) A friendly B&B offering sea views and vegetarian breakfasts.

Deveau's Brasserie (☎ 01620-850241; Open Arms Hotel, Dirleton; mains £10-13; ⏰ noon-9pm) A delightful brasserie serving French and Scottish food, with a convivial country pub next door.

Grange Restaurant (☎ 01620-893344; 35 High St; 3-course lunch/dinner £9/18; ⏰ noon-2.30pm & 6-9pm) Bistro-style place serving good-quality Scottish food.

Scottish Seabird Centre (☎ 01620-893342; mains £4-6; ⏰ 10am-5.30pm Apr-Oct, 10am-4pm Nov-Mar) The centre contains an excellent café with views of the Bass Rock.

Waterside Bistro & Restaurant (☎ 01620-825764; 1-5 Waterside, Nungate, Haddington; bistro mains £7-10, restaurant £15-20; ⏰ noon-9.30pm) A lovely riverside spot, and a great place to have lunch on a summer's day, watching the swans and ducks go by.

ROSSLYN CHAPEL

The success of Dan Brown's novel *The Da Vinci Code* has seen a flood of visitors (plus a Hollywood film crew and actor Tom Hanks working on the inevitable movie) descend on Rosslyn Chapel, 6 miles south of Edinburgh.

Scotland's most beautiful and enigmatic church, Rosslyn was built in the mid-15th century for William St Clair, third Earl of Orkney. The ornately carved interior – at odds with the architectural fashion of its time – is a monument to the mason's art, and rich in symbolic imagery. As well as flowers, vines, angels and biblical figures, the carved stones include many examples of the pagan 'green man'; other figures are associated with Freemasonry and the Knights Templar. Intriguingly, there are also carvings of plants from the Americas that pre-date Columbus' voyage of discovery. The symbolism of these images has led some researchers to conclude that Rosslyn is some kind of secret Templar repository, and it has been claimed that hidden vaults beneath the chapel could conceal anything from the Holy Grail or the head of John the Baptist to the body of Christ himself. The chapel is owned by the Episcopal Church of Scotland and services are still held here on Sunday mornings.

Just south of the chapel are the ruins of **Roslin Castle** (not open to the public), the former seat of the St Clair family. You can descend the path below the castle into **Roslin Glen**, where

TRANSPORT

Distance from Edinburgh 7 miles

Direction South

Travel time 20 to 30 minutes

Bus Lothian Bus 15A runs from St Andrew Sq in Edinburgh to Roslin village (£1 each way, 30 minutes, hourly on weekdays, every two hours on Saturday and twice a day on Sunday).

Car From Edinburgh city centre follow Causewayside and Mayfield Rd south and continue beyond the ring road on the A701 (signposted Penicuik and Peebles). Two miles on, at Bilston roundabout, turn left on the B7006 to Roslin village.

a path leads along the riverbank to a cave where 13th-century Scottish freedom fighter William Wallace is said to have hidden.

Sights

Rosslyn Chapel (☎ 0131-440 2159; www.rosslyn-chapel.com; Roslin; admission adult/child £6/free; 🕒 9.30am-6pm Mon-Sat, noon-4.45pm Sun)

Eating & Sleeping

Roslin Glen Hotel (☎ 0131-440 2029; 2 Penicuik Rd, Roslin; s/d £65/80; mains £7-15) An appealing Victorian townhouse hotel with eight rooms with en-suite bathroom, and a welcoming bar and restaurant, just a few minutes' walk from Rosslyn Chapel.

STIRLING

If you enjoy exploring medieval castles, you'll enjoy a trip to Stirling. Like Edinburgh in miniature, this lively town is dominated by a splendid fortress perched atop a crag, with an atmospheric old town filled with winding cobblestone streets clinging to the slopes beneath.

TRANSPORT

Distance from Edinburgh 35 miles

Direction Northwest

Travel time One hour

Car From Edinburgh city centre, follow West Coates and Corstorphine Rd west, then take the M8 motorway. At junction 2, switch to the M9 then exit at junction 9 or 10 for Stirling.

Train There are trains from Edinburgh to Stirling (standard/cheap day return £9.80/6.20, 55 minutes, at least twice hourly Monday to Saturday, hourly Sunday).

Throughout Scotland's history, Stirling has occupied a strategically important position – hold Stirling and you control the country. This simple truth has ensured that a castle has existed here since prehistoric times. It commands superb views and you cannot help drawing parallels with Edinburgh's grand fortress – but **Stirling Castle** is better. The location, architecture and historical significance combine to make it one of the grandest of all Scottish castles. This means it also attracts visitors like bees to honey, so we'd advise you visit in the afternoon; most of the tour buses have buzzed off by 4pm.

The current building dates from the late-14th to the 16th centuries, when it was a residence of the Stuart monarchs. James VI remodelled the Chapel Royal and was the last king to live here.

The **Royal Burgh of Stirling Visitor Centre** on the Esplanade has an audiovisual presentation and exhibition about Stirling, including the history and architecture of the castle. There's a car park next to the castle (£2 for two hours); visitors with wheelchairs should contact Historic Scotland (HS; www.historic-scotland.gov.uk) for a courtesy vehicle to assist entry into the castle.

Close by the castle at the top of Castle Wynd is the spectacular **Argyll's Lodging**, the most impressive 17th-century town house in Scotland. It's the former home of William Alexander, Earl of Stirling and noted literary figure. It has been tastefully restored and gives an insight into the lavish aristocratic lifestyle of the 17th century. **Mar's Wark**, also on Castle Wynd, is the ornate façade of what was once a Renaissance-style town house commissioned in 1569 by the wealthy Earl of Mar, regent of Scotland during James VI's minority.

Below the castle, the **Old Town** has cobblestone streets that are packed with fine examples of 15th- to 17th-century architectural gems. The town began to grow when Stirling became a royal burgh, around 1124, and in the 15th and 16th centuries rich merchants built their houses here. The steep slopes ensure you'll be ready for a refreshment in a nearby café or pub after exploring for a couple of hours.

Stirling has the best surviving city wall in Scotland, built in around 1547 when Henry VIII of England began his 'Rough Wooing' (see p39); the **Back Walk** follows the line of the wall from Dumbarton Rd (near the TIC) to the castle, continuing around Castle Rock and back to the old town.

Stirling Castle (opposite)

The **Church of the Holy Rude** has been the town's parish church for 500 years; James VI was crowned here in 1567. The nave and tower date from 1456 and the church features one of the country's few surviving medieval open-timber roofs.

Two miles north of Stirling is the impressive **Wallace Monument**, a Victorian tower raised in memory of Sir William Wallace, the Scottish freedom fighter who was hung, drawn and quartered by the English in 1305. The view from of the tower, which takes in no fewer than seven battlegrounds, is as breathtaking as the 67m climb to the top; the monument also contains interesting displays including Wallace's mighty two-handed sword (clearly the man was no weakling).

Another great Scottish hero is celebrated at the **Bannockburn Heritage Centre**, south of Stirling's city centre. On 24 June 1314 the greatest victory in the history of Scotland's struggle to remain independent took place at the Battle of Bannockburn, when Robert the Bruce overcame superior numbers and sent Edward II's English force running for their lives. This victory turned the tide of fortune in favour of the Scots for the following 400 years. The heritage centre tells the story in a simple and eloquent exhibition, including a 12-minute audiovisual display. Outside is the eerie Borestone site, said to have been Robert the Bruce's command post before the battle. Check out his grim-looking statue, dressed in full battle gear and mounted on a charger.

Information

Royal Burgh of Stirling Visitor Centre (☎ 01786-479901; Castle Esplanade; ⏰ 9.30am-6pm Apr-Oct, 9.30am-5pm Nov-Mar)

Stirling TIC (☎ 0870 720 0620; stirling@visitscotland.com; 41 Dumbarton Rd; ⏰ 9am-7pm Jul & Aug, 9am-5pm Jun–mid-Sep, 10am-5pm Mon-Sat mid-Sep–May)

Sights

Bannockburn Heritage Centre (☎ 01786-812664; Glasgow Rd; admission adult/child £5/4; ⏰ 10am-5.30pm Apr-Oct, 10.30am-4pm Feb, Mar, Nov & Dec, closed Jan)

Church of the Holy Rude (☎ 01786-475275; St John St; admission free; ⏰ 11am-4pm May-Sep)

Stirling Castle (☎ 01786-450000; admission adult/child including Argyll's Lodging £8/3; ⏰ 9.30am-6pm Apr-Sep, 9.30am-5pm Oct-Mar)

Wallace Monument (☎ 01786-472140; Abbey Craig, Causewayhead; admission adult/child/family £6/4/15; ⏰ 10am-5pm Mar-May & Oct, 10am-6pm Jun, 9.30am-6.30pm Jul & Aug, 9.30am-5pm Sep, 10.30am-4pm Nov-Feb)

Eating & Sleeping

Aura (☎ 01786-470333; 51 King St; mains £10-13; ⏰ noon-2.30pm & 6-10pm Tue-Sun, noon-2.30pm Mon) Good-quality, fresh, inventive food at reasonable prices, and with an inexpensive new-world wine list to boot.

Cambio (☎ 01786-461041; 1 Corn Exchange; mains £4-7; ⏰ food served 11am-8pm) A trendy, minimalist bar-restaurant serving a range of international dishes.

Darnley Coffee House (☎ 01786-474468; 18 Bow St; snacks £3.50-5; ⏰ 9am-6pm) Located just down the hill from the castle, offering home baking and speciality coffees.

Munro Guest House (☎ 01786-472685; www.munroguesthouse.co.uk; 14 Princes St; s £27-32, d £40-50) A luxurious family-run guesthouse, 10 minutes' walk from the castle.

Stirling Highland Hotel (☎ 01786-272727; www.paramount-hotels.co.uk/stirling; Spittal St; r per person £49-59; P) The smartest hotel in town, housed in the refurbished Victorian high-school building dating from 1854. Very convenient for the castle and old town.

Willy Wallace Backpackers Hostel (☎ 01876-446773; www.willywallacehostel.com; 77 Murray Pl; dm £9-14;) A clean and friendly hostel in the middle of town.

Directory

Directory

TRANSPORT

AIR

There are direct flights to Edinburgh (and Glasgow) airports from England, Wales, Ireland, the USA, Canada, Scandinavia and many countries in western and central Europe.

From the rest of the world you will probably have to fly into a major European hub and catch a connecting flight to Edinburgh: London, Amsterdam, Frankfurt and Paris have the best connections with Edinburgh.

Airlines

Airlines serving Edinburgh and Glasgow airports include:

Aer Arann (RE; ☎ 0800 587 2324; www.aerarann.com)

Aer Lingus (EI; ☎ 0845 084 4444; www.aerlingus.com)

Air Canada (AC; ☎ 0871 220 1111; www.aircanada.ca)

Air France (AF; ☎ 0845 084 5111; www.airfrance.com)

Air Malta (KM; ☎ 0141-847 1111; www.airmalta.com)

Air Scotland (GRE; ☎ 0141-848 4990; www.air-scotland.com)

Air Transat (TSC; ☎ 0870 556 1522; www.airtransat.uk.com)

American Airlines (AA; ☎ 0845 778 9789; www.aa.com)

Austrian Airlines (OS; ☎ 0845 601 0948; www.aua.com)

WARNING

The information in this section is particularly vulnerable to change: prices for international travel are volatile, routes are introduced and cancelled, schedules change, special deals come and go, and rules and visa requirements are amended. In addition, the travel industry is highly competitive and there are many lurks and perks.

Get opinions, quotes and advice from as many airlines and travel agents as possible before you part with your hard-earned cash, and double-check you understand how a fare (and any ticket you may buy) works. The details given in this chapter should be regarded as pointers and are not a substitute for your own careful, up-to-date research into the current situation.

BOOKING TICKETS ONLINE

As well as airline websites, there are a number of useful online resources for buying good-value airline tickets. Recommended websites include:

www.cheapflights.co.uk Lists discount flights to Edinburgh from other parts of the UK and Ireland.

www.opodo.co.uk Site owned by consortium of European airlines; often cheaper than no-frills airlines for short-notice flights.

bmibaby (WW; ☎ 0870 264 2229; www.bmibaby.com)

British Airways/Loganair (BA; Map pp218-19; ☎ 0870 850 9850; www.britishairways.co.uk; 30-32 Frederick St, Edinburgh)

British European/FlyBe (BE; ☎ 0871 700 0123; www.flybe.com)

British Midland (bmi) (BD; ☎ 0870 607 0555; www.flybmi.com)

Continental Airlines (CO; ☎ 0845 607 6760; www.continental.com)

Czech Airlines (OK; ☎ 0870 444 3747; www.czechairlines.co.uk)

Eastern Airways (T3; ☎ 01652-680600; www.easternairways.com)

easyJet (EZY; ☎ 0905 821 0905; www.easyjet.com)

Emirates (EK; ☎ 0870 243 2222; www.emirates.com)

FlyGlobespan (GSM; ☎ 0870 556 1522; www.flyglobespan.com)

GermanWings (4U; ☎ 020-8321 7255; www.germanwings.com)

Icelandair (FI; ☎ 0870 787 4020; www.icelandair.com)

Jet2.com (LS; ☎ 0871 226 1737; www.jet2.com)

KLM Cityhopper (KL; ☎ 0870 507 4074; www.klmuk.com)

Lufthansa (LH; ☎ 0845 773 7747; www.lufthansa.com)

Ryanair (FR; ☎ 0906 270 5656; www.ryanair.com)

SAS (SK; ☎ 0870 607 2772; www.scandinavian.net)

ScotAirways (CB; ☎ 0870 606 0707; www.scotairways.co.uk)

SN Brussels Airlines (SN; ☎ 0870 735 2345; www.flysn.com)

Zoom Airlines (OOM; ☎ 0870 240 0055; www.flyzoom.com)

Airports

Edinburgh Airport (code EDI; ☎ 333 1000; www.edinburghairport.com) is 8 miles west of the city. It has a tourist information and accommodation desk, left-luggage facilities, ATMs, currency exchange desks, shops, restaurants, Internet access and car-hire agencies.

The **Lothian Buses Airlink service 100** (☎ 555 6363; www.flybybus.com) runs from Waverley Bridge, just outside the train station, to the airport (one way/return £3/5, 30 minutes, every 10 to 15 minutes) via the West End and Haymarket; you can buy tickets from the driver.

An airport taxi to the city centre costs around £13 and takes about 20 minutes. Both buses and taxis depart from just outside the arrivals hall (to the left as you exit).

Edinburgh can also be reached from **Glasgow Airport** (code GLA; ☎ 0141-887 1111; www.glasgowairport.com), 56 miles to the west. Scottish Citylink bus 905 runs from the airport to Buchanan Bus Station in Glasgow, where you transfer to bus 900 for Edinburgh (one way £7, two hours, every 15 to 30 minutes).

BICYCLE

Despite its many hills and cobbled streets, Edinburgh is a cycle-friendly city. This is largely due to the efforts of the cycle campaign group **Spokes** (Map p226; ☎ 313 2114; www.spokes.org.uk; St Martins Church, 232 Dalry Rd) and a city council that has pledged to reduce car use.

Visiting cyclists should be aware that the increased popularity of cycling in Edinburgh – and, it has to be said, the inconsiderate behaviour of a selfish minority of cyclists – has caused a backlash and an increase in hostility towards bike riders from both pedestrians and motorists. Follow the Good Cycling Code: be courteous and considerate to others, obey the rules of the road and always give way to walkers, remembering that some people may have impaired hearing or sight. Police have the power to issue on-the-spot fines of up to £40 for offences such as cycling on the pavement, jumping a red light, going the wrong way down a one-way street and cycling after dark without proper lights.

Hire

Biketrax (Map pp224-5; ☎ 228 6633; www.biketrax.co.uk; 11 Lochrin Pl; 9.30am-6pm Mon-Fri, 9.30am-5.30pm Sat, noon-5pm Sun) Rents out a range of cycles and equipment, including kids' bikes, tandems, recumbents, pannier bags, child seats – even unicycles! A mountain bike costs £16 for one day, £12 for extra days thereafter, and £70 for one week. You'll need a £100 cash or credit-card deposit and some form of ID. Has a repair service.

City Cycles (Map pp218-19; ☎ 557 2801; 30 Rodney St; 9am-5.30pm Mon-Sat, noon-4pm Sun) Does repairs and supplies spares and accessories.

Edinburgh Bicycle Cooperative (Map pp224-5; ☎ 228 1368; www.edinburgh-bicycle.co.uk; 8 Alvanley Tce, Whitehouse Loan; 10am-6pm) Does repairs and supplies spares and accessories.

Edinburgh Cycle Hire & Scottish Cycle Safaris (Map p222; ☎ 556 5560; www.cyclescotland.co.uk;

CYCLING EDINBURGH

The city and its surrounding countryside are covered by a wide-reaching network of signposted cycle routes. Many of these are traffic-free and shared by cyclists and pedestrians, but some are simply cycle lanes marked on ordinary roads; the latter are often blocked by parked cars. The main cycle paths follow the routes of former railway lines, and so are delightfully free of any serious hills. The *Edinburgh City Cycle Map* (£4.95), published by Spokes and available from bike shops, shows all the cycle routes in and around the city. Spokes also publishes cycle maps for Midlothian, East Lothian and West Lothian.

The main off-road routes from the city centre out to the countryside follow the Union Canal towpath and the Water of Leith Walkway from Tollcross southwest to Balerno (7½ miles) on the edge of the Pentland Hills, and the Innocent Railway Cycle Path from the southern side of Arthur's Seat eastwards to Musselburgh (5 miles) and on to Ormiston and Pencaitland. There are several routes through the Pentland Hills that are suitable for mountain bikes: for details ask at any bike shop or contact the **Pentland Hills Ranger Service** (☎ 445 3383). There's even a dedicated downhill mountain-biking trail at the Midlothian Ski Centre at Hillend.

For guided cycle tours of Edinburgh, see p50.

29 Blackfriars St; 10am-6pm Mon-Sat) The friendly and helpful folk here rent out top-quality bikes for £10 to £15 a day, £50 to £70 a week; rates include helmet, lock and repair kit. You can hire tents and touring equipment too. It also organises cycle tours in Edinburgh and all over Scotland – check the website for details. Has a repair service.

BUS

Edinburgh Bus Station (Map pp218-19), the terminus for regional and long-distance bus services, is at the northeast corner of St Andrew Sq, with pedestrian entrances from the square and from Elder St. There are information desks, Internet access and left-luggage facilities. For timetable information, call **Traveline** (☎ 0870 608 2608; www.travelinescotland.com).

Public transport within the city is provided entirely by buses; the two main operators are **Lothian Buses** (☎ 555 6363; www.lothianbuses.co.uk), which runs most of the city routes, and **First Edinburgh** (☎ 663 9233; www.firstedinburgh.co.uk), whose buses mainly serve the towns and villages around Edinburgh. You can get timetable information and route maps from the offices listed below. Bus timetables, route maps and fare guides are also posted at all main bus stops.

Adult fares within the city are either 80p or £1; children aged under five travel free and those aged five to 15 pay a flat fare of 60p. On Lothian buses you must pay the driver the exact fare, but First Edinburgh buses will give change. Lothian Buses also offer a Daysaver ticket (£2.30) that gives unlimited travel on Lothian buses for a day; buy from the driver. Night-service buses, which run hourly between midnight and 5am, charge a flat fare of £2.

First Edinburgh Bus Shop (Map pp218-19; Edinburgh Bus Station; 8.30am-6pm Mon-Sat, 9.30am-5pm Sun)

Lothian Buses Lost Property Office (Map pp218-19; ☎ 558 8858; lostproperty@lothianbuses.co.uk; Main Depot, Annadale St; 9am-5pm Mon-Fri)

Lothian Buses Travel Shop Waverley Bridge (Map p222; 8.30am-6pm Mon-Sat, 9.30am-5pm Sun); 27 Hanover St (Map pp218-19; 8.30am-6pm Mon-Sat); 7–9 Shandwick Pl (Map pp218-19; 8.30am-6pm Mon-Sat)

CAR & MOTORCYCLE

Arriving in or leaving Edinburgh by car during the morning and evening rush hours (7.30am to 9.30am and 4.30pm to 6.30pm Monday to Friday) is an experience you can live without. Time your journey to avoid these periods. In particular, there can be huge tailbacks on the A90 between Edinburgh and the Forth Rd Bridge.

Though useful for day trips beyond the city, a car in central Edinburgh is more of a liability than a convenience. Private vehicles are not allowed on Princes St, there is restricted access on George St, St Andrew Sq and Charlotte Sq, many streets are one-way or blocked off, and finding a parking place in the city centre is like striking gold.

There's no parking on main roads into the city from 7.30am to 6.30pm Monday to Saturday. On-street parking in the city centre is controlled by self-service ticket machines from 8.30am to 6.30pm Monday

TOP FIVE USEFUL BUS SERVICES

The following Lothian bus services are particularly useful for visitors.

- **3 and 3A** (every 10 to 15 minutes Monday to Saturday, every 30 minutes Sunday) Runs from Newington along South and North Bridge, along Princes St, through West End and Haymarket to Dalry Rd and Gorgie Rd.
- **23** (every 10 minutes Monday to Friday, every 15 minutes Saturday, every 30 minutes Sunday) Links Morningside to Canonmills via Tollcross, George IV Bridge, the Mound (for National Gallery of Scotland and Princes St) and Hanover St.
- **35** (every 30 minutes Monday to Saturday) Runs from Edinburgh Airport to Ocean Terminal (for Royal Yacht *Britannia*), via the Royal Mile between George IV Bridge and the Palace of Holyroodhouse.
- **41** (every 15 minutes Monday to Saturday, every 30 or 40 minutes Sunday) Runs from Marchmont Rd (Southside) to Cramond via George IV Bridge (for Museum of Scotland and Royal Mile), George St and Charlotte Sq.
- **42** (every 20 minutes Monday to Saturday, every 30 or 40 minutes Sunday) Links Stockbridge, Frederick St (for Princes St), George IV Bridge (for Museum of Scotland and Royal Mile), Causewayside (Southside), Duddingston and Portobello.

to Saturday, and costs £1.60 per hour, with a two-hour maximum. If you break the rules, you'll get a fine, often within minutes of your ticket expiring – Edinburgh's parking wardens are both numerous and notorious. The fine is £60, reduced to £30 if you pay up within 14 days. Cars parked illegally will be towed away. There are large, long-stay car parks at the St James Centre, Greenside Pl, New St, Castle Tce and Morrison St. Motorcycles can be parked free at designated areas in the city centre.

Hire

All the big international car-hire agencies have offices in Edinburgh. There are many smaller, local agencies that offer better rates.

Arnold Clark Car Hire (Map pp214-15; ☎ 657 9120; www.arnoldclarkrental.co.uk; 20 Seafield Rd E; 🕑 8am-6pm Mon-Fri, 8am-5pm Sat, 11am-5pm Sun) One of the most reliable Scottish-based agencies; charges from £23 a day, or £110 a week for a small car, including VAT and insurance. The daily rate includes 250 miles per day; excess is charged at 4p per mile. For periods of four days and more, mileage is unlimited.

Avis Car Rental (Map p217; ☎ 0870 010 0287; www.avis.co.uk; 5 W Park Pl, Dalry Rd; 🕑 8am-6pm Mon-Fri, 8am-1pm Sat, 9am-noon Sun)

Europcar (Map pp218-19; ☎ 556 5210, 0845 758 5375; www.europcar.co.uk; Unit 13, Waverley Train Station; 🕑 24hr)

Thrifty Car Rental (Map p217; ☎ 337 1319; www.thrifty.co.uk; 42 Haymarket Tce; 🕑 8am-6pm Mon-Fri, 8am-4pm Sat & Sun)

TAXI

Edinburgh's black taxis can be hailed in the street, ordered by phone (extra 60p charge), or picked up at one of the many central ranks. Taxis are fairly expensive – the minimum charge is £1.45 (£2.20 at night) for the first 340yd (311m), then 23p (24p at night) for every subsequent 240yd (219m) – a typical 2-mile trip across the city centre will cost around £5. Tipping is up to you: because of the high fares local people rarely tip on short journeys, but occasionally round up to the nearest 50p on longer ones.

The main local companies:

Capital Taxis (☎ 228 2555)

Central Radio Taxis (☎ 229 2468)

City Cabs (☎ 228 1211)

Radiocabs (☎ 225 9000)

TRAIN

The main terminus in Edinburgh is **Waverley train station** (Map pp218-19; Waverley Bridge), located in the heart of the city. Trains arriving from, and departing to, the west also stop at **Haymarket train station** (Map p217; Haymarket Tce), which is more convenient for the West End. You can buy tickets, make reservations and get travel information at the **Edinburgh Rail Travel Centre** (🕑 4.45am-12.30am Mon-Sat, 7am-12.30am Sun) in Waverley station. For fare and timetable enquires, phone the **National Rail Enquiry Service** (☎ 0845 748 4950) or check the timetables at www.firstscotrail.com or www.nationalrail.co.uk. Buy tickets online at www.thetrainline.com.

First ScotRail operates a regular shuttle service between Edinburgh and Glasgow (£9.40, 50 minutes, every 15 minutes).

TRAVEL AGENCIES

American Express (Map pp218-19; ☎ 718 2501; www.americanexpress.co.uk; 69 George St; 🕑 9am-5.30pm Mon-Fri, 9am-4pm Sat)

STA Travel (Map p222; ☎ 226 7747; www.statravel.co.uk; 27 Forrest Rd; 🕑 10am-6pm Mon-Wed & Fri, 10am-7pm Thu, 11am-5pm Sat)

Student Flights (Map p222; ☎ 226 6868; www.studentflight.co.uk; 53 Forrest Rd; 🕑 9.30am-6pm Mon-Fri, 11am-5pm Sat)

Thomas Cook (Map pp218-19; ☎ 226 5500; www.thomascook.co.uk; 52 Hanover St; 🕑 9am-5.30pm Mon, Tue & Thu-Sat, 10am-5.30pm Wed)

PRACTICALITIES

ACCOMMODATION

Accommodation listings in the Sleeping chapter (p160) are broken down first by neighbourhood, then alphabetically within each neighbourhood heading. The average cost of a double room with en-suite bathroom is in the £60 to £100 range, with seasonal variations – the highest rates are charged during August and the Christmas/New Year period.

The Sleeping chapter also has details of accommodation websites, long-term rentals and self-catering.

BUSINESS HOURS

Shops are generally open from 9am to 5pm Monday to Wednesday, Friday and Saturday, and from 9am to 7pm or 8pm Thursday. An increasing number of shops also open on Sunday, typically from noon to 4pm or 5pm. Most supermarkets stay open until 8pm or 10pm daily and a few are open 24 hours.

Approximate standard opening hours:

Banks (9.30am-4pm Mon-Fri, some 9.30am-12.30pm Sat)

Cafés (8am or 9am-6pm) If licensed they may stay open for dinner.

Post offices (9am-5.30pm Mon-Fri, 9am-12.30pm Sat)

Pubs (11am-11pm Mon-Thu, 11am-1am Fri & Sat, 12.30-11pm Sun)

Restaurants (lunch noon-3pm, dinner 6pm-9pm or 10pm)

CHILDREN

Edinburgh has a multitude of attractions for children, and most things to see and do are child-friendly (see p69 for suggestions). Kids under five travel free on Edinburgh buses, and five- to 15-year-olds pay a flat fare of 60p. You should be aware that children under the age of 14 are not allowed into the majority of Edinburgh pubs, even those that serve bar meals; even in family-friendly pubs (those in possession of a Children's Certificate), under-14s are only allowed in between 11am and 8pm, and must be accompanied by an adult aged 18 or above.

For lots of information and advice on travelling with kids, grab a copy of Lonely Planet's *Travel With Children* by Cathy Lanigan.

Baby-Sitting

For full listings of government-approved child-minding services, check out **Childcare-Link** (www.childcarelink.gov.uk), or call **City of Edinburgh Childcare Information Service** (☎ 0800 032 0323).

Some reliable Edinburgh agencies, charging from around £6 per hour:

Family Circle Recruitment (☎ 447 9162; www.familycircles.org; 37 Comiston Rd, Morningside)

Panda's Nanny Agency (☎ 663 3967; www.pandasnannyagency.co.uk; 22 Durham Pl, Bonnyrigg)

CLIMATE

Given how far north it lies (it's on the same latitude as Labrador in Canada), you might expect Edinburgh's climate to be colder than it is, but the Gulf Stream (a warm Atlantic current) keeps the prevailing westerly winds pleasantly mild. May, June and September are generally the best months for dry, sunny weather, but you can expect rain at any time. The weather changes quickly, too – a rainy morning can often be followed by a sunny afternoon. A distinctive feature of Edinburgh's weather is the 'haar', a dense, chilly fog that often blows in from the North Sea when the wind is in the east. You can usually escape it by heading just a few miles inland.

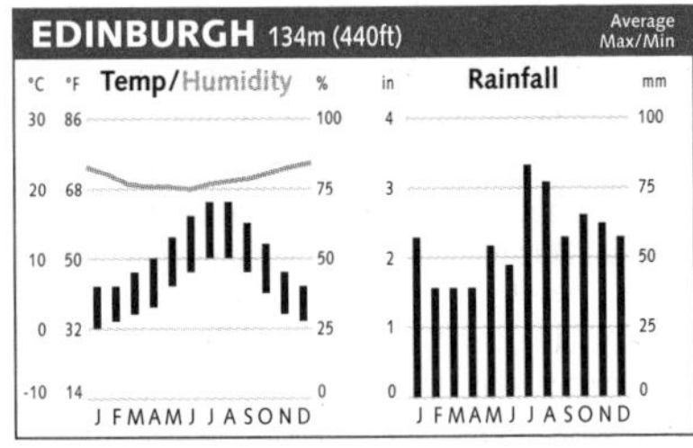

COURSES

Edinburgh University's **Office of Lifelong Learning** (Map pp224-5; ☎ 650 4400; www.lifelong.ed.ac.uk; 11 Buccleuch Pl) runs six- to 11-week courses for adults on a wide range of subjects, including Scottish archaeology, Scottish literature, Scottish history and Gaelic language. A 10-week course exploring the influence of poet Robert Burns costs £75, while the 11-week beginners' Gaelic course costs £80.

Edinburgh is a popular place to learn English as a second language, and is home to many establishments offering a range of intensive courses, summer schools, weekend workshops and specialised English courses (eg for medicine, business or tourism):

Aspect International Language Academy (Map p217; ☎ 220 4278; www.aspectworld.com; 11 Great Stuart St)

Edinburgh Language Centre (Map p217; ☎ 343 6596; www.edinburghlanguagecentre.co.uk; 10b Oxford Tce)

Edinburgh School of English (Map p222; ☎ 557 9200; www.edinburghschool.ac.uk; 271 Canongate, Royal Mile)

Institute for Applied Language Studies (Map p222; ☎ 650 6200; www.ials.ed.ac.uk; Edinburgh University, 21 Hill Pl)

CUSTOMS

Travellers arriving in the UK from the European Union (EU) can bring into the country up to 3200 cigarettes (only 200 cigarettes if arriving from the Czech Republic, Estonia, Hungary, Latvia, Lithuania, Poland, Slovakia or Slovenia), 400 cigarillos, 200 cigars, 3kg of smoking tobacco, 10L of spirits, 20L of fortified wine (eg port or sherry), 90L of wine and 110L of beer, provided the goods are for personal use only.

Travellers arriving from outside the EU can bring in, duty-free, a maximum of 200 cigarettes *or* 100 cigarillos *or* 50 cigars *or* 250g of tobacco; 2L of still table wine; 1L of spirits *or* 2L of fortified wine, sparkling wine or liqueurs; 60mL of perfume; 250mL of eau de toilette; and £145 worth of all other goods (including gifts and souvenirs). Anything over this limit must be declared to customs officers. People under 17 do not get the alcohol and tobacco allowances.

For details of prohibited and restricted goods (such as meat, milk and other animal products), and quarantine regulations, see the HM Customs and Excise website at www.hmrc.gov.uk.

DISABLED TRAVELLERS

Edinburgh's Old Town, with its steep hills, narrow closes, flights of stairs and cobbled streets, is a challenge for wheelchair users. By law, new buildings must be made accessible to wheelchair users, so large new hotels and modern tourist attractions are usually fine. However, many B&Bs and guesthouses are in hard-to-adapt older buildings that lack ramps and lifts. It's a similar story with public transport. Newer buses sometimes have steps or suspension that lowers for access, but it's wise to check before setting out. Most black taxis are wheelchair-friendly.

Many banks are fitted with induction loops to assist the hearing impaired. Some attractions have Braille guides for the visually impaired.

VisitScotland produces a guide, *Accessible Scotland*, for disabled travellers, and the Edinburgh and Scotland Information Centre has accessibility details for Edinburgh (see p200 for information on both organisations). **Historic Scotland** (HS; Map pp224-5; ☎ 668 8600; www.historic-scotland.gov.uk) and the **National Trust for Scotland** (NTS; ☎ 243 9300; www.nts.org.uk) provide details on disabled access and facilities at their properties.

Organisations

Capability Scotland (☎ 313 5510; www.capability-scotland.org.uk; 11 Ellersly Rd, Edinburgh EH12 6HY) Scotland's largest disability organisation, offering advice and info on a range of issues.

Holiday Care Service (☎ 0845 124 9971; www.holidaycare.org.uk; Holiday Care Information Unit, 7th fl Sunley House, 4 Bedford Pk, Croydon, Surrey CR0 2AP) Publishes regional information guides (£5) to Scotland and offers general advice.

Royal Association for Disability & Rehabilitation (Radar; ☎ 020-7250 3222; www.radar.org.uk; Information Dept, 12 City Forum, 250 City Rd, London EC1V 8AF) Publishes a guide on travelling in the UK.

Royal National Institute for the Blind (RNIB; ☎ 311 8500, confidential helpline ☎ 0845 766 9999; www.rnib.org.uk; Dunedin House, 25 Ravelston Tce, Edinburgh EH4 3TP) A good point of initial contact for sight-impaired visitors to Edinburgh.

Royal National Institute for the Deaf (RNID; ☎ 0141-554 0053, textphone ☎ 0808 808 9000; www.rnid.org.uk; Crowngate Business Centre, Brook St, Glasgow G40 3AP) Publishes a large amount of helpful literature, which it mails out free.

DISCOUNT CARDS

The **Edinburgh Pass** (www.edinburgh.org/pass) offers free entry to more than two dozen city attractions, plus unlimited travel on Lothian bus services and one return journey on the Airlink 100 airport bus. It costs £26/34/40 for one/two/three days. As yet, entry to Edinburgh Castle and the Royal Yacht *Britannia* are not included in the Pass.

ELECTRICITY

The standard voltage in Scotland, as in the rest of the UK, is 230V, 50Hz AC. Plugs have three square pins, and adapters are necessary for non-UK appliances; these are widely available in electrical shops in Edinburgh. North American appliances, which run on 110V, will also need a transformer if they don't have one built in.

EMBASSIES & CONSULATES

Most foreign embassies are in London, but a few countries maintain a consulate in Edinburgh:

Australia (Map pp218-19; ☎ 624 3333; 69 George St) For passport applications and document witnessing only; for emergencies contact the Australian High Commission in London (☎ 020-7887 5335).

Canada (Map pp218-19; ☎ 473 6320; Burness, 50 Lothian Rd)

Denmark (Map p217; ☎ 220 0300; 48 Melville St)

France (Map p217; ☎ 225 7954; 11 Randolph Cres)

Germany (Map p217; ☎ 337 2323; 16 Eglinton Cres)

Ireland (Map p217; ☎ 226 7711; 16 Randolph Cres)

Italy (Map p217; ☎ 226 3631; 32 Melville St)

Japan (Map p217; ☎ 225 4777; 2 Melville Cres)

Netherlands (Map pp218-19; ☎ 220 3226; Thistle Ct, 1-2 Thistle St)

Russia (Map p217; ☎ 225 7098; 58 Melville St)

Spain (Map pp218-19; ☎ 220 1843; 63 N Castle St)

USA (Map pp218-19; ☎ 556 8315; 3 Regent Tce)

EMERGENCY

In an emergency, dial ☎ 999 or ☎ 112 (no money needed at public phones) and ask for police, ambulance, fire brigade or coastguard. Other useful phone numbers:

Edinburgh Rape Crisis Centre (☎ 556 9437; edinirc@aol.com)

Lothian & Borders Police HQ (Map p217; ☎ 311 3131; www.lbp.police.uk; Fettes Ave)

Lothian & Borders Police Info Centre (Map p222; ☎ 226 6966; 188 High St; 10am-10pm May-Aug, 10am-8pm Mar, Apr, Sep & Oct, 10am-6pm Nov-Feb) You can report a crime or make lost property enquiries here.

GAY & LESBIAN TRAVELLERS

Edinburgh has a small but flourishing gay scene. The city has a fairly tolerant attitude towards homosexuality, but overt displays of affection aren't wise away from gay venues. The age of consent for homosexual sex in the UK is 16.

The website www.gayscotland.com and the monthly magazine *ScotsGay* (www.scotsgay.com) have information on gay-scene issues.

Useful contacts:

Edinburgh LGB Community Centre (Map pp218-19; ☎ 478 7069; 60 Broughton St)

Lothian Gay & Lesbian Switchboard (☎ 556 4049; www.lgls.co.uk; 7.30-10pm)

Lothian Lesbian Line (☎ 557 0751; 7.30-10pm Mon & Thu)

See also p140 and p167.

HOLIDAYS

On public holidays and bank holidays, banks, post offices and government offices will be closed and public transport may run a reduced service. Many shops stay open, however, except on Christmas and New Year's days.

The following days are public holidays in Scotland:

New Year's Day 1 January

New Year Bank Holiday 2 January

Spring Bank Holiday Second Monday in April

Good Friday The Friday before Easter Sunday

May Day Holiday First Monday in May

Christmas Day 25 December

Boxing Day 26 December

Edinburgh also has its own local holidays on the third Monday in May and the third Monday in September.

INTERNET ACCESS

Most hotels that have Internet connection points in their rooms use ordinary RJ-11 sockets; others use a BT phone socket. For help and information on getting online from hotel rooms see www.kropla.com.

There are around 200 wi-fi hotspots in the city, which can be used to access the Internet if your laptop has a wireless card. You can search for hotspots in Edinburgh on websites such as www.jiwire.com.

There are many Internet cafés spread around the city, and there are also several Internet-enabled telephone boxes (10p per minute, 50p minimum) scattered around the city centre.

connect@edinburgh (Map pp218-19; ☎ 473 3800; ESIC, Princes Mall, 3 Princes St; per 15min 50p; as for ESIC, see p200)

easyInternetcafé (Map pp218-19; ☎ 220 3580; www.easy-everything.com; 58 Rose St; per hr £1, minimum 50p; 7.30am-10.30pm)

e-corner (Map p222; ☎ 558 7858; www.e-corner.co.uk; 55 Blackfriars St; per 20min £1; 7.30am-9pm Mon-Fri, 8am-9pm Sat & Sun)

Internet Café (Map p222; ☎ 226 5400; www.edininternetcafe.com; 98 West Bow, Victoria St; per 30min 60p; 10am-11pm)

Mossco Internet Café (Map p217; ☎ 07775620759; 18 W Maitland St; per min 4p, no minimum; 8am-10pm)

Wired (Map pp214-15; ☎ 659 7820; 1a Brougham Pl; per 20min 50p; 9am-8pm)

LEGAL MATTERS

The 1707 Act of Union preserved the Scottish legal system as separate from the law in England and Wales. Although there has been considerable convergence since then, Scots Law remains distinct.

Police have the power to detain anyone suspected of having committed an offence punishable by imprisonment (including any drugs offences) for up to six hours. They can search you, take photographs and fingerprints, and question you. You are legally required to provide your correct name and address – not doing so, or giving false details, is an offence – but you are not obliged to answer any other police questions. After six hours, the police must either formally charge you or let you go. If you are detained and/or arrested, you have the right to inform a solicitor and one other person, though you have no right to actually see the solicitor or to make a telephone call. If you don't know a solicitor, the police will inform the duty solicitor on your behalf.

If you need legal assistance contact the **Scottish Legal Aid Board** (Map p217; ☎ 226 7061; www.slab.org.uk; 44 Drumsheugh Gardens).

Possession of a small amount of cannabis is an offence punishable by a fine, but possession of a larger amount of cannabis, or any amount of harder drugs, is much more serious, with sentences of up to 14 years in prison. Police have the right to search anyone they suspect of possessing drugs.

It is illegal to drive with a blood-alcohol level of more than 35mg/100mL (anything more than one pint of beer or a glass of wine risks exceeding this).

Drop litter or cigarette ends on Edinburgh's streets and you can be nailed with an on-the-spot fine – a team of red-jacketed litter wardens patrols the city centre on the lookout for offenders. Smoking on public transport is not allowed, and the smoking ban was extended to pubs, restaurants and other enclosed public spaces from 26 March 2006.

WHEN YOU'RE LEGAL

In Scotland the following legal ages apply:

- Drinking alcohol – 18
- Driving – 17
- Heterosexual/homosexual sex – 16
- Marriage – 16
- Smoking – 16
- Voting – 18

MAPS

Lonely Planet's handy, fold-out *Edinburgh City Map* (£3.99) is plastic-coated, virtually indestructible and indicates all the major landmarks, museums and shops. There's also a street index.

The Edinburgh and Scotland Information Centre (ESIC; see p200) issues a free pocket map of the city centre. For coverage of the whole city, the most detailed maps are the AA's *Edinburgh Street-by-Street Z-Map* (£1.50) and the Ordnance Survey's (OS) *Edinburgh Street Atlas* (£3.99). You can buy these at the ESIC and at bookshops and newsagents.

The OS's 1:50,000 Landranger map *Edinburgh, Penicuik & North Berwick* (Sheet No 66; £6.49) covers the city and the surrounding region to the south and east at a scale of 1¼ inches to 1 mile (2cm to 1km); it is useful for walking in the Pentland Hills and exploring East Lothian.

MEDICAL SERVICES

Edinburgh Dental Institute (Map pp218-19; ☎ 536 4958; Fl 3, Lauriston Bldg, Lauriston Pl; 🕒 9am-3.30pm Mon-Fri) For emergency dental treatment, make an appointment here.

Minor Injuries Unit (Map pp214-15; ☎ 537 1330; Western General Hospital, Crewe Rd; 🕒 9am-9pm) For non-life-threatening injuries and ailments, you can attend without having to make an appointment.

Royal Hospital for Sick Children (Map pp224-5; ☎ 536 0000; 9 Sciennes Rd, Marchmont; 🕒 24hr) The main casualty department for children under 13 years of age.

Royal Infirmary of Edinburgh (Map pp214-15; ☎ 536 1000; 51 Little France Cres, Old Dalkeith Rd; 🕒 24hr) Edinburgh's main general hospital has a 24-hour accident and emergency department.

METRIC SYSTEM

Like the rest of the UK, Scotland has officially moved to the metric system, but road distances are still quoted in miles (1.6km) and beer is still served in pints (568ml). Whisky and other spirits are sold in 25ml or 35ml measures, and petrol is sold by the litre. For conversion tables see the inside front cover.

MONEY

The UK currency is the pound sterling (£), with 100 pence (p) to a pound. 'Quid' is a slang term for pound. See the inside front cover for exchange rates.

Several Scottish banks issue their own bank notes. You shouldn't have trouble using them in shops etc in the north of England and in Northern Ireland, but elsewhere they may be refused. Although all UK banks will accept them, foreign banks generally do not.

Euros are accepted in Scotland only at some major tourist attractions and a few upmarket hotels – it's always better to have cash in sterling.

ATMs

There are 24-hour ATMs (called cashpoints in Scotland) all over the city, where you can use Visa, MasterCard, Amex, Cirrus, Plus and Maestro to withdraw cash. Cash withdrawals from an increasing number of ATMs (especially ones in shops) can be subject to a small charge (about £1.50), but most are free.

Changing Money

You can change currency and travellers cheques at exchange counters (known by the French term 'bureau de change') scattered throughout the city centre, and in banks, post offices and travel agencies. Banks generally offer the best rates. Be careful using bureaux de change; they may offer good exchange rates but frequently levy outrageous commissions and fees.

American Express (Map pp218-19; ☎ 718 2501; 69 George St; 🕑 9am-5.30pm Mon-Fri, 9am-4pm Sat)

Bank of Scotland (Map pp218-19; ☎ 465 3900; 38 St Andrew Sq; 🕑 9am-5pm Mon-Fri, 10am-2pm Sat)

Fexco (Map pp218-19; ☎ 557 3953; ESIC, Princes Mall, 3 Princes St; 🕑 as for ESIC, see p200)

Royal Bank of Scotland (Map pp218-19; ☎ 556 8555; 36 St Andrew Sq; 🕑 9.15am-4.45pm Mon, Tue, Thu & Fri, 10am-4.45pm Wed, 10am-2pm Sat)

Thomas Cook (Map pp218-19; ☎ 226 5500; 52 Hanover St; 🕑 9am-5.30pm Mon, Tue & Thu-Sat, 10am-5.30pm Wed)

Credit Cards

Visa, MasterCard, Amex and Diners Club cards are widely accepted, although some places make a charge for using them (generally for small transactions). Charge cards such as Amex and Diners Club may not be accepted in smaller establishments; credit and debit cards like Visa and MasterCard are more widely accepted.

Travellers Cheques

Amex or Thomas Cook cheques are widely accepted in exchange for cash in banks, but (unlike in the US) you can't use them over the counter in shops and restaurants. Bring sterling cheques to avoid changing currencies twice, and take most cheques in large denominations; commission is usually charged per cheque.

NEWSPAPERS & MAGAZINES

Edinburgh's home-grown daily newspapers include the *Scotsman* (www.scotsman.com), a quality daily covering Scottish and international news, sport and current affairs, and the *Edinburgh Evening News* (www.edinburghnews.com), covering news and entertainment in the city and its environs. *Scotland on Sunday* is the Sunday paper from the same publisher.

You can find a wide range of newspapers from around the world at **International Newsagents** (Map p222; ☎ 225 4827; 351 High St, Royal Mile; 🕑 6am-6.30pm Mon-Fri, 7am-6.30pm Sat, 7.30am-6pm Sun Sep-Jul, 6am-midnight Mon-Fri, 6am-1am Sat & Sun Aug).

PHARMACIES

Chemists (pharmacists) can advise you on minor ailments. At least one local chemist remains open round the clock – its location will be displayed in the windows of other chemists. Alternatively, look in the local newspaper or in the *Yellow Pages*. **Boots** (Map p217; ☎ 225 6757; 48 Shandwick Pl; 🕑 8am-9pm Mon-Fri, 8am-6pm Sat, 10.30am-4.30pm Sun) has longer opening hours than most.

POST

Mail sent within the UK can go either 1st or 2nd class. First-class mail is faster (next-day delivery) and more expensive (30p up to 60g, 46p up to 100g) than 2nd-class mail (21/35p). Airmail postcards/letters up to 60g to European countries cost 42/78p; to South Africa, the USA and Canada 47p/£1.42; and to Australia and New Zealand 47p/£1.56. An airmail letter generally takes five days to get to the USA or Canada and around a week to Australia or New Zealand.

If you don't have a permanent address, mail can be sent to poste restante c/o Edinburgh's main post office. Amex offices also hold card-holders' mail for no charge.

Frederick Street Post Office (Map pp218-19; 40 Frederick St; ⏲ 9am-5.30pm Mon-Fri, 9am-12.30pm Sat)

Main Post Office (Map pp218-19; ☎ 0845 722 3344; St James Centre, Leith St; ⏲ 8.30am-5.30pm Mon-Fri, 8.30am-6pm Sat)

St Mary's Street Post Office (Map p222; 46 St Mary's St; ⏲ 9am-5.30pm Mon-Fri, 9am-12.30pm Sat)

SAFETY

Lothian Rd, Dalry Rd, Rose St and the western end of Princes St at the junction with Shandwick Pl and Queensferry St can get a bit rowdy late on Friday and Saturday nights after pub-closing time. Calton Hill offers good views during the day but is best avoided at night.

Women should avoid crossing the Meadows (the park that lies between Old Town and Marchmont) alone after dark – several women have been attacked here. And be aware that the area between Salamander St and Leith Links in Leith is a red-light district: lone women here at any time of day might be approached by kerb crawlers.

TAX & REFUNDS

Value-added tax (VAT) is a 17.5% sales tax that is levied on all goods and services in the UK except fresh food, books, newspapers and children's clothes. Non-EU citizens can claim a refund of VAT paid on most goods bought within the EU, which can make for a considerable saving.

The VAT Retail Export Scheme is voluntary and not all shops participate – look for a blue Tax-Free Shopping sign in the window. Different shops may have different minimum-purchase conditions (normally around £40).

For further details, check out the HM Revenue & Customs website at www.hmrc.gov.uk, call the **National Advice Centre** (☎ 0845 010 9000) or pick up the leaflet *Notice 704 – VAT Retail Exports*, available from all customs arrival points throughout the UK.

TELEPHONE

To call Scotland from abroad dial the international access code (usually ☎ 00) then ☎ 44 (the UK country code), then the area code (dropping the initial 0) followed by the telephone number. The area code for Edinburgh is ☎ 0131.

You'll mainly see two types of phone booths in Scotland: one takes money (and doesn't give change), while the other uses prepaid phone cards and credit cards. Some phones accept both coins and cards. The minimum charge is 20p.

All phones come with reasonably clear instructions in several languages. British Telecom (BT) offers phonecards for £3, £5, £10 and £20; they're widely available from retailers, including post offices and newsagents.

Mobile Phones

Codes for UK mobile phones usually begin with ☎ 07. The UK uses the GSM 900/1800 network, which is compatible with the rest of Europe, Australia and New Zealand, but not with the North American GSM 1900 or the totally different system in Japan (though some North Americans have GSM 1900/900 phones that will work in the UK). If you have a GSM phone, check with your service provider about using it in the UK, and beware

USEFUL CODES

Some codes worth knowing:

International dialling code (☎ 00)

International directory enquiries (☎ 153)

International operator (☎ 155)

Local & national directory enquiries (☎ 118 500)

Local & national operator (☎ 100)

Local call rate (☎ 0345, 0845)

National call rate (☎ 0870)

Premium call rate (☎ 0891, 09064)

Reverse-charge/collect calls (☎ 155)

Time (☎ 123)

Toll-free call (☎ 0800)

of calls being routed internationally (very expensive for a 'local' call). You can also rent a mobile phone – ask a Tourist Information Centre (TIC) for details – or buy a 'pay-as-you-go' UK simcard for as little as £10.

TIME

Edinburgh, along with the rest of the UK and Ireland, follows Greenwich Mean Time (GMT) in the winter and British Summer Time (BST) in the summer. BST is GMT plus one hour; the clocks go forward one hour at 2am on the last Sunday in March, and back again at 2am on the last Sunday in October.

When it's noon in Edinburgh in summer, it's 4am in Los Angeles, 7am in New York, 1pm in Paris (and the rest of Europe), 1pm in Johannesburg, 8pm in Tokyo, 9pm in Sydney and 11pm in Auckland.

Most public transport timetables use the 24-hour clock.

TIPPING

In general, if you eat in an Edinburgh restaurant you should leave a tip of at least 10% unless the service was unsatisfactory. Waiting staff are often paid derisory wages on the assumption that the money will be supplemented by tips. If the bill already includes a service charge (usually 10%), you needn't add a further tip. Tipping in bars is not customary.

Taxis in Edinburgh are expensive, and drivers rarely expect a tip unless they have gone out of their way to help you.

TOILETS

There are well-maintained public toilets conveniently spaced around the city centre and most have facilities for the disabled. Some busy public toilets, such as the ones at Waverley train station and inside Edinburgh Castle, charge 20p.

Some disabled toilets can only be opened with a special key that can be obtained from the TIC or by applying in advance to Radar (see p195).

TOURIST INFORMATION

VisitScotland Edinburgh (www.edinburgh.org) is the city's main provider of tourist information, with an office in the Edinburgh and Scotland Information Centre.

Edinburgh and Scotland Information Centre (ESIC; Map pp218-19; ☎ 0845 225 5121; info@visitscotland.com; Princes Mall, 3 Princes St; ⏲ 9am-8pm Mon-Sat & 10am-8pm Sun Jul & Aug, 9am-7pm Mon-Sat & 10am-7pm Sun May, Jun & Sep, 9am-5pm Mon-Wed, 9am-6pm Thu-Sat & 10am-5pm Sun Oct-Apr) Accommodation booking service, currency exchange, gift and book shop, Internet access, and counters selling tickets for Edinburgh city tours and Scottish Citylink bus services.

Tourist Information Centre (TIC; ☎ 653 6172; Old Craighall Junction, A1) In a service area on the main A1 road, about 5 miles east of the city centre.

Tourist Information Desk (☎ 0845 225 5121; Arrivals Hall, Edinburgh Airport)

VisitScotland (☎ 0845 225 5121; www.visitscotland.com) National tourist board.

VISAS

Currently, if you're a citizen of Australia, Canada, New Zealand, South Africa or the USA, you're permitted to stay in the UK for up to six months (no visa required), but are prohibited from working. See opposite for details of working visas.

EU citizens can live and work in the UK free of immigration control and don't need a visa to enter the country.

All other nationalities should contact their nearest British diplomatic mission to obtain a visa. Six-month/one-year multiple-entry visas cost from £50/85.

There is no extra immigration control for Scotland if you arrive from England or Northern Ireland. For more information, see www.ukvisas.gov.uk or the Lonely Planet website at www.lonelyplanet.com.

Extensions

To extend your stay in Britain contact the **Home Office, Immigration and Nationality Directorate** (☎ 0870 606 7766; Lunar House, 40 Wellesley Rd, Croydon, London CR9 2BY) *before* your existing permit expires. You'll need to send your passport with your application.

WOMEN TRAVELLERS

Women are unlikely to have any special problems, although common-sense caution should be observed, especially late at night (see p199).

For general advice on health issues, contraception and pregnancy, visit a Well Woman clinic – ask at local libraries or doctors' surgeries for the details. In Edinburgh, contact **Well Woman Services** (Map p217; ☎ 332 7941; 18 Dean Tce, Stockbridge; ⏲ 9.30am-7.30pm Mon-Thu, 9am-3.30pm Fri, 9.30am-noon Sat).

The Rape and Abuse Line can be contacted toll-free from 7pm to 10pm every evening on ☎ 0808 800 0123. Or contact the **Edinburgh Rape Crisis Centre** (☎ 556 9437; edinirc@aol.com).

WORK

EU citizens do not need a work permit to work in the UK. Citizens of Commonwealth countries aged 17 to 30 inclusive can apply for a Working Holiday Entry Certificate that allows up to two years in the UK, during which you can take work that is 'incidental' to a holiday. Commonwealth citizens with a UK-born parent may be eligible for a Certificate of Entitlement to the Right of Abode, which allows you to live and work in the UK.

Commonwealth citizens with a UK-born grandparent, or a grandparent born before 31 March 1922 in what's now the Republic of Ireland, may qualify for a UK Ancestry-Employment Certificate, allowing you to work full time for up to four years in the UK.

Visiting full-time US students aged 18 and over can apply for a six-month work permit through the **Council on International Educational Exchange** (☎ 207-553 7600, toll-free ☎ 1-800-40-STUDY; www.ciee.org; 3rd fl, 7 Custom House St, Portland, ME 04101). **British Universities North America Club** (Bunac; ☎ 203-264 0901; www.bunac.org; PO Box 430, Southbury, CT 06488) can also help organise a work permit.

Seasonal work is available in the tourist industry in hotels, restaurants and bars, but in recent years the hospitality industry has seen a flood of young workers from the new EU countries in Eastern Europe. Hostel noticeboards advertise casual work. Bars and restaurants also advertise jobs in their windows.

Those with building trades skills will be in demand. There are also opportunities for secretaries, receptionists, book-keepers and accountants. Other possibilities include telesales work, nursing and nursery care. A wide range of full- and part-time jobs is advertised in the Recruitment section of Friday's edition of the *Scotsman* newspaper, and online at www.scottishjobs.com. The minimum wage in the UK is £5.05 per hour.

Whatever your skills, it's worth registering with a few employment agencies; check the *Edinburgh Guide* website at www.edinburghguide.com/business/recruitment.htm or the *Yellow Pages* (www.yell.co.uk) for listings.

Behind the Scenes

THE LONELY PLANET STORY

The story begins with a classic travel adventure: Tony and Maureen Wheeler's 1972 journey across Europe and Asia to Australia. There was no useful information about the overland trail then, so Tony and Maureen published the first Lonely Planet guidebook to meet a growing need.

From a kitchen table, Lonely Planet has grown to become the largest independent travel publisher in the world, with offices in Melbourne (Australia), Oakland (USA) and London (UK). Today Lonely Planet guidebooks cover the globe. There is an ever-growing list of books and information in a variety of media. Some things haven't changed. The main aim is still to make it possible for adventurous travellers to get out there – to explore and better understand the world.

At Lonely Planet we believe travellers can make a positive contribution to the countries they visit – if they respect their host communities and spend their money wisely. Every year 5% of company profit is donated to charities around the world.

THIS BOOK

This 4th edition of *Edinburgh* was written and updated by Neil Wilson, as were the previous two editions. The 1st edition was written by Tom Smallman. This city guide was commissioned in Lonely Planet's London office, and produced by the following:

Commissioning Editors Amanda Canning, Sam Trafford, Imogen Hall
Coordinating Editor Andrea Dobbin
Coordinating Cartographer Simon Tillema
Coordinating Layout Designer Carol Jackson
Managing Cartographer Mark Griffiths
Assisting Editors Janet Austin, Janice Bird
Assisting Layout Designers Michael Ruff, Liz White
Cover Designer Marika Kozak
Colour Designer Carol Jackson
Project Managers Nancy Ianni, John Shippick, Eoin Dunlevy

Thanks to Alan Murphy, Christina Browning, Michala Green, Bruce Evans, Adriana Mammarella, Celia Wood, Sally Darmody, Carol Chandler, Laura Jane, Mark Germanchis, Ryan Evans, Gerard Walker, Chris Lee Ack

Cover photographs View of the city at night, Visual Photos, Walter Bibikow (top); thousands of visitors walk the Royal Mile during the festival month of August, Chris Furlong (bottom); Scott Monument and Christmas Ferris Wheel, Princes Street Gardens, Jonathan Smith (back).

Internal photographs by Lonely Planet Images and Jonathan Smith, except for the following: p2 (#3), p83 (#2) Chris Furlong; p136, p178 Neil Setchfield; p187 Grant Dixon.

THANKS

NEIL WILSON

Many thanks to the helpful and enthusiastic staff at the Edinburgh & Scotland Information Centre, to the travellers who chipped in with recommendations, and to the various people I pestered for their opinions. Thanks also to Carol Downie for help and advice on restaurants and shopping.

OUR READERS

Many thanks to the travellers who used the last edition and wrote to us with helpful hints, useful advice and interesting anecdotes:

Lindsay Amey, Simone Artaud, Cathy Barker, Robert Cherry, Chris Clements, Fiona Crawford, Rob Davies, Linda Davis, Mary De Winter, Nicole Delong, Gunda Feddersen, Dana Foster, Paula Griswold, Frode Hammer, Marieke Hohnen, Mark Holmes, Debbie Junk, Yuki Kondo-Shah, Charles Kowalski, Andrea Lewerenz, Simon Lowe, Ian Lynch, Kristin Maltman, Brent Marshall, Jamie McBride, Than McIntosh, Langdon Miller, Brenda Miskie, Neil Mitchell, Greg Nance, Voury Nelly, Haydee Notholt y Borel, Craig Richmond, Stewart Robertson, Millicent Scott, Kathie Simpson, Sandra Tegtmeier, Malla Tennila, Yuyun Tsai, Jan Watten, Jamie Westcott, Amanda White, Laura Wood

SEND US YOUR FEEDBACK

We love to hear from travellers – your comments keep us on our toes and help make our books better. Our well-travelled team reads every word on what you loved or loathed about this book. Although we cannot reply individually to postal submissions, we always guarantee that your feedback goes straight to the appropriate authors, in time for the next edition. Each person who sends us information is thanked in the next edition – and the most useful submissions are rewarded with a free book.

To send us your updates – and find out about Lonely Planet events, newsletters and travel news – visit our award-winning website: www.lonelyplanet.com/feedback.

Note: We may edit, reproduce and incorporate your comments in Lonely Planet products such as guidebooks, websites and digital products, so let us know if you don't want your comments reproduced or your name acknowledged. For a copy of our privacy policy visit www.lonelyplanet.com/privacy.

Notes

Notes

Notes

Index

See also separate indexes for Drinking (p210), Eating (p210), Entertainment (p211), Shopping (p211) and Sleeping (p211).

000 map pages
000 photographs

Y

DRINKING

EATING

000 map pages
000 photographs

ENTERTAINMENT

SHOPPING

SLEEPING

000 map pages
000 photographs

MAP LEGEND

ROUTES

Freeway
Primary Road
Secondary Road
Tertiary Road
Lane
Track
Unsealed Road
One-Way Street
Mall/Steps
Tunnel
Walking Tour
Walking Trail
Walking Path
Pedestrian Overpass

TRANSPORT

Ferry
Rail

HYDROGRAPHY

River, Creek
Canal
Water

BOUNDARIES

International
State, Provincial
Ancient Wall
Cliff

AREA FEATURES

Area of Interest
Beach, Desert
Building, Featured
Building, Information
Building, Other
Building, Transport
Cemetery, Christian
Forest
Land
Mall
Park
Sports
Urban

POPULATION

CAPITAL (NATIONAL)
CAPITAL (STATE)
Large City
Medium City
Small City
Town, Village

SYMBOLS

Sights/Activities
Beach
Castle, Fortress
Christian
Islamic
Jewish
Monument
Museum, Gallery
Other Site
Ruin
Swimming Pool
Trail Head
Zoo, Bird Sanctuary

Eating
Eating

Drinking
Drinking
Café

Entertainment
Entertainment

Shopping
Shopping

Sleeping
Sleeping

Transport
Airport, Airfield
Bus Station
Cycling, Bicycle Path
Parking Area
Taxi Rank

Information
Bank, ATM
Embassy/Consulate
Hospital, Medical
Information
Internet Facilities
Police Station
Post Office, GPO
Telephone
Toilets

Geographic
Lighthouse
Lookout
Mountain
National Park

Maps

Firth of Forth
Granton Harbour
Newhaven Harbour
Granton
Wardie
Trinity
Newhaven
Starbank Park
Lower Granton Rd
Trinity Cres
Starbank
Marine Dr
West Granton Rd
Boswall Parkway
Crewe Rd North
Pilton Dr
Granton Rd
Craighall Rd
Silverknowes
Lauriston Castle
Lauriston Farm Rd
Pilton
Ferry Rd
To Cramond; Dalmeny House; The Maltings (0.5mi)
Muirhouse
George Heriot's Sports Ground
Edinburgh Academy
Edinburgh Academy New Field
East Fettes Ave
Inverleith Pl
Inverleith Row
Crewe Rd South
Davidson's Mains Park
Davidson's Mains
Drylaw
Inverleith
Warriston Playing Fields
Canonmills
Hillhouse Rd
To Forth Bridges; South Queensferry; Port Edgar Marina & Sailing School; Inchcolm Island Ferry; Queensferry Museum (4mi); Dundas Castle; Hopetoun House (8mi)
See West End & Stockbridge Map (p217)
Inverleith Park
Comely Bank Rd
Eyre Pl
Broughton
Dundas St
Craigcrook Rd
Craigleith Rd
Corstorphine Hill
Blackhall
Queensferry Rd
Water of Leith
York Pl
Queen St
St Andrew Bus Station
Ravelston
Ravelston Golf Course
Ravelston Dykes Rd
Dean Village
See Old Town Map (p222)
Corstorphine
Murrayfield Rd
Belford Rd
Princes St
Palmerston Pl
Coates
Shandwick Pl
Lothian Rd
Edinburgh Castle
Edinburgh Zoo
Roseburn Tce
West Coates
Haymarket Train Station
Lauriston
Corstorphine Rd
Balgreen Rd
Saughtonhall Dr
Roseburn St
Murrayfield
See Dalry & Morningside Map (p226)
The Meadows
To Dovecote House (0.25mi); Edinburgh Airport (4mi); Ingliston Market (5mi); Glasgow (42mi)
Westfield Rd
Dalry Rd
Dundee St
Union Canal
Tollcross
Melville Dr
Fountainbridge
Whitson Rd
Stevenson Rd
Gorgie Rd
Dalry
Carrick Knowe
Stevenson Dr
Saughton Park
Merchiston
Bruntsfield Pl
Marchmont Rd
Greenhill
Marchmont
Stenhouse Dr
Ford's Rd
Shandon
Saughton Rd
Stenhouse Rd
Chesser Ave
Slateford Rd
Morningside Rd
Saughton Prison
Morningside
Grange
Calder Rd
Murray Burn
Charterhall Rd
Longstone
Inglis Green Rd
Craiglockhart Pond
Blackford Hill
To Ratho; Adventure Centre (6mi)
Craiglockhart Ave
Napier University
Colinton Rd
Glenlockhart Rd
Comiston Rd
Braid Burn
Hermitage of Braid
Craiglockhart
Braid Hills Dr
Kingsknowe
Lanark Rd
To Hillend; Roslin; Rosslyn Chapel; Fairmile Inn; Lothianburn Golf Course; Midlothian Snowsports Centre (0.5mi); Swanston (1mi); Pentland Hills (4mi); Penicuik (6mi)
Braid Hills Golf Course
A901
A903
B9085
A90
A8
A702
A71
A70
A B C D
1 2 3 4 5 6

0 1 km
0 0.5 miles

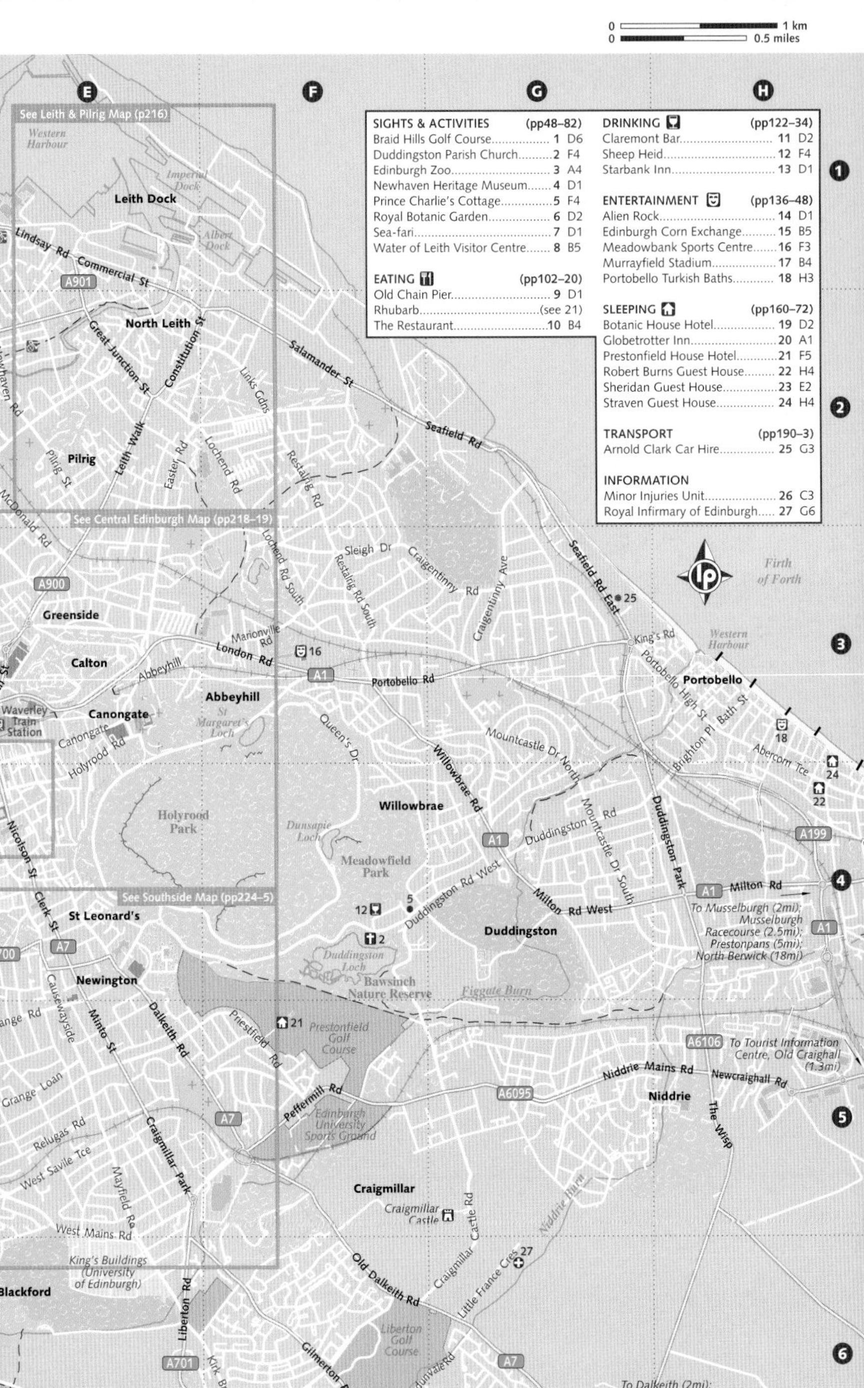

E
F
G
H
1
2
3
4
5
6
See Leith & Pilrig Map (p216)
See Central Edinburgh Map (pp218–19)
See Southside Map (pp224–5)
SIGHTS & ACTIVITIES (pp48–82)
Braid Hills Golf Course 1 D6
Duddingston Parish Church 2 F4
Edinburgh Zoo 3 A4
Newhaven Heritage Museum 4 D1
Prince Charlie's Cottage 5 F4
Royal Botanic Garden 6 D2
Sea-fari 7 D1
Water of Leith Visitor Centre 8 B5
EATING (pp102–20)
Old Chain Pier 9 D1
Rhubarb (see 21)
The Restaurant 10 B4
DRINKING (pp122–34)
Claremont Bar 11 D2
Sheep Heid 12 F4
Starbank Inn 13 D1
ENTERTAINMENT (pp136–48)
Alien Rock 14 D1
Edinburgh Corn Exchange 15 B5
Meadowbank Sports Centre 16 F3
Murrayfield Stadium 17 B4
Portobello Turkish Baths 18 H3
SLEEPING (pp160–72)
Botanic House Hotel 19 D2
Globetrotter Inn 20 A1
Prestonfield House Hotel 21 F5
Robert Burns Guest House 22 H4
Sheridan Guest House 23 E2
Straven Guest House 24 H4
TRANSPORT (pp190–3)
Arnold Clark Car Hire 25 G3
INFORMATION
Minor Injuries Unit 26 C3
Royal Infirmary of Edinburgh 27 G6
Western Harbour
Imperial Dock
Leith Dock
Albert Dock
Lindsay Rd
Commercial St
A901
North Leith
Great Junction St
Constitution St
Salamander St
Newhaven Rd
Links Gdns
Pilrig
Pilrig St
Leith Walk
Easter Rd
Lochend Rd
Restalrig Rd
Seafield Rd
McDonald Rd
Lochend Rd South
Sleigh Dr
Restalrig Rd South
Craigentinny Rd
Craigentinny Ave
Seafield Rd East
Firth of Forth
A900
Greenside
Marionville Rd
London Rd
Calton
Abbeyhill
Abbeyhill
A1
Portobello Rd
King's Rd
Western Harbour
Portobello
Portobello High St
Bath St
Brighton Pl
Abercorn Tce
Waverley Train Station
Canongate
Canongate
Holyrood Rd
St Margaret's Loch
Queen's Dr
Willowbrae Rd
Mountcastle Dr North
Holyrood Park
Willowbrae
Dunsapie Loch
Meadowfield Park
Duddingston Rd
Mountcastle Dr South
Duddingston Park
A199
Nicolson St
Clerk St
St Leonard's
Duddingston Rd West
Milton Rd West
Milton Rd
Duddingston
To Musselburgh (2mi); Musselburgh Racecourse (2.5mi); Prestonpans (5mi); North Berwick (18mi)
A700
A7
Newington
Duddingston Loch
Bawsinch Nature Reserve
Figgate Burn
Causewayside
Grange Rd
Minto St
Dalkeith Rd
Priestfield Rd
Prestonfield Golf Course
A6106
To Tourist Information Centre, Old Craighall (1.3mi)
Niddrie Mains Rd
Newcraighall Rd
Grange Loan
Peffermill Rd
A6095
Niddrie
The Wisp
Relugas Rd
Edinburgh University Sports Ground
West Savile Tce
Mayfield Rd
Craigmillar Park
Craigmillar
Craigmillar Castle
Craigmillar Castle Rd
Niddrie Burn
West Mains Rd
King's Buildings (University of Edinburgh)
Little France Cres
Blackford
Liberton Rd
Old Dalkeith Rd
Liberton Golf Course
Gilmerton Rd
Moredunvale Rd
A701
Kirk Brae
A7
Moredun
To Dalkeith (2mi); Dalhousie Castle (7mi); Borthwick Castle (12mi); Lauder (20mi); Melrose (32mi)
A772
To Penicuik (7mi); Peebles (22mi)
To Gilmerton Cove (600m); Melville Golf Centre (2mi)

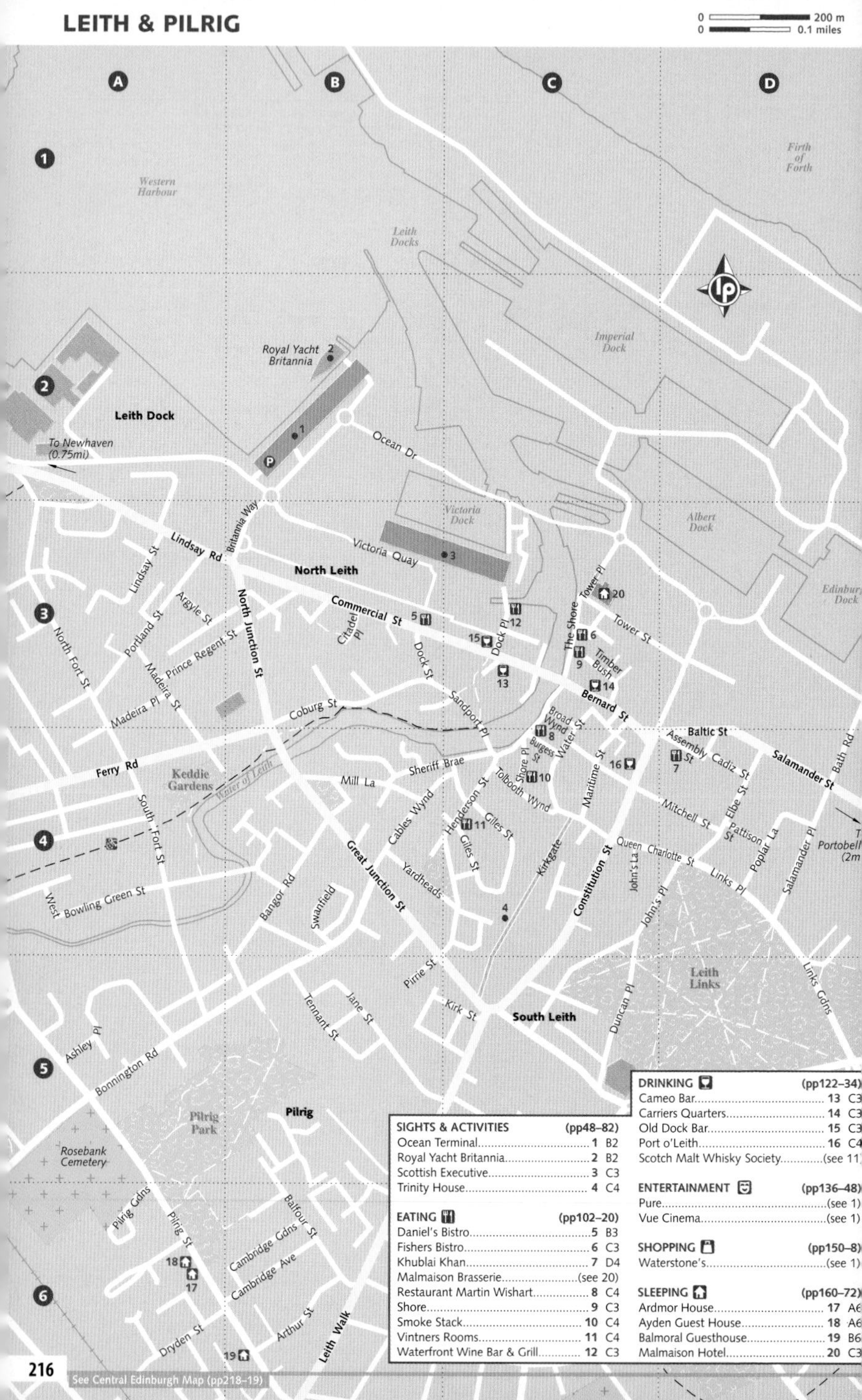
0 200 m
0 0.1 miles
A
B
C
D
1
2
3
4
5
6
Firth of Forth
Western Harbour
Leith Docks
Imperial Dock
Royal Yacht Britannia
Leith Dock
To Newhaven (0.75mi)
Ocean Dr
Victoria Dock
Albert Dock
Edinburgh Dock
Britannia Way
Lindsay Rd
Victoria Quay
North Leith
Lindsay St
Commercial St
Tower Pl
Tower St
The Shore
Timber Bush
Argyle St
Portland St
North Junction St
Citadel Pl
Dock Pl
Dock St
North Fort St
Prince Regent St
Madeira St
Madeira Pl
Sandport Pl
Bernard St
Baltic St
Salamander St
Bath Rd
Coburg St
Broad Wynd
Water St
Assembly St
Cadiz St
Burgess St
Shore Pl
Maritime St
Ferry Rd
Keddie Gardens
Water of Leith
Mill La
Sheriff Brae
Tolbooth Wynd
Mitchell St
Elbe St
Pattison St
Poplar La
Salamander Pl
To Portobello (2m
South Fort St
Cables Wynd
Henderson St
Giles St
Kirkgate
Queen Charlotte St
John's La
Links Pl
Great Junction St
Yardheads
Constitution St
John's Pl
West Bowling Green St
Bangor Rd
Swanfield
Leith Links
Links Gdns
Pirrie St
Jane St
Tennant St
Kirk St
South Leith
Duncan Pl
Ashley Pl
Bonnington Rd
Pilrig Park
Pilrig
Rosebank Cemetery
Pilrig Gdns
Pilrig St
Balfour St
Cambridge Gdns
Cambridge Ave
Arthur St
Dryden St
Leith Walk
SIGHTS & ACTIVITIES (pp48–82)
Ocean Terminal 1 B2
Royal Yacht Britannia 2 B2
Scottish Executive 3 C3
Trinity House 4 C4
EATING (pp102–20)
Daniel's Bistro 5 B3
Fishers Bistro 6 C3
Khublai Khan 7 D4
Malmaison Brasserie (see 20)
Restaurant Martin Wishart 8 C4
Shore 9 C3
Smoke Stack 10 C4
Vintners Rooms 11 C4
Waterfront Wine Bar & Grill 12 C3
DRINKING (pp122–34)
Cameo Bar 13 C3
Carriers Quarters 14 C3
Old Dock Bar 15 C3
Port o'Leith 16 C4
Scotch Malt Whisky Society (see 11)
ENTERTAINMENT (pp136–48)
Pure (see 1)
Vue Cinema (see 1)
SHOPPING (pp150–8)
Waterstone's (see 1)
SLEEPING (pp160–72)
Ardmor House 17 A6
Ayden Guest House 18 A6
Balmoral Guesthouse 19 B6
Malmaison Hotel 20 C3

See Central Edinburgh Map (pp218–19)

WEST END & STOCKBRIDGE

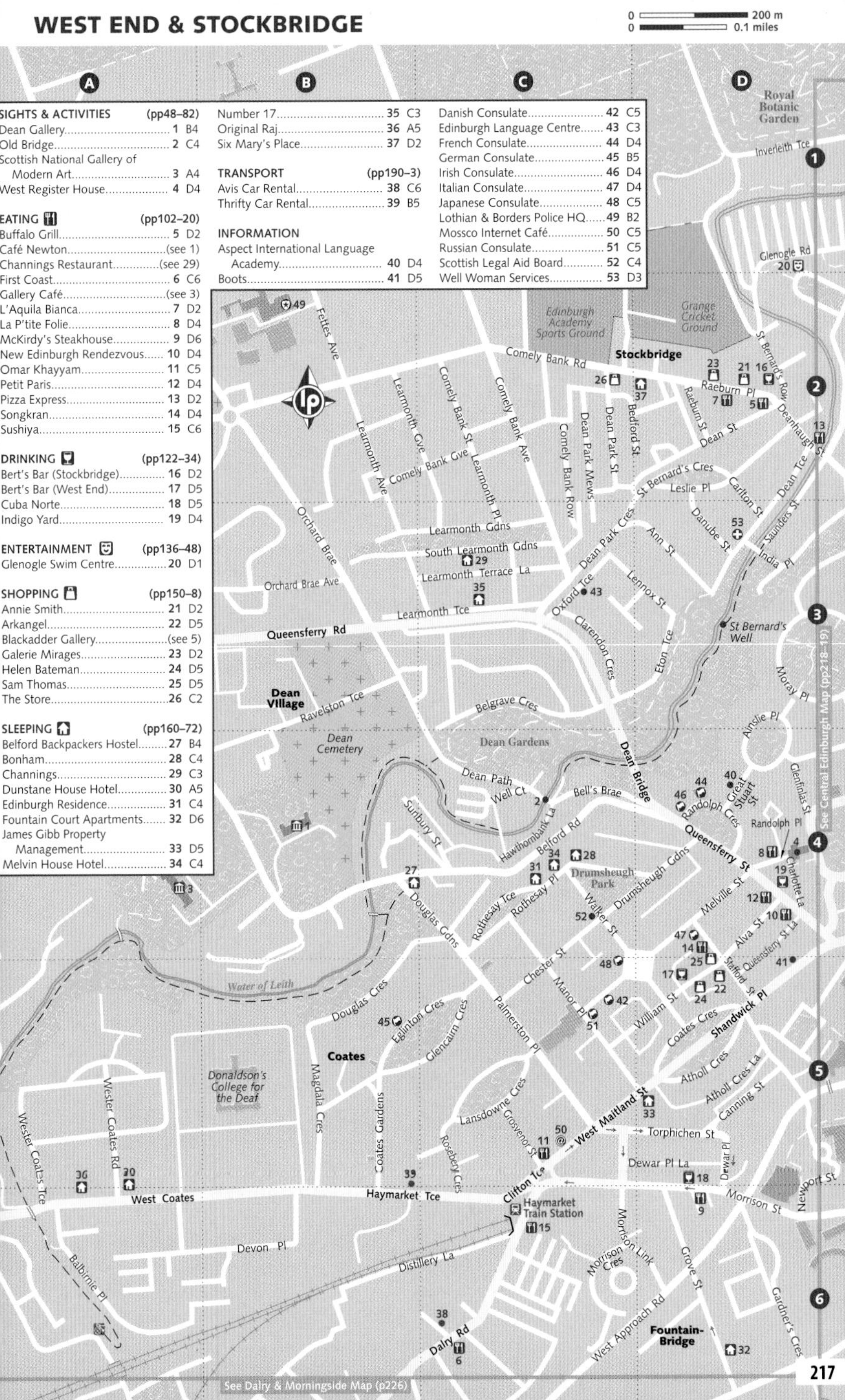

CENTRAL EDINBURGH

See West End & Stockbridge Map (p217)

See Old Town Map (p222)

See Southside Map (pp224–5)

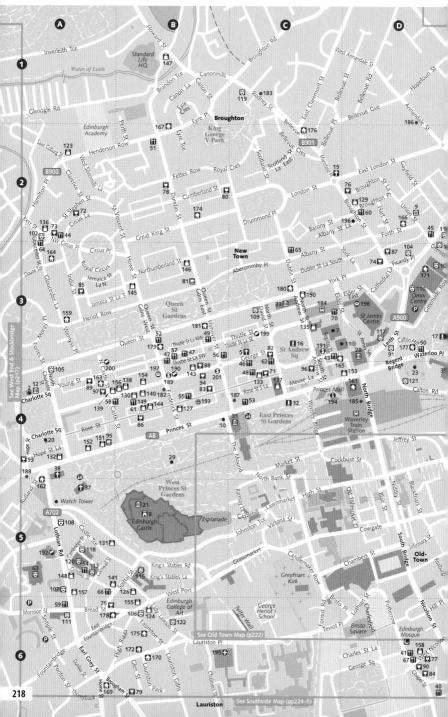

0 200 m
0 0.1 miles
See Leith & Pilrig Map (p216)
E
F
G
H
1
2
3
4
5
6
Iona St
Buchanan St
Dickson St
Eastern Cemetery
St Clair St
Hawkhill Ave
McDonald Rd
Shrub Pl La
Leith Walk
Albert St
Hopetoun Cres
Albion Pl
Easter Road Stadium (Hibernian FC)
101
Allanfield
Annandale St Ln
Albion Rd
Lochend Loch
142
Haddington Pl
Brunswick Rd
Bothwell St
Lochend Park
Brunswick St
South Elgin St
Elgin Tce
Elm Row
69
Montgomery St
Easter Rd
Moray Park Tce
Greenside
Hillside St
Wellington St
Brunton Tce
Rossie Pl
Dalgety Ave
Dalgety Rd
Windsor St
168
Hillside Cres
Leopold Pl
London Rd
East Norton Pl
Royal Terrace Gardens
Marionville Rd
Royal Tce
Carlton Tce
92
Montrose Tce
Wishaw Tce
160
London Rd
Calton
Regent Gardens
A1
Abbeymount
Abbeyhill
Calton Hill
19
22
Regent Road Park
Spring Gdns
Royal Park Tce
Regent Tce
Regent Rd
202
Abbeyhill
Abbeyhill Cres
30
1
Calton New Burial Ground
26
Duke's Walk
Canongate
Calton Rd
13
116
128
27
25
Old Tolbooth Wyn
Horse Wynd
New St
3
St Margaret's Loch
34
134
Canongate
4
18
114
Reid's Cl
173
Holyrood Rd
Queen's Dr
39
98
24
36
St John St
99
Viewcraig St
Pleasance Sports Centre
Dumbledykes Rd
Radical Rd
Salisbury Crags
Holyrood Park
The Pleasance
Viewcraig Gdns
Brown St
Richmond Pl
Richmond La
Arthur's Seat (251m)
125
East Crosscauseway
St Leonard's St
Queen's Dr
14

CENTRAL EDINBURGH (pp218–19)

CENTRAL EDINBURGH (pp218–19)

ENTERTAINMENT (continued)

CC Blooms 100 D3
Easter Road Stadium 101 G1
Edinburgh Floatarium 102 A2
Edinburgh Playhouse 103 D3
Ego 104 D3
Eighty Queen Street 105 A4
El Barrio 106 B6
Filmhouse 107 A5
Gig 108 A5
Jam House 109 C3
Jongleurs 110 D3
Odeon 111 A6
One Spa (see 63)
Planet Out 112 D2
Royal Lyceum Theatre 113 A5
Scottish Poetry Library 114 E4
Stand Comedy Club (see 150)
Stereo 115 B5
Studio 24 116 E4
Thistle Hotel 117 D3
Traverse Theatre 118 A5
Union Yoga 119 C1
Usher Hall 120 A5
Venue 121 D4
Vue Cinema (see 110)
Wee Red Bar 122 B6
Why Not? (see 46)

SHOPPING (pp150–8)

Adam Pottery 123 A2
Avalanche Records 124 B6
Backbeat 125 E6
Boardwise 126 B5
Boudiche 127 B4
Carson Clark Gallery 128 F4
Crombie's 129 D2
Cruise 130 B4
Edinburgh Farmers Market 131 A5
Edinburgh Woollen Mill 132 A4
Fopp 133 C4
Fudge House of Edinburgh 134 E4
Harvey Nichols 135 C3
Ian Mellis 136 A2
Jenners 137 C4
Jo Malone 138 B4
Lime Blue 139 A4
Mappin & Webb 140 B4
McAlister Matheson Music 141 A5
McNaughtan's Bookshop 142 E2
One World Shop (see 38)
Ottakar's 143 B4
Palenque 144 B4
Q-Store (see 196)
Samarkand Galleries 145 B3
Scottish Gallery 146 B3
Second Edition 147 B1
Stationery Office Bookshop 148 A5
Tiso 149 B4
Troon 150 C3
Valvona & Crolla (see 69)
Virgin Megastore 151 A4
Waterstone's 152 A4
Waterstone's 153 D4
Waterstone's 154 B4
West Port Books 155 B6
Whistles 156 B4
Wonderland 157 A5
Word Power 158 D6

SLEEPING (pp160–72)

41 Heriot Row 159 A3
Ailsa Craig Hotel 160 E3
Ardenlee Guest House (see 167)
Balmoral Hotel 161 D4
Caledonian Hilton Hotel 162 A5
Castle Guest House 163 A4
Christopher North House Hotel 164 A3
City Centre Tourist Hostel 165 D3
Clouds Accommodation Agency 166 D2
Dene Guest House 167 B2
Dukes of Windsor Street 168 E2
Edinburgh Central Apartments 169 A6
Edinburgh City Hotel 170 B6
Glasshouse 171 D3
Glen House Apartments 172 B6
Holyrood Hotel 173 F4
Howard 174 B2
Knight Residence 175 B6
Mingalar Guest House 176 C2
Parliament House Hotel 177 D3
Point Hotel 178 A6
Rick's 179 B3
Royal Garden Apartments 180 C3
Ryden Lettings 181 B3

TRANSPORT (pp190–3)

British Airways Travel Shop 182 B4
City Cycles 183 C1
Edinburgh Bus Station 184 C3
Edinburgh Rail Travel Centre 185 D4
Europcar (see 185)
First Edinburgh Bus Shop (see 184)
Lothian Buses Lost Property Office 186 D1
Lothian Buses Travel Shop 187 C4
Lothian Buses Travel Shop 188 A4

INFORMATION

American Express 189 B4
Australian Consulate 190 B4
Bank of Scotland 191 C3
Canadian Consulate 192 A5
connect@edinburgh (see 194)
easyInternetcafé 193 B4
Edinburgh & Scotland Information Centre (ESIC) 194 C4
Edinburgh Dental Institute 195 B6
Edinburgh LGB Community Centre 196 D2
Fexco (see 194)
Frederick St Post Office 197 B4
Main Post Office 198 D3
Netherlands Consulate 199 C3
Royal Bank of Scotland (see 7)
Spanish Consulate 200 A4
Thomas Cook 201 B4
US Consulate 202 E3

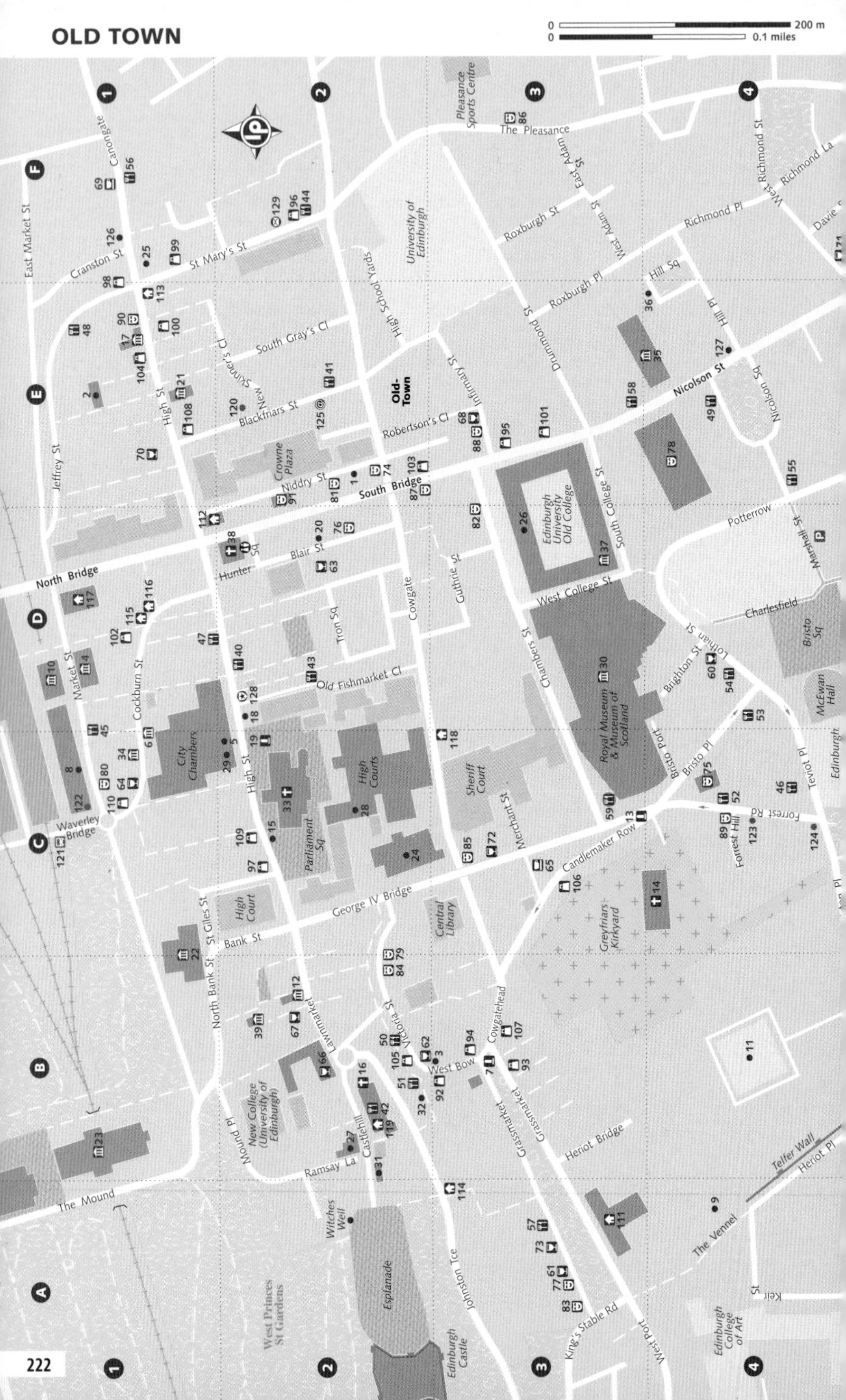
0 200 m
0 0.1 miles
Pleasance Sports Centre
The Pleasance
East Adam St
West Adam St
Roxburgh St
Roxburgh Pl
Richmond Pl
West Richmond St
Richmond La
Hill Sq
Hill Pl
Nicolson Sq
Nicolson St
University of Edinburgh
High School Yards
Infirmary St
Drummond St
Old Town
Canongate
East Market St
Cranston St
St Mary's St
South Gray's Cl
Skinner's Cl
New Skinner's Cl
Blackfriars St
Robertson's Cl
Crowne Plaza
Niddry St
South Bridge
Edinburgh University Old College
South College St
Potterrow
Marshall St
Jeffrey St
High St
North Bridge
Hunter Sq
Blair St
Guthrie St
West College St
Charlesfield
Bristo Sq
Tron Sq
Cowgate
Chambers St
Lothian St
Market St
Cockburn St
Old Fishmarket Cl
Brighton St
McEwan Hall
City Chambers
High Courts
Royal Museum & Museum of Scotland
Bristo Port
Bristo Pl
Teviot Pl
Parliament Sq
Sheriff Court
Merchant St
Forrest Rd
Forrest Hill
Waverley Bridge
Candlemaker Row
St Giles St
High Court
George IV Bridge
Bank St
Central Library
Greyfriars Kirkyard
North Bank St
Lawnmarket
Victoria St
West Bow
Cowgatehead
New College (University of Edinburgh)
Mound Pl
Castlehill
Ramsay La
Grassmarket
Heriot Bridge
The Mound
Witches Well
Telfer Wall
Heriot Pl
The Vennel
Esplanade
Johnston Tce
West Princes St Gardens
Edinburgh Castle
King's Stable Rd
West Port
Keir St
Edinburgh College of Art

OLD TOWN (p222)

SIGHTS & ACTIVITIES (pp48–82)
Auld Reekie Tours......**1** E2
Brass Rubbing Centre......**2** E1
Cadies & Witchery Tours......**3** B3
City Art Centre......**4** D1
City Chambers......**5** C2
Collective Gallery......**6** C1
Covenanters Monument......**7** B3
Edinburgh Dungeon......**8** C1
Flodden Wall......**9** A4
Fringe Office......(see 128)
Fruitmarket Gallery......**10** D1
George Heriot's School......**11** B4
Gladstone's Land......**12** B2
Greyfriars Bobby......**13** C3
Greyfriars Kirk......**14** C4
Heart of Midlothian......**15** C2
Highland Tolbooth Kirk......**16** B2
John Knox House......**17** E1
Loch Ness Discovery Centre......**18** D2
Menzies Campbell Dental Museum......(see 35)
Mercat Cross......**19** C2
Mercat Tours......**20** D2
Museum of Childhood......**21** E1
Museum of Scotland......(see 30)
Museum on the Mound......**22** C1
National Gallery of Scotland......**23** B1
National Library of Scotland......**24** C2
Netherbow Port......**25** F1
Old College (University of Edinburgh)......**26** D3
Outlook Tower & Camera Obscura......**27** B2
Parliament Hall......**28** C2
Pathology Museum......(see 35)
Real Mary King's Close......**29** C2
Royal Museum......**30** D3
Scotch Whisky Heritage Centre...**31** B2
Scottish Genealogy Society Library & Family History Centre......**32** B2
Scottish Storytelling Centre......(see 17)
St Giles Cathedral......**33** C2
Stills Gallery......**34** C1
Surgeons' Hall Museums......**35** E4
Surgeons' Hall Museums Entrance......**36** E4
Talbot Rice Gallery......**37** D3
Tron Kirk......**38** D2
Writers' Museum......**39** B2

EATING (pp102–20)
Always Sunday......**40** D2
Amber......(see 31)
Black Bo's......**41** E2
Café Delos......(see 30)
Café Hub......**42** B2
Café Marlayne......**43** D2
caféteria@thefruitmarket......(see 10)
David Bann......**44** F2
Doric Wine Bar & Bistro......**45** D1
Favorit......**46** C4
Gordon's Trattoria......**47** D1
Heights......(see 111)
Igg's......**48** E1
Kebab Mahal......**49** E4
Maison Bleue......**50** B2
Maxie's Bistro & Wine Bar......**51** B2
Metro Brasserie & Café Bar.....(see 111)
Monster Mash......**52** C4
Namaste......**53** D4
Negociants......**54** D4
North Bridge Brasserie......(see 117)
Original Khushi's......**55** E4
Pancho Villa's......**56** F1
Petit Paris......**57** A3
Suruchi......**58** E3
Tower......**59** C3
Witchery by the Castle......(see 119)

DRINKING (pp122–34)
Assembly Bar......**60** D4
Beehive Inn......**61** A3
Bow Bar......**62** B2
City Café......**63** D2
Ecco Vino......**64** C1
Elephant House Café......**65** C3
Ensign Ewart......**66** B2
Jolly Judge......**67** B2
Malt Shovel......(see 34)
Oxygen......**68** E3
Plaisir du Chocolat......**69** F1
Royal Mile Tavern......**70** E1
Southsider......**71** F4
Three Sisters......(see 118)
Villager......**72** C3
White Hart Inn......**73** A3
World's End......(see 113)

ENTERTAINMENT (pp136–48)
Bannerman's......**74** E2
Bedlam Theatre......**75** C4
Cabaret Voltaire......**76** D2
Dance Base......**77** A3
Edinburgh Festival Theatre......**78** E4
Finnegan's Wake......**79** B2
Hebrides Bar......**80** C1
Honeycomb......**81** E2
Jazz Bar......**82** D3
Jazz Centre......**83** A3
Liquid Room......**84** B2
Netherbow Theatre......(see 17)
Opium......**85** C3
Pleasance Cabaret Bar......**86** F3
Red Vodka Club......(see 85)
Ripping Records......**87** E2
Royal Oak......**88** E3
Sandy Bell's......**89** C4
Scottish Storytelling Centre......(see 17)
Subway......(see 85)
Tass......**90** E1
Whistle Binkie's......**91** E2

SHOPPING (pp150–8)
21st Century Kilts......(see 104)
Aha Ha Ha......**92** B3
Armstrong's......**93** B3
Big Ideas......**94** B3
Blackwell's Bookshop......**95** E3
Casey's......**96** F2
Cashmere Store......**97** C2
Corniche......**98** E1
Cruise......**99** F1
Designs on Cashmere......**100** E1
Flip......**101** E3
Fopp......**102** D1
Forbidden Planet......**103** E2
Geoffrey (Tailor) Inc......**104** E1
Ian Mellis......**105** B2
Joyce Forsyth Designer Knitwear......**106** C3
Mr Wood's Fossils......**107** B3
Palenque......**108** E1
Royal Mile Whiskies......**109** C2
Underground Solush'n......**110** C1

SLEEPING (pp160–72)
Apex International Hotel......**111** A3
Bank Hotel......**112** D1
Brodie's Backpacker Hostel......**113** E1
Castle Rock Hostel......**114** A3
Edinburgh Backpackers Hostel......**115** D1
Royal Mile Residence......**116** D1
Scotsman Hotel......**117** D1
Tailors Hall Hotel......**118** C3
Witchery by the Castle......**119** B2

TRANSPORT (pp190–3)
Edinburgh Cycle Hire & Scottish Cycle Safaris......**120** E2
Lothian Buses Airlink......**121** C1
Lothian Buses Travel Shop......**122** C1
STA Travel......**123** C4
Student Flights......**124** C4

INFORMATION
e-corner......**125** E2
Edinburgh School of English......**126** F1
Institute for Applied Language Studies......**127** E4
International Newsagents......(see 109)
Internet Café......(see 94)
Lothian & Borders Police Information Centre......**128** D2
St Mary's St Post Office......**129** F2

SOUTHSIDE

See Central Edinburgh Map (pp218–19)
See Dalry & Morningside Map (p226)

A B C D
1 2 3 4 5 6

Thornybauk
Brougham St
Panmure Pl
Home St
Lochrin Pl
Union Canal
Tarvit St
Brougham Pl
Lonsdale Tce
St Patrick Sq
Buccleuch Pl
Buccleuch St
Edinburgh University
Meadow La
Gilmore Pl
Hailes St
Valleyfield St
Leven St
Leven Tce
Upper Gilmore Pl
Glengyle Tce
The Meadows
Gillespie Cres
Barclay Pl
Wright's Houses
Bruntsfield Links
Melville Dr
Meadow Pl
Roseneath Pl
Roseneath Tce
Argyle Pl
Sylvan Pl
Melville Tce
Livingstone Pl
Gladstone Tce
Warrender Park Tce
Warrender Park Cres
Marchmont St
Whitehouse Loan
Warrender Park Rd
Leamington Tce
Sciennes Rd
Hatton Pl
Bruntsfield Pl
Bruntsfield Tce
Bruntsfield
Lauderdale St
Spottiswoode St
Arden St
Marchmont Rd
Marchmont Cres
Chalmers Cres
Mansionhouse Rd
Tantallon Pl
Sciennes
Bruntsfield Cres
Spottiswoode Rd
Marchmont
Grange Rd
Seton
Greenhill Gdns
Greenhill Tce
Thirlestane Rd
Beaufort Rd
Cumin Pl
Lauder Rd
Saint Margaret's Pl
Thirlestane La
Greenhill Pl
St Margaret's Rd
Grange Cemetery
Kilgraston Rd
Strathearn Rd
Greenhill
Strathearn Pl
Hope Tce
Church Hill
Clinton Rd
Blackford Rd
Pitsligo Rd
Carlton Cricket Ground
Newbattle Tce
Grange Loan
Saint Thomas Rd
Grange
George Tce
Oswald Rd
Saint Alban's Rd
Astley Ainslie Hospital
South Oswald St
Canaan La
Woodburn Ave
Blackford Ave
West Relugas Rd
Mortonhall Rd
Charterhall Gve
Neil Gve
Charterhall Rd
Blackford Hill Gve
Ladysmith
Midmar Ave
Cluny Gdns
Blackford Pond
Blackford Hill View
Cluny Dr
Blackford Hill
Midmar Dr

2 3 5 6 7 8 9 12 17 19 21 22 28 31 32 33 35 36 37

0 200 m
0 0.1 miles

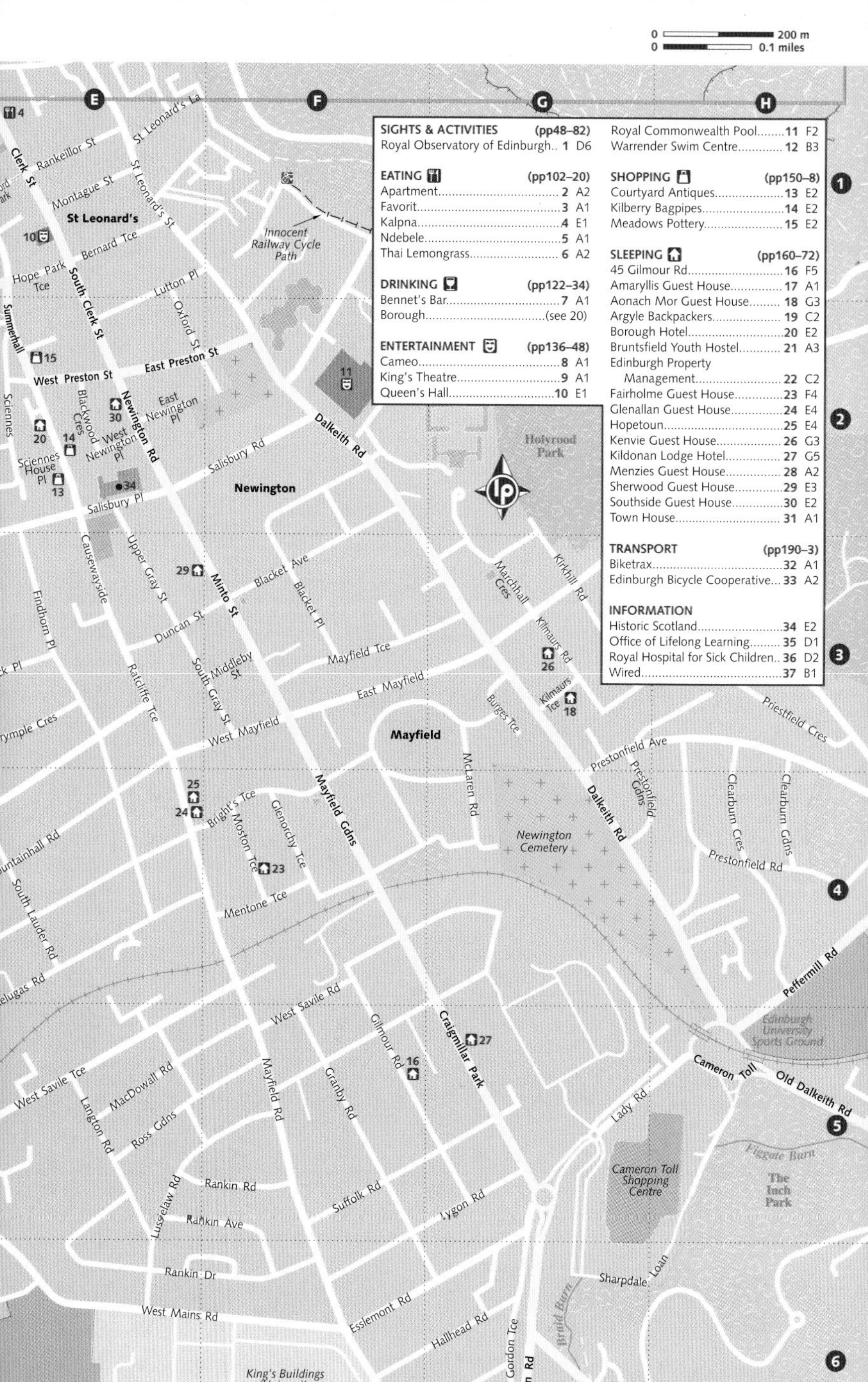

DALRY & MORNINGSIDE